INSIGHT GUIDES

USA The New SOUTH

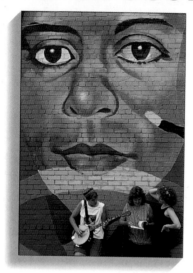

Part of the Langenscheidt Publishing Group

ABOUT THIS BOOK

INSIGHT GUIDE
USA The New SOUTH

Editorial
Project Editor
Martha Ellen Zenfell
Editorial Director
Brian Bell

Distribution

United States
Langenscheidt Publishers, Inc.
46–35 54th Road, Maspeth, NY 11378
Fax: 1 (718) 784 0640

Canada
Thomas Allen & Son Ltd
390 Steelcase Road East
Markham, Ontario L3R 1G2
Fax: (1) 905 475 6747

UK & Ireland
GeoCenter International Ltd
The Viables Centre, Harrow Way
Basingstoke, Hants RG22 4BJ
Fax: (44) 1256 817988

Australia
Universal Publishers
1 Waterloo Road
Macquarie Park, NSW 2113
Fax: (61) 2 9888 9074

New Zealand
Hema Maps New Zealand Ltd (HNZ)
Unit D, 24 Ra ORA Drive
East Tamaki, Auckland
Fax: (64) 9 273 6479

Worldwide
**Apa Publications GmbH & Co.
Verlag KG (Singapore branch)**
38 Joo Koon Road, Singapore 628990
Tel: (65) 6865 1600. Fax: (65) 6861 6438

Printing
Insight Print Services (Pte) Ltd
38 Joo Koon Road, Singapore 628990
Tel: (65) 6865 1600. Fax: (65) 6861 6438

©2004 Apa Publications GmbH & Co.
Verlag KG (Singapore branch)
All Rights Reserved

First Edition 2004

CONTACTING THE EDITORS
We would appreciate it if readers
would alert us to errors or outdated information by writing to:

**Insight Guides, P.O. Box 7910,
London SE1 1WE, England.
Fax: (44) 20 7403 0290.
insight@apaguide.co.uk**

This guidebook combines the interests and enthusiasms of two of
the world's best-known information
providers: Insight Guides, whose titles
have set the standard for visual travel
guides since 1970, and Discovery
Channel, the world's premier source
of nonfiction television programming.

The editors of Insight Guides provide both practical advice and general
understanding about a destination's
history, culture, institutions and people. Discovery Channel and its popular website, www.discovery.com, help
millions of viewers explore their world
from the comfort of their own home
and encourage them to explore the
destination firsthand.

This first edition of *Insight Guide:
USA The New South* is structured to
convey an understanding of all nine
Southern states, as well as the three
balmy and sandy resort areas that
make up the South's over-looked Gulf
Coast. It aims to introduce the
region's people as well as to guide
readers through its fascinating sights
and activities:

◆ The **Features** section, indicated by
a yellow bar at the top of each page,
covers the history and culture of the
Southern states in a series of informative essays.

◆ The main **Places** section, indicated
by a blue bar, is a complete guide to
all the sights and areas worth visiting. Places of special interest are
coordinated by number to a series of
color maps.

◆ The **Travel Tips** listings section,
with an orange bar, provides a handy
point of reference for information on
travel, hotels, shopping, restaurants
and much more.

The contributors

The guiding hand behind this book is **Martha Ellen Zenfell**, a Southerner based in London, England, who has been the project editor of most of Insight's American titles. With a Virginia mama and a Mississippi daddy, not to mention being second cousin to the late Curtis Turner, the flamboyant stockcar racer, Zenfell felt well-equipped to take on the task.

Together she and **David Whelan** traveled through the South, stopping off to see friends and family on the way. On their return, Whelan wrote the chapters, not only on the states they visited, but also the features on gambling, food, movies, literature, and his real love, music.

It's a pleasure to combine good work with good deeds. **Lee Sentell**, a sixth-generation Alabamian, recently published the second edition of his *Best of Alabama* travel guide. Now state tourism director, Lee is donating his writing fees to help restore Alabama's Governor's Mansion.

Fifteen years of writing and editing city magazines in Charlotte, North Carolina, make **Renee Wright** an expert on that scene. Currently, she edits www.carolinasbest.com, dedicated to the finest things to see and do in the Carolinas.

A native to Arkansas, **Jay G. Harrod** has had travel features published in several publications in Arkansas, but this marks his *Insight Guides* debut. **Judy Pennington** is an author who wrote a book on her hometown, Baton Rouge, while **Honey Naylor**, our woman in New Orleans, covered the rest of Louisiana.

Nashville native **Scott Faragher** spent 20 years as an agent for Lou Rawls, Jerry Lee Lewis and Waylon Jennings. His first book, *Music City Babylon* provided an insider's look at the music business; 12 other books have followed.

In the South, the past is never far behind the future. Text from *Insight Guide: Old South* and *Insight Guide: Atlanta* has been adapted for this book and thanks is due to **Tim Jacobson**, **Mary Elizabeth Stanfield**, **Ren** and **Helen Davis**, **Lynn Seldon**, **Louise Forrester Chase**, **William Schemmel**, **Joann Biondi**, **Mary Beth Kerdasha**, **Georgia R. Byrd**, **Connie Toops**, and **Bill Sharp** and **Elaine Appleton**. Photographers include **Lyle Lawson**, **Brian Gauvin** and **Bob Krist**. Travel Tips was compiled by **Jason Mitchell** and **Donna Dailey**. Many thanks, too, to **Cheryl Hargrove**, formerly of Travel South.

Map Legend

– – –	International Boundary
– – – –	State Boundary
⊖	Border Crossing
●	National Park/Reserve
– – – –	Ferry Route
Ⓜ	Subway
✈ ✈	Airport: International/Regional
🚍	Bus Station
ⓘ	Tourist Information
✉	Post Office
✝ ✝	Church/Ruins
✝	Monastery
☾	Mosque
✡	Synagogue
⌘	Castle/Ruins
🏠	Mansion/Stately home
∴	Archeological Site
∩	Cave
𝟙	Statue/Monument
★	Place of Interest

The main places of interest in the Places section are coordinated by number with a full-color map (e.g. ❶), and a symbol at the top of every right-hand page tells you where to find the map.

CONTENTS

Inside front cover:
The New South
Inside back cover:
National Parks, Reserves
and Monuments

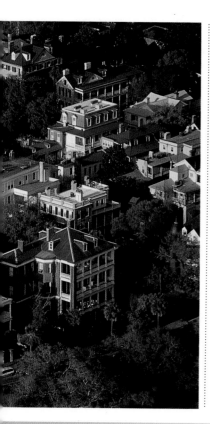

A bird's-eye view of the Historic District of Charleston, South Carolina.

Information panels

SOUTHERN ASPIRATIONS

The romance of the South has not gone with the wind,

but there's a fresh breeze of American creativity blowing

The New South may be the last undiscovered place in the United States. Established images of the South, romantic as they are Gothic, are out of date. Antebellum plantation homes, riverboat gambling and gator-filled swamps are still there, of course, but there is an optimism, a spark, a very American spirit of reinvention.

New Southerners transformed the luscious landscape of the hills of Tennessee, the Mississippi and along the silver sands of the Gulf Coast, from the far-sighted dream-town of Seaside, Florida, to the lighter, more accessible Vegas-style playground in pretty Biloxi. The world-famous architect Frank Geary is producing a landmark art gallery in Biloxi, and, having already illuminated the Atlanta skyline, the architectural assertions of John Portman are gleaming as far afield as San Francisco and Singapore.

An Atlanta neighbor of the world's thirst quencher, Coca-Cola, is the world's 24-hour news journal, CNN, while the world's post office is centered at the FedEx HQ in Memphis. Research and technology thrive in North Carolina's Raleigh-Durham Triangle, and the medical community at Birmingham, Alabama, is recognized worldwide for its contributions to health care and healing. The Right Stuff pumps hard around the jet-jockeys of the world's biggest airbase at Eglin in Florida, as well as the space and rocket centers at Huntsville, Alabama, and Stennis in Mississippi.

The South has always been a hothouse of creativity. Many of the rhythms and syncopations of the 20th century came from the South; the blues, rock 'n' roll, country & western, and jazz were all born under Southern stars. Musicians Britney Spears, REM, Reba Macintyre and Ryan Adams carry that light aloft today. Writers like John Grisham, Anne Rice and Donna Tartt follow literary paths mapped out by William Faulkner, Tom Wolfe and Eudora Welty.

Southern sporting meccas range from the world's oldest, and perhaps most beautiful, baseball stadium at Rickwood Field in Birmingham, Alabama, across the fairways of some of *Golf Digest's* best "Little Golf Towns in the US" on the Gulf Coast, to the Masters Tournament course in Augusta, Georgia. The Atlanta Braves are a team to beat – if anyone can.

The most coveted homebases for the well-to-do movers and shakers in Washington, DC are all in Virginia, and places like Savannah, Georgia and Hot Springs, Arkansas, and the Azalea coast of Alabama feature regularly on lists of America's most desirable places to live. The history and the heritage, the culture and the celebrations, the achievement and the aspirations, are all reasons to visit the New South. ❏

PRECEDING PAGES: sweet soul music, Georgia; Pee-Wee League football team, Tennessee; belles in Easter bonnets, South Carolina.
LEFT: Atlanta's Westin Peachtree Plaza Hotel, a 70-story cylinder of glass and steel.

Decisive Dates

600–1500 AD Ancestors of Native Americans settle at what is now Toltec Mounds State Park, 10 miles (16km) east of Little Rock, Arkansas.

1541 Spanish explorer Hernando de Soto, traveling cross-country from present-day Florida, becomes the first European to see the Mississippi River.

1587 Nearly 150 pioneers sent from England by Sir Walter Raleigh settle on Roanoke Island, Virginia, but are never seen again.

1607 Establishment of Jamestown, Virginia, by British explorers and settlers.

1619 The first slaves arrive in Jamestown, Virginia.

1670 A prosperous city south of Virginia in the Carolinas is established, called Charles Towne (present-day Charleston).

1702 Two French-Canadian brothers establish Fort Louis de la Mobile (present-day Mobile).

1718 Sieur de Bienville founds *La Nouvelle Orleans* on the banks of the Mississippi River.

1733 James Oglethorpe receives a royal charter to estabish the colony of Georgia near present-day Savannah.

1763 The first Arcadians move from Nova Scotia to the swamps of Louisiana.

1767 The Mason-Dixon line is drawn, named for its two principal surveyors.

1768 Charlotte, North Carolina, is named after the wife of King George III, the British monarch.

1781 The Revolutionary War with Britain ends on the Yorktown Peninsula in Virginia.

1789–1825 Four of the first five elected presidents are from Virginia: George Washington, Thomas Jefferson, James Madison, and James Monroe.

1793 Eli Whitney invents the cotton gin, vastly increasing profits and productivity.

1803 President Thomas Jefferson concludes the Louisiana Purchase with France's Napoleon, which doubles the size of the nation.

1811 Steamboats ply the Mississippi River, delivering "King Cotton" to the world.

1815 Americans fight the Bloody British in the Battle of New Orleans in the War of 1812.

1817 Mississippi becomes the 20th US state.

1819 Congress creates the Arkansas Territory.

1820 The combined population of the lands known as "the South" is 4.3 million; 1.5 million are slaves. The Missouri Compromise raises the political profile of the issue of slavery.

1836 Arkansas becomes a US state.

1837 Atlanta (then called Terminus) is established at an intersection of three Georgia roads.

1846 Baton Rogue is named the state capital of Louisiana.

1852 Harriet Beecher Stowe publishes the influential, inflammatory novel *Uncle Tom's Cabin*.

1857 The Dred Scott court case decides that Mr Scott, a black man, is not a citizen and cannot sue for his freedom.

1859 John Brown's raid on the federal arsenal at Harpers Ferry, Virginia (now West Virginia), fans the flames of civil war.

1860 Abraham Lincoln is elected president; South Carolina secedes from the Union.

1861 The Confederate States of America is formed with Jefferson Davis as president; the opening shots of the Civil War are fired at Fort Sumter, South Carolina.

1862 Lincoln's Emancipation Proclamation is a symbolic landmark for Southern blacks.

1863 Vicksburg, Mississippi falls to the Union after a 47-day siege, giving them access to the river.

1864 Rebel victory over Richmond, Virginia, but General William T. Sherman's successful siege of Atlanta is followed by a march across Georgia, plundering everything along the route.

1865 General Robert E. Lee surrenders to Ulysses S. Grant at Appomatox, Virginia. A few days later, Lincoln is assassinated in Washington, DC.

1865–1879 The Reconstruction era.

1886 Atlanta newspaperman Henry Grady coins the phrase "the New South." Coca-Cola is brewed by an Atlanta druggist.

1895 Booker T. Washington becomes a major spokesman for black Southerners.

1915 McKinley Morganfield (Muddy Waters) is born in the small town of Rolling Fork, Mississippi.

1925 40,000 robed KKK members march on Washington, DC. The Grand Ole Opry starts broadcasting in Nashville, Tennessee. The "Scopes Monkey Trial" begins, originally as a test case against Tennessee state law forbidding the teaching of the theory of evolution in public schools.

1925–35 Southern literature garners high acclaim with writers like Eudora Welty, Robert Penn Warren, and Katherine Anne Porter.

1933 President Franklin D. Roosevelt signs the TVA Act, helping to transform a poverty-stricken Tennessee area into a forward-looking community.

1934 Great Smoky Mountains National Park is created, straddling Tennessee and North Carolina.

1935 Elvis Presley is born in Tupelo, Mississippi; his family later moves to Memphis, Tennessee.

1936 Publication of the book *Gone with the Wind*; the film three years later wins eight Academy Awards.

1941 Delta Air Lines moves to Atlanta.

1948 Tennessee Williams is awarded the Pulitzer Prize for *A Streetcar Named Desire*.

1950 Author William Faulkner is awarded the Nobel Prize for Literature.

1955 The Montgomery, Alabama, bus boycott serves as a model for black protest movements around the South.

1957 Attempts to integrate a Little Rock high school are met by a jeering mob and the Arkansas National Guard, requiring the intervention of troops acting on orders given by the US president.

1960 A sit-in by four black college students at a Woolworths lunch counter in Greensboro, North Carolina, is a significant turning point in the Civil Rights movement.

1961 "Freedom Rides" throughout the South organized by Northern activists highlight segregated transportation facilities.

1963 Protests in Birmingham, Alabama, and other Southern cities result in a massive march on Washington, DC, where the Rev. Martin Luther King, Jr gives his "I Have a Dream" speech.

1964 President John F. Kennedy passes the Civil Rights Act.

1965 The Alabama Selma-to-Montgomery march is one of the decisive demonstrations in the southern struggle for civil rights.

1968 Martin Luther King, Jr is assassinated at the Lorraine Motel in Memphis, Tennessee.

1976 James Earl Carter, governor of Georgia, is elected president of the United States.

1980 Ted Turner establishes Cable Network News, based out of Atlanta.

1986 The King Biscuit Blues Festival begins in Helena, Arkansas.

1991 The Louisiana state legislature legalizes

riverboat gambling on the Mississippi River; a year later the state of Mississippi does the same.

1992 William Jefferson Clinton, the governor of Arkansas, is elected to the presidency, with Al Gore, a senator from Tennessee, as vice-president, the first "double-South" ticket since 1860.

1996 The Olympic Games are held in Atlanta. A bomb explodes in Centennial Olympic Park, killing one bystander and injuring 111 others.

2003 Hurricane Isobel lashes the Outer Banks in North Carolina and hurtles along the East Coast, killing 12 people.

2004 A long dispute over the Confederate battle flag being part of the Georgia state flag is decided by referendum; the Rebel image is rejected. ❏

PRECEDING PAGES: the Battle of Kennesaw Mountain, Georgia, 1864, one year before the Civil War ended.
LEFT: king cotton, secret of the South's success.
RIGHT: Atlanta, Olympic city.

The manner of
drawing in of timber
into the forte for the
buylding of a howse

PASCES

BEGINNINGS TO THE GOLDEN AGE

*From rude beginnings as a mosquito-infested colony, to a haunting, romantic
land of myths where cotton was king, the South has always been a place apart*

More than any other part of America, the South stands apart. Some say it's the climate – the thick, oppressive subtropical atmosphere that for eight or nine months every year gives life a unique quality: men and beasts move slower when it's 90 degrees in the shade. Today, however, the South has – and has in abundance – air conditioning, interstate highways, franchise fast-food restaurants, and all the other paraphernalia of American consumerist culture. And still it is the South. Thousands of Northerners and foreigners have migrated to it and work happily in its prosperous cities and beguiling countryside, but Southerners they will not become. For this is still a place where you must either have been born, or have "people" who were born here, to feel that it is your native ground.

Locals will tell you this. They are proud to be Americans, but they are also proud to be Virginians, South Carolinians, Tennesseans and Alabamians. But they are conscious of the pull of another loyalty too, one that transcends the usual ties of national patriotism or of state and local pride. It is a loyalty to a place where life has always been lived in unique ways, a place where habits are strong and memories long. If those memories could speak, they would tell the stories of a region powerfully shaped by its history and determined to pass some of it along to future generations of the New South.

Swampy beginnings

The permanent settlement of what would later become British North America began on the swampy shores of the Chesapeake Bay region in 1607, just four years after the death of England's first Queen Elizabeth and nine years before the death of William Shakespeare. After having known of this continent's existence for more than 100 years, northern Europeans, and

---

LEFT: one of the first British settlements in Virginia, shown in a contemporary drawing.
RIGHT: a rare watercolor of the first of the New World colonists.

in particular Englishmen, undertook what over centuries was to become one of the greatest cultural transplants in recorded history. The region that would evolve into the American South was one of its first and most long-lasting results.

Unlike some of its neighbors to the north, such as Massachusetts and Pennsylvania, the

land halfway down the eastern seaboard that would become Virginia was not settled according to some grandiose scheme. Its history witnesses no effort to rule men by the power of a single grand, inspiring, or fearful idea. On the contrary, Virginia and the civilization that was developed and passed on to the larger South can be understood only if it is seen as a thoroughly earthly effort to transplant the institutions and the general style of living of old England to the soil of a new wilderness world.

If the Pilgrims and the Puritans clung to the rocky shores of Massachusetts Bay in an heroic effort to flee from the Old World's vices, the Virginia colonists hoped to celebrate and fulfill here the Old World's virtues – an Old World with which the majority of them had no serious religious, ideological, or philosophical complaints. Except in one important respect, these were satisfied men.

What drew them across a wild ocean to the edge of a wilder continent was ambition of a largely economic sort, which could find no adequate outlet in Europe. For decades, the Spanish had been extracting fortunes in gold and silver from their southern American preserves – perhaps Englishmen could do the same.

In March 1584, Sir Walter Raleigh obtained a charter from Queen Elizabeth to establish an

English settlement in Virginia and explore the region. Members of the first team of settlers returned to England disgruntled, but Raleigh remained determined to establish an outpost, and in 1587 he sent 150 settlers to the New World once again. Although their original destination was Chesapeake Bay, these settlers landed first at Roanoke Island, on a narrow strip of land off the coast of what is now North Carolina, and remained there.

As the settlers struggled to carve out a niche of civilization, Spain cast its acquisitive eyes toward England, and the British government was forced to divert most of its efforts toward defeating the Armada.

Lost colony

When matters in Europe settled down, Raleigh dispatched another expedition carrying supplies and new settlers to the Roanoke colony. What these settlers found when they arrived in 1590 was not a thriving community. All the original settlers had vanished, and the only clue to their demise was the word "Croatoan," the name of a tribe of Indians carved in the bark of a tree.

Despite the mysterious and frightening end of the 1587 lost colony, Englishmen continued to devise new methods of financing settlements in the New World. Joint-stock companies, such as the London Company and the Plymouth Company, were formed with an eye toward maximum profits and minimum risks.

To that workaday end, the London Company secured from King James I a royal charter to found a colony in the southern part of "Virginia," as the entire region claimed by England was called. Not quite sure of what they would find, the company bosses sold shares and set about recruiting settlers. They paid each settler's passage, and the latter agreed to work for the company for seven years before striking out for himself.

In 1606, 120 men set sail toward Virginia in three ships under the command of Captain Christopher Newport. Their instructions were to establish a fortified post from which they were to trade with the natives and search for a passage to the Pacific Ocean. The ships reached Chesapeake Bay in April 1607, after a four-month voyage that claimed the lives of 16 members of the party. The group sailed 30 miles (48 km) up the James River and selected as their site a densely wooded area bordering a mosquito-ridden swamp. The settlers then split into three groups, each with a specific task: constructing a fort, planting crops, and exploring the region further.

By August, mosquitoes brought an epidemic of malaria, and eight months after their landing, only 38 of the original settlers were still alive. Their salvation was due in part to the efforts of Captain John Smith, who negotiated with the Native Americans and persuaded them to trade with the settlers for maize.

The Native American tribes in the region were loosely bound in a confederacy headed by a powerful chief called Powhatan. A shrewd leader who mistrusted the English objectives, Powhatan resisted efforts by the British to force the native tribes into a tributary status. Peace was achieved between the English and the Native Americans in later years, but it was not just due to the Crown's grand scheme to form a partnership. Instead, it was furthered by a marriage in 1614 between John Rolphe, an English settler, and Pocahontas, Powhatan's brave and stylish daughter.

POCAHONTAS

Pocahontas, daughter of Chief Powhatan, married a white settler named John Rolphe in 1614. She later sailed to Europe and was a huge success, feted by royalty.

Women, children and slaves

In 1609, the first women and children came to Virginia. Their arrival, together with that of the first black slaves in 1619, marked its transition from trading post to colony. As settlers got control of their own parcels of land, they turned to a new crop that was to be their salvation: a broad-leaved plant, grown by the Indians and refined with West Indian stock, that the world came to know and both love and revile as tobacco. Thanks to tobacco, Virginia attracted labor and capital and became a viable commercial colony.

The labor required for the cultivation of tobacco came at first from indentured servants – men and women willing to sell themselves into personal service in return for the price of a passage to Virginia. The problem was that such laborers were white Englishmen who, after a fixed period of time, would have to be paid and would change overnight from cheap bound labor to expensive free labor.

The importation of black slaves ultimately resolved this difficulty. Yet the purchase price of a good African laborer remained substantially higher than the lease price of a good English servant. The relative price of slaves fell only by the end of the 17th century, because the European slave traders and their African suppliers were growing more efficient at their unsavory business. For now, rising life expectancy in the American colonies made it likely that a planter would in fact get a full lifetime's labor out of a slave who had cost him approximately twice as much up front as an indentured servant.

In 1618, the London Company concluded that the most practical way to govern Virginia was to let the colonists govern themselves. Under the leadership of Governor Edwin Sandys, the company allowed the planters to elect representatives to an assembly, which, together with the governor's council, was empowered to legislate for the colony.

The first such assembly, the House of Burgesses, met in Jamestown in August 1619. Free white males over the age of 17 elected two representatives from each of Virginia's 11 towns. It is remembered today as the first colonial legislature to be set up in the New World.

Ætatis suæ 21. Aº. 1616.

The Carolinas

Settlement in the Carolinas got its start in 1653 when colonists from Virginia pushed southward into the area around Albemarle Sound. Eager to escape the taxes and all the trappings of civilization taking hold in Virginia, these settlers found to their dismay that life in the Carolinas was no better: 10 years later, Charles II granted large tracts of land in the region to eight men who had supported the restoration of the English monarchy.

These eight new proprietors were determined to increase the population of their colony and not to depend alone on refugees from Virginia. They promised prospective settlers from

LEFT: power brokers of the new colony.
RIGHT: Pocahontas, daughter of Chief Powhatan.

England freedom from customs duties on wine, silk, capers, wax, and other goods shipped from the colony back to Britian. Then in 1669, the proprietors each agreed to contribute £500 to a proposed settlement at Port Royal. Three ships had set off from England in August 1660, landing first in Virginia to purchase supplies and then in Barbados to recruit more colonists.

That fall, the ships sailed for the Carolinas, but one was wrecked in a gale in the Bahamas. The other two ships took refuge from the storm in Bermuda and after repairs took to the seas again in February 1670. Led by William Sayle, a Puritan settler in the Bahamas and former

governor of Bermuda, the group abandoned plans to land at Port Royal and selected instead a site on the Ashley River. They named their new home Charles Towne in honor of the king.

Glittering city

Shortly after landing, the settlers began constructing another town, which they also called Charles Towne, having renamed their original town Kiawah. By the beginning of the 1680s, the new city was home to around 1,200 people.

Despite the intention of the proprietors to speed growth in both Upper and Lower Carolina, they generally directed most of their attention to the southern region of the colony,

and settlers in the north became dissatisfied. Governors were deposed, and direct appeals were made to the Crown in England. In 1719, the Carolinas' petition to be made a royal colony was at last granted; a few years later Parliament divided the region and made North Carolina yet another royal colony.

The differences between the two colonies ran deep. North Carolina had been settled as early as 1653, 10 years before Charles II granted land to the proprietors. Many of these settlers had completed terms as indentured servants and were eager to grab bits of land for themselves. In addition, ever-increasing numbers of new settlers were attracted by laws that forbade suits over earlier debts, and also by laws that exempted them from taxes for one year.

Tobacco road

Tobacco became the primary crop of North Carolinians, but because of the area's treacherous shoreline, the settlers found it difficult to move their produce to the marketplace. Generally, they were forced to haul their crops overland to Virginia where government agents imposed importation taxes. As a result, for a long time North Carolina remained a region of small farms, where subsistence rather than trade was the main rule.

South Carolina, on the other hand, became a region of great plantations growing easily marketed crops such as rice and indigo. By the 1730s, the commercial possibilities of the rice culture were being realized on a large scale along the length of the tidal and inland swamplands of the Low Country. Indigo, a plant grown for its rich blue dye, thrived on the drier soils unsuitable for rice, ideally complementing it. Neither did indigo require attention in the winter, leaving the slave labor force available for other tasks.

Within a few years of the establishment of the first rice plantations in South Carolina at the end of the 17th century, the black population was greater than the white. Laborers died quickly in the malarial conditions of the swamplands, but planters grew rich and replaced their dead and sick workers with an ever-increasing number of black slaves. Owners of the sprawling plantations often lived in Charleston (formerly Charles Towne) and left the management of their land and workforce in the hands of overseers. Cruel punishments were inflicted on many South Carolina slaves for minor infractions, and overseers were generally more concerned over the commissions they received for harvests than over the health and welfare of the workforce.

Between 1740 and the Revolution – the golden age of colonial South Carolina – prices rose and planters increased production. Rice exports tripled, those of indigo quadrupled, and the annual value of these crops soared five times over. Everywhere planters prospered, many to a degree that would never be experienced again in the South. Both of South Carolina's great crops were much better suited to

ing his interests in a rice company in South Carolina where attacks by the Spanish from Florida were common. He was perhaps no less concerned over the insidious conditions in English debtors' prisons. His two interests coalesced in a scheme to establish a new colony that would serve as a buffer between South Carolina and Florida and would be settled by former debtors' prison inmates who would repay their debts through military service.

Parliament approved the plan and granted to a group of philanthropists the right to establish the colony of Georgia. These proprietors were to govern and supervise the colony for 21 years

large-scale farming units than tobacco, which meant that, even though South Carolina was a much younger colony than Virginia, its plantation system, totally dependent on slave labor, established roots fast and deep.

From Salzburg to Savannah

The last English colony in America, Georgia was also the only colony that formed the focus of a political and social experiment. General James Oglethorpe was concerned over protect-

Left: tobacco, the colony's first successful crop, made for prosperous beginnings.
Above: the glittering city of Charleston, South Carolina.

and then return it to the hands of the Crown.

The first group of settlers (130 men, women, and children) arrived at the mouth of the Savannah River in 1733. General Oglethorpe laid out the city of Savannah almost immediately, and over the next six years, nearly 5,000 immigrants from Salzburg, Scotland and Moravia joined the original group. The proprietors allotted 50-acre (20-hectare) tracts of land to settlers in exchange for military service.

From the colony's founding, Parliament had banned the importation or use of slaves in the region because of fears that the slaves would aid the Spanish in any hostilities that occurred. To help the settlers in farming, the proprietors encouraged indentured servitude, but the costs were too high for many settlers. They envied the large plantations and slave holdings of their neighbors in South Carolina, and only seven years after Georgia's founding, they began to ignore the law banning slavery. By the end of the 1740s, the law was repealed, and the plantation system gained a stronghold in the colony.

Go west

Interest in western lands began as early as 1650 when Captain Abraham Wood led an expedition through the Blue Ridge Mountains to the falls of the Roanoke River. Over the next 50

J.⁰ᴮ ᴸ. MOYNE
⠀⠀⠀BIENVILE

years, many Virginians made fortunes in the fur trade in the west, reaching as far as the fertile Tennessee Valley. In 1716, Virginia's governor Alexander Spotswood led a group of explorers into the Valley of Virginia, returned to Williamsburg, and petitioned the Crown for grants of land in the western territory.

Joining these Tidewater émigrés were settlers from Pennsylvania, whose colonial government encouraged individuals who had completed terms as indentured servants to move south. They moved to areas around Martinsburg and Shepherdstown in what is now West Virginia and to the region around Winchester, Virginia, in 1726. Within just eight years, the Virginian

colonial government had organized Orange County to impose a governmental system on the new western settlements, and four years after that the districts of Frederick and Augusta were established. Further west, the area that contains the present-day states of West Virginia, Kentucky, Ohio, Indiana, Illinois, Michigan, and Wisconsin was named West Augusta.

North Carolina's western region filled up with Scots-Irish and Germans from Virginia, and six counties were formed between 1743 and 1762. South Carolina's western lands were parcelled out to prospective settlers who also received livestock and supplies from the colonial government. The western settlers were of a different temperament to the Tidewater settlers, and their surroundings imposed a contrasting lifestyle. Because of the ongoing difficulty of moving their produce to markets, the western settlers generally operated small farms not dependent on slave labor.

Revolution

In 1763, the year generally regarded as the end of the Colonial period and the beginning of the Revolutionary, the South was inhabited by 700,000 people, not counting Native Americans. Basically of English descent, the white population carried on their cultural traditions in the face of the more recent arrivals of Germans, Roman Catholic Irish, Scots-Irish, and French Huguenots. The population included about 300,000 black slaves. A large number of slaves were American-born, but the slave trade with Africa continued. Virginia had more slaves than any other colony, about 100,000 in 1763, whereas about 50,000 slaves lived in North Carolina and 70,000 lived in South Carolina. These slaves manned the plantations, raising tobacco, rice, and indigo.

As an economic institution and as a system of racial control, slavery defined relations between black and white. Racial prejudice came to these shores with the Europeans, and in the 18th century abstract questions about the morality of slavery were, in the face of that institution's indisputable economic utility, kept muffled and largely private.

On the eve of the Revolution, slavery was practiced in the Northern colonies as well. However, nowhere north of the Potomac River did blacks constitute anything approaching 40 percent of the population, as they did in

Virginia and in most other Southern colonies, to say nothing of the 66 percent currently living in South Carolina.

The war by which America became one united nation was fought between 1775 and 1781 throughout the English colonies, from New England to Georgia. Southerners and Northerners alike shed blood in the attempt to throw off the British yoke. The leader of their armies, George Washington, was a brave Virginian, and a slaveholder. The war began on Northern soil at Lexington and Concord in Massachusetts. It ended on Southern soil, on the Yorktown Peninsula in Virginia, not far from the original colonies of Jamestown and Williamsburg.

In the wake of independence, all the states drew up constitutions, reducing the powers of the Crown-appointed governors, but none granted universal male suffrage. The Church of England was disestablished everywhere, but efforts to create public schools failed. Most Southern states began to abolish the slave trade, but not slavery itself. Many planters felt that the existing order depended on the continuation of a massive black labor force and thus, necessarily, of slavery, and while there was genuine moral aversion to it within the South, it was usually coupled with the conviction that emancipation was unthinkable without "colonization" of the blacks back to Africa.

As the states emerged from war with a great world power, there was much to bind them together despite themselves. They had a common enemy and felt a healthy fear of further British aggression that lasted long into the postwar period. The war had enlisted men in a common army, but could the more populous North, progressively turning toward commerce and manufacturing, coexist contentedly with a staunchly agricultural South?

Virginian George Washington was 57 when he was inaugurated the first president of the United States under the new Constitution in 1789; he was also one of the richest men in America. Washington was succeeded in office by John Adams, but it was the presidency of Thomas Jefferson (1801–09), architect, gentle-

man, and author of the Declaration of Independence, that ushered in the palmy days of what came to be known as the "Virginia dynasty." For the next 25 years, Virginian planters occupied the White House and presided over a young nation generally enjoying a flush of nationalism and optimism about its prospects.

The Louisiana Purchase

Jefferson "the nationalist" bought the vast Louisiana Territory – reaching from the Mississippi River to the crest of the Rocky Mountains that doubled the size of the nation – from Napoleon in 1803, although there was nothing

in the Constitution that gave the president the right to acquire new lands. In 1805, he asked Congress for money to buy the territory of Florida from Spain.

At the time of Louisiana's transfer to the US from France, New Orleans was a small, provencial town of just over 8,000, with black people accounting for slightly more than half of the population. More than 50 percent were slaves, but the number of free blacks was also substantial. Creoles of French, African, and Spanish descent were in the majority, but there was also a significant element with other origins. Physically, the town consisted of about 1,300 structures situated almost entirely in the area

LEFT: Sieur de Bienville, founder of New Orleans.
RIGHT: Thomas Jefferson: the president, architect, and statesman who doubled the size of the nation with the Louisiana Purchase in 1803.

that is today called the *Vieux Carré* — or, more commonly, the French Quarter.

The South itself was undergoing change. As the price of staple crops tumbled 75 percent and the Industrial Revolution took hold in the North, old sectional realities, based since colonial times on very subtle but profound cultural differences, re-emerged now heightened by economic grievances. When this was combined, from the 1830s onwards, with the emergence of the slavery issue as the most powerful agent of sectionalism, one era in Southern history gave way to another.

The nationalist South, which had won inde-

pendence in concert with the North, written the Constitution, and forged the federal republic, gave way to the sectional South, which, due to the burden of slavery and its own understandings of the American polity and the good life, finally forsook that republic for a nation of its own imaginings.

Antebellum era

There is something about the history of the South between the Revolution and the Civil War that makes it, in the popular imagination, loom larger and more vividly than any other moment. That period is strewn with durable images of masters and slaves and Southern

belles, of plantation houses with white pillars and broad fields of cotton. This is the South immortalized in Margaret Mitchell's *Gone with the Wind* and trivialized in countless subsequent volumes of historical romance. It is a South that seems both content and sure of itself as being a place apart from, and superior to, the rest of America, even as it headed for disaster. It is a picture that only truly characterizes the South of the late antebellum period and then only unevenly, and it is a South that was the product of a gradual evolution.

A place apart

To understand that point of arrival, it helps first to consider the texture of Southern life before the divisiveness of sectionalism took hold, and then to observe the political flashpoints that marked the South's increasing self-awareness as a place apart, with a destiny all its own.

On the eve of the antebellum era, the South had ample reason to be satisfied with America's national affairs. The Republican Party – then the only political party worthy of the name, and not to be confused with the anti-slavery party of Abraham Lincoln, which was not founded until the 1850s – was strongly influenced by Southerners.

James Monroe, a Southerner and the last of the "Virginia dynasty," was still president; William Crawford of Georgia, John C. Calhoun of South Carolina and William Wirt of Virginia constituted half of Monroe's cabinet.

The flush of nationalism from the Revolution itself and from the second war with Britain in 1812 – culminating in the successful Battle of New Orleans – still warmed the land. Five signatories of the Declaration of Independence were still alive. Thomas Jefferson, its author, was still master of his magnificent house, Monticello, in Virginia, and was also still a reminder of the boldness of the American national experiment, and of America's genius for a new kind of politics.

But if the South was politically still at peace with the rest of America, there were palpable differences in its cultural and economic life from which political particularism, aggravated by the debate over slavery and western expansion, would grow. At the time the Constitution was written, and for some years into the early history of the young republic, it appeared that the population of the Southern states would at least equal, and perhaps even exceed, that of the North. The national census in 1820 still mirrored the old colonial demographics. One in every four Southerners was a Virginian, yet not even one in 25 people lived in Louisiana. Maryland, Virginia, and North Carolina boasted half of the entire Southern population, while the three most southwestern states of Mississippi, Alabama, and Louisiana were home to less than one-tenth of the population.

But these were the areas that were growing most quickly. Between 1810 and 1820, the white population of Tennessee, Alabama, Mississippi, and Louisiana increased by as much

King cotton

In the 18th century, the South's great crops had been those of seaboard Virginia and South Carolina: tobacco and rice. In the 19th century, sugar was the chief crop in Louisiana, which required great investment in both land and slaves. Sugar was unique among Southern staple crops in its dependence on tariff protection. But short-staple cotton, which could be grown anywhere, either by gangs of slaves or by white yeomen, on rough land as well as fertile, was becoming more popular.

The Deep South states of Louisiana and Mississippi especially thrived on the new crop's

as 50 percent, while that of Maryland, Virginia, and the Carolinas rose just 12 percent. There were also significant variations with regard to slavery. At one extreme, slaves constituted nearly 53 percent of the population of South Carolina and were also in the majority in Louisiana; in Tennessee they accounted for just 19 percent of the total. But despite these statistics, it was only in the states of Tennessee and Kentucky that blacks accounted for less than one-third of the population.

LEFT: the Battle of New Orleans, 1815.
ABOVE: by the early 1800s, 90 percent of the Southern economy was engaged in agriculture.

popularity, but cotton fields also expanded westward across Alabama and Mississippi into Arkansas and Texas.

The introduction of Eli Whitney's cotton gin in 1793 had made possible the rapid combing of the plant and vastly increased the South's cotton output and its profitability. By 1820, cotton had already surpassed all other Southern produce, and three-quarters of the crop of 353,000 bales went for export. Over the next 30 years, the price declined steadily but yields increased, almost doubling in every decade leading up to the Civil War.

For many people, cotton represented their big chance, not just of making a living but of achieving real success, and the legendary path from dogtrot cabin to white-columned splendor was genuinely trodden by countless Southerners who started with little, but who, by the 1850s, took their proud place as grandees of "The Cotton Kingdom."

Steamboat's a comin'

Before the railroad era, which did not reach much of the South until the 1840s and 1850s, the need to transport bulky 500-lb (230-kg) bales of cotton to market put a premium on water transportation and briefly sustained the fleets of steamboats that had plied the Missis-

it be emancipated. The American Colonization Society was founded in 1816 and was headed by Southerners James Madison, James Monroe, and John Marshall from Virginia. In 1826, of the 143 emancipation societies in existence in the country, 103 had been founded in the South, many of them by Quaker Benjamin Lundy, who spread the abolition message through the mountainous regions of Tennessee and North Carolina. In addition, there were several anti-slavery newspapers in the South, including the *Emancipator* in Tennessee.

Some blacks were in fact "colonized" back to Africa, and the west African nation of Liberia

sippi River from 1811. Slavery, which had attached itself to the South in colonial times, proved well adapted to the cotton trade and helped fuel its expansion. However, much of the enlightened opinion of the age, both in the North and the South, had doubts about the morality of the institution.

In the 1770s, Thomas Jefferson, a slaveholder until the day he died, proposed repatriating ("colonizing" as it came to be known) black people back to Africa. Slavery was obviously a Southern problem and one that involved both the moral problem of holding other humans in perpetual bondage and the practical problem of what to do with an alien race should

owes its existence to the movement; its capital city, Monrovia, was named for President James Monroe. But the numbers were simply too daunting – and the economic stakes too high – for "colonization" ever to be tried widely.

Besides, there was the pull of cotton, which was so compatible with slavery, and which not only profited the Southern planters but also represented the bulk of United States exports and fueled the entire national economy. For a new country trying to establish itself, Southern cotton, whether or not it was grown by slaves, constituted a tremendous economic resource that no one, not even Northerners, were prepared to put at risk.

Triangular trade route

The South's increasing reliance on staple-crop agriculture had consequences both inside and outside the region that no one could fully foresee. Indeed then, with cotton constituting the lion's share of American exports, that reliance did not seem excessive. But Southerners relied heavily on others to transport their precious staples to faraway markets, as they themselves sailed few ships and built almost none.

Thus, like it or not, they found themselves locked into a sort of triangular trade, in which cotton from the South went to England, and manufactured goods from England and Europe

Southerners generally felt well served by it. With their exports exceeding $30 million a year, some Southerners enjoyed great credit far and wide, displaying it splendidly.

Insofar as Southerners manufactured things for themselves, they made relatively simple items necessary to service the needs of their agricultural society. They worked with wood, iron, and hides, and they ground grain into meal, grits, and flour. In most of the South, the white artisan class, which also had to compete with trained plantation and urban slaves, were too few in number and too dependent on agriculture to become as important as they would be in

came to New York, and then sold to the South. It was a far-flung economic system, which in general relied on the factories of the Old World, the commercial and transportation services of the American Northeast, and the staple agricultural products of the American South.

As a key player in such an international system, Southerners came early and strongly to believe in free trade as a cornerstone for prosperity. Potential for abuse existed, but the pattern usually fitted the region's needs, and

LEFT: steamboats, later supplanted by the railroads, were engines of the South's golden age.
ABOVE: duels were fought in New Orleans' City Park.

the North. Such trades were all small-time, with usually only two or three men to a shop, and they served largely local markets.

By contrast, tobacco and iron were sometimes worked in establishments of considerable size. Virginia, which was the nation's largest coal producer, turned out pig iron, castings, nails, firearms, and farm implements. Tobacco factories transformed half the tobacco crop into plugs and twists for chewing, snuff, pipe tobacco, and cigars. And yet, there were probably more field hands in some single counties of the South Carolina Low Country in 1820 than there were factory workers in the whole of the South.

It would be a mistake to regard the South, at this point still 40 years before the Civil War, as a place powerfully united by either character or conviction. Two types of internal tension in particular strained the unity of Southern life, creating political ramifications as the antebellum years wore on. The conflict between Low Country and Up Country reached back to colonial times, when the coastal regions of South Carolina and Virginia had boasted more advanced social institutions, more ample material possessions (including more slaves), and larger towns than the remoter regions.

In Tennessee, it was the fertile central and

western regions that corresponded to "Low Country," while the mountainous eastern sections played the role of "the backwoods." Obviously much could depend on which of these groups controlled the state governments, and the unity of the South would depend in part on whether the same type of groups were in power in each of the states.

The second source of internal division was between the upper South and the cotton, or Deep, South. Agriculture in Virginia was more diversified, and much produce was sold domestically; it boasted more commerce and manufacturing and enjoyed greater proximity to the outside world. In most of the Deep South,

cotton was the predominant money crop, with rice and sugar at the edges, and it sold abroad on the world market. The upper South had more free blacks; the Deep South had the heaviest concentration of slaves. Of all the Southern states, South Carolina probably shared the least with anybody else. Virginia still enjoyed the most revered heritage but seemed somehow to be losing its economic and political grip. And the transmontane states such as Tennessee were assuming new vigor and importance every year.

Civil unrest

With "colonization" providing an outlet for moral frustrations about slavery, and with cotton constituting a key to national prosperity, it would seem that the matter of slavery might not necessarily have led, as it did, to the dissolution of the Union and civil war. Indeed, slavery was basically left as something to be regulated by the states as they themselves saw fit. So it might have remained, at least for a much longer time, had the new American nation been a fixed, static place, as most older nations were by then. But America in the early 19th century was a land on the verge of both economic growth and geographical expansion, the likes of which the world had not seen before, and it is in this context that slavery – localized in the South but linked to the growth of the cotton trade – became the explosive issue of the later antebellum era. It invited the resurgence of sectionalism, which increasingly came to mean the slavery question, and finally provoked the constitutional crisis that nearly ended the American experiment.

Thomas Jefferson called this forging "an empire for liberty" – the process of state-making outlined in the Northwest Ordinance of 1787, which became the manual for the orderly growth of the American republic westward across the continent. Slavery ceased to be merely a local Southern matter, and Southern sectionalism, which was increasingly aggravated by both anti- and pro-slavery arguments, pushed the nation toward disunion. In 1819, there were 22 states, 11 slave and 11 free – the careful result of admitting first one type and then the other so as to maintain equal representation in the Senate. The problem came in the House of Representatives when the slave states, falling behind their Northern sisters, filled 81 seats compared with the North's 105.

At this early stage, it is foolish to dwell too closely on purely sectional divisions in the halls of the national government. The Republican Party was a national organization with major constituents, united by class and interest, on both sides of the Mason-Dixon Line – the state boundary between Maryland and Pennsylvania considered to be the dividing line between North and South.

The Missouri Compromise

In 1820, what focused attention so sharply on the matter of Congressional balance was the imminent admission to the Union of the state of Missouri. It was an occasion with precedent-setting potential for, if Missouri went "free," Southerners had reason to fear that so might the whole of the trans-Mississippi West. If that happened, the South, with its "peculiar institution" comprising hordes of black slaves, would find itself in a permanent minority in the government. Should that government then ever choose to amend the Constitution so as to attack slavery, the South would be at its mercy.

On March 3, 1820, a government compromise was reached in which Missouri would be admitted as a slave state but was to be paired with the admission of Maine as a free state. That much seemed fair to everyone and portended no ill for the future admission of other states. What did set off alarm bells and a new precedent was Congress's extension of the 36/30 latitude straight west across the whole Louisiana Purchase, for the purpose of dividing future free from future slave territory.

On the surface and in retrospect, this would seem a plausible enough thing to have done, but that is not to take into account the expansive spirit of nationalism that was then suffusing

American life and whose compelling symbol was the Great West.

Congress, now boldly legislating with regard to slavery in the new territories acquired in the west since the Revolution, banned it from some of that territory not yet even organized into states. The 36/30 line cut across the boundless spirit of the age and left a livid scar that said the west was now split. Thomas Jefferson most memorably captured the long-range meaning of what had happened. The compromise struck him, he said, as a fire bell in the night, and he warned the nation that any such fixed geographical line that divided the North and the South and was identified with political and

LEFT: plantation slaves made a prosperous economy.
ABOVE: some Southern cities had stores that specialized in domestic labor.

moral principles could never be erased peacefully. In the compromise, the Southern nationalists heard a distant death knell for the Union.

Free trade

The South's marriage to both staple-crop agriculture and the system of slave labor that made this possible continued to set the region apart from the rest of the country, even as cotton became an ever more valuable national asset. Cotton's value was tied to conditions in the world market, and the more the trade expanded and prospered, the more Southern agricultural interests became convinced that everything depended on free trade. So it was that, at the end of the 1820s, the issue of the tariff became as sectionally divisive as the issue of slavery expansion. The problem for a staple-crop producer was a classic dilemma of selling cheap, if the world price happened to be low, and buying-expensively, for the manufactured goods that Southern planters had to buy came at prices that were artificially inflated by tariff protection.

As far as Northern factory owners were concerned, protective duties encouraged growth in the early stages of industrialization; as far as the South was concerned, the duty imposed by the tariff was robbing them of valuable profit.

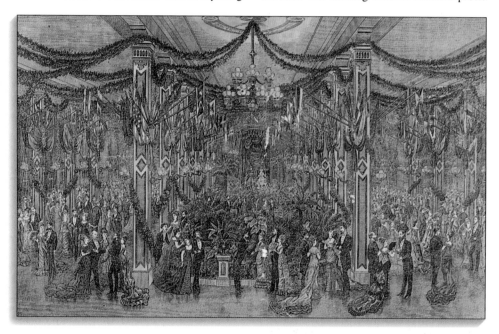

MARDI GRAS MYSTERY

Although the South may present itself to outsiders as a gracious, united land, rivalries between states and cities have been known to occur. Nowhere is this more apparent than in the American origin of Carnival, or Mardi Gras. Traditionally associated with New Orleans, Mobile in Alabama lays claim to having hosted the first celebration.

Certainly, the French in New Orleans were attending masked balls and parties as early as 1718, which continued until the Spanish authorities banned them. But Mobile dates its first celebration to 1703, when the Cowbellion de Rakin Society took loudly to the streets armed with rakes, hoes, and cowbells. Although they marched on New Year's Eve and not Fat Tuesday, Mobilians claim they were a true antecedent of Mardi Gras. Later, some of the Mobile members of the Cowbellian de Rakin Society traveled to New Orleans and were instrumental in the formation of the Mystick Krewe of Comus which, all agree, was New Orleans' first and most prestigious Mardi Gras society, established in 1857. It was then that the event gained status and momentum.

Carnival was suspended during and after the Civil War, but from around 1866 onwards, both cities resumed the parades, floats, masking, and general merriment that makes Mardi Gras so memorable.

Unhappy with the Union

As the nation expanded to the west and as the North's growth and vigor began to outdistance the South's, support would grow for secession from the Union. Even as the tariff declined as a divisive issue, that of slavery, infinitely more complex and emotional, took its place. To the very large extent that no Northerner was being asked to bear the burden of emancipation, it seemed to many Southerners that the North's allegedly noble convictions about the universal rights of man were actually very cheap convictions to hold. Like no other issue before it, anti-slavery laid bare the critical rifts inherent in the American nation, even as that nation was striving to reproduce itself in the west. To oppose slavery was, to Southerners, to oppose the way the South lived and prospered.

In a sense, either side could claim that it was the other side that threatened the Union. Northern anti-slavery voices argued that no nation founded on liberty could live up to those first principles as long as it tolerated slavery anywhere in its midst.

Southern pro-slavery voices argued that when the Union was put together in the 1780s, it was done in the complete knowledge of the existence of slavery in the Southern states, for whose economic concern alone slavery must remain. To attack it, therefore, was to attack the contract that had been established between the states that constituted the Union, putting something else – a "higher law" – above the Union. This was, of course, exactly what Northerners would accuse Southerners of when the latter spoke of nullification and the right of a state to secede: of putting something else – states' rights – above the Union. It all depended on just where a man stood, and from the 1830s, Southerners stood more and more firmly on defensive ground.

As the anti-slavery movement and the abolitionists shouted about a "higher law," Southerners responded by erecting an elaborate structure of economic, ethnological and Biblical arguments defending it. They warned of abolition's dire consequences, which would mean economic ruin for the South and the nation, destitution for the black people, and extermination of the white people. They argued that the Old and the New Testaments were strewn with references to masters and servants. Paul had commanded obedience, and Christ himself had never spoken against the institution, which was all around him. Slavery had obviously worked well for the Greeks and Romans, whose civilizations 19th-century Americans professed to admire.

Immutable laws of nature, pro-slavery apologists argued, ordained a "mudsill class," on whose crude labors a higher culture could be built by those of superior knowledge and

power. In the South, so the argument went, this meant a cultured and leisured white planter class at the top and, at the bottom, black slaves whose natural burden it was to hew the wood and haul the water, but whose inestimable benefit it also was to have been redeemed from African savagery and converted to Christianity. The slaves suffered no greater physical hardships than did Northern "wage slaves," and they enjoyed a good bit more security.

And so, as the end of the 1850s approached and as the threats to slavery multiplied, even once moderate Southerners again raised radical doubts about the wisdom of union with the American nation. ❑

LEFT: by the 1800s, Mardi Gras, or Carnival, was in full swing in Mobile and New Orleans.
RIGHT: Eli Whitney's cotton gin mechanized the combing of cotton, and vastly increased profits.

FROM THE WAR BETWEEN THE STATES TO WORLD WAR II

The first modern war devastated a land that saw itself prosperous and powerful.

It would be many, many years before the South could rise again

The American Civil War was a war the likes of which no one had seen before. It was the first real war of the industrial age; it was the first war in which armies were supplied by railway; it was the first war to be conducted by telegraph and so able to be reported quickly to homefront populations. It saw the introduction of the observation balloon, the repeating rifle (an early form of machine gun) and, at sea, the iron-clad, steam-powered warship. When it first began in the spring of 1861, there was much talk on both sides of a quick and neat conflict with the boys being home for a heroes' Christmas.

Naive Northerners saw it merely as a police action to curb the recalcitrant South. Naive Southerners boasted that one dashing young Southern cavalier could whip ten cowardly abolitionists. More thoughtful men on both sides, including Abraham Lincoln and Jefferson Davis, understood that the sectional controversies of four decades had aroused deep passions and that in all likelihood, once the war began, blood would flow until some final settlement was achieved.

Seeds of secession

The intemperate economic arguments over tariffs that strained the Union in the 1850s, and the South's reputation as the "wealth producing" section of the country, giving reason to believe it could go it alone, went hand in hand with perceived moral and cultural rifts. Demand rose in the South for Southern textbooks and Southern teachers and for the South to emancipate itself from literary dependency on Northern and European writers.

The most tangible cultural bond had already snapped in 1845 when the two largest Protestant denominations in America, the Methodists and the Baptists, had divided over the slavery question into Northern and Southern groupings. In each case, the stigma of immorality was placed on the slaveholding South. But it was the

publication of one particular book in 1852 – *Uncle Tom's Cabin or Life Among the Lowly* – that contributed to the course of disunion more than any other single cultural event. Author Harriet Beecher Stowe's experience of the South's peculiar institution was limited, to say the least, but the impact of her novel was not. Stowe, a member of a Northern anti-slavery family, drew heavily on the highly negative reports of conditions in the South to be found in Theodore Dwight Weld's propagandistic *Slavery As It Is*, and she reflected all its simplicities: overseers (Simon Legree) were universally sadistic; slaves (Uncle Tom) were angels in ebony. Slavery was worse in the Deep South.

LEFT: Fort Sumter, South Carolina, where the opening shots of the Civil War were fired on April 12, 1861.

RIGHT: Robert E. Lee, offered the command of the Union forces, turned it down to lead the Confederate army.

Explosive literature

While Stowe shared all the white racist attitudes of her time, slavery and not racial equality was her point, and she made it brilliantly. In the South, reaction to Stowe's book was vehement. Attacking the author and the book equally, newspaper editors claimed that Stowe had no knowledge whatsoever of the conditions of slaves in the South, possessed no "moral sense," and had plagiarized Charles Dickens. The book achieved a permanent place in American literary history, but at that particular time it also added the explosive element of moral self-righteousness to the slavery debate

by strengthening the stereotype of slavery as a malevolent institution that stood, literally and morally, in the path of national progress. Thousands of Northerners, having previously held themselves aloof from the moral question, were swayed by the book to join the abolition cause.

Self-righteousness settled on both sides, as the South counterattacked the libel on its character with no less than 15 novels of its own and with sweeping arguments that Northern wage earners were actually worse off than slaves. For in the late 1850s, as troubled as the political landscape had become, the South's actual landscape of plantations and farms enjoyed enormous prosperity. For this reason, the myth that

cotton was indeed king grew strong. This myth lent acceptability to the momentous decision to leave the Union by many Southerners who reasoned that a cotton-hungry Great Britain would have to give support to the South if that country itself were to survive. But places other than the South grew cotton, and the only calculation that went into Britain's decision about whom to support in the American Civil War was the cool calculation of which side it was that was most likely to win.

Dred Scott

Each of the remaining three years of the decade had brought grim omens. In 1857, the Supreme Court, five of whose nine justices were Southerners, waded into the slavery controversy with the Dred Scott Decision. The case involved the migrations of a black slave, Dred Scott, who during the 1830s had been carried by his master, John Emerson, an army surgeon, from the slave state of Missouri to Illinois, where the Northwest Ordinance of 1787 forbade slavery, and then to Wisconsin Territory, where the Missouri Compromise also forbade slavery. Scott finally returned to Missouri and sued for his freedom on the grounds that his stay in free territory made him a free man.

In a broad decision, the court seemed determined to vindicate the South and inflame the anti-slavery North. As a black and as a slave, the court decided, Dred Scott – and therefore all other black slaves and their descendants – was not a citizen and could not sue for his freedom.

John Brown's raid on the federal arsenal at Harpers Ferry, Virginia, in October 1859, also had an irrational impact on the course of events. John Brown, destined to become a mythical figure in American history, may well have been a madman. Certainly his scheme to liberate a number of slaves, whom he would then turn into guerrilla bands in the Virginia mountains, had a bizarre quality about it, while his tactics in trying to carry it off suggest greater theatrical than military genius.

His band of 21 included his own sons and several blacks, and no local slaves came to their aid, as had been anticipated they might. When a passing train alerted the outside world to their attack, Brown's raiders proved no match for the contingent of Marines, commanded by Robert E. Lee, who were sent to quell them.

Most Northerners, while disapproving the

raid's methods, lauded its aims. Moderate Southerners responded slowly at first, but hardened their attitudes when it was revealed that Brown had been financed by a secret cadre of wealthy Northern abolitionists. As extreme reactions set in on both sides, the raid became a turning point in the fast-developing secession crisis. Southerners who came to identify John Brown with the North – an oversimplification certainly, but a compelling one – concluded that they must secede to be safe, and that the fear that moved them was real and immediate.

South Carolina, predictably, responded first and, in December 1860, set in motion the train of secession. By February 6, 1861, all five of the other Deep South states – Mississippi, Florida, Alabama, Georgia, Louisiana – had followed, along with Texas. The states of the Upper South – Virginia, North Carolina, and Tennessee – hesitated, as did Arkansas, but warned that they would resist any attempt by the federal government to coerce any state that left the Union. President Abraham Lincoln, in his inaugural address on March 4, attempted to walk a fine line aiming to preserve what was left of the Union and to reassure the South: "I have no purpose directly or indirectly to interfere with the institution of slavery in the states where it exists." He also asserted that secession was legally not possible: "No state upon its own mere action, can lawfully get out of the Union." Both sides hesitated to make a move toward violence, and while the first shot was fired by the South, it was said to have been in response to overt Northern aggression.

Coercion, or at least the appearance of it in the South's eyes, came in April 1861 when Lincoln, after much delay, attempted to resupply Fort Sumter in Charleston harbor, one of the few federal military installations in the Deep South that had not surrendered to state authority. The garrison commander, Major Robert Anderson, refused South Carolina's ultimatum, and at 4:30am on April 12, South Carolina forces commenced a bloodless bombardment of the island fortress. The national colors came down 34 hours later.

LEFT: teenage cadets from the Virginia Military Institute helped win the Battle of New Market.
RIGHT: top to bottom: the Bonnie Blue flag of Texas (not official); the Stars and Bars; the Battle Flag; 1863 National Flag; 1865 National Flag.

A Southern nation

The confrontation instantly galvanized the North in defense of the Union, and Lincoln issued a call for 75,000 three-month volunteers to put down the, as he put it, "insurrection." Lincoln's call for troops at last forced the hand of the states of the moderate border South: Virginia seceded on April 17, Arkansas on May 6, Tennessee on May 7, and North Carolina on May 20. Slaveholding Kentucky, Maryland, and Missouri did not leave the Union but with their Southern sisters, they joined to declare the independence of a new Southern nation, the Confederate States of America.

While neither side ever lacked the resolution to see the fight through to the bitter end, the North had the clear advantage in numbers and economic strength. The 23 Northern states contained a population of 22 million, augmented by heavy foreign immigration. The North could, even in a long conflict, replace its losses. Though heavily agricultural like the South, it had a more balanced economy with an advanced industrial establishment, strong financial institutions, an excellent railroad grid, a navy, and a merchant marine. The 11 states of the Confederacy had a population of some 9 million, a third of whom were slaves. Its manufacturing was undeveloped and tied to

Jefferson Davis

One of many disparaging remarks the "Sphinx of the Confederacy" endured during, and after, the Civil War was that he was "overmatched and outplayed." Scholars have even suggested that if their roles had been reversed, and Lincoln had been president of the Confederacy, the Union might well have lost the war. Jefferson Davis, the only president of the Confederacy, was a complicated and enigmatic personality who never sought, and didn't want, the job.

In 1824, Davis attended the United States Mili-

tary Academy at West Point, graduating 23rd out of a class of 33. Love for Sara Knox Taylor, daughter of his commanding officer, Colonel Zachary Taylor (later president of the United States), caused Davis to resign from the army in 1835 because the colonel opposed the match. They married anyway and moved to Mississippi where Davis bought a plantation. But Sara died from malaria within three months. Davis spent the ensuing 10 years working his farm, and by all accounts his manner toward his slaves was patriarchal rather than brutal. He was a well-regarded local figure.

Davis married Varina Howard in 1845, the same year he was elected to the US Congress as representative for Mississippi. When war against Mexico was declared, he fought and returned a hero. A seat in the US Senate soon followed.

Henry Clay's 1850 Compromise Slave Act was anathema to Davis who, as a strong supporter of states' rights, felt Clay's bill violated the terms of the US Constitution. Davis resigned and went home to Mississippi. In 1853, Washington once again beckoned and President Franklin Pierce made Davis Secretary of War. He served with distinction until he was re-elected to the Senate in 1857.

The election of Abraham Lincoln in 1860, and his declaration that there would be no additional slave-owning states admitted to the Union, broadened the schism between North and South. In January 1861, Mississippi seceded. Davis resigned his Senate seat and was appointed major-general of the state's troops. The following month, the deadlocked Confederate Congress, meeting in Montgomery, Alabama, found in Davis a compromise presidential candidate upon whom all could agree, and elected him to the Confederacy's highest office. Davis received the news with something less than joy: "I thought myself better adapted to command in the field."

In the beginning, he was a popular choice; "honest, pure and patriotic" were some of the adjectives showered upon him. His cabinet included men of ability, and he listened to the advice of his generals. But 1863 saw a turn in Davis's fortunes. Becoming autocratic, he meddled in army matters, countermanding orders and promoting favorite officers. Many felt he had usurped powers not granted by the electorate, and called him a despot. Until the war's last days, Davis insisted it would be won by the Confederacy, and refused to consider any peace proposals except those that left the South independent.

When Lee surrendered at Appomattox in April 1865, Davis attempted to flee with his family to Mexico, but was caught and imprisoned, first in the shackles of a common criminal, at Virginia's Fort Monroe, where he was confined until 1867. After his release, Davis settled on a plantation near Biloxi, Mississippi *(see page 195)*, where he wrote his version of the Confederacy's history, *The Rise and Fall of the Confederate Government*. Mississippians wanted to return Davis to the US Senate, but he refused to ask for a federal pardon.

Jefferson Davis died peacefully on December 6, 1889 in New Orleans, Louisiana. His body now rests in Richmond, Virginia. ❏

LEFT: Jefferson Davis, president of the Confederacy.

agriculture; it had no substantial iron industry, and it made no heavy armaments. Its railroad network was still rudimentary and utterly unready for the massive load soon to be placed upon it.

Yet the discrepancy in resources, which Southerners recognized, was not initially compelling, for the South was taking a calculated risk on several counts. These were that the North would not actually fight to save the Union; that Great Britain and France, hungry for Southern cotton, would intervene on the South's behalf; and that the South's control of the Mississippi River would weaken western support for the Northern war effort. In each case, the South guessed wrong.

YANKEE OR REBEL?

Dissension over the war in parts of Virginia led to the adoption of a separate constitution. The new state of West Virginia was admitted to the Union in April, 1863.

70 years. They elected Jefferson Davis of Mississippi as president and Alexander H. Stephens of Georgia as vice-president. In military preparations, the Confederacy had some genuine advantages. Davis issued a call for 100,000 volunteers, and most who answered were well armed and clothed.

In its officer corps, the Confederacy had Robert E. Lee, who had served as the superintendent of the crack military academy West Point and was attached to a western command at the time of secession. Lee had been offered command

ABOVE: the burning of Richmond, the capital of the Confederacy, on April 3, 1865.

The government of the new Confederacy got its start on February 4, 1861, in Montgomery, Alabama, where representatives of the six states that had by then seceded met at a convention. The representatives adopted a provisional constitution, modeled faithfully after the Constitution but specifically clarifying issues of states' rights that had become muddled over the past

of the Northern armies but had turned it down, resigned from the US Army, and returned to his home state of Virginia where he was named major-general of the Virginia Confederate troops. Almost immediately upon hearing this news, more than 380 other officers resigned their commissions and took new positions in the Confederate forces.

While Davis was engaged in fielding his new armies, dissension grew in the southern Allegheny region of western Virginia and east Tennessee. The western counties of Virginia had not been represented at the convention that had approved the state's secession. On June 11, 1861, western delegates met to denounce secession and form a new government. The delegates elected Francis H. Pierpont governor, selected senators, and adopted a new state constitution for West Virginia, which was admitted to the Union in April 1863. In east Tennessee, only the establishment of martial law kept Unionists from following West Virginia's lead.

The opening shots of the war were fired on Fort Sumter, South Carolina, in April 1861. Exactly four mind-numbingly tragic years later, in April, 1865, General Robert E. Lee surrendered to Ulysses S. Grant in Appomattox. (*For a report on the major conflicts and battlefields, see "Civil War Sites" on page 93*).

The physical costs of the Civil War were huge on both sides. The war killed between 600,000 and 700,000 young men in a nation totaling only 33 million: a fatality rate around double that suffered by American forces in both world wars. The nation, both North and South, lost not only these men, however, but the children and the grandchildren amd the great-grandchildren who never were, a cultural loss that is beyond calculation.

The South suffered the most physically, for its cities, towns, and plantations were devastated and its economy ruined. During its brief and turbulent existence, the Confederacy, which

CIVIL WAR FACTS AND IRONIES

● The Civil War goes by many names. Some of these include: the War of Northern Aggression; the War of Rebellion; the Brothers' War; and "the Late Unpleasantness."

● Four of Abraham Lincoln's brothers-in-law fought on the side of the Confederates.

● Winchester, Virginia, changed hands 72 times.

● Missouri sent 39 regiments to fight in Vicksburg, Mississippi: 17 to the Confederacy and 22 to the Union.

● April 14, 1865, the date of Lincoln's assassination, was also the fourth anniversary of the surrender of Fort Sumter in South Carolina. It has been said Lincoln was invited to the ceremony, but declined in order to go to the theatre.

● Some 10,500 armed conflicts occured during the war. According to a study done by the Civil War Sites Advisory Commission, 384 of these were principal battles that took place in 26 different states. The Southern states that were engaged in 15 or more major conflicts include:

Virginia	123 battles
Tennessee	38 battles
Georgia	28 battles
Louisiana	23 battles
North Carolina	20 battles
Arkansas	17 battles
Mississippi	16 battles

had failed to stay the run and establish Southern nationhood, had at least crystallized Southern distinctiveness.

Reconstruction era

As the Confederacy crumbled and the Union took control of region after region in the South, President Lincoln was determined not to direct malice toward the conquered people. Despite heavy opposition in his party, the president devised a "Proclamation on Amnesty and Reconstruction." This plan called for the restoration of civil rights to all Southerners, except highly ranked civil and military officials, after they took an oath of allegiance to the Constitution. The plan also specified that when 10 percent of the state's voters had taken the oath, the state could then re-establish a government. The president's plan had not been signed when, on April 14, 1865, John Wilkes Booth assassinated Lincoln at Ford's Theatre. With Lincoln's death, the Reconstruction debate fell to President Andrew Johnson.

Johnson, a former tailor from North Carolina and then Tennessee, was a self-educated man who had slowly risen through the ranks of political office from alderman to US Senator. He had retained his seat in the Senate after Tennessee seceded – the only Southern senator to do so – and after the fall of Nashville, President Lincoln had appointed him military governor of Tennessee. Johnson's plan for Reconstruction was announced on May 29. It included all the provisions of Lincoln's plan but added that individuals with property valued at $20,000 or more were excepted from amnesty.

Carpetbaggers

In this way, Johnson attempted to alter Southern society. No lover of the wealthy, white, planter class, Johnson wanted to make room for small farmers and poor whites in the Southern political scene. There were also wide-reaching reforms for blacks. But these same reforms opened up the doors to scalawags (unscrupulous white Southerners who supported Republican policy) and carpetbaggers (Northerners who came South to take advantage of the conditions for personal gain).

LEFT: Robert E. Lee surrendered to Ulysses S. Grant at Virginia's Appomattox Court House on April 9, 1985.
RIGHT: remembering the past in an Atlanta cemetary.

For years afterward, most white Southerners couldn't say enough bad things about these times, and it became a sacred part of Southern myth that Reconstruction constituted the "blackout of honest government" and the unforgivable insult to the white race. Others – literate blacks and radical partisans – recalled it as a noble and well-intentioned experiment in which the native virtue and sterling performance of black people was matched only by the unadulterated malice of their Southern white adversaries.

For all their ineptitude, the Republican governments in the South did more than take bribes and swindle the taxpayers. Even though the

presence of blacks in public office would soon pass away, these regimes made marks that would last longer than they did themselves. The state constitutions on which they rested were superior to, or at least more modern than, their antebellum predecessors. Participation in politics was broadened to universal white manhood suffrage. Even black people, now guaranteed the vote by the Fifteenth Amendment, usually favored the vote for all whites regardless of the latters' past association with the Confederacy and the defense of slavery.

The first black man to sit in the United States Senate was Hiram Revels, an ordained minister and a schoolteacher from Mississippi. Revels was the first black to fill the chair once occupied by Jefferson Davis, and he was followed soon after by another black man, Blanche K. Bruce, who had been born a slave in Virginia, escaped bondage to become a teacher, and then returned to the South in 1869 to settle in Mississippi. Black people from Florida, Louisiana, Mississippi, Georgia, North and South Carolina, and Alabama served in the United States House of Representatives, and while not all of their careers in public life were especially memorable, neither were they any less remarkable nor any more prone to corruption than those of many of their white counterparts.

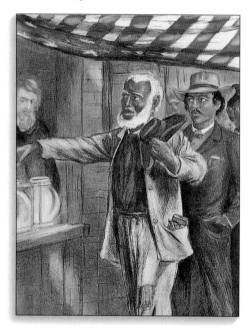

The new constitutions asserted the right of children to schooling, and the new state governments backed this up with appropriations that at least began to support such institutions. These administrations also began to give some tentative legal protection to women, who in much of the region had until this time to rely pretty much on their wits and their sex to get along in a man's world.

The government also did what it could to promote the economic rebuilding of the South, though in this it was severely limited by powerful prevailing notions about the limited role the state itself should play in the economy. The constitutions established both agencies to promote immigration into the South and, especially important, programs to promote industrialization. And of course these were the governments that for the first time gave blacks a real, though limited, chance to show what they could do in positions of power, trust, and responsibility.

But Reconstruction is only part of the story, for better or worse, of the Republican regimes in the state capitals. The South was not just a place being acted upon, but it was also a place filled with people acting on their own behalf to maintain their values and assert their influence on the nation.

Sabotage

From today's perspective, in the wake of the Civil Rights movements of the 1950s and 1960s, it is easy to look back on the white Southerners of the Reconstruction era with contempt for a people so morally dulled as to sabotage such a noble experiment in racial justice. But viewed by the standards of that age, it was they and not their reformist antagonists who represented the American mainstream. These were men convinced of the absolute impossibility of the black and white races coexisting in one place, except in a relationship of complete white control and, therefore, complete black submission.

Their commitment to white supremacy sprang from tradition, and in the 1870s and 1880s, it was also bolstered by the best scientific opinion. Herbert Spencer and William Graham Sumner pioneered a fierce brand of social Darwinism that dovetailed nicely with the practice of white supremacy at home and abroad. White Southerners were not alone; they were not an isolated, embattled minority of evil people who never outgrew nasty habits of whipping their slaves and keeping millions of blacks in their place.

Nevertheless, the idea of the Ku Klux Klan was conceived at Pulaski, Tennessee, in 1865. It began as an organization of unemployed Confederates and, by the late 1860s, had become an extralegal paramilitary brotherhood, wrapped in legendary bedsheets and shrouded in exotic ceremonies and rituals.

Large themes such as "racial adjustment" always take up prominent places in the history books, but there is a danger in this. For thousands of Southerners, the years after the Civil War were not judged by some far-off national reference points. They were a time neither of the perceived disaster of black alien rule, nor of the sparkling dawn of brotherhood and ultimately, racial equality. Rather, they were years without very much, if any, extraordinary moral dimension at all, when Southerners were not as preoccupied as we are commonly led to believe with either momentous political choices or intractable racial dilemmas.

These were years spent trying to make a dollar, and trying to solve the immediate, local, concrete problems that come with trying to stay alive in changed and changing circumstances. The South then was a world of harvest yields, of the weather, of freight rates to market, of prices in that market, of technological change, of social resistance to change. The 1870s were hard times in the South, as elsewhere, and it was the limits of the Southern economy as much as anything else that determined that the radical reforms of Reconstruction would not succeed. In a poor region, concern for prosperity far outweighed concern for civil rights and would continue to do so until that far distant day when the South finally got to its feet.

Sharecroppers

Slavery had been replaced by sharecropping, and all of those alleged new farms were not in fact worked by happy yeomen but by dour, overworked tenants, poor as ever and far from independent. Sharecropping was a simple arrangement whereby the landowner decided what crops were grown and then arranged for their marketing.

The proceeds were split into thirds: one for the labor, one for the land, one for the seeds and implements. Or put another way: one-third for the cropper, two-thirds for the owner. The plantations once worked by slaves were divided into plots worked by tenant families – and it was each of these new units that was counted in the census as a "farm." Thus the general structure of the Old South plantation – land held in parcels and worked by cheap labor with no other options – persisted.

Thousands of Northerners had come to realize that the underdeveloped South presented vast opportunities. It offered ingredients of early-

stage industrial development in abundance: land, timber, coal, water power, and cheap labor. "How to get rich in the South" propaganda streamed out of the North, and countless after-dinner speeches to eager groups of Northern businessmen and investors began with ringing admonitions to "Go South, young man ..."

Many Southerners, eager to put away the rancor of the war and its after-years, seemed keen to embrace their share of the nation's new industrial destiny. In a spirit of sectional reconciliation undergirded by a common desire for profits and prosperity, they welcomed the Yankee investors and industrialists, and not just with words.

With expanding railroads, by far the most magical technology of the age, the way was opened for the development of the South's vast iron ore and coal deposits and for the growth of cities such as Birmingham, Alabama, which Southerners John T. Milner and Daniel Pratt did their best, quite successfully, to turn into the Pittsburgh of the South. By 1898, Birmingham had become the largest source of pig iron in the United States and the third largest source in the whole world – yet, in 1860, there had been nothing there at all.

Beginning in the middle and late 1880s, the South's oldest cash crop, tobacco, proved that it too offered new market opportunities. But the

LEFT: after the Civil War, black men were granted the right to vote; this is a drawing from 1867.
RIGHT: by the 1870s, small farms replaced plantations.

greatest substance and the greatest symbolism of the new industrializing South grew from the crop most closely identified with the region: cotton. More than anything else, the cotton mill came to typify the effort of the South to be more like its former enemy, the North. Between 1880 and 1900, the number of Southern mills rose from 161 to some 400, which far outstripped the rest of the country.

Viewed on the surface, the South's industrial progress seemed impressive, and yet it was still tarnished not far below. The region had induced capital and manufacturing to come to it by offering everything at its command more

cheaply – taxes, power, land, raw materials, and especially labor. But once the initial processing had been done in the South, the final, more valuable (and infinitely more lucrative) work was done somewhere else, imprisoning the South in a self-defeating "colonial economy" of Southern enterprises controlled from Northern boardrooms and Southern factories feeding the profits of Northern shareholders.

This newer South fitted comfortably within this mainstream. The South had to start from a lower point than the rest of America, and it seemed that Southerners always had to run harder just to keep up. But about the worthiness of the race itself, prophets of this newer

South had no doubts. So spacious was their faith that there was even room in it for the South's most forgotten man – the black man.

Booker T. Washington

Booker T. Washington, born a slave in the Virginia back country, became the greatest black spokesman that the New South produced. He concluded that no sane white man, who truly hoped for the progress of his section, could profit by keeping millions of blacks in a condition of perpetual serfdom. It went against the grain of practicality not to allow everyone on the bandwagon, even though it went without saying that black Southerners would only ride at the rear.

But riding at the rear was better than not at all, and it was, Washington understood, about the best that could be expected. It was more essential for a black to be able to earn a dollar at a good job than to be able to spend a dollar in the same opera house as a white man. So he put forward his famous program for the vocational education of blacks both in skills, to enable them to support themselves and their families in modest comfort, and in trades, to give them some claim to the prosperity brought about by wider economic changes.

Booker T. Washington's enduring monument is Tuskegee Institute in Alabama (see page 147), an industrial training center where he hoped to educate blacks in the most practical ways of being useful to their own community. Today, Washington's measures seem mild, half-hearted, and to some even "Uncle Tomish." Then, however, they appeared prudent and not without a genuine vision for the black race. But the United States Supreme Court effectively scotched any notions of black social equality with its famous doctrine of "separate but equal." Racial segregation in public accommodation and education, the court said, could not be construed as "unequal" or as "discriminatory" so long as the facilities available to both races were comparable in quality.

Even though things in the South were, in fact, almost always separate but unequal, "separate but equal" remained the law of the land for race relations in all of the United States until as late as the 1950s. And in the South, which was where the vast majority of blacks still lived, a rigorous pattern of social segregation – known as the era of Jim Crow – clamped down on the many black people with unrelenting discipline. (The name Jim Crow comes from a song in a black minstrel show.)

World War I

With the outbreak of hostilities in Europe in 1914, key cotton exchanges did not open, and prices initially tumbled. But due both to its congressional influence and its felicitous climate, making year-round training possible, military camps and bases proliferated, and many cities continued on in peacetime. Southern ports became important embarkation points and home to an ever more immense American fleet.

with pent-up energy. The industrial boom triggered by the war expanded and, in the water-power rich South, was driven by electricity. The chemical and textile industries especially profited, and the region of the Carolina Piedmont overtook New England as the nation's primary consumer of the South's raw cotton.

The fashion for cigarettes and an increasing number of female smokers gave new life to the South's oldest source of wealth, tobacco, and it was at this time that names such as "Camel" and "Lucky Strike" entered the American vernacular. But none of these could match the Southern beverage that had first been brewed by an Atlanta

The wartime boom – once the initial cotton panic had passed – gave fresh substance to the New South's not so new boasts that industrialization was the path to a prosperous future. Munitions factories in Tennessee and Virginia, chemical plants in Alabama, and textile mills everywhere pulled Southerners out of the fields and, in what was a new experience for many, gave them a taste of earning real money.

The whole nation dashed toward the 1920s

druggist in 1886 and then made famous by Robert Woodruff in the 1920s: Coca-Cola. Everywhere there were new roads, automobiles, movie palaces and real estate subdivisions. But by 1920, the 11 American states with the lowest per capita income were all Southern, with Alabama at the bottom and Louisiana at the top. Thus poverty joined with race, religion, and the memory of defeat to set the South apart as America's most sectional of sections.

LEFT: Booker T. Washington founded Alabama's Tuskegee Institute; it still prospers today.
ABOVE: the Ku Klux Klan started in Tennessee in 1865 and was reborn in Georgia 50 years later.

The KKK

The Ku Klux Klan, which was reborn on Stone Mountain in Georgia on Thanksgiving night, 1915, still skulks about the South today, representing the anachronistic voice of white supremacy. Then, it was the authentic voice not only of the South's unrelenting race prejudice but also of the more general fear among a rural people that change was making a mess of old moral certainties. In this respect, the Klan did not mirror only Southern anxiety, and indeed some of its greatest "successes" came from places as far afield as Indiana, where it actually operated a successful political machine.

But the Klan's general lack of a well articulated program bespoke its truer nature – that of the defense mechanism, and death rattle, of a dying America and a more slowly dying South.

For such ill-educated people, whose daily lives were an endless (and for many hopeless) routine of planting cotton and waiting for it to grow, the rituals and mystique of the exotic hooded order fostered a sense of camaraderie and belonging amid the distress of an otherwise grim agricultural existence. The price of admission was $10 and it bought a knighthood in the Invisible Empire of the Ku Klux Klan, where there were wizards and cyclopses – and always someone else to blame.

Although the Klan became an influence in state politics, it never had a platform and could never boast the powerful political leadership needed for long-term success. Most of the

major urban newspapers of the day vociferously opposed it, and the KKK ultimately fell victim to its own excesses.

The 1930s

It was President Franklin Roosevelt, not the KKK, who had the greater impact on Southerners' lives during the 1930s. Roosevelt, a New York blue blood with a house in Warm Springs, Georgia, always claimed to know the South well – indeed to love it and understand its problems. Among many other projects, he was instrumental in furthering the Tennessee Valley Authority (TVA), one of the largest public works projects ever attempted.

The TVA's genesis reached back to 1916 to the federal authorization, for reasons of national defense, of power and nitrate plants on the Tennessee River at Muscle Shoals in Alabama and to a belief that there should be a public yardstick for measuring the cost of private utilities. At stake was water power, the generation of electricity, the production of fertilizer, flood control, navigation, conservation, and other facets of regional planning. The project encompassed an area touching on parts of seven states and nearly as large as England.

The TVA became a powerful ally of the New South once recovery came, adding immensely to the region's attractiveness for industrial development. The orchestration of resources by the TVA helped attract Northern capital anew. Along with the continued growth of textile and garment manufacturing, paper milling and furniture manufacturing, and increasingly chemical and petroleum industries, the TVA proved that, despite the drawbacks of outside investment –

CIVILIAN CONSERVATION CORPS

Anyone camping near the Skyline Drive or Blue Ridge Parkway in Virginia's Shenandoah Valley, or picnicking in Tennessee's Great Smokies National Park, is probably reaping the rewards of one of Franklin D. Roosevelt's most successful 1930s relief programs, the Civilian Conservation Corps (CCC). Enrolees were generally underprivileged young men who were assigned outdoor work in national parks near where they lived. At the same time, they were given educational opportunities to improve their social and occupational skills. Projects included building camp grounds and picnic areas, hiking trails, cabins and other lodging facilities, many of which are still in use.

and thus of outside control – if there were enough of it to go around, there would also be sufficient profits for the South.

Huey P. Long

Louisiana's Huey P. Long posed the only serious threat to Roosevelt in the early 1930s. By then a senator, Long provided crucial help in securing the Democratic Party nomination for Roosevelt in 1932 and at first pledged support. Two years after the election, that support evaporated as Long issued diatribes against the president's economic and labor policies. Long's dreams were not bounded by state lines. In

estimated Long could win six million votes as a third-party presidential candidate in the 1936 election. That prediction was never proved. In September 1935, Long was assassinated by Dr Carl Austin Weiss in the Louisiana State Capitol. The presumed motive was that Weiss was infuriated over Long's attempts to oust Weiss's father-in-law from his judgeship. That, too, was never proved. After firing the shot that killed Long, Weiss was gunned down by the senator's bodyguards, and the mystery remains.

Frivolous, but no less meaningful events, also took place in the 1930s. Atlantan Margaret Mitchell's book, *Gone with the Wind*, set the

1932, he announced his "Share-Our-Wealth" program, through which he proposed the liquidation of large personal fortunes; guarantees of $2,500 in annual wages to every worker; adequate pensions; and college educations for all qualified students.

Two years later, Long took his program nationwide and soon claimed that 7.5 million members belonged to his 27,000 clubs. His popularity soared to the point that poll-watchers

LEFT: Huey P. Long, Louisiana's high-profile politician.
ABOVE: Atlanta author Margaret Mitchell (left), and Clark Gable (right) at the starry premiere of *Gone With the Wind* in 1939.

imagination of the nation alight, prompting a glamorous ascent that culminated in a starry premiere of the MGM movie three years later.

World War II was shorter and less traumatic for the United States than for most of the other participating nations, but for a country that still clung tenaciously to old notions of innocence and isolation, it brought the cares – and the challenges – of the world crashing down on American shoulders with resounding finality. Both the goal and the means employed to achieve victory were loaded with important implications for the South, whose people once again eagerly flocked to their country's colors. Those implications meant change. ❏

MODERN TIMES

Racial conflict in the 1950s and '60s seared the air, but the emergence
of "the Sun Belt" as an ecomonic force foreshadowed the New South

The changes of the past 100 years had been profound ones for the South. From a profitable, self-sufficient land of plantations and Old World values, it had been transformed into a place of small farms and light industry, dominated by Yankee know-how and dependent on Northern investment. The years after 1945 saw the development of the much vaunted "affluent society" in America, and Southerners made it known once and for all that they intended to be full partners in it.

Southern boosters proclaimed afresh all the region's advantages: abundant natural resources and sources of energy, congenial state legislatures at the ready with favorable tax laws and additional incentives, a cheap and plentiful supply of labor, and long-deprived markets for durable and consumer goods. The conversion of wartime plants helped start the boom, which soon became self-sustaining as factories multiplied, producing air conditioners, washing machines, farm implements and in time even automobiles, in addition to the old stand-bys such as textiles and chemicals.

Southern zeal

Exhibiting a zeal that matched the bonanza-sized opportunities, Southern leaders in both public and private life ceaselessly put the South's case as the undoubted site of America's next industrial revolution.

Southerners thus kept alive the old scalawag tradition of enticing Northern investment, using the lures of relatively low expenses and high prospective profits. Large Northern-based corporations did enter the South to build plants and factories and hired Southern workers to staff them. Management, while commonly non-Southern at first, was eventually recruited from the native work force.

Industrialization wrought extremely visible

changes in the South's economic life. These ranged from the complete domination of the economies of small towns such as Camden, South Carolina, and Waynesboro, Virginia, by Northern-based corporate giants such as Du Pont and General Electric, to the complete remaking of regional landscapes. This is what

happened in the Tennessee Valley where, by the early 1970s, the dams and power plants of the Roosevelt-era Tennessee Valley Authority were turning out 10 percent of the United States' electricity needs.

Along the Mississippi River, oil refineries and petrochemical plants lined the shore all the way from Baton Rouge to New Orleans. Defense contracts provided an artificial, though highly tangible, boost to industrial growth, and as Cold War military budgets swelled, the South's share of them grew disproportionately. America's space race was run from Southern headquarters whose names became famous throughout the world in the 1960s and '70s:

LEFT: Martin Luther King, Jr and Ralph Abernathy (right) lead the Selma-to-Montgomery march, 1965.
RIGHT: racial conflict brought the attention of the world to the South.

Cape Canaveral in Florida, the Marshall Space Flight Center in Alabama, and the Mission Control Center in Houston, Texas.

Change also came to the land itself, which remained for many Southerners, however they made their living, at the core of their identity. Once the "land of cotton" whose "kingdom" stretched from Virginia's Tidewater to Texas, Southern agriculture of the post World War II years turned decisively to other more profitable commodities, and at long last it lived up to the New South's original admonition to farmers to diversify, diversify, diversify. By the 1960s, tree farms were as common as cotton fields and pro-

duced approximately a third of the nation's lumber. Southern pastures, which likewise profited from the region's generous growing season, fed beef cattle that produced an income for Southern farmers three times that earned by "the great white staple" of yore.

Commercial poultry production soared, and from the long, low-roofed sheds that became a fixture on thousands of Southern farms there came millions of chickens and eggs. Almost all of America's tobacco continued to be grown in Virginia, Kentucky, and North Carolina, and the South still produced the lion's share of America's cotton, though most of it came from regions west of the Mississippi.

The Sun Belt

Whatever the ancestral and economic pull of the land, however, the demographics of the post-1945 South told a different story. It was a story of the seemingly ineluctable migration of Southerners from the countryside and small towns to the cities. Industrialization speeded urbanization and breathed new life into old-fashioned towns such as Augusta, Georgia; Nashville, Tennessee; Montgomery, Alabama; and Richmond, Virginia.

The South's premier city, Atlanta, Georgia, which had always made much of rising from the ashes left by William Tecumseh Sherman's Federal Army in 1864, set the pace, establishing itself as the commercial and transportation hub (first in the era of the railroad and later in the airline age) of the entire Southeast. Less than half a million people were living there in 1940; thirty years later the figure was as great as 1.2 million. Such growth was fueled publicly as well as privately. This, coupled with the enduring lure of a mild climate and a generally lower cost of living, gave birth to the lucrative Sun Belt phenomenon.

Southern cities grew out, not up, and they grew in a hurry. There was no time for, and little interest in, the agglomeration of dense inner-city neighborhoods; the Sun Belt cities sprouted in the middle-class, white-collar era, and because of an ethnic homogeneity utterly unlike the older industrial cities of the North, their residents tended to sort themselves along simple lines of income and, even after segregation was made unlawful, of race. In this sense, the cities' growth conformed to old Southern characteristics. But in their renewed promise of an utterly transformed physical and social landscape, the cities clashed sharply with the region's fundamental conservatism.

The single change in the South that very few lamented, and that no one would admit to lamenting anyway, involved the issue that most visibly went to the heart of Southern distinctiveness: race.

In 1954, the landmark Supreme Court decision of *Brown v. Board of Education* set aside "separate but equal" and opened the door on a tense period during which the forces of state and nation faced off as they had not done since the secession crisis of 1860 and 1861. This time no one talked of leaving the Union, but segregationist Southerners did make a series of last stands in a not altogether unsuccessful attempt to slow the steamroller of federally mandated racial equality.

Civil Rights acts

In 1957, Republican President Dwight D. Eisenhower sent federal troops to Little Rock, Arkansas, to protect black students at the newly integrated Central High School *(see page 226)*, and the next years witnessed much talk among Southern governors of "state interposition" and "massive resistance" to hold back the tide. They were not alone, and thousands of ordinary white Southerners rallied to their cry.

But the times had changed decisively, and there were now thousands of native Northerners who had come to the South in the post-war economic boom and who were at best indifferent to the system of segregation. States' rights held little allure for them, and in the years of the "sit-in" and the "freedom march," the old racial arrangements of the South crumbled because of two factors: outside pressures and internal weariness.

Federal force was used again in the early 1960s against recalcitrant state governors such as Ross Barnett of Mississippi and George Wallace of Alabama. But it was the nonviolence of black leaders in the South – best exemplified by Martin Luther King, Jr, who had come to prominence during the Montgomery Bus Boycott of 1955 and was brutally assassinated in Memphis 13 years later *(see pages 141 and 242)* – that eventually triumphed. The spectacle of peaceful black demonstrators being met with the clubs and dogs and water cannon of white police departments, brought instantly into people's homes by television, revolted the moral conscience of the nation and moved moderate-minded people everywhere to the judgment that the South's racial prejudices no longer had a place in modern America.

That consensus was reflected in the passage of the Civil Rights Act of 1964 and of the Voting Rights Act of 1965, which finally completed the work begun in the Reconstruction era following the Civil War. That the pattern of racial arrangements changed so quickly, and with so little social disruption, is testimony both to how truly outdated it had become and to the salient fact that white Southerners, who were in a majority in most parts of the region, no longer needed to fear the tyranny of a vengeful black majority.

In the absence of the bogy of race, and despite the persistent populism that boiled to the surface in the third-party presidential bids of Alabama Governor George C. Wallace and, finally, in November 1976, in the election of Georgian Jimmy Carter to the presidency on an anti-Washington platform, a sturdy new sense of self was developing among the prosperous citizens of this newest New South.

It was helped, of course, by the election of

another Southerner, Bill Clinton from Arkansas, to the presidency in the early 1990s.

Bible Belt

But it was not in politics but in religion – in the unadulterated orthodox faith of their fathers – that Southerners continued to find the solace of continuity amid rapid social and economic change. Almost half of Southern church members are Southern Baptists, a denomination so all-embracing and so influential that it has fairly been called the folk church of the South. The secular impact of such religious identification, and of the faith it reflects, is notoriously hard to judge, but there's no doubt that it contributes

LEFT: chemical plant in Louisiana.
RIGHT: Georgian Jimmy Carter, president 1977–81.

mightily to the conservative cultural cast of the region. The black church, which provided so much of the nurturing ground and leadership for the great victories of the 1950s and 1960s Civil Rights movement, remains today still almost totally black. On both sides of the color line, it seems, the church doors are open, but no one chooses to pass through of his own free will. Nor is it something that troubles most Southern Christians, black or white.

Small-town values

By contrast, another main theme of Southern history seems to have rather less of a future

today, at least in the form that most Southerners once knew it. Ruralism is on the wane, and whatever parallels might be drawn between the small farms idealized in the 1920s, and the "green revolution" of the 1960s and 1970s, the fact remains that, by 1970, 65 percent of Southerners were classified by the census as urban.

Yet this was urbanism Southern-style, and in most cases it was on a smaller scale than elsewhere. Only 25 percent lived in cities with populations over 100,000; 40 percent lived in suburbs or in the 4,500 "cities" of less than 100,000 people. It is frequently remarked that most Southern cities, even the big ones, retain the quality of overgrown country towns.

Indeed, many urban residents have only recently come from the country and still have ties there. And, in the 1970 census, there was that hefty 35 percent who were still officially "rural." These were not the rural folk of myth: four out of five earned a living "in town," commuting by car to an office or factory while remaining very much country people in outlook. And while the truly rural population was small, it remained divided much as it had been throughout its long history into planters, yeomen, and landless laborers, with all the social distinctions to match.

Finally, poverty and a perceived powerlessness will cease to shape the South's future as they once shaped its past. The new prosperity of the Sun Belt boom is not imaginary; this is the New South in the flesh at last, after all those years of blustery talk. It is no coincidence that the world-wide headquarters of the courier company Federal Express are located in Memphis, Tennessee; that North Carolina, home of the vastly profitable R. J. Reynolds tobacco company, boasts both the headquarters of the airline US Airways and a highly recognized "Silicon Valley" computer corridor near Raleigh-Durham; or that the soaring architectural towers of Atlanta, inspired by local son and internationally respected architect John Portman, house many corporate headquarters mentioned in the Fortune 500.

There is no reason to suppose that the new prosperity of the South will not grow even greater in the future. It should not be surprising that the region should at last have opted for a newer South. Backwardness, after all, is picturesque only in fiction and old movies. Like Americans in colder climates, Southerners perceive the good life through a lens that is largely materialistic. They are subject to the same economic pressures and temptations as other people and, in general, they make their choices from the same broad set of options.

And yet there remains a difference that is impossible to quantify and that has nothing at all to do with colonial economies, sharecropping, textile mills, high-tech industries or per capita income. Rather, to use the Southern idiom, it is a matter of accent, and to talk about it means having to deal with matters of taste and personal standards.

Consider the following: it is a cliché that any real Southerner will remain polite until he gets mad enough to kill. Not that many kill (although deer hunting and the stalking of small animals remain popular outdoor pursuits, and the prevalence of gun stores takes many a foreign visitor by surprise), but it's true that most Southerners remain polite even in this age of "candor" and enlightened free expression. In sophisticated New South cities and on urbane university campuses, one can still witness a certain charming deference of man to woman, of youth to age, of student to teacher.

Only the deaf or ill-attentive can fail to notice the still pervasive "no, ma'ams" and "yes, sirs" that punctuate ordinary everyday conversation

Relative values

Consciousness of kin – the saints and the sinners alike – remains powerful and, in a much attenuated form, so does consciousness of class. Despite the great movement of people and wealth into the South from outside, a select gentry survives comprising descendants of antebellum planters who owe their existence more to the power of tradition than to money or influence, which have long since passed to others. There is a distinction in the South between "good family" and "good people" that is not often made in Iowa or Pennsylvania. Admittedly, it is only the shade of an aristocratic

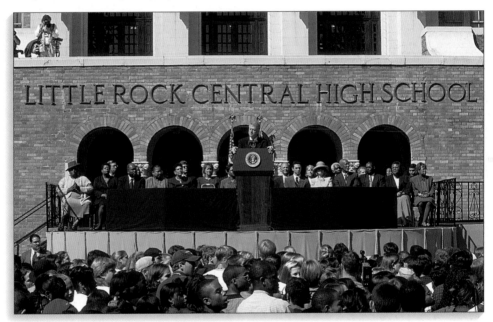

– leftovers for sure of a more class-conscious age but showing few signs of retreat even in these rigorously egalitarian times. Many of the rituals and restraints of etiquette that seem to have fallen out of use elsewhere in the world still thrive in the South, perhaps less in their more outlandish Sir Walter Scott forms than simply as traditions of courtesy and good manners. Church, home, and family still serve as a prime source of social conventions and of cultural and moral values.

LEFT: modern methods are used to produce tobacco.
ABOVE: President Bill Clinton at Little Rock's Central High School, scene of racial strife in 1957.

tradition, but one that, shorn of its less lovely trappings, has been redeemed.

Its heirs can be stuffy and pretentious at their worst – undistinguished in either abilities or assets. But at their best, they can be a happy exception to the boredom and tastelessness of modern mass culture, through which every man is automatically accorded equality with every other man to achieve a uniformity of low regard. Besides this, character traits such as personal integrity, honor, understated graciousness, and the cultivation of "good living" (as distinct from simply making a good living) are praiseworthy wherever they are found. In this case, all over the New South. ❑

SOUTHERNERS

From good ole boys and Southern belles to modern dot-commers
and international bankers – Dixie charms 'em all

Southerners divide the world into two parts: the South, and everywhere else. The authority for this view is unassailable. *Dixie*, the South's anthem, declares that "the world was made in just six days,/ And finished off in various ways/ Look away! Look away! Look away, Dixie Land!/ God made Dixie trim and nice,/ But Adam called it Paradise,/ Look away! Look away! Look away, Dixie Land." To be a non-Southerner, therefore, is to be excluded from Paradise.

Infinite variety

Those unfortunate enough to be outsiders generally base much of their knowledge of Southerners on one novel and its movie version: Margaret Mitchell's 1936 bestseller *Gone with the Wind*, immortalized three years later by MGM. What the entire world has imagined – many as they read the novel in translation, and later had confirmed while watching the film on Ted Turner's TV station – was Scarlett O'Hara with skirts billowing as she floated over Tara's sweeping lawns under blossoming magnolias.

This was a limited view of the South even in the 1860s. Trying to fit all Southerners into the mold of Mitchell's main characters is to deny the infinite variety of human beings. Yet Southern types as distinct and classifiable as their well-documented Southern accents do exist – as long as you know what to look for.

The past in the South defines the present. Once you cross the Mason-Dixon line, that imaginary border between North and South, the past ceases to be the past. It just won't lie down. Knowing who did what, and when, in history is just as important as knowing what year Elton John bought his lavish apartment in Atlanta, or which restaurant in Birmingham, Alabama, made *Gourmet*'s Top Five list.

PRECEDING PAGES: Charlotte Motor Speedway, North Carolina; Dollywood theme park, Tennessee.
LEFT: Southerners divide the world into two parts: the South, and everywhere else.
RIGHT: eating and drinking are preoccupations.

You might easily find, for example, on a summer afternoon, heated discussions taking place on the porches of numerous homes in Rutherford County, Tennessee, about the details of daring cavalry raids under the command of Lt-General Nathan Bedford Forrest in 1864. The men who rode with him were known as Forrest's Escort

and most came from the immediate vicinity. The discussion is as animated as if the raid had occurred this morning and news of it had just arrived. Who participated. Who did what. The outcome – as if it were still in doubt. As if it still mattered. But it does matter, to them. If it were known that yo' great-grandpappy did *not* ride with Forrest's Escort, you would be permitted no part in the conversation.

The "living in Paradise" attitude dates back even farther in Southern consciousness. Settlers bound for Virginia were assured in an ode by Michael Drayton (1563–1631) that Virginia is "Earth's only Paradise." The Cavalier/ planter/ Christian gentleman figure appeared hauntingly in the novels of antebellum writers long before he actually trod the soil of Virginia as that ultimate Southern icon, General Robert E. Lee.

Today's descendants may still own the same land or may be two generations away from it, engaged in a high-tech business in the city. But there will still be an historical recollection, a family group memory. The land confers a sense of place on an individual. It's a rootedness rare in other Americans, whose historical continuity is more fragmented.

Contemporaries who have broken with the past, however, point out problems faced by those held in its thrall. "There's nothing wrong with

Mr S—," they might say, "except that he's got ancestors." There's an almost Asian strength to ancestor worship in the South, the Virginia variety being especially intense, with the Carolinas not far behind.

The semi-tropical landscape of South Carolina's Low Country, with its weirdness and melancholy, was the setting for Edgar Allan Poe's story *The Gold Bug* – specifically, Sullivan Island at the entrance to Charleston Harbor. Today, dank tarns and funereal, coastal woodlands still abound in legends and superstitions.

One of the most celebrated tales of the Low Country started in the back alleys of Charleston and graduated to successful productions in New York and major European cities, including a performance at Milan's La Scala. The odyssey of a work about South Carolina Gullah African-Americans began with the publication in 1925 of DuBose Heyward's novella *Porgy*. The author, an admirer of the poetry and pathos in the lives of those in Charleston's dilapidated quarter, turned his novella into a play two years later. In 1935, George Gershwin's music joined Heyward's libretto to become the folk opera *Porgy and Bess*. Hollywood followed in 1959.

Catfish Row is no minstrel world of stereotypes, though. There's Porgy, crippled but a true hero; Bess, a genuinely seductive heroine; Crown, embodiment of erotic primitive brutality; the bootlegger Sporting Life; the matriarch Maria. No clowns, no Uncle Toms, no Mr Interlocutor. It made a refreshing change.

In pinning down the appeal of these characters, the punchline in an apocryphal Southern anecdote may prove as illuminating as critical analysis. As the story goes, a well-meaning white employer suggests that if his employee's conduct over the weekend had not been so improvident, he would be feeling much better and more like working on Monday morning. The employee replies: "Yessir, boss, that's true, but you ain't never been a black man on a Saturday night." Heyward appreciated what he called this "unique characteristic" in the lives of African-Americans. He saw the person of African descent as the "inheritor of a source of delight" that he would have given much to possess.

Southern belles

A bestselling country song once advised unwary males that "there's girls, there's women, and there's ladies." The first and last terms are references to Southern belles and Southern ladies, Scarlett O'Hara and Melanie Wilkes being the two best known in their respective categories. Matriarchs and spinsters are a sub-class of Southern ladies. "Women" includes all other females from independent female tycoons to Appalachian mountain beauties to prostitutes.

The code word for Southern belle among those who are and do not have to concern themselves with definitions is "real cute girl." For a divine example of the "real cute girl" syndrome, read Rebecca Wells's *The Divine Secrets of the Ya-Ya Sisterhood* (HarperCollins, 1998), about a daughter, her mother and her mother's high-stepping society pals in Louisiana. Never refer in public to a young woman as a Southern belle. No one with pretensions to a high social intelligence quotient would prattle in such a manner. Southern belle is a term of convenience applied by outsiders in their attempts to understand an inexplicable life form. Over time, the persona of the Southern belle has changed. The definitive description was penned in 1959 by Frances Gray Patton for *Holiday* magazine. The modern belle, Patton found, sees her "essentially passive" role at odds with a society increasingly with hazards of coarseness and strident ambitions." But then did the "gently nurtured Southern girl" ever really exist outside the gothic Southern imagination? Her personal aura comprises equal parts of purity and passion. And, no matter what she has been doing all day, she can dance all night in high heels to the melodies generated by juke box, rock band or full orchestra. Her smile makes the old feel young and the poor feel rich.

In her presence any male – be he nine or 90 – feels alternately soothed and energized, gallant, competent, invincible. She does exist, and she

> ### BELLES AND BOWS
> A southern belle's smile makes the old feel young and the poor feel rich. She can also dance all night in high heels.

based on assertiveness. She must "excite admiration without appearing to demand it, create an illusion of fragility without looking sick and sustain an atmosphere of gentle gaiety without seeming bat-brained." Her physique, shaped by too many vitamins, proteins and work-outs, doesn't help: no fourth-generation belle can slip into her great-great-grandmother's wedding dress or tiny white kid gloves.

As an added burden, her socioeconomic position means that she is "thrown early into competition with the opposite sex – a position rife confirms his expectations by always doing what is expected of her.

Steel magnolias

The Southern female – now typically called a "steel magnolia" – was originally categorized as a Southern lady who, if she survived multiple childbirths, became a matriarch. In Virginia, there's a saying that it takes three generations to make a gentleman, four to make a lady. Ladies had the responsibility of formulating and ritualizing the social conventions that well-bred girls from Little Rock, Mobile, and all over the South would be taught from their cradles. Such a lady referred to her husband only by his title and his

LEFT: man and beast.
ABOVE: proms are popular, especially in small towns.

surname, a custom that has not entirely disappeared. Forced by circumstances to manage and oversee huge plantations while their husbands and other male relatives were away from 1861 to 1865, the ladies were loath to return to "china doll" status after the Confederacy's collapse. Today they can be found staffing charity auctions in Atlanta, or as trustees of art institutes in New Orleans.

Rural realities

The contrast between rural past and urban present is fresher in the Southern consciousness than in other regions because the change from one to

the other is so recent. It wasn't so long ago that 85 percent of Southerners made their living from the land, and the number remains high. These are ordinary folks, yeoman farmers, lower class and lower middle class, many of German and Scots-Irish descent.

In the Carolinas they are textile workers and tenant farmers who raise tobacco; in the mountain South they are coal miners, loggers and hardscrabble farmers, tilling rocky, unforgiving soil called "creek farms" in eastern Tennessee, where "bottom land," rich loamy soil is scarce and very precious.

These people live a few miles "out from town" in a house trailer on county-maintained roads

that were once wagon ruts and loggers' roads. The Mountain South, especially around Tennessee and Virginia, has long been home to small groups whose occupation has excited inordinate interest. In the mountain idiom, they are moonshiners. Like farming, moonshining – the illegal distilling of whiskey – was a family business. Producing mountain dew or white lightnin', two other terms for home-distilled whiskey, was a cash crop in a region where a diligent farmer could end the growing season with a lot of corn and not a single penny in his overalls.

The generations-old family activity was criminalized when a remote federal government decided to collect a tax on the making of such whiskey. The change led to years of violence in the Appalachian hills and, curiously enough, to the development of the South's favorite sport after football. Stock-car racing grew out of the ability of the bootleg runner's high-performance car to outrun the cars of agents.

Bubbas and good ole boys

Three terms used to describe white Southern males are not synonyms – bubba, redneck, and good ole boy. Bubba is a fellow whose reactions are constrained by his limited intelligence. Two of a bubba's three standard reactions involve shooting: (1) shoot it and have it stuffed for a wall trophy; (2) shoot it and cook and eat it; and (3) marry it. Today's bubba can be rural or urban, may even be the overindulged, spoiled-brat son of a small-town lawyer.

A redneck is rural. The term, not originally derogatory, referred to those who labored in the field (today on the construction site) under the South's hot sun. As a result, their neck acquired a red, ridged appearance. The original rednecks were from humble, but honorable, beginnings. Andrew Jackson, seventh president of the United States, came from such folk.

Today's rowdy redneck often has a fairly hefty income, which he spends on camping equipment, fishing, and on weekends at stock-car races. Away from the racetrack, the redneck can still be recognized. All drive pick-up trucks. All have profoundly conservative politics.

A good ole boy exemplifies all the masculine virtues esteemed by his region. His life is equally devoted to guns, hunting, fishing, drinking, football and women, seasoned with a dash of nostalgia for trains. He is affable, amiable, likeable, and stubborn beyond belief – "sot [set] in his ways." One of his main activities is swapping anecdotes with his buddies ("stories" would be his word) in some social group variously called a gun, rifle, or hunting club. Typically, the group owns a number of acres in an isolated rural area on which members hunt or target practice on a regular basis.

For the good ole boy, hunting acquires mythical proportions. Good ole boys can be found at both the high and low ends of the economic scale. The ones whose fathers never got any farther from home than 'coon hunting in the next county or one trip to the state capital will today casually mention just having returned from a

hippies, but with cable TV and interesting jobs or hobbies. In the more remote areas, though, conflict can arise. "Those damn hippies, they don't want to change a thang," grumbled one elderly storekeeper in Virginia whose five-and-dime was now outfitted for tourists who want to experience an old-timey past. "They just don't understand progress."

Escape is also the game plan for thousands of rural youngsters who flock to the cities, dreaming of becoming tycoons and computer software designers. And in the New South, this is feasible, something their grandparents would never understand. Joining them at Delta Airways and

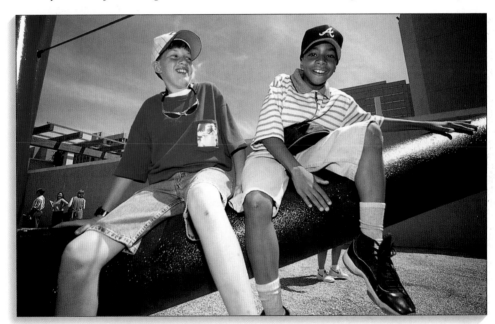

month in Kenya or Tanzania. Many a lawyer, politician or CEO, who could pose for the cover of *Gentleman's Quarterly*, calls himself a "good ole boy" when interviewed.

New Southerners

New Southerners also come in three varieties. The first are distinctly rural, escapees from the city who live in the green hills of the Blue Ridge Mountains, or lovely Victorian villages like Eureka Springs, Arkansas. Educated, literate and longing for a simpler life, these are modern-day

other corporations are transplanted Yankees who work in John Portman-designed Atlanta towers, and sweat it out in the gym after dining on shrimp and grits in a wood-and-chrome, award-winning wine bar. Although this last category can never be considered truly Southern, parents up North are apt to comment on their child's slower way of talking, and how that frenetic New York jog has transformed into an amiable, ambling gait.

Given the fact that there are so many different types of Southerners, don't let anyone tell you, in Southern phraseology, that "there's no such of a thing left." They do exist – in all shapes and accents – all over the South. ❑

LEFT: lecture at Morehouse College, Atlanta.
ABOVE: friends at the Birmingham Museum of Art.

THE NEW SOUTH

A strong spirit of reinvention gave the world Coca-Cola, CNN,
Wal-Mart, the Sweet Potato Queens and Books-A-Million

When Atlanta newspaperman Henry W. Grady delivered an address entitled "The New South" on December 21, 1886, in New York City, he began a movement that long outlived him and that future generations each in their turn and in their own way would call "new." Twenty years after the Civil War, as the South was still faltering, Grady had in mind the economic rejuvenation of his region. The time had come, he said, to put away animosity and to forget the rancor of war and its aftermath. It was now time for the South to reinvent itself.

This spirit of reinvention is probably the single most defining quality of the New South. From Little Rock to Richmond, the warehouses that once were stacked with bales of cotton or crates of produce have been reborn as art galleries, dining areas, and loft accommodation for the young singles who flock to clatter the keyboards of the new economy.

Change and rejuvenation

Change and rejuvenation doesn't stop there. Savannah has reinvented itself as a party town and, courtesy of the Savannah College of Art and Design (SCAD), has renovated fine and distinguished buildings all around town as classrooms and student accommodation. Now the school attracts students from all around the world. The Raleigh-Durham area of North Carolina has become a humming center of high-tech innovation and excellence.

Birmingham, Alabama, has a world-famous medical center that specializes in open-heart surgery, diabetes treatment and Aids research. Memphis, Tennessee, has transformed its downtown area into a world capital of blues, rock 'n' roll and soul music, as well as an international freight-forwarding hub based around the Federal Express headquarters.

LEFT: Cable News Network is only one of Atlanta's mega-corporations; three-quarters of all *Fortune* 1,000 companies have a presence in the city.
RIGHT: females are now a force to be reckoned with.

Jackson, Mississippi, integrated itself into the new economy, and along the way spawned a social phenomenon: the Sweet Potato Queens. In 1999, Jill Conner Browne wrote a book, *The Sweet Potato Queens' Book of Love* (Crown Publishing) that kicked the dust right out of any clichés of simpering Southern belles. Miz

Browne and a group of girlfriends, women of indeterminate age with a fondness for dressing up in garish red wigs and green sequinned ball gowns, began dancing on a float in the annual St Patrick's Day parade.

Such was their gutsy élan, that other women in Jackson wanted to be queens, too, flinging ladylike decorum to the air, and surrendering to the charms of their number one consort, Lance Romance. The phenomena swept out of the flat Mississippi countryside and into the hearts of American women from coast to coast, and in no time at all the Queens' cookbooks, calendars, and alumni chapters were dancing and sashaying around the nation.

Birmingham, Alabama, is one of the towns free from Old South baggage, having made its mark six years after the end of the war. The statue that heralds over the lush green mountains around the city is a tribute to the industrial heroism of steelmaking, not a Confederate hero or a founding father. Undefined by their histories, these cities have been free to do things their way, time and time again.

Skyline cities

Two New South cities virtually unrecognizable from the dusty settlements they were when cotton was King are Charlotte, North Carolina,

and Atlanta, Georgia. Perhaps it's no coincidence that these cities, lacking the seaports or navigable rivers that could have guaranteed an easy living from shipping and cargo, made their ways with creative entrepreneurism right from the very start.

Charlotte's skyline has been transformed in the past 30 years, principally by the efforts of two of the nation's largest banks, Wachovia and Bank of America. In an effort to outdo each other, the companies built in succession several skyscrapers, each one taller than the last. In 1992, when the Bank of America building was completed, it was taller than Wachovia's (then known as First Union). Locals tell the tale that Bank of America kept its design secret until First Union's was shown to the world. Bank of America architects took one look and threw a crown on top of their tower in order to walk off with the title "tallest in the city."

The uncontested "capital of the New South" is Atlanta. From John Portman-designed skyscrapers with dizzying atriums spring a staggering array of high earning, high-profile company headquarters. Metro Atlanta's *Fortune* 1,000 companies generate more than $250 billion in sales revenues, with three-quarters of all the *Fortune* 1,000 companies having a presence in the city. The names of Atlanta-based companies ring loud and proud: CNN, Home Depot, UPS, Delta.

It is a fact that some New South corporations are Yankee transplants, lured from the chilly North by good weather, cheap rents, and proximity to mountains and the sea. But homegrown talent fares well, too. Top of the list is Coca-Coca *(see below)*, while coming up

PUTTING THE FIZZ IN COCA-COLA

Coca-Cola is the most ubiquitous consumer product in the world, and it all began in Georgia. In 1886, a pharmacist by the name of "Doc" Pemberton invented a thick, sweet syrup as a soda fountain drink. His partner was a Yankee named Frank Robinson, and his flowing Victorian handwriting is still embodied in the company's logo. When Pemberton died in 1888, never having tasted the sweet success of his invention, the product was sold to Asa Candler.

A marketing genius, Candler handed out free coupons for people throughout the South to sample the novel drink, and produced high-quality calendars and posters to keep the name in the public eye. In 1916, to thwart rival cola drinks,

the distinctive waist-shaped bottle was introduced. Seven years later, Atlantan Robert Woodruff took charge and steered the company for more than five decades. Under his helm came the radio jingles recorded in the 1960s by Aretha Franklin, Ray Charles, and Roy Orbison.

During World War II, Woodruff ensured than every G.I. overseas got a Coke for 5¢, a plan that paid off handsomely later. Norman Rockwell was hired to draw illustrations, as was Haddon Sundblom. Supposedly it was Sundblom's Yuletide ads that got Americans thinking of Santa Claus as the tubby, white-bearded man in a red tunic who graces contemporary Christmas cards.

behind are a trio of well-established locally born corporations with businesses and reputations to be reckoned with.

Sam Walton and his wife Helen opened their first variety store in 1945. They were joined by Sam's brother, J.L. (Bud) Walton and together they had nine stores by 1959. The first store bearing the Wal-Mart name was in Rogers, Arkansas, in July, 1962. The dynamic company that evolved from those modest beginnings has been called the retailing phenomenon of the 20th century.

ATLANTA ARCHITECTURE

The architecture of downtown Atlanta has been described as "roco-cola."

Founded in 1917 as a street corner newsstand in Florence, Alabama, Books-A-Million, Inc. has grown to become the premier book chain in the Southeast, and the third largest book retailer in the US. Based in Birmingham, the company currently operates more than 200 stores in 18 states and in the District of Columbia. Most branches keep an impressive range of magazines, and there is always company in the entertaining Southerners sipping coffee in the Joe Muggs cafés.

These dynamic companies of the New South invariably owe their success in some part to

Krispy Kreme began as a family business in 1933. Four years later, Vernon Rudolph moved to Winston-Salem, North Carolina, with $25, rented the front of a store and talked the grocer into loaning him the ingredients to make doughnuts. By 2001, Krispy Kreme had gained such a reputation that, rumor has it, sales rose dramatically in the aftermath of the World Trade Center attacks as Americans sought relief and comfort from a home-grown brand that was tasty and safe.

LEFT: recent economic gains support 21st-century businesses such as this Nashville wine bar.
ABOVE: the New South outruns the Old South, Mobile.

traditional Southern values like loyalty and consistency, values harking back to the Old South. The past is never too far away here; it wafts on the air like a sweet, haunting perfume, giving a keynote to the present, drifting in the direction of the future.

Old and new motif

The logo for Charlotte's Levine Museum of the New South, created by a local firm, Crescent PR, pays tribute to both. Three converging horizontal lines suggest the plowed fields of the rural past, while, rising from the horizon, three vertical lines symbolize the factory stacks, or skyscrapers, of a new, glittering future. ❏

LAS VEGAS BY THE SEA

Across formerly sleepy resorts and barren cotton fields,
the jangle of slot machines drifts on the moist night air

On the lovely Bay of Biloxi, out of a sleepy resort town of the 1980s, a little tinsel town has burst like a firework display. In 1998, Biloxi's mayor A. J. Holloway said, "We don't want to be the Las Vegas of the South. We want to be – and we are – the playground of the South," and there is truth in that. Behind the waterfront neon extravaganza, there is still a pretty coastal Mississippi town with cafés, art galleries and as musty a rare bookshop as any quiet community could nurture. But what hits the eye is the massive sea-wall of casinos.

Along the coast road, there are beautiful antebellum homes on stilts, across the street from Gulf Coast silver-white sands by the water, followed by a crescendo of towering hotels, sparkling with brash neon and with large annexes poking out over the bay.

The 1,800-room Beaux Rivage is a glittering fantasy of Steve Wynn's in the image of his Las Vegas landmark, Bellagio, complete with a private marina, an enormous showroom, and a bar wild enough to draw recruiters for reality TV shows. Mississippi actively casts its net for casino operators by making one of the lowest tax-takes in the country, less than half that of its Louisiana neighbors. The gaming license fees are also about a quarter of those charged in Louisiana, but there is still a local undercurrent of moral disquiet about the business.

No limits

America's love-hate affair with gambling has made a massive turn-around in the past 15 years. In 1988, gaming was legal in only two states, Nevada and New Jersey. Now there are only two states – Utah and Hawaii – where it is illegal. Mississippi, one of the leading enthusiasts for the revenue spilling off the green baize tables, probably has the most schizophrenic legal position.

There are no restrictions on the number of

gaming licenses that a county or district may issue, nor on the amount of gaming space that a casino can use, but dealer schools are prohibited. Biloxi, being by the sea, pioneered the toleration of wagering sports as early as the 1980s when "cruises to nowhere" were permitted by the state legislature, taking guests out into inter-

national waters and then immediately opening up the tables, slot and craps pits.

Bobby Mahoney of Mary Mahoney's Biloxi restaurant said: "The statute in Mississippi preventing dealer schools from operating, just means all the best [casino] jobs go to folks from out-of-state." On the other hand, Nonnie DeBardeleben, a politician from the nearby town of Pass Christian, said: "My supervisor's only complaint is that he can't get a wheelbarrow big enough to carry the money across the street to the bank."

The anomalies began with the original dockside casino legislation, passed in Congress in 1990. Eight conservative senators were pledged

LEFT: the Bay of Biloxi, Mississippi.
RIGHT: Mississippi law requires casinos to be located on water; this "moat" in Tunica serves the purpose.

to vote against the bill, but all suffered mysterious stomach upsets on the day of the vote. One may wonder if they lacked the gastro-intestinal fortitude to vote against such a spew of revenue.

Cash floats

Mississippi state law requires all casinos to be sited on the waterfront, ostensibly on the site of a comparable structure. What kind of a "comparable structure" preceded the eye-popping six-story brick-built replica galleon of Treasure Bay casino, one can only wonder. The "dockside" rule is that the gaming house itself has to be a separate structure, wholly over the

there were more than 6,000, and almost as many more to come. Residents in the nearby town of Clarksdale tell of how Tunica County had so little infrastructure, there wasn't even a chief of police, and they had to lure away Clarksdale's, leaving the larger town without a senior lawman for many worrying months.

Tunica has positioned itself, literally, as a center-point, accessible from Memphis, and also from Arkansas, Alabama and the rest of southern Tennessee. This has enabled Mississippi to achieve what might have seemed impossible – it has enticed gaming business away from Nevada. To this end, operations like the Gold Coast and

water, meaning that the money-making part of Beaux Rivage and Casino Magic, for instance, float on vast pontoons, but are connected internally to their landside hotels. From inside, it's difficult to tell where one structure ends and the other begins.

In Tunica County, it seems that although a previous dockside development had to exist, somehow the water didn't have to be there. An entirely new canal was dug for the row of Harrah's, Horseshoe and Gold Coast casinos to perch over, raising a landscaped fantasy of resort hotels in what were flat, empty cottonfields a few years before. Tunica County had only 20 hotel rooms in 1992. Six years later

Biloxi's Beau Rivage market themselves not just as gambling houses, but as resort destinations. Spas, large showrooms and entertainments like the Blues and Legends Hall of Fame in the Tunica Horseshoe are all part of the "complete entertainment package." So far, though, there is no sign of the trumpeted "family friendliness" that Las Vegas was so keen on, up until recently. Neither has Biloxi given in too overtly to the sleazier end of "adult" recreation which is so often a feature of gambling destinations.

However, the reborn riverboats have certainly brought their share of woes along with them. In 1993, after the *Lady Luck* riverboat casino opened in Natchez, Adams County judge

Charles Vess said, "Our civil cases ballooned – auto repossessions, furniture repossessions, a big influx of bad checks." There is also evidence that, if anything, poor people have gotten poorer since the arrival of the dealers.

Louisiana

If Mississippi has had an uneasy relationship with the slots and tables, Louisiana has been positively struggling. The only land-based casino in New Orleans, Harrah's, has distinguished itself by teetering on the verge of bankrupcy since opening in 1992. Infighting between local and state government, as well as the high

a case brought by Seminole Indians in Florida, a decision by Congress in 1988 conceded that a reservation in a state where gaming was legal could conduct games of their own, without state interference. Indian councils have taken this opportunity, and unemployment among Indians has dropped from around 30 percent to almost nothing as a result. Nearly all states that allow gambling now have reservation gaming. At first, the traditional casino operators forcefully resisted the trend, but in a pragmatic, "if you can't beat them, join them," spirit, they are increasingly partnering up with the Indians.

Even with the partnerships, reservation casi-

rates of Louisiana gambling taxes are blamed. Presumably none of Louisiana's legendary political murky dealings were involved. There are also Mississippi-style waterfront casinos on Lake Pontchartrain. Otherwise, Louisiana has a bizzare complex of laws that permit closed off gaming rooms in some bars and gas stations, mostly featuring slot machines, and the isolated and frankly alarming "truck-stop" casinos.

The other major change on the betting landscape has been the rise of Indian casinos. After

nos are not usually as lavish as their resort counterparts, and this is in part because banks are unwilling to lend money for development. The reason given is that they cannot sieze property if a loan is defaulted. There are reservation casinos in all the states of the New South, except for Arkansas, Tennessee, and South Carolina.

The Bible Belt is adapting to the congregations of Mamon, streaming into temples of chance with their devotion to numbers, dice, and dollars, but for many it isn't an easy relationship. Still, the jangle of slots, the snap of the cards, and the clatter of a silver ball in a wheel are accompaniments to 21st-century Southern life that look set to stay. ❏

LEFT: almost all of the states in the New South now allow some form of gaming.
ABOVE: roulette on the river, Vicksburg.

WHAT'S COOKING

The styles of Southern cuisine are as melodic as the accents
and as varied as the landscape from Virginia to Louisiana

Southern cooking arrives like the embrace of Southern hospitality, courteously warm and comforting, but varied, spicy and elegantly unfussed. Like everything in the South, dining is familiar, but the accent is softer, and proceedings are a good deal less hurried.

Cajun and Creole

Cajun cooking is based on simple traditions and ingredients, but with herbs that the Atchafalaya settlers learned from the Indians, and the red peppers used by the Spanish. Like everything Cajun, the food is cooked in no kind of a hurry. It features the crawfish, catfish, shrimp, crab and alligator the bayous offered in abundance, mixed in with rice, peas and yams.

Authentic Cajun fare is a rarity in New Orleans restaurants, whatever it may say on the menu. Although tasty, this food in its native form is not appealing to the eye, and most establishments tend to dress it up. To sample Cajun for real, try to get to a private house or a party in rural Louisiana. The culinary artistry of the Cajun's French heritage shines through in bisques, boullions, and boudins. Solidly French dishes like rack of lamb *en croûte* are almost as likely as the ever-tasty gumbo soups, made with chicken, shrimp, or smoked duck. The name "gumbo" comes from an African word meaning okra, invariably mixed into the pot.

Except in regional Louisiana, Creole and Cajun dishes are almost intertwined now, but Creole dishes tend to be based on rich and creamy roux sauces, and spicier than the Cajun, clinging to the three essential ingredients; black pepper, white pepper and red pepper.

Soul food

Soul food means chitlins, collard greens, pork neck bone, and pigs' feet. It's country. If there's meat other than chitlins (deep-fried small pigs'

LEFT: a Nashville attorney lunches at the Satsuma Tea Room, famous for home-style fayre.
RIGHT: crawfish festival at Breaux Bridge, Louisiana, deep in the heart of Cajun Country.

intestines) or pigs' feet, it'll be pork or chicken. There will probably be potatoes, rice, and peas, or maybe corn to accompany. This all harks back to the simple meals using the cheapest ingredients that sustained the poor, mostly black, sharecroppers and urbanites. Now, like much poor food of the past, soul food can be

found in fashionable restaurants. The town of Salley in South Carolina holds an annual chitlins festival, feeding as many white folks as black.

Plantation-style dining

Sweltering in large kitchens, usually detached from the plantation mansions, cooks blended the richness of fresh ingredients with oysters and rabbit, catfish or tasty pecans. In the melting pot of Louisiana, sauces were derived from Creole recipes, adding a dash of spice.

Elsewhere, presentation leaned more toward traditional French cuisine, picked up from plantation owners' frequent trips to Europe and given a Southern twist. Poached capons and stuffed game hens featured along with classic stews, Kentucky Bourbon grilled steaks and – like most Southern dining – ham and corn.

Nouvelle Southern

Louis Osteen, while at Louis's Charleston Grill in South Carolina, aimed to keep these traditions alive, believing the plantation was "where the finest food in the South was made." Now, as the chef and owner of Louis's at Pawleys on Pawley's Island, and in the true New South spirit of reinvention, he has become a leading exponent of what is called "New Southern," or sometimes even, "Nouvelle Southern" cuisine.

Its creations are inspired by traditional American cooking techniques, but combining the signature ingredients of the South. These might include collard-green egg rolls with tasso, red pepper purée and peach chutney. Local fish may be grilled, and served with a hoisin and ginger or Szechwan peanut sauce sauce. Foie gras could even be served with a hush puppy.

Barbecue

Anywhere else, barbecue simply means cooking outdoors on an open grill. In the South, it's a sacred art, more likely to involve a whole pig than any kind of a fiddling-ribs affair. Virginia

SOUTHERN FOOD TERMS

Boudin: a red-hot Cajun sausage made with rice, herbs, and onions. Pronounced *boo-dan*.

Chitlins: yummy deep-fried small pigs' intestines.

Collards: a large, green-leaf vegetable traditionally served on New Year's Day with pork and black-eyed peas.

Green tomatoes: sliced thin green tomatoes rolled in white cornmeal and fried in hot fat.

Grits: coarsely ground hulled corn, boiled and eaten for breakfast or served at night with shrimp or catfish.

Hush puppies: round puffs of cornmeal mixed with minced onion, and sometimes beer, then deep fried.

Jambalaya: served on top of yellow rice, the best contains anything in the kitchen: sausages, seafood, vegetables.

Kale: green vegetable with a delightful bitter tang.

Moonshine: also called "white lightning," the legal corn whiskey is best taken straight; the illegal kind can kill you.

Okra: a long pod vegetable with seeds, okra came to the New World with slaves, who hid the seeds in their hair.

Spoon bread: made from corn and baked like a custard, the bread is so soft it must be eaten with a spoon.

Tomato pudding: cubed old bread softened in tomatoes, covered with crumbs and baked. Popular in Appalachia.

Yams: similar to sweet potatoes, but usually served "candied," or sliced and flavored with syrup and spices.

barbecue sauce is tomato-based, with a dash of vinegar and pepper. South Carolina has a unique barbecue with mustard. "That's for hot dogs," was all a Georgia gourmet would say. North Carolinians pack the pork with coleslaw.

Tennessee-style barbecue, called "dry rub barbecue," has a blend of spices rubbed dry onto the pork skin. Memphis plays host to the World Barbecue Championship, a major highlight in the "Memphis in May" festival.

Down a dark, unpromising alley near the Peabody Hotel, Charlie Vergo's Rendezvous is the Memphis shrine of barbecue. A popular local tale is that one of the early owners was charged

world over, and sent by Virginians to friends and relatives unfortunate enough to be out of state for any length of time. In another "poor-food chic" twist, the British TV chef Nigella Lawson promotes a trailer-trash recipe for ham cooked in Coca-Cola. It's delicious, too.

Catfish

Catfish are plentiful in the South – so much so in Lousiana that they are often scooped into sacks right off the shore, and in Mississippi, catfish farms are taking over from cotton plantations. The soft, white fish shows up in jambalaya and étouffe, but all over the South is

with murder. He said he'd caught the dead man in bed with his wife, and shot him. The judge said that was no excuse for murder. The chef pleaded, "But she'd told him my secret barbecue recipe." "In that case," said the judge, "you should have shot her, too. Case dismissed."

Culinary artform

The curing, smoking, hanging and preparation of rich, succulent hams is another devotional Southern artform. Virginia hams are prized the

most likely to arrive at table deep-fried. Other fish like trout and mullet show up for supper and, around the coasts, redfish and snappers.

Grits

The South's own breakfast treat is the recipe that settlers probably learned from the Indians, hominy grits – sometimes strange to the foreign palate but a delicacy when the taste is acquired. Corn is treated with lye water (potash water, as it was known in the old days) to make it swell and produce hominy. This is then dried and ground to produce grits. The best grits are smooth and creamy, served hot with butter, salt and pepper, and with a fried egg on the side.❏

LEFT: fine dining in Natchez-under-the-Hill, but also in New Orleans, Charleston, Birmingham and Atlanta.
ABOVE: Taylor, Mississippi: good food and good people.

DANCING IN THE STREETS

From blues and soul to country, from jazz to rock 'n' roll,
many of the rhythms that swept the world originated in the South

There is music everywhere in the South. Walk around the French Quarter in New Orleans, Beale Street in Memphis or just about any-where in Clarksdale, Mississippi, and in no time your feet will be syncopating. Most of all, there's music and poetry in the droll, sparkling South-ern talk. From this cultural richness, the Southern United States became the most fertile musical lands of the 20th century. Country, gospel, jazz, the blues, soul, and rock 'n' roll were all con-ceived in the South. So too, were their many off-spring such as Cajun, Zydeco, country & western, and rhythm & blues.

James Brown and Ray Charles came from Georgia, Jerry Lee Lewis from Ferriday, Louisi-ana, blues legends Robert Johnson, Muddy Waters, Willie Dixon, and John Lee Hooker hailed from the Mississippi Delta, as did rock & roll and soul innovators Ike Turner and Sam Cooke. Jazz giants Louis Armstrong and the Marsalis family, and the Neville Brothers all came from New Orleans. The father of country music, Jimmie Rodgers, was a Mississippian from Meridian, and Hank Williams was born in Olive Hill near Georgiana, Alabama. Then there was Sam Phillips in Memphis. Most of the great artists that his Sun Studio produced came from the South, including a boy from Tupelo, Missis-sippi, name of Elvis Aaron Presley.

European folk music began the musical seed-ing. Settlers from Scotland and Ireland brought their fiddles and harmoniums, and a hearty trad-ition of jigs and reels to dance to. They blended in with folk styles from Holland, Spain, and Ger-many. Church music and the rhythms of Africa were also key ingredients.

Added to the mix in Louisiana, a French influ-ence came by way of Canada with the Acadians, and developed into the jubilant Cajun music. Nearly all the vocals are sung in French, showing the fierce independence of Cajun spirit as the

language was banned from Louisiana schools in the 1930s. Around Mardi Gras time in Eunice, Lafayette and all over bayou country, there are Cajun and Zydeco bands getting the dancers up from the crawfish *étouffée* and jambalaya. Hank Williams took a Cajun tune to fame with his country classic *Jambalaya*.

Soul

Soul music was an evolution of rhythm & blues, a more solidly black dance beat than the slightly sanitized rock 'n' roll making white radio play. Often with a heavy, rhythmic brass section, soul was more raw and emotional, more an amplifi-cation of the spirit of its blues roots.

The two Southern cauldrons of soul, Stax Records in Memphis and the Fame Studio in Muscle Shoals, Alabama, both started at the beginning of the 1960s. Stax was formed by the white brother and sister team of Jim Stewart and Estelle Axton. They took the label name from the first letters of their surnames: STewart, AXton. Stax recorded in an old cinema, under a marquee

---

LEFT: Elvis Presley, Jerry Lee Lewis, Carl Perkins and Johnny Cash in December, 1956, at Sun Studio.
RIGHT: Wilson Pickett recorded *Mustang Sally* at the Fame Studios in Muscle Shoals, Alabama.

proclaiming it "Soulville USA." Here they recorded Rufus and Carla Thomas, Otis Redding, Sam and Dave, Wilson Pickett, and Isaac Hayes, most of them over the house band which was basically Booker T and the MGs, recording stars in their own right.

In Muscle Shoals, Rick Hall owned the Fame studio and label, and produced Arthur Alexander's *You Better Move On*, later covered by the Rolling Stones, and Etta James' hugely successful *Tell Mama* album, both in 1961. There was a crossover with Stax when Otis Redding brought Arthur Conley to Muscle Shoals to record the classic *When a Man Loves a Woman*. Fame was

the studio where a Memphis girl named Aretha Franklin cut some of her early hits, while the Muscle Shoals Rhythm Section went on to back big-name rock bands in the late 1960s and '70s.

Jazz

Jazz may be America's greatest contribution to the music world, and it all started in the South. New Orleans, to be exact, although the word itself may come from the name of Charles "Chas" Washington, a drummer from Vicksburg, Mississippi. Jelly Roll Morton claimed to have coined the term in 1902 to distinguish it from ragtime, but researchers have pointed out that he was only 12 years old at the time.

Around the turn of the 20th century, a new kind of sound began to develop in the form of African rhythms, marching bands, Creole and gospel sounds, and the parlor piano. The emerging motifs of the blues, some syncopation and the cultural mix of New Orleans contributed. The city's talent pool provided extraordinary musicians to define the new form, players like pianist Jelly Roll Morton, then later, trumpeter Louis Armstrong. Many of them traveled North, or even to Europe, to achieve recognition and popularity for themselves and for the new art, and from Chicago to New York, to Paris, London and Helsinki, it caught on pretty fast.

The first jazz records were made, paradoxically it seems now, by a white ensemble, The Original Dixieland Jazz Band. They weren't original, they were covering black music, and they recorded for the Victor Company in New York, but they were formed in New Orleans. Every spring the greatest names in jazz make pilgrimage to New Orleans, as they have since 1959, to listen and play at the spectacular JazzFest.

Gospel

European church music was an influence for two distinct strands of what is now called gospel music. White gospel comes from Protestant roots, and ranges from small vocal harmony groups, through choirs with bands, to massed choirs in assembly rooms. Before the Civil War, revival and campfire meetings were accompanied by the hymn-like singing of songs, later collected into songbooks like *Gospel Hymns and Sacred Tunes* (1875) and *The Christian Harp* (1877).

Black gospel music traces its roots back to the late 19th and early 20th centuries. Rhythms and harmonies from the working songs, spirituals, the blues, and ragtime all came to church, and mixed with the cadences of the revival hymns. In turn, some of the choirs and preachers took their music back out to the secular world. James Brown and blues legend Son House were both preachers, and B.B. King learned his early musical lessons in the church choir.

With the recent popularity of Christian music in America spawning record labels and radio stations, the music and its message are flourishing. Mahalia Jackson, a major gospel star, spurned all offers of secular engagements, but she did record *Come Sunday* with Duke Ellington, and sang at the inauguration of President Kennedy, as well as Martin Luther King, Jr's funeral.

Blues

Archaeologist Charles Peabody first documented the working songs of the black laborers on a dig in 1903 at Stovall, Mississippi. He later described it in the influential *Journal of American Folklore* as "weird in interval and strange in rhythm; peculiarly beautiful." That same year, musician WC Handy heard the sound of a guitar played with a knife-blade as a slide and set about popularizing it in his repertoire.

Robert Johnson, the undisputed king of the

IT ROCKS

The blues had a baby and they named it rock 'n' roll, sang Muddy Waters, asserting the bluesman's parental claim on the infant sound.

cians playing on street corners. BB King was among them, and his skills eventually bought him one of the corners for his Beale Street restaurant. A very influential outlet for the blues was radio's "King Biscuit Time," which still airs each day at 12:15pm out of KFFA in Helena, Arkansas.

The Blues had a Baby

Sam Phillips worked as a disc jockey in Muscle Shoals, Alabama, but when he decided to set up shop with a recording studio in 1945, his enthusiasm for country music and the blues drew him to Memphis. His 706 Union

Delta bluesmen, lived from 1911 to 1938. The influence of the 29 songs recorded in the last two years of his life inspired artists from Muddy Waters to Robert Cray and Eric Clapton. The Mississippi Delta was the stomping ground of the early blues, and nowhere more than in Clarksdale *(for more on Clarksdale, Johnson and Handy, see pages 176–79)*. In the 1920s and 1930s Delta blues musicians started migrating; electric players followed Muddy Waters to Chicago; others were drawn to the studios in Memphis. Beale Street was crackling with musi-

Avenue studio has been available for rent by the hour ever since. The Memphis Recording Service's first customer was Ike Turner, who later cut *Rocket 88* in the modest studio in 1951. This track is one of the true contenders for the title of "the first rock 'n' roll record," and was part of Phillips' motivation to open his own record label.

Charlie Rich, Carl Perkins, Jerry Lee Lewis, Roy Orbison, and Johnny Cash all reached the ears and dancing feet of the world through Phillips' label, along with the man he described as "My greatest discovery. When he sings, you can hear clear down to his soul" – the legendary Howlin' Wolf. Then there is the story of a shy young man coming in to record a song for his

LEFT: Louis Armstrong, New Orleans' finest.
ABOVE: Riley (Blues Boy) King, otherwise known as BB.

mother's birthday in 1953. In fact, Phillips turned Elvis away at least once, but when he sang Arthur Cruddup's *That's All Right, Mama,* Sam heard what he had been searching for – a white kid who could bring rhythm & blues to a white audience. After 10 record releases, Phillips sold his contract with Elvis to RCA for just $35,000, a tiny sum by modern standards. Sam died aged 80 on July 30, 2003.

Phillips aimed to synthesize something between the dark, exciting rhythm & blues and vibrant, electric country. The results, including Elvis's early records, were called "rockabilly." Another Phillips discovery, Arkansan Johnny

Cash's outlaw, hard-life image, honed in prison gigs, bridged the rock 'n' roll and country styles perfectly until his death in 2003.

Country

The history of modern country music dates back to 1927, when Ralph Peer set up recording equipment in Bristol, Tennessee, scouting for the New York Victor label. Near the border with Virginia, the Bristol sessions attracted both the Carter Family and Jimmie Rodgers. The Carter family popularized traditional songs of England and the rural South with strong and distinctive harmonies, and Maybelle Carter developed a style of melodic rhythm guitar picking that is still a country main-

stay. Rodgers returned to Victor to record *Blue Yodel,* a white blues that set a standard for songs of the working man's struggles.

At a young age, Earl Scruggs instinctively developed the three-finger picking banjo style that became the emblem of bluegrass. Bill Munroe coined the term "bluegrass" for his band the Bluegrass Boys, where Scruggs and Lester Flatt first played together.

The biggest star of the Grand Ole Opry, though, was Alabamian Hank Williams. He learned from the age of eight to play the blues on the guitar from a mentor, Rufus Teetot Payne, and his vocal style drew on Roy Acuff's *Grand Ole Opry* broadcasts. Williams's song *Move It On Over* anticipated Bill Haley's hit *Rock Around the Clock* by 10 years. A tough childhood and a stormy love life with his wife Audrey inspired poetry that still reaches out. *Cold, Cold Heart,* which he first recorded in 1951, is still regularly covered, recently on a Grammy-winning album by Norah Jones.

Chet Atkins and Owen Bradley were leading producers in Nashville, and in the mid-1950s, when the American audience was deserting for Elvis and rock 'n' roll, they developed a smoother, more commercial country style to recapture the market. Chet produced Jim Reeves's *Four Walls,* and made the transition from a hillbilly dance-hall image to a lush, intimate sound drenched in sentiment. Owen Bradley produced Brenda Lee singing *I'm Sorry* in the same style and sold 15 million records.

The tamed, suburban Nashville sound of the 1960s was born. Nashville had moved from the songs of working peoples' troubles and blues to a smooth, marketable product. That left the raw, sincere heart of country out to be stolen.

It was picked up by non-Southerners like Willie Nelson, Merle Haggard and Gram Parsons, who brought a liberal viewpoint and synthesized country with rock. Now, Garth Brooks and KD Lang may be a long lost highway from Hank Williams, but the country roads still run either to or from Nashville, Tennessee.

To this day, from North Carolina's innovative lyrical son Ryan Adams to Louisiana's pop prodigal wild child, Britney Spears, the South still has a whole lot of shakin' going on.   ❏

LEFT: "King Biscuit Time" still airs in Arkansas.
RIGHT: Grand Ole Opry players often stop by Nashville's Tootsie's Orchard Lounge between gigs.

PLACES

*A detailed guide to the South, with principal sites
clearly cross-referenced by number to the maps*

Shiny-new cities like Charlotte in North Carolina, Birmingham in Alabama, and Atlanta are emblems of transformation in the cultural landscape. Savannah, Memphis and Biloxi are rising as modern vacation playgrounds, vying with New Orleans for the party crowd, although little can compete with the Big Easy's annual Jazz Festival or Mardi Gras.

From the Atlantic shores of Virginia and the Carolinas to the silver sands and emerald sea of the Gulf Coast, and from the Great Smoky Mountains to the swamps and bayous of Louisiana, the country is lush and epic. The Art Deco panache of Hot Springs, Arkansas and Alabama's tranquil, wooded Azalea Coast offer bijoux B&Bs and sumptuous places for pampering, all served up with a uniquely Southern welcome.

Plantations and antebellum mansions drape the hills throughout the South. Graceful places to visit, and often to stay, since many offer overnight hospitality, they keep alive a picture of how the South was. In the New South, the other side of that currency has found expression. The Martin Luther King Foundation in Atlanta and the National Civil Rights Museum in Memphis, along with countless museums and sites of heritage across the land where cotton was King, attest to the struggles of the more recent past.

Anywhere in the South is worth visiting for the food alone. Creole and Cajun spice, along with variations on traditional French sauces whet and satisfy appetites across Louisiana. The abundance of seafood in coastal regions is matched only by the varieties of culinary heritage that go into its preparation. Regional barbecue specialties set lips smacking from North Carolina to Nashville, and plantation-style dining is still a rich and elegant affair.

The southern beaches from South Walton to Pass Christian attract travelers of all kinds – the family-fun crowds flock to Panama City beach and anglers love the bayous and coastal waters at the edge of the Gulf, while golfers lug their woods and irons to the world-famous links at Augusta and South Carolina near the Atlantic coast. The wild, unspoiled shorelines offer hikers, birdwatchers and campers a natural nirvana. The haunting wilderness around the Natchez Trace and the spectacular Skyline Drive in the Blue Ridge Mountains make for driving trips that linger and echo in the memory. The history and the heritage, the culture and the celebrations, the aspirations and the achievements are all reasons to visit the New South. ❑

PRECEDING PAGES: the hazy blue hills of *Cold Mountain* country; leaves color the landscape of a Virginia farm; Atlanta skyline at night.
LEFT: like its namesake on the Nile, Memphis is dominated by a pyramid; this one is 32 stories high and used as a sports arena.

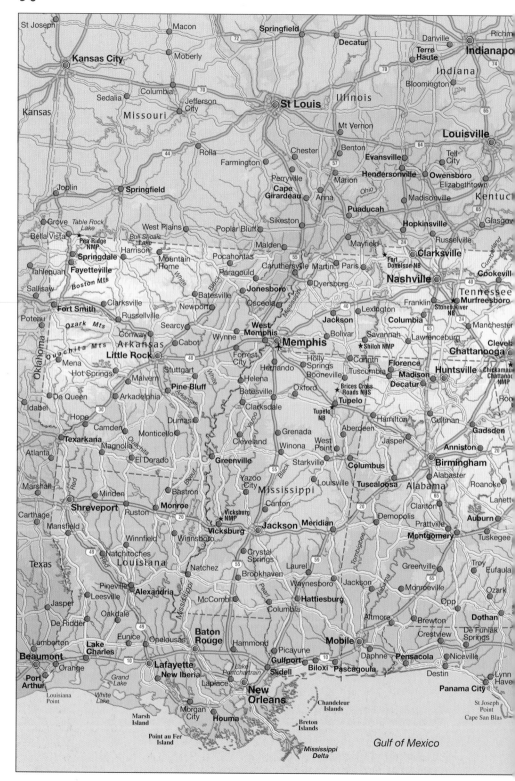

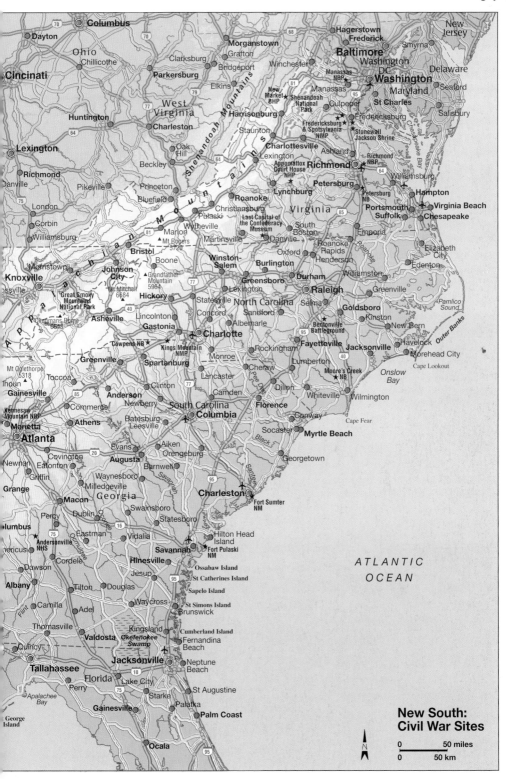

New South:
Civil War Sites

0   50 miles

0   50 km

CIVIL WAR SITES

The War Between the States killed more than 600,000
young men, and changed the South forever.
Its sites are moving and poignant reminders

Map
on pages
90–91

In his famous address at Gettysburg, Abraham Lincoln spoke movingly of hallowed ground. Many of the most important battlefields of the Civil War are part of the National Park Service, and for Americans none of the other land that the nation has set aside for preservation bears the emotional force of these consecrated places. Brutal battles were fought here, pitting kinsmen against kinsmen in an awful conflict that scarred the national psyche. Fighting raged across most of the eastern states for four years, killing more than 600,000 men and nearly destroying the young republic.

The sites administered by the Park Service include battlefields, cemeteries and memorials. Some are clustered together and can easily be visited in a day or two. Others require long-distance driving and a serious investment of time. Almost all are open every day except major holidays, but it's best to call ahead to check; to find the location of each historic site, see the individual state maps.

The opening shot

In 1860, Lincoln was elected president, and momentous events came in a rush. On December 20, an angry South Carolina convention voted to secede from the Union, followed quickly by Alabama, Florida, Georgia, Louisiana and Mississippi. The Confederate States of America formed in February 1861, electing Jefferson Davis as president *(see page 38)*, and nearly all Federal forts in the South were seized by Confederate forces.

In South Carolina, Major Robert Anderson realized that the building at what is now **Fort Sumter National Monument** (tel: 843-883-3123) was the only defensible fort of the four Federal installations in Charleston, and he consolidated troops there. When Lincoln took office on March 4, 1861, he made clear that he would hold the fort. At 4:30am on April 12, Confederate batteries opened fire on Fort Sumter, and the Civil War had begun.

Anderson surrendered late the next day. The Union Army laid siege to the fort for 22 months, but never retook it; Confederate troops remained until 1865. Today, boats licensed by the National Park Service carry visitors to Fort Sumter, which is situated on an island in Charleston harbor.

Just west of Washington, DC, **Manassas National Battlefield Park** (tel: 703-361-1339) in Virginia was the site of two major clashes. General Irvin McDowell led 35,000 Union troops toward a key railroad junction at Manassas on July 18, 1861, expecting to take Richmond, the Confederate capital, easily and end the war quickly. But waiting there, near the Stone Bridge on Bull Run Creek, was General Pierre G.T. Beauregard and 22,000 Confederate troops. Another

LEFT: re-enactment at Clinton, Georgia.
BELOW: instruments of war.

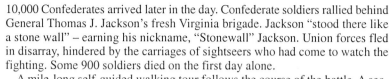

Union troops laid siege to Fort Sumter for 22 months in vain.

10,000 Confederates arrived later in the day. Confederate soldiers rallied behind General Thomas J. Jackson's fresh Virginia brigade. Jackson "stood there like a stone wall" – earning his nickname, "Stonewall" Jackson. Union forces fled in disarray, hindered by the carriages of sightseers who had come to watch the fighting. Some 900 soldiers died on the first day alone.

A mile-long self-guided walking tour follows the course of the battle. A second walk covers the area of the Stone Bridge; Union troops who were wounded here received aid and medicine in an effort organized by Clara Barton. At the age of 40 she had quit her US Patent Office job, and would later found the American Red Cross. Visitors can tour the **Ben Lomond Manor House**, which was possibly used as a hospital, and watch the battle depicted in a film shown in the visitor center.

The second Battle of Manassas (Bull Run) came more than a year later, this time involving not raw recruits but veteran soldiers. Robert E. Lee, the new commander of the Confederate Army of Northern Virginia, dispatched Stonewall Jackson's force to engage General John Pope's Union troops. After several battles and tactical mistakes by Pope during the engagement, Jackson sent Union forces fleeing once again. The confrontation killed 3,300 men. A 12-mile (19-km) driving tour covers much of the large area of the second battle of Bull Run.

General George B. McClellan rebuilt the fleeing Federals into the 100,000-man Army of the Potomac and in May 1862 marched on the heavily fortified Confederate capital at Richmond, Virginia. On May 15, Confederate fire drove off five Union ironclad ships that had been moving up the James River toward Richmond. June 26 was the start of seven days of fierce battles on Richmond's eastern outskirts. Lee's forces repulsed McClellan's Union troops, with casualties on both sides numbering 35,000.

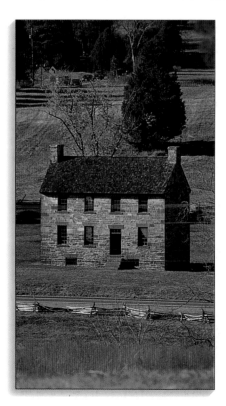

BELOW: Manassas, where two battles took 4,200 lives.

Richmond was not safe for the Confederates, however. Battles in regions north of the city continued through the coming months and years. In March 1864, Ulysses S. Grant became commander of the Union field forces, and immediately proclaimed as his chief objective the capture of Richmond.

The battlefield at **Cold Harbor** sits midway between two roadside taverns. When Grant's soldiers attacked there on June 3, they suffered 7,000 casualties in 30 minutes, forcing him to change to a siege strategy. Union soldiers, including several regiments of African-American troops, took Fort Harrison on September 29. Richmond held on until April 1865, falling only after Lee's forces withdrew. It's possible to trace the whole of the encounter at the 10 units of **Richmond National Battlefield Park** (tel: 804-226-1981). A complete tour requires an 80-mile (130-km) long drive.

War for the west

Far to the west, both sides coveted the state of Missouri, with its strategic position on both the Missouri and Mississippi rivers. The battle for Missouri moved to a climax at the beginning of 1862, when Union Brigadier General Samuel R. Curtis launched a drive to push Confederate forces from the state. Rebel troops regrouped south of Fayetteville in Arkansas under Major General Earl Van Dorn. Van Dorn's forces marched toward Missouri but met Curtis's troops at what is now **Pea Ridge National Military Park** (tel: 479-451-8122 ext 227), 10 miles (16 km) northeast of Rogers, Arkansas, which ultimately saved the state of Missouri for the Union.

Until 1862, the Union military had seemed unable to gain an important victory. Confederate defensive lines had few weak points, but Union commanders decided to test the line in western Tennessee, where Fort Henry on the Tennessee River and Fort Donelson on the Cumberland River sat just 12 miles (19 km) apart. Union ironclad gunboats commenced fire on **Fort Henry** on February 6, 1862, while the virtually unknown Brigadier General Ulysses S. Grant led a ground assault. Grant was slow in reaching the fort, and by the time he arrived, the ironclads had destroyed it, and almost the entire garrison had left, fleeing for Fort Donelson.

When Union forces attacked on February 14, gunboats could not duplicate their feat against Donelson's heavier guns. Changing tactics, Grant encircled the fort and laid siege. The Confederates surrendered on February 16. These were the Union's first big victories, and the newly tested General Grant had made a name for himself. Driving and walking tours are available at **Fort Donelson National Battlefield** (tel: 931-232-5706), a mile west of Dover in Tennessee. Visitors can also see the **Dover Hotel** (Surrender House), whch has been restored to its Civil War appearance.

Army of the Tennessee

After the losses at Fort Henry and Fort Donelson, Confederate forces withdrew. In Mississippi, General A. S. Johnston consolidated a force of 44,000 troops at Corinth, planning to overwhelm Grant. Grant, in turn, moved his own 40,000-man Army of the Tennessee to an encampment around **Shiloh Church**, 22 miles (35 km) northeast of Corinth. Grant drilled his new recruits but set up almost no defenses. Johnston's attack on April 6, 1862, caught Union forces by surprise. Grant's troops spent the entire day in fierce, retreating battles at locations such as **Hornet's Nest**.

Confederates used a barrage of 62 cannons – the largest artillery assault of its day – to inflict huge losses on a Union division. Johnston was killed in action and P. G. T. Beauregard assumed command. By the end of the day, Grant's remaining forces reached **Pittsburgh Landing** and set up a position fortified by gunboats and thousands of men.

By the morning of April 7, Grant's forces numbered 55,000, but, unaware of the reinforcements, Beauregard attacked. By the time Beauregard retreated, his troops were low on ammunition, and Confederate casualties swelled to 15,000. **Shiloh National Military Park** (tel: 731-689-5696) includes a visitor center and a self-guided driving tour.

Even before the battle at Shiloh, Union forces were preparing to attack Fort Pulaski, a newly completed fort, now in Confederate hands, which guarded the river approaches to Savannah in Georgia. After taking Hilton Head island, Union forces moved 10 experimental rifled cannons into position on Tybee Island, a

Map
on pages
90–91

BELOW: monument to Stonewall Jackson.

mile away from the fort. On April 10, 1862, the Union's new cannons opened up on Pulaski's brick walls, which ranged in thickness from 7 to 15 ft (2–5 meters). Confederate Colonel Charles H. Olmstead and his troops held on through 30 hours of devastating high-technology barrage.

By noon on April 11, explosive shells opened an outer wall and exposed the fort's main powder magazine. Fearing that an explosion might destroy not only the fort but also the men inside, Olmstead surrendered. **Fort Pulaski National Monument** (tel: 912-786-5787) is reached via Highway 80 from Savannah.

As 1862 drew to a close, Major General William Rosecrans took command of the Union Army of the Cumberland, charged with driving Confederate forces under General Braxton Bragg out of Tennessee. Rosecrans found Bragg waiting for him in a grove of cedars near the Stones River in **Murfreesboro,** Tennessee, 27 miles (46 km) southeast of Nashville.

Troops on both sides acted out one of the heartbreaking ironies of warfare as they camped within sight of one another on December 30, 1863, singing rousing songs well into the evening. Then, at dawn on December 31, in a day that went badly for Union forces, they were driven back nearly a mile before establishing a new line. There was neither music nor fighting on New Year's Day.

On January 2, Bragg's forces drove Union soldiers back to Stones River, where Rosecrans's superior artillery was waiting. Bragg lost 1,800 soldiers at the river, and the battle ended as his forces retreated. The Confederates had lost Tennessee. The casualties after two days of pitched fighting were 13,000 Union soldiers and 10,000 Confederate soldiers. **Stones River National Battlefield** (tel: 615-893-9501) lies in the northwest corner of Murfreesboro and includes a very informative driving tour.

Only 30 miles (48 km) west of Jackson, the Mississippi state capital, is **Vicksburg National Military Park** (tel: 601-636-0583), the site of the last Confederate stronghold on the Mississippi River (*see page 163*). After a crippling 47-day siege, on July 4, 1863, Confederate Lieutenant General John C Pemberton surrendered to Grant. When Port Hudson fell five days later, the Mississippi belonged to the Union.

Emancipation Proclamation

Tragic as Vicksburg was, it was only one example of the horrors of this war. Autumn of 1862 brought the costliest battle of the Civil War – the Battle of Antietam, fought on both sides of Antietam Creek in Maryland, where more than 23,000 men fell.

Although the Confederates had not lost, its army had taken a step toward losing the war. On September 22, President Lincoln issued the Emancipation Proclamation, which on January 1, 1863, freed slaves in states "in rebellion against the United States." Only then did emancipation become a formal objective of the war.

It was possible to "take the pulse" of the war at **Fredericksburg** in Virginia. The city's proximity to Washington, DC, and Richmond – it lies halfway between – had been a blessing before the war, but after secession its strategic location became a curse. One hundred thousand men died near Fredericksburg in four major battles. **Fredericksburg and Spotsylvania National Military Park** (tel: 504-373-6122) encompasses 7,775 acres (3,146 hectares) of land that includes four battlefields and three historic buildings. **Fredericksburg Battlefield** is where General Ambrose E. Burnside's Union troops crossed the Rappahannock River in December 1862 to attack Lee's forces, commanded by Stonewall Jackson. Heavily defended on hills west of Fredericksburg, Jackson handily won the battle, inflicting big losses on the Federal troops. More than 15,000 Union soldiers are buried at **Fredericksburg National Cemetery**, while **Chatham Manor**, a Georgian mansion used as a field hospital, is where volunteer Clara Barton and poet Walt Whitman tended to injured soldiers.

Death of a rebel hero

A drive west leads to the **Chancellorsville Battlefield**, where in May 1863 Jackson's forces again won a victory against Federal troops. Here Jackson was shot by "friendly fire." Following the amputation of his left arm on May 4, General Lee wrote to him, "You are better off than I am, for while you have lost your left, I have lost my right arm." Jackson died of pneumonia on May 10 at **Guinea Station**, 15 miles (24 km) south of Fredericksburg, where the **Stonewall Jackson Shrine** now stands.

To the west is **Wilderness Battlefield**, where, a year later, on May 5–6, 1864, Lee and Grant first faced each other in an indecisive battle. Grant broke away to march toward the Spotsylvania Court House. Lee's army actually reached Spotsylvania first, and he fended off several small Union attacks. When more Union troops arrived, along with a thick fog, the fighting grew more savage. After 20 hours of hand-to-hand combat and several days of a staunch

Map on pages 90–91

Fredericksburg in Virginia saw heavy battle in 1862.

BELOW: flag lowering ceremony at Fort Sumter.

TIP

If you can afford it, hiring a personal guide to a Southern Civil War site, especially in one of the smaller parks, can be memorable. Guides are very often local people who not only grew up playing in the parks, but can recount family stories about the war.

Confederate defense, Grant pulled his troops out and called the fight at "Bloody Angle" a Union victory, a key to winning the war.

Lee lost his right-hand man in Stonewall Jackson, but not his fighting spirit. On June 3, he began a march west into Pennsylvania. This was to lead to the fateful Battle of Gettysburg, where his 70,000 soldiers would clash with General George G. Meade's 93,000 Union troops. In three days, the two armies suffered 51,000 casualties – the greatest losses incurred in any battle ever fought in North America.

Struggle for the South

A visit to **Chickamauga and Chattanooga National Military Park** (tel: 706-866-9241) in Georgia, just miles outside Chattanooga in Tennessee, stirs the imagination and provides insight into the four-year struggle for the South. Hiking over its fields, hills and hardwood forests, picture two battles – one an empty Confederate victory on September 18–19, 1863, at **Chickamauga Battlefield**; the next, a Union triumph in the Battle of Chattanooga on November 23–25. The best way to imagine this battle is by hiking up to **Point Park** on **Lookout Mountain**. From here all of Chattanooga can be seen.

After Ulysses S. Grant was named supreme commander on March 9, 1864, the Union Army traveled south from Chattanooga toward **Atlanta** – "too important a place in the hands of the enemy to be left undisturbed," as General Sherman put it. The Federal Army wanted to get its hands on the weaponry, the foundries "and especially its railroads, which converged there from the four great cardinal points," Sherman said.

Kennesaw Mountain National Battlefield Park (tel: 770-427-4686)

BELOW: re-enacting camp followers.

SAVE OUR CIVIL WAR SITES

More than one-third of all principal Civil War battlefields have either vanished or are hanging on by the slenderest of threads. According to a study conducted by the Civil War Sites Advisory Commission, around 10,500 armed conflicts occured and of these 384 have been identified as of historical significance. The National Park Service is in a position to maintain only the most important of these battlefields, while 43 percent of the other major sites remain solely in private hands, subject to the whim of their owners. The report does not even include the countless smaller sites, such as cemeteries, forts, prisons and other buildings that are at risk.

One of the problems is the changing nature of the South, as it moves from a rural to an urban economy. As long as the battlefields were agricultural land, they were relatively safe. But along with the building of superhighways, especially around Washington, DC, came increasing residential and commercial development, especially in the green hills of Virginia, the site of more than 50 percent of all battles. The South is again under siege, but this time the enemy is as likely to be a greedy Southerner as any damn Yankee. For information, contact the American Battlefield Protection Program or go to www.cr.nps.gov/military.htm

memorializes the 1864 Atlanta campaign, which began when Sherman led 100,000 troops out of Chattanooga in early May, only to confront 65,000 Confederate troops in the mountains of northwest Georgia. For months the two armies battled for key points along the Western & Atlantic Railroad, which ran from Chattanooga to Atlanta. A climax was reached on June 22 at **Kennesaw Mountain**, just northwest of Atlanta. Hand-to-hand combat killed more than 2,000 of Sherman's men at Kennesaw, while the Confederates lost several hundred men in winning the battle.

Map on pages 90–91

March to the Sea

Still, Sherman pushed General Johnston's Confederate troops south into Atlanta by July 9. After several attacks, Sherman placed the city under siege, concentrating on the railroads. He won the last one, the Macon & Western, on August 31, and telegraphed the fall of Atlanta to Washington on September 2. Riding the victory, Lincoln was re-elected on November 8. A week later, Sherman began his ruthless March to the Sea – still recounted by Southerners today – destroying or stealing nearly everything in his path: crops, buildings, railroads, horses. He promised to "make Georgia howl."

Hiking trails from 2 to 10 miles (3–16 km) lead to the most important sites. These are Kennesaw Mountain, with a vista of northern Georgia, and where the armies clashed; **Pigeon Hill**, where a foot trail leads to Confederate entrenchments; **Cheatham Hill**, site of the most savage fighting; and **Kolb's Farm** (not open to the public), headquarters of General Joseph Hooker.

Two small parks in Mississippi mark strategic points in the ongoing conflict between North and South. Sherman's army needed to defend the

BELOW: *USS Cairo* at Vicksburg.

Nashville–Chattanooga Railroad, a critical Union supply line. In June 1864, the Confederates, under General Nathan Bedford Forrest, an unschooled farm boy who had become a millionaire, routed Union soldiers at Brices Cross Roads, displaying brilliant military tactics and taking advantage of torrential downpours that mired Union troops in mud. Victory in battle, however, didn't help the Confederate position, as Sherman was still able to defend the railroad. It is possible to see the battlefield and markers at the small **Brices Cross Roads National Battlefield Site** (no tel, closed Mon).

Only a month later, arid, hot weather created as many difficulties as did the earlier rain, tiring soldiers on both sides. Again Federal troops battled Confederate men to protect their southern supply line. On July 14, the two sides met at **Tupelo**, Mississippi, with exhausted, ill-fed Union troops winning a close victory. For two months, the two sides skirmished. Finally, in September, Confederate troops pushed north past Federal soldiers into Tennessee. But Sherman's forces no longer needed to protect the railroad; they had already won Atlanta and were on their way to the sea. **Tupelo National Battlefield** is located within Tupelo city limits, about a mile east of the **Natchez Trace Parkway**. Information on both sites is available by telephoning 662-680-4027.

Grant's army was everywhere during the spring of 1864. Even while Sherman waged the Atlanta campaign and smaller forces defended the Nashville–Chattanooga Railroad, Federal troops were focused on Richmond. The Union Army reached Petersburg, Virginia, which Grant called "the key to taking Richmond," in mid-June 1864. For 10 gruelling months, Grant kept Petersburg under siege. He cut Lee's supply lines from the south, diminishing troop strength through direct attack, hunger and demoralization. Petersburg finally surrendered on April 2, 1865. On the same day, the proud capital of Richmond fell.

One of the most tragic sites at **Petersburg National Battlefield** (tel: 804-458-9504) is the **Crater**. Here, the 48th Pennsylvania Infantry, which included many former coal miners, dug a tunnel toward a Confederate fort at Pegram's Salient. In this tunnel they blew up 4 tons of gunpowder, planning to send Union troops through the gap it would create, with the intention of shortening the siege. The explosion, which blew up Confederate artillery, created a crater 170 feet (52 meters) long, 60 ft (18 meters) wide and 30 ft (9 meters) deep. The Union Army went directly into the crater but were unable to go farther, and lost 4,000 men when Confederate troops attacked. The battlefield is within Petersburg city limits.

The final day

From here, it is possible to visit the 27 historic structures lying 20 miles (32 km) east of Lynchburg within the restored village of **Appomattox Court House National Historical Park** (tel: 434-352-8987), where Robert E. Lee, with a solider's dignity, surrendered to Ulysses S. Grant only one week after Richmond fell. The national park site encompasses nearly 1,800 acres (730 hectares) of rolling hills in rural Virginia, which include the **McLean home** (where the surrender took place) and the **Appomattox Court House.**

BELOW: Confederate artilleryman.

A lasting legacy

One of the saddest sites of the Civil War is to be seen at **Andersonville National Historic Site** (tel: 229-924-0343) in Georgia. Andersonville was the largest encampment housing Federal prisoners, and a third of those confined here, almost 13,000 Union soldiers, died. When it was built in 1864, most people thought the war would soon be over. The Confederate government had built the prison to hold 10,000 captives, but soon there were 32,000 men suffering in the filthy, unsanitary conditions of the prison camp. Prisoners died from disease, poor sanitation, malnutrition, overcrowding or even exposure to the elements.

Following the war, the prison commander, Captain Henry Wirz, was hanged as a war criminal, although his crimes were simply those of the ailing Confederate government, which had no money or resources with which to feed and house its own troops, much less its prisoners. Andersonville's life as a prison ended in early 1865.

In the months of July and August, Clara Barton, working together with Dorence Atwater, a former prisoner who had chronicled the prisoners' deaths, identified thousands and thousands of grave sites.

While at Andersonville, visit the **National Cemetery**, the atmospheric prison, and **Providence Spring House**, which the Women's Relief Corps built in 1901 as a tribute to the site where, during a downpour on August 9, 1864, a spring began to flow. Prisoners thanked "Divine Providence" for the fresh water. Today, this historic site is a memorial not only to the men who were imprisoned and who died at Andersonville, but also to all Americans ever confined as prisoners of war – the only such national park in the country. ❑

Map on pages 90–91

BELOW: a small section of the Vicksburg National Cemetery.

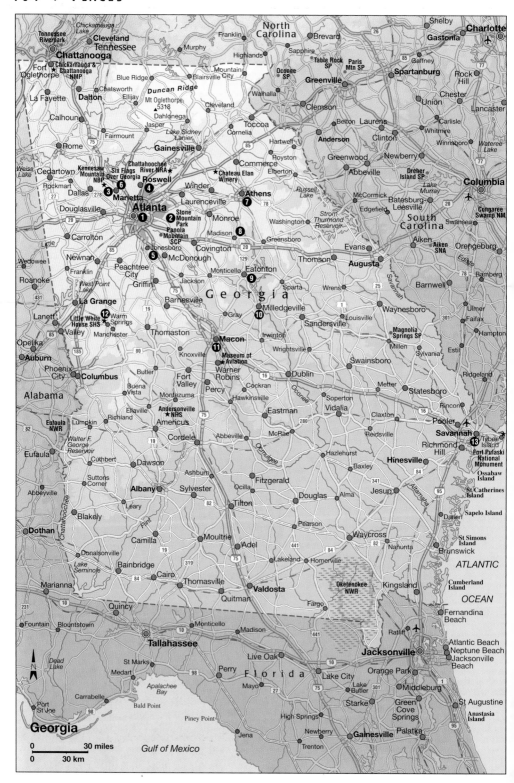

Georgia

0   30 miles

0   30 km

Gulf of Mexico

GEORGIA

*A detailed guide to the entire state, with principal sites
clearly cross-referenced by number to the maps*

The song *Georgia on My Mind*, sung by native son Ray Charles, is as poignant and elegant as the state itself. From the green forests of the northern hills to the moss-draped streets of "Slow-vannah," as the colonial town of Savannah is called, Georgia treads a fragrant path through the past and the future. Savannah was created by royal charter in 1733 by James Oglethorpe, the first settlement in "the colony of Georgia in America." He designed the town on a grid of broad thoroughfares, interspersed with public squares. Today Savannah is as design-conscious as it was then, for the highly successful Savannah College of Art and Design (SCAD) not only renovates buildings all around town, but attracts a hard-working, fun-loving group of international students.

Ray Charles himself is immortalized in Macon, an antebellum town with an upbeat lilt, which bills itself as "the song and soul of the South." Celebrated along with Charles in the Georgia Music Hall of Fame are fellow musicians Alabamian Little Richard, Otis Redding, Lena Horne, R.E.M., Brenda Lee and Johnny Mercer.

Macon is just one town along what has become known as the "Antebellum Trail," a series of towns – Athens, Madison, Eatonton, Milledgeville– where tree-lined streets shade 1860s Italian and Greek Revival mansions. The trail, ambling through rolling countryside, is so relaxed that it's difficult to make even the one and only decision: whether to stroll a while or sit a spell.

The future is Atlanta, the undisputed capital of the New South. Atlanta leads the ranks in new jobs, new businesses and new opportunities. As early as 1859, Greene B. Haywood was writing in *Sketch of Atlanta*: "the population of the city is remarkable for its activity and enterprise. Most of the inhabitants came here for the purpose of bettering their fortunes." And come they did.

Henry W. Grady, editor of the *Atlanta Constitution* and originator of the phrase "the New South," in 1886 wrote: "I want to say to General Sherman... that from the ashes he left us in 1864 we have raised a brave and beautiful city; that somehow or other we have caught the sunshine in the bricks and mortar of our homes." Today, this "sunshine in the bricks and mortar" is reflected in the Victorian mansions of neighborhoods like Druid Hills and Inman Park, and bounces, bright as a new penny, off the steel and chrome skyscrapers of Downtown, designed by internationally known Atlantan John Portman. The buildings are brash and audacious, as is the manner that has contributed to the city's success. Portman himself remarked after the successful bid for the 1996 Olympics: "Clearly we don't just let things happen – we make them happen." ❑

PRECEDING PAGES: the Morgan County Court House in Madison is listed on the National Register of Historic Places.

ATLANTA

Map on page 108

Called "The Capital of the New South" by Henry Grady, the bold skyscraper city of Atlanta has CNN, Coca-Cola, history, and ambition to go

Ringed by tree-lined suburbs, Alanta's Chamber of Commerce likes to call Downtown "the sweetest part of the peach." But Downtown is a brash place, an urban maze where canyons of towers are relieved by softer relics like the Flatiron building, a smaller version of New York's landmark. There's an international bustle, people of all races, colors and creeds, young and old, mingling in cafés, bars and restaurants. In "the town that's too busy to hate," some bemoan Downtown's almost sterile environment, but a short MARTA ride soon reaches the airier surroundings of older homes, super-malls and parks.

The entertainment and shopping complex of **Underground Atlanta** (Peachtree and Alabama streets, tel: 404-523-2311, open daily) is the ideal place to begin a tour, as this is where Atlanta was born. With no navigable river or seaport, Atlanta's birth was a coincidence of favorable topography and the expansion of the railroads. Today, the rail lines just north follow the same route as these original beds, laid down over 150 years ago.

LEFT: atriums appeal to Atlantans. **BELOW:** statue in Downtown Atlanta, *Emerging*, created by Marc Smith.

Downtown Atlanta

Step inside and explore the old buildings that are now home to shops, bars, and cafés encompassing six city blocks above and below ground. Just as in the late 19th century, **Kenny's Alley** is a center for nightlife and entertainment. There's a walk-in **Atlanta Visitors Center** on the upper level.

A major attraction near the Underground complex is the **World of Coca-Cola** (55 Martin Luther King, Jr Drive, tel: 404-676-5151, www.woccatlanta.com, open daily). One of Atlanta's most visited attractions, exhibits feature both rare and familiar Coke memorabilia, a theater showing the soft drink's big hit television commercials, a pleasantly reproduced soda fountain from the past, and brightly colored displays of the Coke advertising art that has made so many generations reach for the "pause that refreshes."

At the end of a visit, top off your tour with free samples of more than a dozen soft drink flavors. No one is sure what will happen to the site once Coca-Cola moves its entertainment complex farther north in 2005–6 *(see page 109)*, but a rumor circulating locally is that the grounds might be purchased by the state for a future Georgia History Museum.

Across the street from Coca-Coca is the Gothic-style **Shrine of the Immaculate Conception**. On the crest of the hill, east of the church, is the gold-domed **State Capitol Building** (open for tours). Follow Peachtree Street northward, past the MARTA Five Points Transit Station to arrive at **Five Points** , the symbolic heart of Atlanta. Here, north of the railroad tracks, at the intersection of Marietta, Peachtree, and Decatur,

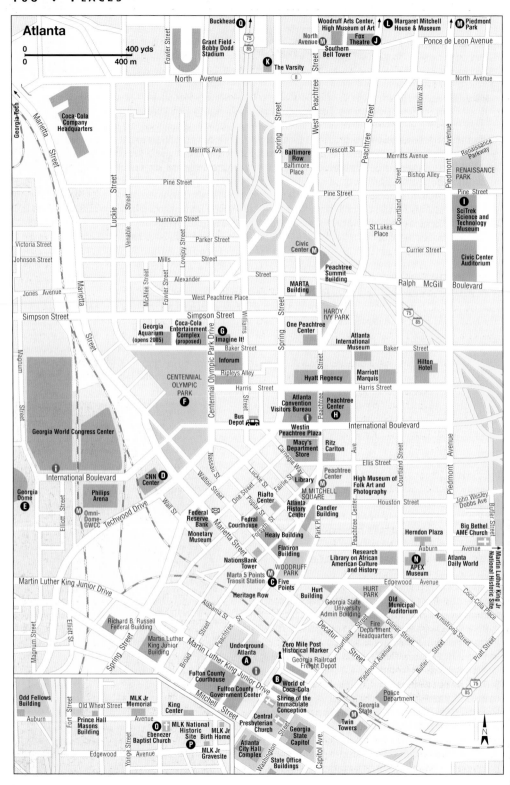

Atlanta

0 ─────────── 400 yds
0 ─────────── 400 m

Fowler Street
Buckhead Ⓠ
Grant Field - Bobby Dodd Stadium
Woodruff Arts Center, High Museum of Art
Ⓛ Margaret Mitchell House & Museum
Ⓜ Piedmont Park
North Avenue Ⓜ
Southern Bell Tower
Ⓙ Fox Theatre
Ponce de Leon Avenue
North Avenue
Ⓚ The Varsity
North Avenue
Georgia Tech
Marietta Street
Coca-Cola Company Headquarters
Merritts Ave
Spring Street
West Peachtree Street
Peachtree Street
Prescott St
Merritts Avenue
Bishop Alley
Willow St
Piedmont Avenue
Renaissance Parkway
RENAISSANCE PARK
Luckie Street
Pine Street
Baltimore Row
Baltimore Place
Pine Street
Courtland
St Lukes Place
Pine Street
Ⓘ SciTrek Science and Technology Museum
Venable Street
Hunnicutt Street
Parker Street
Mills Street
Civic Center Ⓜ
Currier Street
Civic Center Auditorium
Victoria Street
Johnson Street
McAfee Street
Fowler Street
Lovejoy Street
Alexander Street
Peachtree Summit Building
Jones Avenue
West Peachtree Place
MARTA Building
Ralph McGill Boulevard
Simpson Street
Marietta Street
Williams Street
Simpson Street
One Peachtree Center
HARDY IVY PARK
Atlanta International Museum
Baker Street
Hilton Hotel
Georgia Aquarium (opens 2005)
Coca-Cola Entertainment Complex (proposed)
Ⓖ Imagine It!
Baker Street
Spring Street
Magnum Street
CENTENNIAL OLYMPIC PARK
Centennial Olympic Park Drive
Inforum
Ripleys Alley
Harris Street
Hyatt Regency
Marriott Marquis
Harris Street
Peachtree Street
Ⓕ
Georgia World Congress Center
Bus Depot
Atlanta Convention Visitors Bureau
Peachtree Center Ⓗ
International Boulevard
Westin Peachtree Plaza
Macy's Department Store
Ritz Carlton
Peachtree Center Ave
Ellis Street
Courtland Street
Piedmont Avenue
International Boulevard
Elliott Street
Techwood Drive
CNN Ⓓ Center
Nassau St
Walton Street
Luckie St
Carnegie Way
Fairlie St
Peachtree Center
Library
High Museum of Folk Art and Photography
Houston Street
John Wesley Dobbs Ave
Georgia Dome Ⓔ
Ⓜ Omni-Dome-GWCC
Philips Arena
One Street
Poplar St
Rialto Center
M.MITCHELL SQUARE Ⓜ
Atlanta History Center
Candler Building
Herndon Plaza
Big Bethel AME Church
Butler Street
Georgia Dome
Wall St
Marietta Street
Federal Reserve Bank
Monetary Museum
Federal Courthouse
Healy Building
Park Pl
Peachtree Center
International Boulevard
Spring Street
NationsBank Tower
Flatiron Building
WOODRUFF PARK
Research Library on African American Culture and History
Auburn Avenue
Ⓝ APEX Museum
Atlanta Daily World
Martin Luther King Jr National Historic Site
Martin Luther King Junior Drive
Marta 5 Points Transit Station Ⓒ Five Points
Heritage Row
Hurt Building
HURT PARK
Old Municipal Auditorium
Edgewood Avenue
Coca-Cola Place
Elliott St
Alabama St
Richard B. Russell Federal Building
Martin Luther King Junior Building
Broad Street
Peachtree Street
Forsyth Street
Decatur Street
Georgia State University Admin Building
Fire Department Headquarters
Gilmer Street
Armstrong Street
Pratt Street
Spring Street
Magnum Street
Martin Luther King Junior Drive
Underground Atlanta Ⓐ
Zero Mile Post Historical Marker
Georgia Railroad Freight Depot
Courtland Street
Butler Street
Police Department
Odd Fellows Building
Old Wheat Street
MLK Jr Memorial
King Center
Fulton County Courthouse
Fulton County Government Center
Mitchell Street
Ⓑ World of Coca-Cola
Shrine of the Immaculate Conception
Central Presbyterian Church
Georgia State Ⓜ
Twin Towers
Fort Street
Prince Hall Masons Building
Ⓞ MLK National Historic Site
Ebenezer Baptist Church
MLK Jr Birth Home
Ⓟ
MLK Jr Gravesite
Atlanta City Hall Complex
Georgia State Capitol
Police Department
Yonge Street
Auburn Avenue
Edgewood Avenue
Washington Street
State Office Buildings
Capitol Ave.
75 85
N

Atlanta's bustling business district grew in the early 1840s. Following Marietta Street west, stop off at the **NationsBank Tower**, 35 Broad Street, built in 1901 and redesigned in 1929 by noted architect Philip Trammell Shutze, and admire the main banking floor.

Farther west on Marietta is the **CNN Center**  (tel: 404-827-2300, open daily), hub of the worldwide television news service founded by Ted Turner. For a behind-the-scenes **Studio Tour** of Cable News Network, take what is claimed to be the world's largest free-standing escalator upstairs for the guided tour. Along the way you can watch a news story travel through the newsroom to the anchor's desk, where it is delivered live on camera, or discover the secrets of weather broadcasting. Advance reservations are recommended, and are subject to change. Online booking is available at www.cnn.com/StudioTour.

Behind CNN is the **Georgia Dome** ❺ (tel: 404-223-9200, tours available), the world's largest cable-supported dome, and a venue for the 1996 Olympics. Next door is the **Georgia World Congress Center**, one of the largest conference facilities in the nation.

Parks, pop and Peachtree

Bordered by Marietta Street and Techwood Drive is the 21-acre (9-hectare) **Centennial Olympic Park** ❻. This urban parkland features an outdoor amphitheater, a café, and the Fountain of Rings with four sound-and-water shows a day. More infamously, it was the site of a fatal bombing during the 1996 summer Olympics. The **Centennial Visitor Center** dispenses information and recounts a history of the games; there's also a coffee shop attached.

At the corner of Baker and Centennial Olympic Park Drive is **Imagine It!** ❼, the Children's Museum of Atlanta (tel: 404-659-5437, open daily). Aimed at two- to eight-year-olds, this interaction museum is one of the city's newest. In fact, this entire area, formerly derelict, is gearing up for major tourist activity. The brand-new **Georgia Aquarium** opens in 2005, promising to be both entertaining and educational.

Sharing the 20-acre (8-hectare) site will be the new **Coca-Cola entertainment complex**, designed by the Jerde Partnership. Few details have been released, but judging by the partnership's previous enterprises – CityWalk in Los Angeles and the Fremont Street Experience in Las Vegas – it will certainly be a dazzling and innovative landmark.

Capping a string of Atlanta's finest skyscrapers, at the summit of a ridge is the **Westin Peachtree Plaza Hotel** at 210 Peachtree Street. This soaring 70-story cylinder of glass and steel, built in 1976, was for many years the tallest hotel in the world. At the top of the building is the Sundial Restaurant, voted as having "the best views in Atlanta."

The **Peachtree Center** ❽ complex is architect and developer John Portman's vision of a Southern-style Rockefeller Center, which has been a work-in-progress for more than 35 years. Portman, who also designed the Westin, has redefined the Downtown business district and parlayed his experience here into prestigious commissions around the world. Possibly

Map on page 108

Ted Turner was not only responsible for CNN, but also owns the Braves baseball team. Visit the Braves Hall of Fame, tel: 404-614-2311.

BELOW: Bank of America tower.

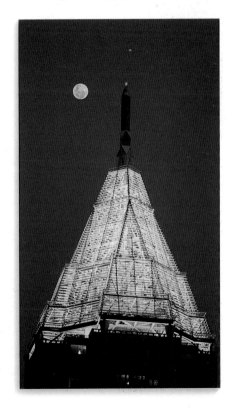

the most recognizable building in the center is the 1967 **Hyatt Regency Hotel** with its soaring 22-story atrium lobby and rotating, flying saucer-like restaurant, Polaris, on the roof. An evolution of this theme is the 48-story open, curving atrium lobby of the nearby **Atlanta Marriott Marquis Hotel**. Described by some as "Jonah's view of the belly of the whale," a glance downward from the upper floors of the hotel is not recommended for the faint of heart.

The elaborate **Mall at Peachtree Center** is located beneath the corporate towers at 231 Peachtree Street. A feature more commonly found in northern cities than in the sunny South are the climate-controlled pedestrian walkways that connect all the Peachtree Center buildings together. These walkways also provide a respite from Downtown's more unsavory urban aspects.

Halfway between Downtown and Midtown at 395 Piedmont Avenue is the **Atlanta Civic Center** and **SciTrek ❶** (tel: 404-522-5500, open daily), the science and technology museum of Atlanta. The Civic Center houses the city's theatrical auditorium, while SciTrek, one of the top 10 science centers in the US, features more than 150 hands-on displays and the Challenger Learning Center, a two-room simulator of a space station.

Midtown

If Downtown is the business and historic heart of Atlanta, Midtown is where the city's cultural lifeblood flows strongest. While Midtown may be more a state of mind than a district measured by rigid boundaries, its center is the busy area around the intersection of Peachtree and 14th streets. Proximity to four MARTA Transit Stations – Civic Center, North Avenue, Midtown, and Arts Center – makes access to all points fairly easy.

BELOW:
Midtown's High
Museum of Art.

The highlight of a visit to Midtown's southern region is one of America's great movie palaces, the Moorish-style **Fox Theatre** ❶ at 660 Peachtree Street, built in 1929 and with an interior reminiscent of an Arabian courtyard. An ideal way to see the interior of the Fox is on a guided tour offered by the Atlanta Preservation Center (tel: 404-876-2041).

Two buildings dominate the area's skyline. One is the 52-story **Southern Bell Center**, at 675 West Peachtree Street; the other, to the south, is the **Bank of America Plaza**. Still one of the world's tallest buildings, the Bank of America is topped with an open pyramidal structure sometimes called Atlanta's Eiffel Tower.

A few blocks west is a landmark of a completely different kind. At Spring Street and North Avenue is **The Varsity** ❸, an Atlanta culinary tradition since 1928. The current Art Moderne building, erected in 1940, has long been a gathering place for Georgia Tech students and an essential stop for locals showing out-of-town guests the best chili-dogs, onion rings, and hamburgers.

Georgia Tech

Across Interstate 75/85 on North Avenue, residential facilities built as part of the Olympic village for the 1996 games mark the entrance to the campus of the Georgia Institute of Technology, or **Georgia Tech**. Established only two decades after Atlanta was devastated in the Civil War, Georgia Tech was a tangible outcome of journalist Henry Grady's call for a "New South" combining business, industry, and agriculture.

Architectural highlights include the Tech Tower (1888), the Aaron French Building (1899) and the Carnegie Building, which was the school's first library and a 1907 gift from Andrew Carnegie.

John Portman, Atlanta architect extraordinaire, started with just two people; he now has offices worldwide.

BELOW: the World of Coca-Cola.

A few blocks northeast, the **Margaret Mitchell House and Museum** (tel: 404-249-7015), erstwhile home of the author of *Gone with the Wind*, sits at the corner of 10th and Peachtree streets. Though the house, which Mitchell ingloriously referred to as "the Dump," is sometimes rented out for parties, tours normally take place daily. A short film describes the struggle to restore the building; the tour then continues to the apartment in which Mitchell penned her celebrated novel. A museum, opened in December 1999, honors the 60th anniversary of the premiere of "GWTW," as aficionados call the movie. The museum contains everything you could wish to know about one of the South's defining films, and displays include the original Tara doorway from the film set; fans will surely swoon.

At 1280 Peachtree Street is the **Woodruff Arts Center** (tel: 404-733-4200), which hosts concerts of the Atlanta Symphony, performances by the Alliance Theatre and the Children's Theater, and works from the Atlanta College of Art. Adjacent to the Arts Center is the striking, modern **High Museum of Art** (tel: 404-733-4444), designed by the architect Richard Meier. The name has nothing to do with the museum's exalted position but reflects the generosity of art patron Harriet High who, in 1926, donated her home for use as an art museum. The present building is of white porcelain-enameled steel, and the permanent collection includes Sub-Saharan African Art.

The upscale neighbourhood of **Ansley Park** has fine old homes, and the elegant Beaux Arts-style **First Church of Christ, Scientist** (1914). But its enduring popularity is, in part, for its convenience to both Peachtree Street and Atlanta's largest public park, **Piedmont Park** . Since its days as a mustering ground for Confederate veterans' reunions, Piedmont Park has been a gathering place for Atlantans from all walks of life. The largest event takes place every 4th of July, when 55,000 runners sweat it out in the Peachtree Road Race. A place to cool off again in the north of the park is the **Atlanta Botanical Garden**, featuring one of the world's largest permanent displays of tropical orchids. For a closer look at Ansley Park or Piedmont Park, join a volunteer from the Atlanta Preservation Center on one of their guided walking tours.

Sweet Auburn Avenue

Auburn Avenue, east of Downtown beyond Interstate 85, is best known for its associations with Dr Martin Luther King, Jr. The street's nickname "Sweet Auburn Avenue" was earned through its prosperity. Between 1890 and 1960, Auburn Avenue was always jumpin'. By day, black men and women thronged the black-owned businessses like banks and insurance companies, beauty salons, retail stores, barber shops, and grocery stores. Nights were even livelier, with people strolling in the street, and jiving in the nightspots.

The **Preservation District** is the western portion of the street which leads to the Martin Luther King, Jr National Historic Site. Both are overseen by the National Park Service. Poised at the "gateway" to Auburn Avenue, at the corner of Courtland Street, is the **Auburn Avenue Research Library on African American Culture and History.** Next to the library heading east is the Afro American Panoramic Experience, more commonly known as the APEX **Museum** (tel: 404-523-APEX). It features traveling exhibits from all over the world. The APEX is the official starting point for the "Freedom Walk," the walking tour of Auburn Avenue. Along the walk, important sites are identified by informative National Park Service plaques.

The music you hear from the moment you set foot on Auburn Avenue usually comes from the **Royal Peacock**. In the 1950s, the Peacock was the hottest of night spots. On weekends, black people from all over town would pack the Peacock to hear the Four Tops, B.B. King, or Gladys Knight and to dance on the polished dance floor. **Big Bethel A.M.E. Church** grew out of a church organized before the Civil War. The freedmen who founded Big Bethel established Atlanta's first school for black children.

Martin Luther King National Historic Site

At 407 Auburn is the most famous church in the South, **Ebenezer Baptist Church** . It is the family church of the late Dr King, with a legacy that dates back to Dr King's maternal grandmother. Martin Luther served as co-pastor of the church with his father.

Today, Sunday services are held in the large Horizon Sanctuary across the street. Tours of the original church are given throughout the week and on Sunday afternoons. There's the added possibility of hearing one of Dr King's sermons, which are regularly piped into the sanctuary. Just past the church is the complex that attracts many more visitors than any other in the Atlanta area, the **Martin Luther King National Historic Site** (tel: 404-526-8900, www.nps.gov/malu). The **Visitor Center** has a video program and can help

Map on page 108

LEFT: Martin Luther King's Birth Home has been restored to its appearance during the years the King family lived here.
BELOW: outside the Martin Luther King Memorial.

Map on page 108

with questions, while the **Plaza** contains a rose garden, amphitheater and a poignant statue called *Behold*. Based on the MLK Center for Nonviolent Social Change founded in 1968 by King's widow Coretta and others, headed by the King's younger son is the **King Center**, Dexter Scott King. The organization continues to work for economic and social equality. The centerpiece of the memorial is the great man's resting place. His **gravesite**, a white marble tomb, tops a circular red brick base, at the foot of a long blue-watered pool.

Preserved homes dot the avenue all the way to Boulevard Street, but for many visitors Auburn's Freedom Walk ends with a beginning – at the steps of a modest, two-story, yellow and brown house at 501 Auburn Avenue – the **Martin Luther King, Jr Birth Home**. The Queen Anne-style house has been restored to its appearance during the years 1929 – when King was born – to 1941, when his family moved to another house nearby.

Buckhead

Buckhead **Q**, about 4 miles (6.5 km) north of the city's central Downtown area, is Atlanta's best address. If Atlanta were a super-highway, Buckhead would be the fast lane. All the best, brightest, and most marketable projects the city has up its sleeve are based in Buckhead. All Atlantans want to live here, and at weekends it often seems that all Atlantans, and every university student in Georgia, *do*. The area is served by three MARTA stations: Lenox, Buckhead and Lindbergh. The perfect place to learn about Buckhead – and indeed, Atlanta itself – is at the **Atlanta History Center** (130 West Paces Ferry Road, tel: 404-814-4000). This attractive, tree-shaded campus occupies more than 30 acres (12 hectares) and includes the **Museum of Atlanta History**. It's advisable to spend the best part of a day here, since the cool, flower-laden grounds and tranquil atmosphere are a perfect antidote to the urban bustle that swirls around so much of the city.

In a compact area along Buckhead's Roswell Road, Peachtree, and adjacent side streets such as Pharr Road, Buckhead Avenue, Irby Avenue, and East Andrews Drive, is an eclectic mix of cafés, clubs, restaurants, shops and theaters that draws shoppers during the day, diners in the evening, and partygoers into the night. There's always something to do here; it's no wonder that the governor of Georgia has a house in the neighborhood.

If Buckhead is Atlanta's shopping mecca, then Phipps Plaza and Lenox Square are the ultimate destinations for millions of plastic-wielding pilgrims. At the corner of Lenox and Peachtree roads, **Phipps Plaza**, a monument in polished brass and marble, is the Taj Mahal of malls. Tiffany's, Lord & Taylor, Gucci, Versace and Saks are here, as well as a movie theater complex. Built in 1959, **Lenox Square**, on East Paces Ferry Road, was Atlanta's first mall and, with continual expansion, is the largest in the Southeast. The four-level mall is home to over 250 stores, 27 of them unique to Atlanta. An **Atlanta Visitors Center** information booth offers brochures and maps of the city, and pointers to the highlights of Buckhead's varied and often notorious nightlife. ❑

BELOW: Buckhead watering hole.
RIGHT: Scarlett goes out on the town.

AROUND GEORGIA

*Elegant wineries, a relaxed college town and a fine park are just
miles away from Atlanta, while nestled deep in the countryside
are homes so beautiful even Sherman couldn't bear to burn them*

Map
on page
104

From Atlanta outwards, the hills and history of Georgia have an Antebellum Trail, Athens, famous for its music and football, and the astonishing Stone Mountain. This massive hunk of almost-bare granite poking high out of the earth has a massive carving of Confederate generals Robert E Lee and Stonewall Jackson riding alongside the Southern president Jefferson Davis. Stone Mountain makes a great day trip from Atlanta.

Known to the Creek Indians as *"Therrethlofkee,"* or "the mountain on the side of the river (Chattahoochee) where there are no other mountains," Stone Mountain is the world's largest outcrop of granite and commands the horizon 16 miles (26 km) east of **Atlanta ❶**. A day exploring this magnificent rock and enjoying the activities and attractions of the park that surrounds it, easily shows why **Stone Mountain Park ❷** (tel: 770-498-5690, open daily) is the most popular tourist attraction in Georgia.

Stone Mountain Village is a throng of vintage buildings and quaint shops. The 1857 **Stone Mountain Railroad Depot** survived the Civil War and is now the village's town hall. The **Stone Mountain General Store** at Main and Manor streets offers a wide selection of crafts and antiques. Just east of the depot is **Memorial Hall** featuring geological and human history displays of the mountain, photographs, and artifacts from the carving work, plus a museum of Civil War weapons.

Touring Stone Mountain

Most tours start with a ride on the **Stone Mountain Scenic Railroad**. From the depot on Robert E. Lee Boulevard, the vintage steam engine rocks and sways along a 5-mile (8-km) loop around the mountain's base, providing a pleasant overview of the park's attractions and the area's landscape. If you want to stretch your legs, hike to the top along the **Stone Mountain Walk-up Trail** which ascends nearly 800 ft (240 meters) meandering through several climate zones – from the Appalachian forest at the base, to the harsh environment of the summit. The **Stone Mountain Skylift** offers a breathtaking, five-minute gondola ride from the base to the summit and provides the park's best close-up view of the carving.

Antebellum Plantation, on John B. Gordon Drive, re-creates a working plantation. The centerpiece of this exhibit is the **Charles M. Davis House**, a beautifully proportioned neoclassical structure built in 1850 as the main residence of a 1,000-acre (400-hectare) plantation near Albany, Georgia. There are also two 150-year-old **Slave Cabins**. These primitive structures stand in stark contrast to the elegant homes of the plantation owner and overseer. If the undeniably lovely plantation has whetted your appetite for a

LEFT: Stone Mountain Park.
BELOW: Chateau Elan is a popular winery and resort.

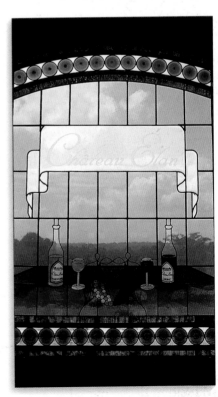

taste of the "Old South," travel east on Lee Boulevard to the **Riverboat Dock** on the shores of **Stone Mountain Lake**. Here, an enjoyable passage can be booked on a sternwheeler. On the lake, listen out for the soft musical tones of the **Stone Mountain Carillon** (consisting of 732 bells) on the western bank of the lake.

At the western base of the mountain, near the Memorial Drive entrance, **Confederate Hall** features a three-dimensional map of Georgia that depicts General Sherman's 1864 invasion. The acres of white sand at **Stone Mountain Beach**, on the eastern shore of Stone Mountain Lake, bring a touch of the ocean inland, and are ideal for relaxing and swimming.

Near Atlanta

The **Chattahoochee River National Recreation Area** (CRNRA) stretches like a "strand of pearls" from Atlanta's western suburbs to Lake Lanier. Its woodlands and shoreline make for great fishing and water sports. To the northwest and simmering with small-town Southern charm is **Marietta ❸**, founded in 1833. The town square is ringed by historic buildings, cafés, restaurants, and antique shops. The **Marietta Welcome Center** (tel: 770-429-1115, open daily) is in the 1898 railroad depot at 4 Depot Street. Just across the street, **Kennesaw House** (tel: 770-528-0431, open daily) was built in 1855 as the Fletcher House Hotel. James J. Andrews' Federal raiders met here on April 11, 1862 to iron out their plan to steal a locomotive and head north toward Union lines, and destroy the railway behind them. It now houses Marietta's Museum of History.

For a racier time, hit the indoor go-karts at the **Andretti Speed Lab** (tel: 770-992-5688, open daily), an entertainment complex devoted to Formula One racing located in **Roswell ❹**, 20 miles (32 km) north of Atlanta. The town also has

a wealth of historic buildings. The fine 1846 **Smith Plantation House** (tel: 770-641-3978, closed Sun) at 935 Alpharetta Street is one of the city's best preserved landmarks. In 1853, town founder James Bulloch's daughter Martha married Theodore Roosevelt in the dining room of **Bulloch Hall** at 180 Bulloch Avenue. Their son, Theodore junior, would lead the "Rough Riders" in the Spanish-American War, and later served as the 26th president of the United States.

East of Roswell, in the town of Duluth, the entertaining **Southeastern Railway Museum** (tel: 770-476-2013, hours vary) houses an extensive collection of antique railroad cars and artifacts.

The **Chateau Elan Winery** (tel: 678-425-0900, call for opening times) on Georgia 211 at Interstate 85 includes a visitor center, wine shop, restaurant, and art gallery. There is also an elegant inn, tennis center, golf course, European-style spa, and equestrian center.

Continue through the green rolling hills of Henry County to **Panola Mountain State Conservation Park** (tel: 770-389-7801, open daily) a 600-acre (242-hectare) park that is a smaller version of its neighbor, Stone Mountain.

Margaret Mitchell drew inspiration for her epic, *Gone with the Wind* at **Jonesboro ❺**, 16 miles (25 km) south of Atlanta via I-75 and Georgia Highway 54. As a child, Margaret visited ageing relatives here and heard their stories of the Civil War. Several antebellum homes still remain in the town. **Stately Oaks** (tel: 770-473-0197, closed Sun), an 1830s Greek Revival mansion is the site of the annual "Tara Ball." Go to the **Railroad Depot** for *Gone with the Wind* souvenirs. Just south of Jonesboro on Talmadge Road is **Lovejoy Plantation**. The visits young Margaret Mitchell made to her great-grandfather Philip Fitzgerald's house, now on these grounds, was the model for *Twelve Oaks* in her book.

Finally, any visit to Atlanta would be incomplete without spending a day at **Six Flags Over Georgia** ❻ (tel: 770-948-9290, call for opening times). Located on Six Flags Parkway and I-20, Six Flags features over 100 rides, including wild roller coasters such as the Ninja – the Bruce Lee of roller coasters.

Map on page 104

Athens

For many Georgians, **Athens** ❼ means one thing and one thing alone – football – and the 90,000 rabid, red-and-black-clad University of Georgia fans who descend for Saturday afternoon matches. Out-of-state visitors are more likely to think of the home of REM and other successful American rock bands. Either way the city's enormous university is the focus of life here.

Chartered in 1785, the **University of Georgia** was the first state university established in the new United States. The fine wrought-iron gateway to the campus – **The Arch** – is on Broad Street, at College Avenue. Just to the south is **Old College**, the school's first permanent structure, erected in 1806. The bell in the magnificent Greek Revival-style 1832 **Chapel** once summoned students to compulsory religious services, now it tolls to celebrate athletic triumphs. The **Main Library**, with a collection of over 3 million documents, includes the original Confederate Constitution, which was handwritten in 1861.

UGA (University of Georgia in Athens) mascot, warm in a school sweater.

BELOW: this gateway to UGA was erected in 1858.

The **Georgia Museum of Art** (tel: 706-542-4662, closed Mon) has more than 7,000 works, including the Kress Collection of Italian Renaissance Art and Asian prints and drawings. The **Athens Welcome Center** (tel: 706-353-1820) at 280 East Dougherty Street is in the restored 1820 **Church-Waddel-Brumby House**, the oldest standing residence in Athens. Across Dougherty Street is the **History Village**. Atop the hill across Hancock Street is **City Hall** and the celebrated **Double-Barreled Cannon** cast for the Confederate Army at the nearby Athens Foundry in 1863. The gun, designed by John Gilleland, was supposed to fire two balls tethered by a chain to "mow down Yankees like a scythe cuts wheat." Tried only once, the cannon was never used in combat. South on College Avenue toward Broad Street is where Athens' students and business people meet and mingle. Behind the facades of 19th-century commercial buildings are popular eateries and clubs where the beer is cold and refreshing, the music loud, and the fun fast-paced.

Local landmarks to look for include the fabled **40 Watt Club**, at 285 West Washington Street, where Athens-based bands such as the B-52's and REM started out in the 1970s. Walk north to Prince Avenue and follow it west to some of the finest antebellum houses in Georgia. The **Joseph H. Lumpkin House**, at 248 Prince Street, was built in 1841. Just south, at 279 Meigs Street, is the 1833 **Joseph Camak House**,

an early Federal-style brick house with beautiful wrought-iron details. At 489 Prince Street is **Fire Hall No. 2**, a triangular, single-bay Victorian brick station constructed for horse-drawn engines in 1901. Across Prince, at 698 Pope Street, the 1835 **Howell Cobb House** was home to a notable figure in Georgian history: Cobb served as Governor, Secretary of the US Treasury under President James Buchanan (1856–60), president of Georgia's 1861 Secession Convention, and as a general in the Confederate Army.

Three miles (5 km) south of Athens, at 2450 South Milledge Avenue, is **The State Botanical Garden of Georgia** (tel: 706-542-1244, closed Sat, Sun) set above the Middle Oconee River on 313 forested acres (127 hectares). Visitors come to enjoy the gardens, hike the miles of nature trails, and take classes in various aspects of gardening.

Antebellum Trail

The Antebellum Trail isn't really a trail, in the romantic, magnolia-laned way the name suggests, but it does take in middle and east Georgian historic towns, and Civil War battle sites. Much of the quintessential – and mythical – Old South romanticized by *Gone with the Wind* is here to explore; the type of territory foreigners think Atlanta should be, but isn't. It even includes Br'er Rabbit, the South's most famous critter.

From Atlanta, pick up the Antebellum Trail by driving I-20 for 30 miles east (48 km) through Social Circle, Rutledge and then into **Madison** , renowned as the town so beautiful even General Sherman couldn't bear to burn it. There are dozens of palatial Greek Revival mansions built in the 1830s that survived the ravages of war, the Great Depression, and progress. At the **Madison County Welcome Center** (tel: 706-342-4454, open daily) on East Jefferson Street, pick up brochures to the town's historic buildings. The **Morgan County Court House** is listed on the National Register of Historic Places.

Two well-known authors were born in **Eatonton** ❾. Stories from antebellum plantations inspired Joel Chandler Harris (1848–1908) to write the folksy *Tales of Uncle Remus*. Later on, Alice Walker turned her early experiences here into the Pulitzer Prize-winning *The Color Purple*. Harris's tales of Br'er Rabbit, Br'er Fox, The Tar Baby and other "critters" are commemorated at the **Uncle Remus Museum** (tel: 706-485-6856, open Sep–May daily). A walking/driving tour guide is easily available at the Chamber of Commerce on the courthouse square and takes visitors past landmarks in the life of Alice Walker.

Until 1868, when Atlanta was given the honor, **Milledgeville** ❿ served as Georgia's capital. Stop at the **Milledgeville Welcome Center** (tel: 478-452-4687, closed Sun), 200 West Hancock Street, for tour maps and information. One of Georgia's most cherished historic landmarks, the lovely **Old Governors' Mansion**, built in Palladian Greek Revival style between 1835 and 1838, has a prized ticket to the 1825 ball commemorating the Marquis de Lafayette's farewell tour of America. The well-known novelist and short-story writer **Flannery O'Connor** found Milledgeville's traditions and Old South Gothic para-

BELOW: Br'er Rabbitt goes to court, Eatonton.

Map on page 104

doxes an ideal foil for her Irish Catholic wit. In the library at **Georgia College** – her alma mater, across from the Old Governors' Mansion – the **Flannery O'Connor Room** displays manuscripts and mementoes from her career.

Macon

At the exact center of the state, **Macon ⓫** is the largest city on the Antebellum Trail. A bridge over the **Ocmulgee River** honors Macon-born soulman Otis Redding. "Little Richard" Penniman (*Tutti Frutti*) hailed from here, as did the Allman Brothers Band. The **Macon-Bibb County Visitors' Bureau** (tel: 478-743-3401, open Mon–Sat) is in the old Terminal Station, Downtown at 200 Cherry Street. The **Georgia Music Hall of Fame** (tel: 478-750-8555, open daily), at 200 Martin Luther King Boulevard, showcases the above musicians and also other talented home-grown stars who found fame on the world stage. The **Hay House** (tel: 478-742-8155, open daily) is the must-see house-museum. Completed in 1859, the grand Italian Renaissance palazzo is visually stunning inside and out. The **Tubman African-American Museum** (tel: 478-743-8544, open daily), Downtown at 340 Walnut Street, celebrates local and national African-American achievements.

Ray Charles is honored in Macon's Georgia Music Hall of Fame.

Warm Springs ⓬ is forever associated with President Franklin Delano Roosevelt. The future four-time president first came in 1924 to soak his polio-afflicted legs in Warm Springs' mineral waters. He built his six-room cottage, *The Little White House*, in a heavily wooded site (tel: 706-655-5870, call for opening times). Some of the strategic legislation of his "New Deal" was formed in these pine-paneled rooms. On April 12, 1945, Roosevelt suffered a fatal stroke while posing for a portrait in the dining room. His unfinished portrait is still on the easel. ❑

BELOW: historic home on the Antebellum Trail, Madison.

SAVANNAH

Only a short plane ride from Atlanta's gleaming skyscrapers, Savannah is cool, classy and just made for cocktails

Map on page 104

Author and local resident Rosemary Daniell once observed: "Savannah is the kind of town where drunken, irreverent fun, and thumbing one's nose at propriety are still permissible, even popular. It is said the first thing one is asked in Atlanta is, 'What do you do?'; in Charleston, 'Who were your ancestors?' and in Savannah, 'What would you like to drink?'"

Only a 40-minute plane ride away from the gleaming skyscrapers of Atlanta, **Savannah ⓭** is the oldest city in Georgia. People are attracted here by the leisurely pace and because, although there are fine houses and museums, the jewel is the town itself; there are few absolutely "must see" attractions. Some outsiders call the city "Slow-vannah" for this reason. Perhaps it's the high humidity that makes locals move that way. They speak slowly, drive slowly, and eat slowly. So take your time: there's no reason to hurry here.

In 1733, James Oglethorpe received a royal charter to establish "the colony of Georgia in America." Two of the many reasons for this were to protect the lands from Spanish Florida, and to produce wine and silk for the British Empire.

Oglethorpe designed the town on a grid of broad thoroughfares, punctuated at regular intervals with spacious public squares. Today, 21 of the 24 squares have been refurbished, forming the nucleus of Savannah's **Historic District** – one of the largest, loveliest urban, National Historic Landmark districts in the country, covering a 2½-mile (4-km) radius.

LEFT: Savannah's Monterey Square. **BELOW:** bespoke fish drainpipe.

Distinctive squares

Each square has a distinctive character, defined by the structures that encompass it, whether a towering cathedral, a Confederacy statue, or an ornate fountain. **Bull Street**, running the length of the district north to south, links the most beautiful squares to each other. These excel in Savannah's most characteristic details: fancy ironwork and Spanish moss. The ironwork, scrolled and lacy enough to rival New Orleans' finest, decorates fountains and monuments or balconies suspended from Greek Revival mansions. Sometimes the metal is in the shape of animals and put to use as water spouts or foot scrapers.

A walking tour allows visitors to set their own pace, but it is difficult to cover the entire Historic District in one afternoon, especially when the heat is at its most oppressive. There are a selection of transportation options, however, including horse-drawn carriage tours and free shuttle buses.

A good place to start is the **Savannah Visitors' Center** (open daily), 14 blocks south of the river and just to the west of the Historic District, on Martin Luther King, Jr, Boulevard. Sharing premises with the **Savannah History Museum**, where the exhibits

include the Oscar earned by local son and nationally known composer Johnny Mercer for the song *Moon River,* the center is in the former Civil War-era Central Georgia Railway depot. The visitors' center is the place to check for elegant accommodation. A handful of the houses in the Historic District have been turned into bed and breakfast inns, which are luxurious, and luxuriously expensive. The main area for more modestly accommodation is the motel strip near the Visitors' Center, a 30-minute walk away from the restaurants, shops and attractions Downtown.

SCAD

Opposite the center is the campus of the **Savannah College of Art and Design** (SCAD). The college has restored 56 buildings around town – including a couple of funky 1950s movie houses – many of which are used as classrooms or student accommodation. SCAD's little white vans and colorfully-clad, international residents are ubiquitous, and the college's influence on making Savannah such a vital, fun town cannot be overestimated.

A few blocks east in **Telfair Square** is the **Telfair Museum of Art** (tel: 912-232-1177, open daily), one of the oldest art museums in the South. It is housed in a Regency mansion designed by British-born William Jay. The museum has a fine permanent collection of paintings and furniture. Another opulent division of the Telfair Museum is through Wright Square to **Oglethorpe Square**, the **Owens-Thomas House** (tel: 912-233-9743, closed Mon). A splash of distinctive architectural details, like a sideporch supported by four Corinthian columns, were the first American work by William Jay; he designed it when he was only 20 years old and then he came to Savannah to supervise the building's construction. The house shows a major portion of the Telfair's decorative arts collection. Also featured on the grounds are rare intact examples of urban slave quarters with objects on long-term loan from the Acacia Collection of African Americana.

BELOW: the Mercer House, scene of a *Midnight* murder.

The Telfair's newest building, the **Jepson Center for the Arts**, is scheduled to open in early 2005 and will house 20th- and 21st-century art.

All of Savannah's squares are dotted with daily activity, as well as vendors of art, hot-dog stands, and freelance musicians. Summer brings festive free jazz concerts to Johnson Square, near the river, while impromptu weddings are performed in the gazebo at Wright Square. A spring visit is the most opportune time to savor the myriad of colors when the landscape is in full bloom. At night, fountains and monuments are lit by street lanterns, and although the squares may be tempting they also provide a breeding ground for purse snatchers and pan-handlers: it's best to enjoy their attractions before the sun goes down.

Wright Square is a gorgeous example of Savannah landscaping. A huge boulder marks the grave of Tomo-Chi-Chi, the Yamacraw Indian chief who welcomed General Oglethorpe and the other early settlers. On the east side is the Lutheran Church of the Ascension, a celebrated landmark dating back to 1772, which has a beautiful Ascension window in the main sanctuary.

Between Wright Square and **Chippawa Square** is the **Juliette Gordon Low Birthplace** (tel: 912-233-4501, closed Wed). While living in Britain, Low was introduced to a scouting program and, on her return to Georgia in 1912, founded the Girl Scouts of America, a movement that rapidly spread throughout the country. The house, built between 1818 and 1821 and rich with furnishings, can be enjoyed in a 30-minute tour guided by a local in period dress. Be prepared to share the tour with Girl Scouts, as the house is now a national scouting headquarters.

Around *Midnight*

The most talked about residence in recent memory is the lovely **Mercer House** on **Monterey Square**, built by composer Johnny Mercer's grandfather. The residence was the home of the late antique dealer Jim Williams, the subject of John Berendt's book *Midnight in the Garden of Good and Evil* and the 1997 movie directed by Clint Eastwood and starring Kevin Spacey.

In 1981, eccentric but debonair millionaire Williams shot his 22-year-old male companion. The victim had a reputation for wildness and excess, and Williams claimed self-defense. Convicted twice of murder, jailed and released and tried a third time to a hung jury, the fourth time he was tried and successfully acquitted.

Williams died of a heart attack the year he was freed. His sister occupied the house for many years, a magnificent structure filled with antiques. Popular local rumor has it that the late Jacqueline Onassis once tried to buy the house herself. The shutters are nearly always drawn tight, and the house is definitely not open to the public.

Cover of an early edition of "Midnight in the Garden of Good and Evil."

BELOW: some of Savannah's most beautiful homes are now B&Bs.

The Historic District's procession of squares ends at beautiful **Forsyth Park**, a 31-acre (13-hectare) setting for constant outdoor activity: jogging, frisbee tournaments, walking, and football. At the centerpiece of the park stands an elaborate fountain similar to the one in the Place de la Concorde, Paris.

River city

The development in Savannah of Eli Whitney's cotton gin *(see page 27)* in 1793 kick-started the American Industrial Revolution. In turn, it also heralded a massive boom in shipping, and by 1795, US exports were 40 times greater than in previous years. Savannah, positioned neatly on the Atlantic Ocean and looking out toward Europe, quickly became the largest port in the Southeast. In the early 19th century, Savannah's commerce thrived, and the launch of the steamship *SS Savannah* opened up new shipping routes.

Factors Row, a cobblestoned walkway near the river, is lined with 19th-century buildings, and the lovely 1852 **US Customs House**. The **Old Cotton Exchange** was constructed in 1887 when Savannah was the leading cotton exporter in the world.

The five-story brick warehouses and former shipping offices have now become a meeting point for tourists, reached by a series of steep steps. The buildings provide a nostalgic setting for thriving businesses, lavish inns, rustic restaurants, and novelty gift shops the length of **River Street**, where the ramps and walkways are covered with attractive stones imported from Europe. If you plan an evening on the town here, it might be wise to forgo the high heels.

The riverfront air is always filled with music, from South American natives playing soothing pan pipes to jazz saxophonists and threesomes picking banjos

BELOW: Tybee Island is known as "Savannah's beach."

and guitars. This all makes for a wonderful stretch of waterfront to eat, drink, shop, and generally to while away some pleasant time.

Slow-moving ships hauling everything from melons, bananas and pineapples, to kaolin clay, pass at a leisurely pace just yards away. The *Georgia Belle* and the *River Queen* replicate the paddlesteamers that plied the waters during the city's heyday, and both offer sightseeing cruises.

A signature Savannah sight is the touching riverside statue of *The Waving Girl*, erected in 1971 in remembrance to Florence Martus. Florence lived with her brother, the lighthouse-keeper, at the Elba Island Lighthouse in the mouth of the Savannah River. Every day for 44 years she waved a white handkerchief in welcome to each incoming ship. She had begun by hoping that any one of the ships might bring home the sailor she loved. Once she had started, it just didn't seem right to stop.

If the port evokes a yearning for food, River Street merchants offer an eclectic range of cuisine from fresh seafood to honey-dipped chicken fingers to fried onion rings. The area really comes to life at night and on St Patrick's Day, when the city plays host to the second-largest celebration in the country – not a party for the faint-hearted.

The riverfront skyline, dominated by the 185-ft (56-meter) tall great **Savannah Bridge**, was long known locally as "the bridge with no name." More revelry, restaurants and nightlife can be found in **City Market**, four blocks of restored buildings within walking distance at Jefferson and West Saint Julian Street near **Franklin Square**. In the daytime, City Market is the place to climb aboard for a horse-drawn carriage tour of the town, or to shop for upscale souvenirs and gifts.

Leaving Downtown and heading east on **Victory Drive** – known for its palm trees, handsome houses, and flowering azaleas – in the direction of the coastal islands, it's possible to catch a glimpse of old wealth in **Ardsley Park**. The stately, columned homes grace middle-to-upper class neighborhoods shaded by giant trees, and driving around at random provides a visual treat.

By the sea

Nearby is **Bonaventure Cemetery**, a luxurious final resting place for Savannah's most distinguished citizens. A former plantation, Bonaventure is wistfully beautiful, dripping with moss, and overflowing with azaleas, jasmine, magnolias, and live oak trees. (*Midnight's* memorable cover illustration is a tombstone from Bonaventure.)

Fifteen miles (24 km) east of Savannah, on Highway 80 heading toward Tybee Island, is **Fort Pulaski National Monument** Civil War site *(see page 96)*. **Tybee Island**, 18 miles (29 km) east of Downtown is known as "Savannah's beach." The small barrier island has a 3-mile (4.8-km) long beach that's backed by sand dunes covered with sea oats. It's a low-key resort with a well-known landmark, the **Tybee Island Light Station**. The lighthouse offered mariners safe entrance into the Savannah River for more than 270 years and is open to the public everyday except Tuesday. ❑

Map on page 104

BELOW: the riverside area was once known for cotton; now it's known for cocktails.

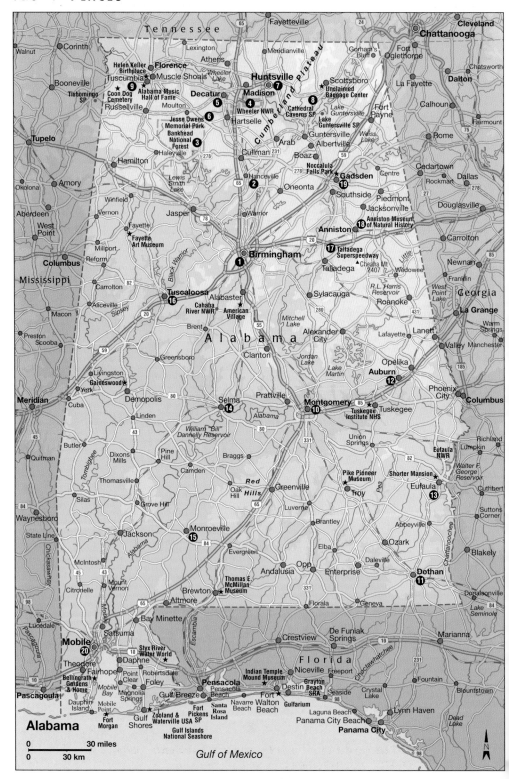

Alabama

ALABAMA

A detailed guide to the entire state, with principal sites clearly cross-referenced by number to the maps

A woman, it is said, is a candidate for Mobile's Mardi Gras queen only if she was conceived under an azalea bush, the azalea being a trademark flower of the state. Family roots matter in Alabama, and most of the people who were born here tend to stay here. Four singers who formed a band called – funnily enough – Alabama, created an anthem titled *My Home's in Alabama*. They might well be singing about a number of notables whose houses across the state are open for tours. Hank Williams's frame boyhood home is in Georgiana. Martin Luther King, Jr lived in a parsonage within walking distance of where Jefferson Davis resided during the early months of the Confederacy. The novelist F. Scott Fitzgerald wrote *Tender is the Night* in his home a few blocks away. W.C. Handy, "the father of the blues," grew up near Helen Keller, the deaf and blind woman famous from the play and the movie, *The Miracle Worker*.

Almost as important as family is food. Alabama has landscape from haze-covered mountains to sandy beaches, and its culinary choices are equally wide-ranging. In north Alabama, barbecued pork is smothered with a unique vinegar sauce; in the south a tomato-based sauce is the popular choice. Award-winning restaurants in Birmingham honor grits, tomatoes, and black-eyed peas. German automakers at the Mercedes plant and locals alike crave the dripping barbecued ribs at Dreamland in Tuscaloosa, while Alabama shrimp and oysters netted on the Gulf Coast are served up "fried, stewed, and nude." It's not surprising, then, that *Gourmet* magazine named Birmingham's Highlands Bar & Grill restaurant among the nation's top five eateries.

What can be surprising, though, is the diversity of Alabama's attractions – sports, space, and civil rights sites, for instance. Golfers discover that some of the nation's best-value golfing can be enjoyed along 100 miles (160 km) of public courses that Robert Trent Jones, Sr designed for the state pension fund. Others learn that the first rockets that sent American astronauts into space came from a facility in Huntsville. Alabama was the scene of many Civil Rights battles, and heritage museums show how non-violent protests successfully overturned a system of discrimination, and became a source of inspiration to oppressed minorities.

Huge expanses of forests, rivers, and mountains give credence to the nickname "Alabama the Beautiful." Birmingham has two sprawling wildlife areas within minutes of Downtown, and more than two dozen state parks are scattered statewide.

Family, food and fantastic scenery. No wonder everyone calls it *Sweet Home Alabama*.

PRECEDING PAGES: antebellum maids on the Azalea Trail, with the beautiful Bragg-Mitchell mansion in the background.

BIRMINGHAM

With a smart, affluent workforce of medical and engineering professionals, great food, and a creative arts scene, Birmingham is a major player in the New South

Map on page 134

Aloft on the foothills of the Appalachian Mountains, a massive statue of *Vulcan* is a proud tribute to the industrial heroism of steelmaking. The 56-ft (17-meter) high Roman god of fire and the forge was Birmingham's signature representative at the 1904 World's Fair in Saint Louis, and just as much today, proclaims Birmingham as one of the pioneering capitals of the New South. Named after the industrial powerhouse town in England, Birmingham achieved prominence in 1871, shortly after the Civil War, as a commercial hub at the crossing of two major railroads. Carrying none of the antebellum baggage or Old South history that its neighbors were steeped in, the "Magic City" was forged in the very beginnings of the New South, and grew through commerce and industry, rather than agriculture.

Long known as "the South's capital of football," Birmingham even took that reputation out onto the international soccer field (in the rest of the world, the word "football" refers to soccer) at the 1996 Olympic Games, when the soccer championships were held at Legion Field. Sports of all kinds play a healthy role in the life in the city, not least at the Alabama Sports Hall of Fame museum.

LEFT: *Vulcan,* Roman god of fire and the forge.
BELOW: *The Storyteller* at Five Points South.

Dynamic metropolis

Vulcan Park Ⓐ (151 Vulcan Park Drive, tel: 205-933-1409, open daily) is a good place for an overview of Birmingham and its evolution. The statue of *Vulcan*, restored for its centennial, now presides over an entirely different kind of city. Born in the smelting pots and hammered during the civil rights clashes in the 1960s, Birmingham survived the nation's 20th-century downturn in steel production to become a dynamic and integrated metropolis of a million people. Now, they are more likely to be working in modern service industries like health care, education or banking than to be sweltering in manufacturing.

After seeing the cityscape from this high vantage point by the second-largest statue in America, head down the mountain to the city. **Five Points South** Ⓑ, the business district along Highland Avenue at 20th Street, is home to several of Birmingham's four-star restaurants. Many of the city's younger generation like to hang out around the fountain near Frank Fleming's *The Storyteller* sculpture of a goat reading to turtles and other animals.

Barbecue and "country cooking" like fried green tomatoes remain permanently popular choices, but the city has earned a reputation for a new type of food. Chef Frank Stitt III opened **Highlands Bar & Grill** (2011 11th Avenue South, tel: 205-939-1400) in 1982, and its success has led him to open two more, Bottega and Chez Forfor. In these high-powered kitchens,

Frank perfects his trademark dishes, using Southern staples like grits and bacon to prepare gourmand creations. *Gourmet* magazine has ranked Highlands as one of America's top five restaurants, and the *New York Times* equates Stitt's popularity with that of athletic superstars.

Lakeview dining

Go north on 20th Street and turn east on University Boulevard (8th Avenue) to 29th Street for the **Lakeview District C**, a cluster of popular restaurants and bars. Dining choices here range from local pork barbecue topped with tomato sauce to beef and good Southern seafood. Five blocks north is the **Pepper Place** design and antiques district, named for the Southern classic soda, Dr Pepper, which was once bottled here. In summer, Second Avenue South between 28th and 29th streets is transformed into a lively Saturday market for organic produce, chef demonstrations, and entertainment. A member of one of the city's steel families used her wealth to enable some of the restoration projects.

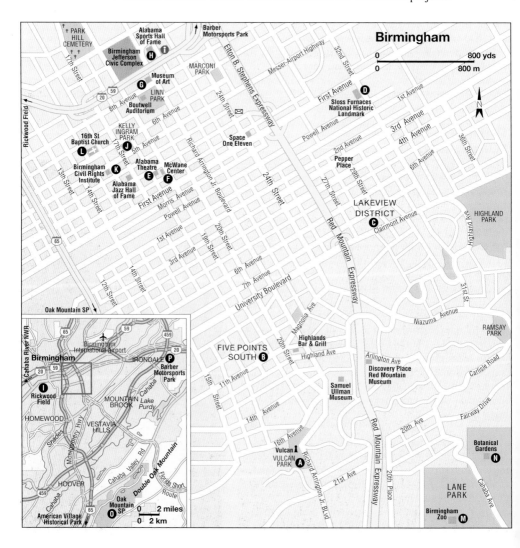

The spirit of reinvention

Return to 20th Street and head north to leave Southside for Downtown. Turn east on First Avenue North to 34th Street, then left on Second at 32nd to tour **Sloss Furnaces National Historic Landmark** ❹ (tel: 205-324-1911, closed Mon). This monument to early 20th-century industry is the largest preserved steel plant in the world, and also a festival site. Kids or even grown-ups who aren't interested in learning how to make steel are usually intrigued by ghost stories, including one of a furnace worker who died a particularly grisly death in a cauldron of molten steel.

Two other urban landmarks are neighbors on Third Avenue. Each has a proud history, and has had new leases of life in recent years. The marquee outside the **Alabama Theatre** ❺ (1817 Third Avenue North, tel: 205-252-2262) has offered entertainment choices since it opened on Christmas Day, 1927. On the sidewalk are metal stars honoring Alabama-born entertainers like actress Tallulah Bankhead (born in Huntsville), Disney star Dean Jones (from Decatur), and television comedian Jim Nabors (from Sylacauga).

The opulent 3,000-seat theater reigned like a dowager for more than a half century, closing when department stores followed customers to the suburbs. When demolition loomed, fans of the theater's Wurlitzer organ raised money to buy the building. Now a delightful venue for classic movies and concerts, it's worth the price of admission just to see the lobby's gold-leafed hexagonal ceiling, and the auditorium's sumptuous Moorish spiral terracotta columns.

A former nearby department store also has a new purpose. The old Loveman's, next to the theater, now houses the **McWane Center** ❻, one of the South's largest children's hands-on science centers. Financed by one of the

Map
on page
134

Science is fun, not serious at the McWane Center, which also has an IMAX theater.

LEFT: Sloss Furnaces is now an industrial museum.
BELOW: Alabama entertainment.

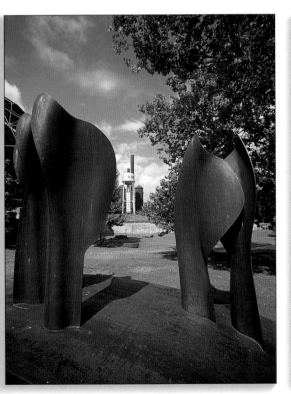

city's steel families, children are encouraged to romp through subtle science lessons. One floor hosts touring museum exhibits that appeal to adults, while the domed IMAX theater is a particular treat.

A few blocks north is the **Birmingham Museum of Art G** (2000 Eighth Avenue North, tel: 205-328-7628, closed Mon), the South's largest public art museum. The first floor has work from a wealth of 17th-century Dutch and Flemish painters, plus 18th-century English and 19th-century French artists; these include Monet, Rodin, Sargent, and Gainsborough. The Wedgwood collection is the largest outside of England.

A public park facing the art museum is named **Linn Park** for a prominent family. A century ago, when boosters coined the nickname "Magic City," it was named Capitol Park in anticipation of Birmingham becoming the state capital. (That didn't happen; Alabama's state capital is Montgomery.) The Downtown park is the hub of the state's largest music festival, held annually on the third weekend of June. City Stages attracts hundreds of thousands of fans, and acts range from church choirs to superstar headliners. The festival is a fine time to meet people from Birmingham at their best.

Just north of the elevated interstate highway near the **Birmingham Jefferson Civic Complex** is a museum that pays tribute to Americans' love of sports. The **Alabama Sports Hall of Fame H** celebrates athletes with Alabama connections. Dioramas highlight the achievements of Olympic track legend Jesse Owens (born near Decatur), football's Bart Starr and Coach Paul Bryant and baseball's Hank Aaron (born in Mobile), not to mention Willie Mays. Boxing heavyweight Joe Louis was born in the east Alabama town of Lafayette.

Another Magic City steel-era legacy is **Rickwood Field I** (1137 Second Ave), the world's oldest ballpark. Take the Interstate 59 Arkadelphia Road exit south to Second Avenue West. The Coal Barons team was formed in 1885 and steel magnate Rick Wood built the wooden park for his team in 1910. Today's Birmingham Barons play in a newer concrete park in nearby Hoover, but it's worth visiting one of Ted Williams' favorite fields. "It was a wonderful hitter's park, not because the fences were short… but the way the ball sounded when it hit the bat," he said.

BELOW: this stained-glass window from the Sixteenth Street Baptist Church was a gift from the people of Wales.

Honoring the past

During the first half of the 20th century, in what seems like a parallel universe, African-Americans owned businesses and enjoyed movies in a district just a few blocks from the Alabama Theatre and Loveman's. Blacks frequented beauty parlors, barber shops, clothing stores, churches, insurance offices, and banks, all run by people of their race.

With whites leaving Downtown for the affluent suburbs of Mountain Brook, Homewood, Hoover, and Vestavia Hills, black people have dominated local governments and boards for several decades. Richard Arrington, the city's first African-American mayor, received active support from both races for his progressive and positive leadership.

To begin healing past race divisions, he encouraged the establishment of shrines from what were formerly civil rights battlefields. Three of these are of particular significance. The indelible images of Birmingham police facing down young demonstrators, with snarling dogs and fire hoses, was played out along a four-block area in 1963 between **Kelly Ingram Park**  (corner of 16th Street and 5th Avenue North) and City Hall. Walk through the now peaceful park to see sculptures of two children through jail bars, a trio of praying ministers, and a particularly gripping image of a German Shepherd dog menacing a black man. Alabama's largest statue of Dr Martin Luther King, Jr faces the Sixteenth Street Baptist Church, scene of the grimmest incident in the struggle for civil rights *(see below)*.

The Birmingham Museum of Art is the South's largest public art museum.

Civil Rights Institute

The **Birmingham Civil Rights Institute** ❿ (tel: 205-328-9696, closed Mon), immediately west of the park, is part history lesson and part audience participation, proof of how the city has passed the ugly chapter of the 1960s. Moving and evocative photos, videos, audio recordings, and exhibits show just how African-Americans were treated under local segregation laws.

Look for the cell where Dr King wrote his famous *Letter from the Birmingham Jail*, galvanizing bystanders to become active in the movement. "White" and "colored" drinking fountains, and a 1950s lunch counter symbolize segregation in public places. The danger of the movement hits home in the charred shell of a Greyhound bus, burned by racists near Anniston when blacks and whites rode together in a challenge to the state's segregation laws. When the institute opened in 1992, *The New York Times* headlined "Facing Up to Racial Pains of the Past, Birmingham Moves On." Just north across the street is the **Sixteenth Street Baptist Church** ❿ (tel: 205-251-9402, closed Sun, Mon).

BELOW: inside the Birmingham Civil Rights Institute.

TIP

To learn more about the 1963 Sixteenth Street Baptist Church bombing, watch Spike Lee's acclaimed 1997 movie, *4 Little Girls*.

Photographs show the aftermath of a bomb planted by white racists in 1963. Near the pulpit are class pictures of the four young girls who were killed while preparing for Sunday school. In the balcony is a stained-glass black Christ, crucified, with the words "You do it unto me," which was a gift from the people of Wales. The congregation of about 300 holds a memorial service on the Sunday closest to the date of the bombing, September 15.

Botanicals and bikes

First-time visitors to Birmingham are pleasantly surprised by the city's beautiful mountains and lush blankets of trees. This is a city that provides facilities for a wide range of outdoor leisure activities. East on US 280 to Mountain Brook are two of the most popular. The **Birmingham Zoo** Ⓜ (2630 Cahaba Road, tel: 205-879-0408, open daily) is home to Siberian tigers, white rhinos, gorillas, and orang-utans. Across the street is the **Birmingham Botanical Gardens** Ⓝ (tel: 205-414-3950, open daily), containing 25 display gardens. The South's largest clear-span greenhouse shelters tropical plants, camellias, and a cactus collection. Scores of plants native to the South are showcased in a garden sponsored by *Southern Living* magazine, the arbiter of Southern hospitality, design and cooking, based in nearby Homewood.

To get away from urban stess, just 15 minutes south of Downtown take I-65 exit 246 through a tangle of fast-food restaurants and gasoline stations to the tranquility of **Oak Mountain State Park** Ⓞ, Alabama's largest. Facilities for hiking, swimming, fishing, golf, and horse riding, and a challenging mountain bike course, are all available. Tranquility is not, however, on the minds of motorcycle enthusiasts, who love to gaze at the world's largest collection of bikes at the

BELOW: the Alabama Jazz Hall of Fame is housed in the historic Carver Theater.

Barber Motorsports Park ⓟ (tel: 205-699-7275, open daily). It's 20 minutes from Downtown at I-20 exit 140. When third-generation dairyman George Barber began buying vintage motorcycles in 1988, he probably didn't have it in mind to amass the world's pre-eminent collection, but that's what he's done. He opened a makeshift museum in the old repair shop of the dairy's truck fleet in 1995, and constructed a showplace for his collection. Just for good measure, he built a racetrack to FIA and FIM standards that has come to be known as the "Augusta National of Racetracks."

By the time he opened the museum in 2003 he had about 800 bikes, including some dating back to 1904. He selects from his collection and can display about 350 vintage and current models at a time. Barber's bikes aren't only for show, but for racing, too. His race team restores bikes and races the historic models. The engines are packed with lubricant, but most models can be made race-ready at just an hour's notice.

Choppers

Barber, who lent a gorgeous 1929 Scott Squirrel to the acclaimed Guggenheim *Motorcycle* exhibition said, "Nothing annoys me more than when I'm traveling and I tell people where I'm from and they get this blank look on their face. An awful lot of eyeballs watch motor racing on television, and I aim to make their first impression of Birmingham an impressive one." How many bikes will it take to satisfy him? "I'll keep collecting until they carry me away in a white jacket." His newest obsession is Lotus Formula One racecars. Barber believes he has the largest collection of these, too. Vintage choppers can be seen being restored in the basement of the museum. Coming for a race? Surprisingly, the 2.38-mile (3.8-km)

BELOW: the Barber Motorsports Park, with one of its pre-eminent exhibits.

Map on page 134

racecourse, considered the finest road course in North America, has no bleachers; it's surrounded by a grassy hillside. The Grand Prix-caliber track rises and falls over 50 ft (15 meters), and from any one spot 70 percent of the switchback circuit is visible, eliminating the need for grandstands. Just bring a blanket or folding chairs. The races are televised on the Speed channel.

Into the countryside

The longest free-flowing river east of the Mississippi slices right through the Birmingham Metro area, and forms the southern boundary between Jefferson County and its rapidly developing neighbor Shelby County.

The **Cahaba River** is said to have more species per mile than any other river in the continental US, and is home to more than 60 rare species of plants and animals. A 4-mile (6.5-km) stretch in Bibb County forms the **Cahaba River National Wildlife Refuge** that shelters the largest known stand of rare Cahaba lilies, which bloom in May. Go west on I-59 to exit 97 and turn left on US 11, then west on State Route 5. Turn left on County Route 24 and go 4½ miles (7.2 km), then park west of Piper Bridge.

Virginians wandering around south of Birmingham may do a double-take when they might think they've seen George Washington's Mount Vernon home, Williamsburg's Bruton Parish Church, and a 1770 Courthouse. These Colonial landmarks have been meticulously recreated at the **American Village historical park** (tel: 205-665-3535, closed Sat, Sun) where guests can learn more about the theories of liberty and self-government. Visitors can rally with the Sons of Liberty, protest against the imposition of British taxes, and serve as delegates to the Constitutional Convention. Leave I-65 at exit 234. ❑

BELOW: peanuts are now a more common sight than cotton in the fields of Alabama.

Civil Rights

During the Reconstruction era after the Civil War, amendments to the US Constitution gave freed slaves the right to vote and own property. By the beginning of the 20th century, Southern states had passed segregation laws to limit these rights.

Half a century later, congregations in black churches – virtually the only institution not controlled by whites – demonstrated to overturn segregation laws. In 1955, seamstress Rosa Parks was arrested for refusing to give her seat on a Montgomery bus to a white person, as required by city ordinance. A young minister, Martin Luther King, Jr, organized the year-long Montgomery Bus Boycott.

Meanwhile, blacks could not vote, drink from the same water fountains as whites, eat in white-owned cafés, or try on clothes in stores before buying them. Complainers in Birmingham were often harassed or beaten by thugs linked to the police. When black people in Birmingham took their complaints to City Hall in 1963, Police Commissioner Bull Conner turned fire hoses on them, and filled the jail with children who had marched. Within days of Dr King's famous "I Have a Dream" speech at the March on Washington, Ku Klux Klansmen bombed a Birmingham Baptist church active in the Civil Rights Movement, killing four young girls. The bombing prompted some white Alabamians to oppose the brutality. Three white men were convicted of the church bombing, one as recently as 2002.

African-Americans in Selma, frustrated by official tactics preventing them from registering to vote, attempted a 51-mile (82-km) march on the state Capitol. Under orders from segregationist Gov. George Wallace, state police attacked them as they left Selma. President Lyndon Johnson pushed the stalled Voting Rights Bill through Congress. In 2000, President Bill Clinton attended a re-enactment of the 1965 Selma-to-Montgomery march. Clinton said that before the Voting Rights Act "was signed in ink in Washington, it first was signed in blood in Selma."

As African-Americans elected public officials and impacted local ordinances, they swept their old foes from office. Voting majorities gave them control of city and county governments in Birmingham and the Black Belt west of Montgomery. A repentant Wallace received their support in 1982, and subsequently appointed many African-Americans to public office. An African-American judge was elected to the Alabama Supreme Court with broad support from both races.

The state tourism office publishes an Alabama Civil Rights Trail brochure showing major sites and the Selma to Montgomery National Voting Rights Trail. The Birmingham Civil Rights Institute is by the Sixteenth Street Baptist Church *(see page 137)*. Museums are also open in Selma and Tuskegee. ❏

RIGHT: in 1955, Rosa Parks refused to give up her seat on a bus to a white person, prompting the Montgomery Bus Boycott.

AROUND ALABAMA

Rugged mountains in the northern part of the state segue gently into the central plains and beyond, revealing a space center, civil rights sites and a NASCAR Superspeedway

Map on page 130

The first towns settled by English-speaking people in present-day Alabama were around what George Washington called "the great bend" of the Tennessee River. The mighty bend swoops down through the hills of Chattanooga, crosses Alabama, then winds north to merge with the Ohio River. The river town of Decatur, 77 miles (124 km) north of Birmingham, is a good place to stop overnight and think about traveling west to tour the Helen Keller home, or heading east to the birthplace of America's space program.

The terrain becomes more mountainous north of **Birmingham ❶** on Interstate 65. A remarkable religious destination – a compound reflecting 13th-century Romanesque Gothic architecture – lies in the hills 17 miles (27 km) east of the interstate near **Hanceville ❷**. Mother Angelica, whose Eternal Word television channel is broadcast to Catholics around the world, built her **Shrine of the Most Blessed Sacrament** (tel: 256-352-6267, open daily) for the order of nuns cloistered here. Take exit 291, turn east on State Route 91 for 13 miles (21 km), then right onto County 747 and right on County 548. The magnificence of the golden chapel interior is worth the pilgrimage detour. Respectful dress is required to enter the chapel, please; no shorts or sleeveless shirts.

Wild and scenic river

One of the South's most pristine wilderness areas is west of the interstate at **Cullman**. To reach the sprawling **Bankhead National Forest ❸** (tel: 205-489-5111, open daily) take I-65 exit 308 and head west for 30 miles (48 km) to **Double Springs**. Go 12 miles (19 km) north on State Route 33 to County Road 60 and the Sipsey Wilderness. Congress has designated Sipsey a "wild and scenic river." Three areas in the forest permit overnight camping, but be sure to make reservations well in advance.

Resume the northern trek to Decatur on Interstate 65 and exit on State Route 67 for 2 miles (3 km) to the visitors center of the **Wheeler National Wildlife Refuge ❹** (tel: 256-350-6639, open daily). Migrating waterfowl spend the winter here in the backwaters of the Tennessee River. Raised boardwalks within the refuge are excellent places to photograph the birds and animals.

Turn left on State Route 67 and right on US 31 to reach the commercial and residential areas of **Decatur ❺** (pop. 54,500). Most of the town, except for an 1833 bank, was destroyed by Union troops in the Civil War. The bank anchors the Old Decatur historic district with a number of Victorian and bungalow houses. Take a side trip west to the community of **Oakville**, birthplace of track star Jesse Owens. Go west on Old Moulton Road 14 miles (23 km) from State Route 67

LEFT: Montgomery's Palladian-style cultural center houses two theaters where Shakespeare is performed.
BELOW: 1851 state capitol.

and follow signs to the **Jesse Owens Memorial Park**  (174 County Road 241, tel: 256-974-3636, closed Mon), with its museum. An Ohio State coach taught the athlete "to run as if the track is on fire." In sight is the **Oakville Indian Mounds Park** where a replica of a seven-sided Native American council house contains a museum of Indian artifacts.

Back in Decatur there's a choice to be made; whether first to head west into the Shoals region, where Helen Keller and W.C. Handy were born, or go east to "the rocket city" of Huntsville and Scottsboro, the home of Unclaimed Baggage. For Huntsville, head north on US 31 and cross the broad river to Interstate 565. Just past the I-65 interchange, take exit 2 and park in the tiny village of **Mooresville** (pop. 92). Many of the houses here are occupied by fifth-generation descendants of the builders. If the "new" post office built in 1840 is open, the 48 wooden call boxes from the 1825 Tavern are still in use. Mooresville played Mark Twain's hometown in a "Tom and Huck" Disney movie.

Huntsville

Less than 15 minutes from the 19th-century village of Mooresville on Interstate 65 is the birthplace of America's space program. The US Army chose the cotton mill town of **Huntsville**  (pop. 160,000) in 1950 as the research center for German rocket scientists captured during World War II. Dr Wernher von Braun's rockets launched America's first satellite and *Mercury* astronauts before the *Saturn V* rocket took *Apollo* astronauts to the moon. NASA's Marshall Space Flight Center is within the Army's Redstone Arsenal. Test rockets and astronaut-training equipment are displayed at the **US Space & Rocket Center** museum (Interstate 565 exit 15, tel: 256-837-3400, open daily). If you're interested in **US Space Camp** and aviation programs, call to check in advance which age groups are scheduled for sessions. Two miles (3 km) east of the space museum is the **Huntsville Botanical Garden** (tel: 256-830-4447, open daily), known for its aquatic garden, a butterfly house, and a collection of day lilies. Attendances peak between Thanksgiving and New Year during the holiday lights season. North of the space museum is Cummings Research Park, the nation's second largest technology center.

Take exit 19-C for the **Huntsville Visitor Center** (tel: 256-551-2230) on Church Street not far from the **Historic Huntsville Depot**. Because of the city's space image, its role as the first capital of Alabama is less heralded. Settled at a spring in 1805, the town was the largest in the territory when Alabama's population qualified it for statehood in 1819. Costumed guides demonstrate pioneer chores inside the restored **Alabama Constitution Village** (tel: 256-564-8100), a block south of the courthouse square. The village, where the state's constitution was first written, is a convenient starting place for a walking tour past the several dozen pre-Civil War homes and churches in the **Twickenham Historic District**. The oldest is the 1814 mansion of town promoter LeRoy Pope. The 1819 **Weeden House** behind the Episcopal church is a museum named for a painter-poet. The self-guided tour ends at Harrison Brothers Hardware. Open for a

BELOW: Ivy Green, the birthplace of Helen Keller.

century on the square, it sells more gifts than nails and chains. Screen actress Tallulah Bankhead was born in an apartment facing the courthouse. The **Huntsville Museum of Art** (tel: 256-535-4350, closed Mon), located in Big Spring Park, houses a notable collection of Italian silver Buccellati animals. The ideal time for a visit to Huntsville is in late September, when Downtown turns into one huge street fair for the Big Spring Jam music festival.

Go east for 30 minutes on US 72 to tour the large limestone cavern at the **Cathedral Caverns State Park ❽** (tel: 256-728-8193, open daily), with a stalagmite "forest" and a massive column 243 ft (74 meters) around. The footpaths are smooth and wide enough for wheelchairs. It's worth bringing a jacket for the guided tour, as it's always 60°F (16°C) inside.

Lost luggage

Continue east for another 15 minutes to reach the famous Scottsboro **Unclaimed Baggage Center** (509 W. Willow Street, tel: 256-259-1525, closed Sun), described as "one of the country's best-kept shopping secrets." Browse through travelers' lost merchandise for potential bargains, or just enjoy wondering, "who packed *those*?" For a restful retreat and a mountaintop view of miles of open space, seek out **Gorham's Bluff** (tel: 256-451-8439), about an hour east of Huntsville. There are spectacular views of the Tennessee River valley below. An inn with a fine restaurant has the perfect view.

To reach **Florence** and the Shoals region from Decatur or Huntsville, go west on State Route 20. In **Tuscumbia ❾**, follow directional signs for "Ivy Green," the local name for the **Helen Keller Birthplace** (300 W. North Commons, tel: 256-383-4066, open daily). The emotional story of "The Miracle Worker"

Map on page 130

The birthplace of the space program was Huntsville, Alabama; visit the US Space & Rocket Center.

BELOW: Huntsville was the engine for Alabama's early history.

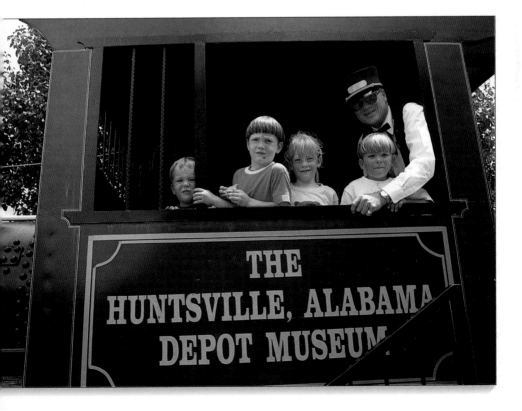

unfolded in the 1820s house and a detached cottage. The metal pump where teacher Anne Sullivan spelled w-a-t-e-r in the deaf child's hand is under a shelter behind the house. Local actors perform the play outdoors in summer. A mile south, the **Alabama Music Hall of Fame** (tel: 256-381-4417, closed Christmas Week and Jan 1) celebrates achievements of natives including Hank Williams, Lionel Richie, Jimmy Buffet and the country band Alabama. This is also the home of the famous **Muscle Shoals** Fame recording studios (603 E. Avalon Avenue, tel: 256-381-0801), where everyone from Aretha Franklin to ZZ Hill made soul music history *(see page 77)*. Seeking Southern oddities? Turn off US 72 onto State Route 247 and go 12 miles (19 km) south to see the graves of legendary hunting dogs in the **Coon Dog Cemetery**.

Jefferson Davis and Martin Luther King

The distance from Birmingham to the state capital of **Montgomery** ❿ (pop. 205,000) is 91 miles (146 km) to the south via Interstate 65, but architecturally the distance is about a century. Birmingham's rush of building creativity peaked about 1927. Most landmarks in Montgomery predate the Civil War, and many are close enough together to explore on foot. A word of advice: carry a bottle of water in the summer because the city is humid, even by Southern standards. A side benefit of the humidity is the proliferation of gray Spanish moss that drips from the trees.

The **State Capitol**, an 1851 Greek Revival structure, looks down Dexter Avenue. The bronze star under the front portico marks where Jefferson Davis took the oath in 1861 as the president of the Confederate States of America. The Old Senate Chamber has been faithfully restored to the time when Southern delegates established the Confederacy. Murals painted inside the dome in 1927 romanticize significant periods of the state's history.

BELOW: Executive residence for Dixie, 1861.

FIRST WHITE HOUSE OF THE CONFEDERACY

Designated Executive Residence by the Provisional Confederate Congress February 21, 1861. President Jefferson Davis and his family lived here until the Confederate Capital moved to Richmond summer 1861.
Built by William Sayre 1832-35 at Bibb and Lee Streets.
Moved to present location by the First White House Association and dedicated June 3, 1921.

Walk a block west of the Capitol for the red brick **Dexter Avenue King Memorial Church** (tel: 334-263-3970, open daily) where 25-year-old Martin Luther King, Jr organized the Montgomery Bus Boycott in 1955. A block behind the church is the **Civil Rights Memorial** designed by sculptor Maya Lin. Feel the sheet of water flowing over the names of 40 civil rights martyrs. The houses in which Jefferson and King lived a century apart are only six blocks from each other.

From the south wing of the Capitol, cross the street to the **First White House of the Confederacy** (tel: 334-242-1861, closed Sat, Sun). Then drive the few blocks to the **Dexter Avenue Parsonage** (309 S. Jackson, tel: 334-263-3970, open daily), southwest of the Capitol. A plaque on the porch marks a bomb blast in 1956. The site of Mrs Parks's arrest *(see page 141)* and the **Rosa Parks Museum** (tel: 334-241-8661, open daily) is down Dexter Avenue and left on Montgomery Street at the intersection with Commerce Street.

To see more than 40 relocated 19th-century buildings, including the 1818 Lucas Tavern, drive north across Dexter Avenue to **Old Alabama Town** (301 Columbus, tel: 334-240-4500, closed Sun). One of the city's most popular destinations has nothing to do with American history, but British theater. Construction magnate Winton (Red) Blount donated the Palladian-influenced building, which houses two impressive theaters at the **Alabama Shakespeare Festival** (tel: 334-271-5300, open daily). Take Interstate 85 exit 6 and follow signs to Woodmere. Even if you don't attend a play, stroll the grounds of the **Blount Cultural Park** and see the art collection Blount gave to the **Montgomery Museum of Fine Arts** (tel: 334-244-5700, closed Mon).

Map on page 130

Take a 45-minute side trip east on Interstate 85 to reach the **George Washington Carver Museum** (tel: 334-727-6390, open daily) at the famed **Tuskegee Institute**. The black scientist developed hundreds of by-products from sweet potatoes and peanuts. After a boll weevil infestation in 1915, Carver convinced many South Alabama planters to forsake cotton and plant peanuts. Farmers in the Wiregrass area around **Dothan ⓫** were so appreciative they invited Carver to visit, which led to the annual National Peanut Festival. Drive south on US 231 or 431 to the southeast corner of the state to see murals painted on sides of commercial buildings.

Statue of Booker T. Washington, founder of Tuskegee Institute.

Football fans and art lovers should continue east on Interstate 85 from Montgomery to the college town of **Auburn ⓬**. The **Jule Collins Smith Museum of Fine Arts** (901 S. College Street, tel: 334-844-1484, closed Mon) displays 36 mid-20th-century works by artists including Louis Guglielmi, Jacob Lawrence and Ben Shahn that Congress deemed "un-American" and ordered sold at "government surplus" auction in 1947. Auburn's $1,072 investment is now valued at $10 million. Sports memorabilia is housed in the **Lovelace Athletic Museum** near Jordan-Hare Stadium on the campus.

BELOW:
Brown Chapel AME Church, Selma.

To see the state's most spectacular collection of Italianate mansions with wide verandas and overhanging eaves, drive about 90 minutes southeast of Montgomery along US 82 to the river town of **Eufaula ⓭**. North Eufaula Avenue is as pretty as any street in Alabama. **Shorter Mansion** (tel: 334-687-3793, open daily), a neoclassical Revival landmark resembling a wedding cake, was built in 1884. (It featured in the 2002 movie *Sweet Home Alabama*.) West of Montgomery are sleepy Black Belt towns with elaborate mansions built by slaves when cotton was king.

Selma

The 51-mile (82-km) route along US 80 to **Selma ⓮** (population 20,500) is best known for the Selma-to-Montgomery march of 1965 (see page 141). There's been remarkably little change along the roadway since to disturb the cows grazing in broad rolling pastures. The National Park Service is building interpretative centers at each end – and in the middle – of this important historic route.

Cross the Edmund Pettus Bridge and turn left on Water Street to see photos of the protest in the modest **National Voting Rights Museum**.

For an impressive example of the opposite end of the wealth spectrum, turn west off Broad onto Jeff Davis. Go two blocks and turn left onto Mabry Street for **Sturdivant Hall** (tel: 334-872-5626, closed Mon), built in 1853. Six fluted Corinthian columns support

BELOW:
the late, legendary Dale Earnhardt at the Talladega Superspeedway, site of the racer's final win before his death in 2001.

a massive portico that leads to a mansion interior dominated by elaborate plaster friezes. The 1837 **Saint James Hotel** (1200 Water Avenue, tel: 334-872-3234), beautifully restored after being shuttered for decades, is the state's oldest. Take a break in the ground floor Drinking Room to hear tales of resident ghosts who don't check out. An hour west of Selma is **Demopolis**, a town founded in 1818 by exiled aristocrats loyal to Napoleon. Leave US 80 for US 43 North to arive at **Gaineswood** (805 South Cedar, tel: 334-289-4846, open daily), an elegant Greek Revival villa with a ballroom of reflecting mirrors. The house is a National Historic Landmark.

South towards Mobile

Monroeville 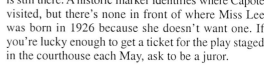 (pop. 6,862), about halfway between Montgomery and Mobile, is a treat for fans of the novel or the movie *To Kill a Mockingbird*. The spirits of Scout and brother Jem still pervade the small home town of reclusive novelist Harper Lee. Take Interstate 65 to exit 96 and head west on County Road 20 for 21 miles (34 km). The 1903 courthouse in the town square houses the **Old Courthouse Museum** (tel: 251-575-7433, closed Sun). A movie crew replicated the interior of this very courtroom for the scenes where attorney Atticus Finch (Gregory Peck) defends a handicapped black man accused of attacking a white girl. You can also see photographs of the novelist and her childhood friend Truman Capote.

The major houses mentioned in the novel are gone, and the Lee family home at 216 South Alabama St (10 doors south of the square) was torn down in the 1960s to make way for a hamburger drive-in. The house next door where Capote (Dill, in the book) visited is gone, too, but the rock wall mentioned in the story is still there. A historic marker identifies where Capote visited, but there's none in front of where Miss Lee was born in 1926 because she doesn't want one. If you're lucky enough to get a ticket for the play staged in the courthouse each May, ask to be a juror.

Mercedes and Nascar

Interstate 20 that slices through Birmingham has earned the nickname "wheels alley" because of the Mercedes-Benz plant to the west and the Barber Motorsports Park *(see page 139)* and "the world's fastest speedway" to the east.

Some 58 miles (93 km) west of Birmingham on Interstate 20/59 is **Tuscaloosa** ⑯ (pop. 78,000), a former state capital and home of the University of Alabama. It's best known now for the **Mercedes-Benz** assembly plant and visitor center (tel: 205-507-2253, closed Sat, Sun). Take exit 86 to see historic vehicles and walk through the clean assembly plant on a guided tour. It's the company's only plant outside of Germany.

Football fans follow signs to the university campus and the **Paul Bryant Museum** (tel: 205-348-4668, open daily) near Bryant-Denny Stadium. Exhibits and films highlight important victories over Penn State, Notre Dame, Miami, and arch-rival Auburn. Football fans rarely visit T-town without finding time for a plate of barbecued ribs at Dreamland, the "roadhouse" restaurant off Jug Factory Road.

On two Sundays a year upwards of 180,000 racing fans make a pilgrimage 50 miles (80 km) east of Birmingham to the **Talladega Superspeedway** ⓱ (tel: 256-362-2261 for race tickets) to watch the top NASCAR drivers circle the tri-oval track at speeds approaching 200 miles an hour (320 km/h). (Not a race fan? Be sure to avoid **Talladega** (pop. 15,143) and Interstate 20 on race days; a few beer-drinking fans feel the need for speed after the race is over.) Guided tours in a slow van are available on days the track isn't being used for races or testing. You can inspect dozens of famous racecars inside the **International Motorsports Hall of Fame** (tel: 256-362-5002, open daily) next to the track. Some of the mangled vehicles may make you wonder how drivers survived the wrecks.

Map on page 130

Stuffed animals

If racing is too hectic, drive east to **Anniston** ⓲ (24,276), where one museum is devoted to stuffed animals, and another to military weapons. Drive east on Interstate 20 and turn north on US 431 for 6 miles (10 km) to Lagarde Park and the **Anniston Museum of Natural History** (tel: 256-237-6766, closed Mon except in summer). Dioramas of birds and animals date from the 19th century. Next door at the **Berman Museum of World History** (tel: 256-237-6261, closed Mon except in summer) is a remarkable collection of pistols, rifles, bronzes, paintings, and personal objects that belonged to such diverse figures as Hitler, Mussolini, Napoleon, and Jefferson Davis. Farley and Germaine Berman were American spies during World War II who retired to Anniston.

Continue north on US 431 for 30 miles (48 km) to **Gadsden** ⓳ (pop. 38,978) to **Noccalula Falls Park** (1500 Noccalula Road, tel: 256-549-4663, open daily) to view a series of pioneer buildings next to a towering, refreshing waterfall. ❏

BELOW: horsehead fountain in front of the 1837 Saint James Hotel, the state's oldest.

MOBILE

Feted by the French, the Spanish, and the British,
Mobile retains the unhurried Southern grace
of an elegant Grand Dame

Map
on page
130

Shaded by ancient live oaks dripping in Spanish moss, and bordered with azalea bushes as big as sea-trunks, **Mobile ⑳** (pop. 198,915) is steeped in 300 years of history. Fought over by the French, the Spanish, and the British, the city displays trophies from her past occupations, and still is every inch a genteel and hospitable Southern belle.

Follow directional signs at Interstate 10 exit 26 (Water Street) to the **Fort Conde Welcome Center** (150 S. Royal Street, tel: 251-208-7569, open daily), a faithful re-creation of a 1724 fort built by the French colonists. The ruins of the original, razed in 1820, were found during excavations for the interstate interchange. Costumed guides recount lively tales of Mobile's founders, and fire off cannons and muskets (minus the ammunition, of course) to demonstrate how the French kept rival Europeans at bay until the English took possession in 1763. The Spanish occupied from 1780 until Mobile joined the US in 1813, 37 years after the Founding Fathers signed the Declaration of Independence, which reinforces the feeling of it being a place apart from the rest of Alabama.

It's a pleasant idea to leave the car in the visitors lot across the street from Fort Conde, since much of Mobile can be explored on foot. This compact architectural feast for the senses offers museums and historical sites at every turn. One of the South's finest city museums is across Royal Street. The **Museum of Mobile** (tel: 251-208-7569, closed Sun) is in the 1857 City Hall. Exhibits describe Jean Baptiste Le Moyne, Sieur de Bienville, founding the outpost in 1702 as the French capital of a vast empire stretching from the Gulf of Mexico into present-day Canada. In 1718, the French moved the seat of power 141 miles (227 km) west to New Orleans, but Mobile survived the loss of prestige, and remained an active trading port even through the military conflicts that followed.

LEFT: blessing of the fleet on Alabama's Gulf Coast.
BELOW: water wheel exhibit at Mobile's Gulf Coast Exploreum.

The home of Mardi Gras

Mobile started something else in the early years, later "exported" to New Orleans. Mardi Gras (literally "Fat Tuesday," the last day before Lent) was first celebrated here in 1703 and became more formally organized in 1830. Two Mobilians who had been members of a mystic society or *krewe* moved to New Orleans and were instrumental in forming that city's first secret society. A man and a woman with deep roots in Old Mobile society reign as King Felix III and his queen over galas and float-filled, family-friendly parades. Don't miss the museum's display of handmade, jewel-encrusted coronation costumes worn by Mardi Gras royalty. Queens' gowns and trains, including court costumes from 1910, are as regal and expensive as in any museum in the nation.

Upstairs is the Civil War section with a replica of the Confederate submarine *H.L. Hunley*, built in Mobile in 1862, and recently recovered off the South Carolina coast. Mobile's best-known military figure is Admiral Raphael Semmes, the daring Confederate raider who captured 66 ships during the Civil War. A sterling silver presentation sword and his gravestone are presented in the museum. A bronze statue of Semmes, called "Old Beeswax" by his crew for his flamboyant moustache, faces Mobile Bay from the median in Government Street. Adjoining the museum is the **Gulf Coast Exploreum**, a hands-on science center with an IMAX theater.

Steamboat captain

Mobile has many house museums, and two that definitely should not be missed. Walk to the first museum, located Downtown, as this is a great way to enjoy the architecture along the way. From the Semmes statue, go four blocks west on tree-lined Government Street to the Radisson Admiral Semmes Hotel (built in 1940), then north seven blocks on Joachim Street (the restored 1927 Saenger Theater is along the way). A steamboat captain built the **Richards-DAR House** (256 North Joachim Street, tel: 215-208-7320, open daily) in 1860. The Italianate home is noteworthy for its ornate, iron-lace trim with a "four seasons" motif over the brick facade.

Collect the car from Fort Conde via Claiborne, two blocks west of Joachim, to tour the 1835 **Cathedral of Immaculate Conception** on Dauphin Street. The twin towers date from 1890, and the 12 stained-glass windows are richly detailed. A railed entrance descends to the crypt, and to the tombs of bishops. Pope John XXIII designated the cathedral a minor basilica in 1962.

BELOW:
the *USS Alabama*
Battleship, Mobile's
top attraction.

To reach the **Oakleigh Mansion** (tel: 251-432-1281, closed Sun) from Royal Street, drive 2 miles (3 km) west, under a canopy of live oaks along Government, and turn left on George or Roper streets. The white-raised cottage, commenced in 1833, has period furniture and a Thomas Sully portrait of a Mobile grand dame, Madam Octavia Walton LeVert. The best times to visit are when the azaleas bloom in spring, and Christmas. Sunken gardens outside began when slaves dug the clay for the bricks used in the house.

Mobile's **Magnolia Cemetery** is one of the state's oldest and largest. To reach Magnolia, turn south on Ann Street at the intersection of Government and go one mile. Some of the most elaborate tombs are near the center, close to the Virginia Street gate. Iron markers and a variety of mausoleum styles are represented. The 1860 Slatter Family Tomb has the finest ornamental cast iron in the cemetery. Some 1,100 Confederate casualties, including the first crew of the *H.L. Hunley* submarine, are buried near the statue marking the Confederate Rest opposite Ann Street.

The battleship and the bay

Mobile's most popular attraction, **Battlefield Park**, can be seen from any point on the riverfront. The *USS Alabama* Battleship (tel: 251-433-2703, open daily) is berthed off the causeway in Mobile Bay alongside a World War II submarine. The battleship assisted the

Map on page 130

British in protecting convoys through the North Sea against German warships and aircraft in occupied Norway. The *Alabama* saw 37 months of active duty and was never damaged by enemy fire. Several of the battleship's nine battle stars were earned while serving with a strike force in Japan and Okinawa. The ship sailed with a crew of 2,500 sailors and Marines, until she was retired in 1947. The Navy announced that she would be scrapped, and Alabama school children donated $100,000 in dimes to a $1 million fund to tow her the 5,600 miles (9,000 km) from Seattle through the Panama Canal to her berth in Mobile Bay.

Start the self-guided tour with a video of crewmen describing the ship's features. The submarine *USS Drum* also played an important role in the war, and became the hero of the western Pacific in 1942, with the highest total of enemy tonnage sunk, including the *Mizuho*, the largest Japanese vessel lost in the war.

TIP

For more sites along lovely, sweetly scented Mobile Bay, see "The Gulf Coast," page 188.

Alabama's golf trail

Golfers from all over the world are now drawn to Mobile, Birmingham, Huntsville, Opelika, Dothan, and Florence, with green fees not much above those at municipal courses. In all, the **Robert Trent Jones Golf Trail** (tel: 800-949-4444) includes 450 holes of golf at 11 locations. Most of the half million golfers who play the trail each year are from out of state, including 6 percent from outside the US. State pension fund chief David Bronner invested retirement funds in golf courses to encourage tourism. Moderately skilled players complain about the difficulty of his courses, reinforcing Jones's axiom: "Nobody remembers easy courses." A decade after the first courses opened, *Golf Digest* magazine readers voted the trail the best value, and also placed it in the top 10 for quality among the world's 30 best-known golf destinations. ❑

BELOW: a reconstruction of life in the 1700s at Mobile's Fort Conde.

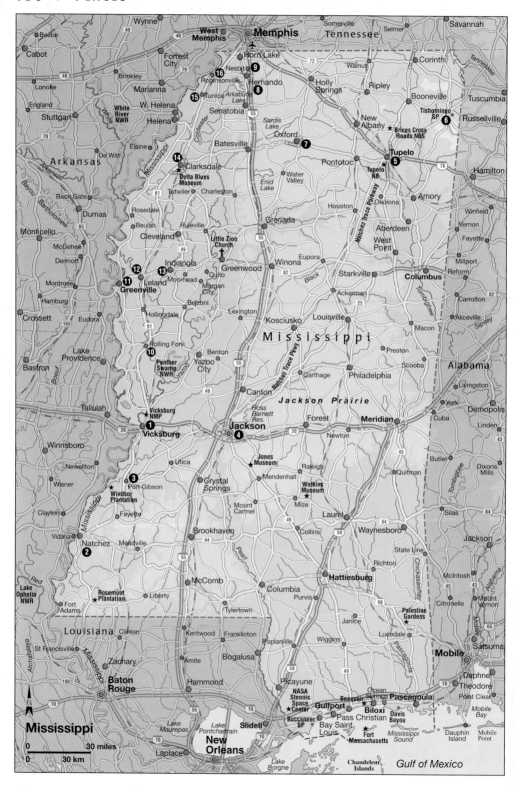

MISSISSIPPI

*A detailed guide to the entire state, with principal sites
clearly cross-referenced by number to the maps*

Named for the river that has been America's great trading route,
and ranged around the fertile Delta that blazed musical and
literary richness, as well as agricultural wealth, Mississippi
has an abundant and complex heritage to explore. The Magnolia
State offers ancient delights on the Natchez Trace, and Tishomingo
Park in the foothills of the Appalachian Mountains.

The Civil War was writ large across the map of Mississippi. Vicksburg was the site of one of the longest sieges in American history, and
the Battlefield Park is a quietening evocation of just how hard and
bitter the young country's wrestle with itself was. Jackson has risen
from the ashes of the "Chimneyville" burnings by Sherman, but the
scarcity of old buildings can't fail to make a resonant impression.
Heartbreakingly beautiful Natchez, paradoxically, still bears the scars
of coming through the "recent unpleasantness" intact.

As bitter, and still in many ways incomplete, the civil rights struggle was nowhere more raw than in Mississippi. From the cotton plantations to the race riots in Oxford, many of the dark milestones on the
march to freedom are along the roads of Mississippi. As well as battlefields, there are elegant antebellum mansions to discover, many of
which offer the grace of Southern hospitality that the term "bed and
breakfast accommodation" can't begin to describe.

The vivid and sometimes stark contrasts may be one explanation
for the wonderfully perplexing fountain of literary talent that springs
from the Mississippi mud and soil. This state has given the world the
words of Eudora Welty, Richard Wright, Tennessee Williams, and
John Grisham, to name just a few. William Faulkner, the father of the
20th-century American novel, lived in Oxford, amid lucrative sojurns
to Hollywood in its heyday.

Born in the cotton fields from working songs, gospel elevations,
and African rhythms, the blues in turn propagated the seeds for musical innovations which themselves conquered the 20th century world;
jazz, soul and rock 'n' roll. Elvis, the King of rock 'n' roll, was born
in the pretty town of Tupelo. The blues is, or are, still alive and shout-
ing, from its nursery in Clarksdale, through the alma-maters of
Greenville and Jackson. Classical education flourishes, too, in the
gentle northern slopes of Oxford, where the antebellum campus has
a romantic air fit to compare with the "dreaming spires" of the town's
English namesake.

Along with the innumerable senators, scientists, sports stars, and
scribes, Ole Miss can claim a prodigious number of former Miss
Americas among her august alumni. There's definitely something
about Mississippi. ❑

PRECEDING PAGES: Margaret's Grocery, north of Vicksburg where the Reverend
Dennis built bizarre structures, including a schoolbus church, for his wife.

VICKSBURG

Straddling a bluff on a bend in Ole Man River,
Vicksburg's Civil War history may be somber and poignant,
but its attractions are modern and popular

Map
on page
160

A t the southern point of the Mississippi Delta in 1811, the Methodist Reverend Newitt Vick found a bluff 200 ft (61 meters) above the great river, overlooking the bend where the Yazoo River joins the Mississippi. He bought 1,220 acres (490 hectares) of land from the government of the territory, and planned a town on the 200 acres (80 hectares) north of the river. Reverend Vick never saw it completed, since both he and his wife succumbed to yellow fever less than a year later, but the Vicks left 13 children, and, together with the reverend's executors, they developed the town that carries their name.

Known later as "the Gibraltar of the Confederacy," Vicksburg is a commanding position on the mighty river. So much so that in the Civil War, Abraham Lincoln called it "the key." He and General Ulysses S. Grant were agreed that its capture would cut off Texas, Louisiana, and Arkansas from the Confederacy. The strategy led to a 47-day siege, and one of the two decisive engagements of the war.

The white flag was hoisted on the court house on July 3, the same day as Robert E. Lee's defeat at Gettysburg. Grant took the surrender from General John C. Pemberton on the 4th of July, 1862. There is a popular belief that Vicksburg did not celebrate Independence Day for another 100 years, but newspapers in the library describe picnics and commemorations. The festivities, though, did take on a different tone as the town remembered the suffering of the war, and the siege. People from the North also visited on the 4th of July, and still do, to be at the site of their fathers' and forefathers' victory.

LEFT: Walnut Hills, where Lazy Susan lunches are served at round tables. **BELOW:** the Old Court House, 1858.

Vibrant Vicksburg

Modern Vicksburg offers, as well as the solemn tranquillity of the Battlefield Park, a vibrant and ambitious blues museum, riverboat-style casinos, an attractive historic downtown district, and a number of beautiful antebellum mansions, some of which provide gracious B&B accommodation. Vicksburg also has a place in the American history of music. On a visit to the River City Blues Museum, the city's distinguished and charming Alderwoman Gertrude Anderson Young said, "You know, jazz got its name from a Vicksburg drummer."

Just south of Vicksburg's Washington Street, on old US 61 by the Ameristar casino, is the attractive and informative **Mississippi State Welcome Center**.

The first of Vicksburg's antebellum mansions is in the historic garden district; it's a short way farther north on Washington, left onto Klein and at the intersection with Oak Street. Offering delightful B&B accommodation and an acclaimed restaurant, **Cedar Grove ⒶA** (2200 Oak Street, tel: 601-636-1000) is a graceful

plantation house, set near the river among formal gardens, and giving wide-sweeping views of the Mississippi from a roof garden. John Alexander Klein built the columned mansion in 1840 as a home for himself and his bride, Elizabeth. On their year-long European honeymoon, they acquired Italian marble fireplaces, French empire gasoliers, and Bohemian glass for the doorway. Elizabeth was related to General Sherman, who personally escorted the family to safety early in the siege, and the house later served as a Union hospital. Although a cannonball remains embedded in the parlor wall, the family's connection with that most hated of Union soldiers didn't endear them to Vicksburg society.

Most of the **Downtown Riverfront** actually fronts onto the Yazoo River, with the waterfront dominated by riverboat-style casinos. Just to the south are the **Isle of Capri**, the **Ameristar**, and **The Flamingo** casinos. None of the boats actually sail, they merely conform to the letter of Mississippi's idiosyncratic gaming laws *(see page 91)* but they do give an attractive flavor of the old riverboat style, and are spectacularly illuminated after dark. The Ameristar is popular for its Thursday night events, often with a blues theme.

Chess and Cobra

BELOW: moonshine jugs at the Corner Drug Store.

Farther north and to the right, about level with where the former Harrah's casino is "moored," a short street has been named **Willie Dixon Way** in dedication to Vicksburg's most famous bluesman. The great bass player, producer, and arranger was a mainstay of the Chess and Cobra labels, and supplied Muddy Waters with the diamond-hard riff and brash lyric for *Hoochie Coochie Ma*n. The street goes from nowhere to nowhere much else, and nothing happens on the way. Story of the blues.

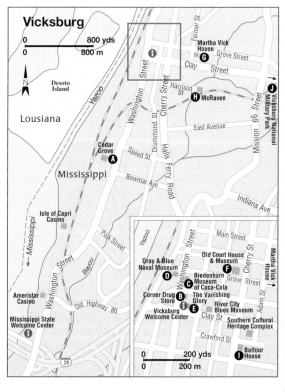

The Downtown historic district is about five blocks around the intersection of Washington and Clay streets, and still has a 19th- and early 20th-century appearance. Less than a block north is the friendly and helpful **Vicksburg Welcome Center**. The cosy, brick-lined office has a wealth of information about attractions, events, and accommodation in town.

Still on Washington, the **Corner Drug Store ❸** (1123 Washington Street, closed Sun) is more than a useful stop for travelers, providing drugstore requisites like toothpaste, medicines, and shampoo. The store wears its saloon-bar history proudly in the crystal chandeliers still hanging from the ceiling. There are fascinating exhibits of Civil War cures, including jars of angustura bark, some evil-looking potions that might have deterred sickness more than curing it, and a number of bullets bearing deep teeth-marks. There is a display of moonshine whisky with a recipe (still available locally, according to the proprietor), and numerous Civil War weapons, jugs, and surgical instruments. The store also sells more esoteric cures such as St John's wort and natural melatonin.

The place where the gooey, fizzy stuff was bottled for the first time in 1894 is now the **Biedenharn Coca-Cola Museum ❹** (1107 Washington Street, tel: 601-638-6514, open daily), a small and friendly museum that could not be more different than its glitzy cousin in Atlanta. Inside, it feels like a step into a sepia postcard. The original bottling equipment is replicated, which had to be operated in protective clothing, since the bottles were given to exploding. At the rear, through a red-brick courtyard, is a replica of a 1900s soda fountain with wire-backed chairs and small, round tables.

Upstairs from the Daily Grind Café is the **Attic Gallery**, selling innovative fine art from local artists like the charming Earl Simmonds, as well as art from

Map on page 160

Vicksburg has an easy-going, small-town feel about it.

BELOW: Vicksburg's downtown area, high above the Mississippi River.

Southern artists further afield. Across the street, the **Gray & Blue Naval Museum** has, they claim, the largest collection anywhere of Civil War Naval models and an impressive diorama of the Siege of Vicksburg, with just a trace of bias. The proprietor asserts, "we're not politically correct, but we are historically accurate." The **Biscuit Company Café and Bar** provides great views of the river to go with the food and drinks. There's often live music in the evenings, too. Back to Clay Street and a block up on the left, the story of the siege is vividly portrayed in ***The Vanishing Glory*** ❺ (717 Clay Street, open daily), a wide-screen presentation conjuring the event from eyewitness accounts, letters and diaries, of soldiers and citizens. The show is hourly on the hour.

Further along Clay Street, the **River City Blues Museum** features rare guitars, records and photographs, as well as, in the foyer, some instruments for visitors to play. Housed in the wood-paneled rooms of the former YMCA, the collection shows the enthusiasm of the curator and sponsors. So if the mojo's working, this could be the place to bring it.

A courthouse with cats

For one of Vicksburg's most delightful attractions, continue up Clay Street to Cherry Street and make the climb to the top. High on the hill, the **Old Court House** ❻ (Court Square, tel: 601-636-0741, open daily) was a favorite target for Union artillery during the siege, until someone had the idea of moving in Yankee prisoners. The courthouse survived and now houses a charming museum, guarded by a company of watchful cats. The museum illuminates the lives of the locals more than larger and more distant historical events.

The cosy exhibits evoke the rustic pioneer and dark polished antebellum home life. An engaging black history display includes a feature on "blacks who wore grey." There is a Confederate flag from Fort McCree which was never surrendered, a post-war "blacklist" of "unreconstructed individuals," newspapers printed on wallpaper during the siege, cannonballs, and shot. The museum is punctuated with stories of the origins of terms like *Dixie* and *Yankee*. Tours are advertised as "self-guided," but if Gordon Cotton, the curator, catches your eye, you'll likely be swept along by his twinkling enthusiasm for just about any and every subject of local history and lore. Very little can have happened in Vicksburg in the last two centuries about which Gordon won't gladly enlighten and entertain in his kindly schoolteacher style.

Turn left out of the courthouse and down Grove Street for a couple of blocks to the **Martha Vick house** ❼ (1300 Grove Street, tel: 601-638-7036, open daily), the last surviving home from the founding Vick family. Dating from the 1830s, the house is furnished with English and American antiques of the period.

Take Farmer Street for a few blocks and go left up Harrison Street. In this uncommonly haunted state, **McRaven** ❽ (1445 Harrison Street, tel: 601-636-1663) may be the most haunted house in Mississippi. Furniture moves by itself, footsteps are heard when there's no one there, and lights go on and off for no obvious reason. Three distinct styles of architecture

BELOW:
the 47-day siege of Vicksburg killed over 19,000 soldiers.

Map
on page
160

are clearly visible in the house's additions; frontier from 1797, Empire in 1836, and the last, Greek Revival from 1849. In the grounds, barely a hundred yards (91 meters) behind the house, the confronting trench lines of the Confederacy and the Union remain, just a few short steps apart.

The elegant **Balfour House** ❶ (1002 Crawford Street, open daily) is another home that offers B&B accommodation. In her journals, Emma Balfour gave Mississippi one of its most treasured first-hand accounts of the siege. She wrote with description and compassion of seeing "mortars from the west passing entirely over the house," and "…our poor soldiers have no rest, as we have few reserves." The house itself is one of Mississippi's finest examples of the Greek Revival style, and features an elliptical spiral staircase.

Individual and poignant

Follow Clay Street towards US 61 to **Vicksburg National Military Park** ❷ *(see page 96)*. The park covers much of the ground of the 47-day siege, as well as the extensive memorial gardens. All of the Confederate states and all but six of the US states of the time (20 states in all) have significant memorials to their fallen soldiers here; the siege killed over 19,000 men in total. Each monument is individual and poignant, and it would take a lifetime to tell all the tales. The park is a major draw for visitors from all over America, but it includes no statue or monument to General Sherman. Under a special pavilion is the *USS Cairo*, an ironclad fighting ship sunk in the conflict, raised from the riverbed 100 years later *(see photo on page 99)*. Much of the ship was so well preserved in the Mississippi mud that a watch found on board was still in working order. The running watch is displayed in an adjacent exhibition. ❑

The monument to Illinois in Battlefield Park commemorates Albert D.J. Cashier, a soldier who was discovered to be a woman. Jenny Hodger successfully carried out her masquerade for almost 50 years.

BELOW: view of the Mississippi from Vicksburg.

AROUND MISSISSIPPI

Graceful plantations, a gorgeous college town, a capital where commerce is king, and the ghosts of Elvis and Faulkner – Mississippi beguiles the mind

Map on page 156

Known first for the mighty, misty Mississippi River, this lyrical and literary state has history, musical and cultural heritage, and beautiful scenery. The verdant hills of northern Mississippi look out over one of the most fertile plains on earth – the Mississippi Delta. Having once been America's capital for cotton and rice, the ever-adaptable Mississppians are now raising soybeans and fat catfish under that big, sweltering sky.

Mississippi has fine plantation homes, especially in Natchez and Port Gibson, both of which escaped most of the ravages of the Civil War, or "the recent unpleasantness," as it is still sometimes known. Adding in the towering Mississippian giants of musical and literary heritage, plus a few state parks, and great Southern food and hospitality; well, child, what kept you so long? Don't be shy, y'all come now, y'hear?

Natchez

South of **Vicksburg ❶** about 70 miles (112 km) on US 61, **Natchez ❷** once was the capital of Mississippi. It was held and governed first by the French, then the English, followed by the Spanish. It shimmers with fading antebellum grace, thanks to the still arguable distinction of surviving the Civil War intact. Natchez surrendered without opposing Grant's occupation, and, because of the awful suffering that Vicksburg endured in its 47-day siege, Natchez citizens still feel a bitterness from their near neighbors. Most Vicksburgers seem to harbor no such feelings, though, believing that since President Jefferson Davis refused to garrison Natchez, the town could never have withstood an invasion.

A good first stop is the visitor center. Follow Highway 61 south of Natchez and join Highway 84. Overlooking the magnificent box girder bridges that carry trains and cars over the steep banks of the Mississippi, the **Natchez Visitor Center** (640 Canal Street, tel: 1-800-647-6724, open daily) offers a great viewing platform. A massive model of the town and the big river illuminates sites of historic and other points of local interest.

Left out of the Visitor Center on Canal Street, take the first left under the bluff by the river. Literally below the town, **Natchez-under-the-Hill** was once Natchez's dockside area of ill-repute, a strip of bars and brothels. Its act has cleaned up with restaurants and shops to attract tourists, but still carries echoes of its rowdy port-of-call days. The **Isle of Capri casino** offers some of the recreations that got the blood pumping back then, and the **Silver Street Inn**, a former 19th-century bordello, is a romantic, evocative remnant with good food and great views of the

LEFT: Natchez-under-the-Hill.
BELOW: Magnolia Hall, built in 1858 by planter Thomas Henderson.

Monmouth is set in beautiful landscaped gardens and listed by Zagat's as among the nation's top 50 inns. Tours are available during the day (tel: 601-442-5852).

BELOW: Mammy's Cupboard, a fun but politically incorrect restaurant outside Natchez.

river from its decorative balcony. Return to Canal Street and turn left. Just a couple of blocks on, at the corner of State Street, tickets are available for Natchez Spring and Fall Pilgrimages (tel: 601-446-6631, March, April and October – call for exact dates), a range of tours that take in over 30 plantation and antebellum historic houses. Follow State to Commerce and into the faded glory, antebellum grace and 20th-century decay of Downtown. The **Historic Natchez Foundation** (109 Commerce Street, tel: 601-442-2500) has information about the Historic District, an eight-block area, mostly by the river.

Plantation heaven

Lovely **Monmouth** *(see picture)* is a good introduction to the Natchez plantations, most of which are open every day. From Monmouth, turn right, then right again almost immediately onto Melrose Avenue. On the left is **Linden** (1 Linden Place, tel: 601-445-5472), an impressive mansion with a long, columned gallery. The house was commenced in 1792 and added to by later owners, though it has remained in the same family for the past 150 years. B&B accommodation is available. The first of Natchez' Greek Revival-style white columned mansions, **Auburn** (400 Duncan Avenue, tel: 601-442-5981) is furnished with antiques, some Regency and some Rococo. The unsupported spiral staircase in the foyer is particularly graceful.

Longwood (140 Lower Woodville Road, tel: 800-647-6742) is an octagonal brick mansion surrounded by columned porches and balconies and topped with a shining, Moorish onion dome. The house is even more remarkable for being externally grand, and internally incomplete. Like a movie facade, the interior beams and rough brick of the unfinished upper floors remain exposed.

Head across Highway 84 to Homochitto Street for about half a mile, to the stately white columned plantation house of **Dunleith** (tel: 601-446-8500). Sitting among 40 acres (16 hectares) of green pastures and wooded bayous, the house and grounds are open for daytime tours, and offer romantic and secluded B&B accommodation.

Natchez Indians

Described by one French settler as "one of the most polite and affable nations on the Mississippi," the attempts of the Natchez Indians to coexist with the white newcomers were constantly frustrated. In 1729, the Natchez tried to reclaim their homeland with an attack on Fort Rosalie. The French garrison was wiped out, but the colonists retaliated by killing most of the Indians and driving the rest away. Listed as a National Historic Landmark, the **Grand Village of the Natchez Indians** (400 Jefferson Davis Boulevard, tel: 601-446-6502) has an authentically re-created hut and three mounds, plus some arts and crafts on show in the friendly visitor center. To get there, return along Homochitto Street, take Highway 61 south and turn left onto Jefferson Davis Boulevard to the Grand Village entrance.

About 40 miles (64 km) north, Highway 61 leads straight into **Port Gibson ❸**. Grant's decision to spare the town from the torches means that it is one of the few old Mississippi towns to be preserved almost intact.

Three user-friendly self-guided tours are marked by green signs – a Grand Gulf battlefield tour, a Windsor battlefield tour including the ruins of evocative Windsor Plantation, and the Port Gibson tour covering historic homes and 19th-century churches.

Map on page 156

BELOW: Longwood is beautiful on the outside and unfinished on the inside.

On Church Street, which is part of Highway 61 itself, is the **Chamber of Commerce Visitor Center** (tel: 601-437-4351, open daily) in a house built by the city's founder Samuel Gibson in 1805. Also along Church Street, among the chinaberry trees, are a candy-box selection of church architectural styles, from high Victorian Gothic to Romanesque. Most distinctive of all is the **First Presbyterian Church**, a white, stone, plain, gothic steepled building topped by a huge gold hand, pointing informatively, instructively or as a warning, it's hard to tell. Whichever the message, it points skywards.

Windsor Plantation (tel: 601-437-4351, on route 552, 10 miles (16 km) west of Port Gibson, open dawn–dusk) is well worth a detour. Built in 1861, and held to be the most lavish of Mississippi's Greek Revival expressions, the house was destroyed – not by the advancing Union troops, but by an accident in 1890. All that remains are Doric columns, ironwork and a spectral beauty. Visits near dusk make the most powerful impression.

Just south of Port Gibson, pick up the glorious **Natchez Trace Parkway** (*see pages 245 and 246*) and take it for about 60 meandering miles (100 km) to the town of Jackson. The parkway offers wonderful spots for hiking, walking, picnics, and quiet solitude. Bring your binoculars for spotting unusual birds.

Jackson

Jackson ❹ was named after Major General Andrew Jackson for his distinction in the War of 1812 and the Battle of New Orleans. In 1822, the Mississippi state capital moved here from Natchez to be more central.

Mississippi was fertile ground for the civil rights movement, spawning activists and events of the era. Jackson is where Medgar Evers was murdered in 1963, and each June the town hosts the Medgar Evers Mississippi Homecoming

BELOW:
the haunting,
evocative ruins of
Windsor Plantation.

Map
on page
156

sponsored by B.B. King. Today, Jackson is a clean and green commercial center, humming with pioneers in technology and medical sciences.

The **Old Capitol** (100 South State Street, tel: 601-576-6920, open daily) houses the **State Historical Museum**. The seat of government later moved to the Beaux Arts building, known since 1903 as the **New Capitol** (400 High Street). The **Eudora Welty Public Library** is one block north of the Old Capitol, at the intersection with Yazoo Street, with a reading room featuring many of the amazing number of Mississipian literary luminaries, including William Faulkner and Tennessee Williams.

For blues aficionados, Jackson was something of a hotspot, and nowhere more than at **225 North Farish Street**, the site of the Henry C. Spier's original store. Go one block south on State, right on Amite Street to North Farish, then right again. There's not that much to see now, but the footsteps of Spier's pioneering musical discoveries led here, including Charley Patton, Willie Brown, and legendary singer Son House. Spier's well-tuned ear was not infallible, though; he passed on Jimmie Rodgers, the "father of country music." A few blocks farther north along Farish Street, on the opposite side, is the **Record Mart** (309 North Farish Street) where Lillian McMurry produced Sonny Boy Williamson II and Elmore James, and numerous other blues greats for Trumpet Records in the Diamond Recording Studio in the same building.

Take I-51 north and turn left onto Lakeland Drive for just under a mile to the **Mississippi Museum of Natural Science** (2148 Lakeland Drive, tel: 601-354-7303, open daily), which is on the left. It includes a forest area, a large greenhouse and an aquarium forming a swamp exhibit, housing lazy turtles and snappy alligators.

Go north on I-55 to exit 98, and turn onto Lakeland Drive for the **Mississippi Sports Hall of Fame** (1152 Lakeland Drive, tel: 601-982-8264, closed Sun). The facility has memorabilia from Mississippi's luminaries of track and field, including baseball heroes Dizzy Dean and Charles "Pee Wee" Armstrong. Across the parking lot is the **Jim Buck Ross Agriculture and Forestry Museum** (tel: 601-713-3365, closed Sun) containing living re-creations of life on a mid-18th-century farm and a 1920s town. The museum adjoins the **Chimneyville Crafts Gallery** where native traditional and modern members of the Craftsmen's Guild of Mississippi are showcased.

Elvis slept here

The most pleasant way to reach **Tupelo ❺** is to rejoin the Natchez Trace for the 170-mile (273-km) drive. The airy **Natchez Trace Visitor Center** is in Tupelo at parkway milepost 266 (tel: 800-305-7417, open daily). There are restrooms, camping facilities and hiking trails – real Southern hospitality.

Neat little Tupelo draws more than 100,000 visitors annually to the small shotgun shack at 306 Presley Drive, the **birthplace of Elvis Presley** (open daily). The 30 ft x 15 ft (10 meter x 5 meter) single-story house is restored to the condition it would have been in when the King was, well, a princeling, presumably. With just two square rooms and no indoor

Approximately 30 percent of Mississippi workers are still engaged in agriculture. Although much of this is catfish farming, the state still makes $432 million from cotton.

BELOW:
find out about
Dizzy Dean and
Charles "Pee Wee"
Armstrong here.

MISSISSIPPI
SPORTS HALL OF FAME

Statue of Elvis as a young man in front of the King's modest Tupelo birthplace.

BELOW: Elvis was born here in 1937; in 1957 he bought the house back.

plumbing, it resembles the layout and proportions of the sharecroppers' shacks common in the Delta. The house was built in 1934 by his father Vernon and uncle, Vester, with $180 that Vernon borrowed from a Mr Bean. Elvis was born in the shack on January 8, 1937. Three years later the family were unable to meet the repayments and Bean repossessed the house.

On his way to stardom in 1957, Elvis was playing at a local fair when he spotted the house and bought it back. The property has been maintained since as a kind of shrine, and it certainly conjures the humble beginnings of the first rock 'n' roll megastar. The house is attended by enthusiastic and well-informed guides, and makes for a rewarding visit.

Rather less value, information and courtesy are available from the tiny adjacent **Elvis Museum** although they do keep an appropriately tacky gift shop. At the top of a small hill is a chapel that plays Elvis's spiritual records. The chapel is in great demand for weddings, and needs to be booked months ahead.

Tupelo is also home to the fascinating **Tupelo Automobile Museum** (1 Otis Boulevard, tel: 662-842-4242, closed Mon). Turn left out of the Elvis shrine, then left again onto Otis Boulevard for about half a mile, and the museum is on the right. On a showroom floor the size of an aircraft hangar, more than 100 cars from 1886 to 1994 gleam and luster in row after row. All are in showroom condition with adjacent loudspeakers ready to purr out historical and technical details. A 1959 Edsel Corsair, a salmon pink Chrysler 300 V8 with white wall tires, and Liberace's incredible black Barister Corvette, fitted with gold radiator grille, pipes and candelabra, all crouch in neat, gleaming lines. You'll never be happy with a Honda again.

The **Lyric Theater** (Broadway and Court streets, tel: 601-844 1935,) is an attractive Art Deco auditorium with a candy-colored foyer. Just south of Main Street, on the outside it's a mild-mannered, unassuming **McDonalds** (372 Gloster Street). Inside, it's a temple for the Elvii, with walls lined with framed photographs and memorabilia.

Oxford is just a couple of hours drive west from Tupelo, but first, here is a delightful side trip to a state park in the northern Mississippi hills. Rejoin the Natchez Trace Parkway north to **Tishomingo State Park ❻** (tel: 662-438-6914, Mile marker 304 from the parkway), named for the famed Chickasaw chief.

In the foothills of the Appalachian Mountains, the park is on the National Register of Historic Places, and its 1,530 acres (620 hectares) of unique geology include rock formations dating back to the Paleozoic era, carpeted and canopied by rare ferns and wildflowers in the shade of the ancient woodlands. The park has one of North America's largest white-tail deer populations, as well as many wild turkeys and ducks. Another attraction is the scarce and wonderfully symbolic Bald Eagle, often seen throughout the winter months.

Oxford

From Tupelo, head west for about 50 miles (80 km) into **Oxford ❼**. Nestling in the gentler slopes of northern Mississippi, the town, like its English namesake, has an outstanding university. "Ole Miss," as the famed **University of Mississippi** is known, was chartered in 1844. The first university in the South to accept black students, in October of 1962 the entry of James Meredith was the sparking point for race riots and one of the key moments in the birthing pains of American civil rights.

Among Ole Miss's many garlands of learning, the university has the world's largest archive of blues music in the University Blues Archive. A stroll around the beautiful campus, dorms and faculty houses, with venerable names like *Faulkner*, is just like a walk among cloisters of learning.

Oxford looks and feels like a lovely, elegant, civilized town. The graceful main square is lined with upscale restaurants and shops, including the well-stocked **Square Books**. Just off the square among the antique shops are numerous bars popular with students.

Writers past and present

Befitting a seat of learning, strong literary roots are planted here. William Faulkner, considered by many to be the American founder of the modern novel, made his home behind oak and rowan trees, in **Rowan Oak** (Old Taylor Road). Faulkner extended the white wooden plantation-style house, mostly with his own hands. It is open for public viewing, although hours can be erratic and information hard to come by, but it is lovingly curated by Ole Miss, its present owners. Even if the house itself is closed, the grounds, shaded by huge, cool trees, are enjoyable to stroll around. Rowan Oak recently benefited from substantial renovation, $500,000 being granted by the state of Mississippi.

Oxford has also been home to John Grisham, popular author of *The Firm*, *The Pelican Brief* and *The Client*, successful books mainly set in the South that have

Map on page 156

BELOW: Ole Miss (University of Mississippi) campus in the elegant town of Oxford.

Map on page 156

The University of Mississippi was chartered in 1844.

become successful movies. His is the large yellow house just west of town south of MS 270. West on MS 278 for a little over 20 miles (32 km), then north for about 30 miles (48 km) on I-55 is **Arkabutla Lake**, popular for water sports, hiking, and camping, and a great spot to watch the local quail, wood ducks, and white-tail deer.

Just over 7 miles (11km) north and a left turn off I-55, is the country town of **Hernando ❽**. From the bluff at the west edge of town is a panoramic view of the Mississippi Delta, much as the explorer De Soto first saw in 1542 when he discovered for the Europeans this verdant plain, stretching out as far as the eye could see.

Jerry Lee Lewis

Farther north about 5 miles (8 km) on I-55, in **Nesbit ❾** is the **Jerry Lee Lewis Ranch** (1595 Malone Road, closed Sat, Sun). Signed on the high, white security gates as, "The Killer," over symbols of pianos, the Killer himself is unlikely to make an appearance, but much memorabilia of the singer's work is in evidence here. So, too, are some of his vintage Harley-Davidson motorcycles, his huge swimming pool in the shape of a grand piano, and his favorite dog, a chihuahua called Tapioca.

West of MS 31 and Goodman Road is the **Flower Patch** (5921 Goodman Road, tel: 662-781-2344) in **Horn Lake**, a little flower shop advertising itself as "Elvis' Honeymoon Cottage." This modest white house with black shutters is where the King brought his young bride Priscilla after their Las Vegas wedding in 1967. The shop offers Elvis-themed bouquets in a shrine that draws the Elvii in droves. ❏

The Mississippi

Ole Man River, as Jerome Kern's lyric christened it, has been a way of life for many civilizations, a source of inspiration, and one of North America's main trading arteries. Writing of his days as a Mississippi riverboatman before the Civil War, Mark Twain said, "It is not a commonplace river, but on the contrary is in all ways remarkable." Samuel Clemens chose the pen name of Mark Twain from a mark on the side of a cargo freighter by which its load was measured. He aspired to captain a riverboat because he considered the position to be that of a "king without a keeper." T.S. Eliot was so moved as to call the mighty waterway "a great, brown god."

The first European to set sight on the river was Hernando De Soto, in 1542, when the English Queen Elizabeth was still in her teens, and Michaelangelo's paint was wet on the ceiling of the Sistine Chapel in Rome. Hernando stood high on the land, then called "Quigualtam" by the Indians, where the Mississippi town, Hernando, is named after him *(see page 172)*, and saw spread out the alluvian plain now known as the Mississippi Delta. (An alluvial plain is a valley filled with sand and silts deposited by water runoff). Because of European indifference, and also perhaps De Soto's demise shortly afterwards, it was another 150 years before a white European paid any further attention to the immense river.

Running more than 2,000 miles (3,200 km) from its source at Lake Itasca in Minnesota, the Mississippi empties into the Gulf of Mexico at New Orleans. It is the longest river in North America, and the third longest in the world. At its widest, it spans over a mile, and its waters run 198 ft (60 meters) deep at Baton Rouge. Providing such a massive navigable trade route, the Mississippi was important, not only in the development of the South, but also to the developing United States, and remains so to this day. It carried cotton through the center of the South, and out to the ocean for export. Its ability to provide the same function for the industrial towns of the North made it a major objective for Lincoln in the Civil War, perhaps even an objective for the war itself.

In the 19th century, paddle steamers were packed outside and in with bales of cotton, and stacked to the gunnels with passengers. As romanticized by countless western tales, they also served as floating casinos, far adrift from tiresome laws and lawmen on land. In the 1990s, riverboat gambling returned to the muddy waters, with static casino boats from Saint Louis to New Orleans.

The battle for control of the Mississippi didn't end in the 19th century; in the 1930s, when Louisiana governor Huey Long oversaw a new bridge at Baton Rouge, it is said that he ensured its span was too low for ocean-going vessels to pass under, compelling freighters to dock in Louisiana.

Great trains of barges still slip through the mist and below the wide spans of box-girder bridges, floating cargo between Missouri and New Orleans, and the Mississippi is still, from any glance, a river of dreams. ❑

RIGHT: the *American Queen* runs excursions along the Mississippi.

MISSISSIPPI BLUES TOUR

*The Delta spreads from the lobby of the Peabody Hotel
in Memphis to Catfish Row in Vicksburg. In between,
in these fertile cotton fields, the blues were born*

Map
on page
156

US Highway 61 – the Blue Highway – runs North to South right through the Mississippi Delta, and was immortalized in the title of Bob Dylan's album *Highway 61 Revisited*. As well as connecting much of Mississippi, the road took players from the Delta to the riches of Memphis. State Highways 61 and 49 were the tracks of trade for Delta musicians in the first half of the 20th century, linking most of the major music venues, and where 61 crosses Highway 49 in Clarksdale is a large crossroads sign, with three blue guitars. Clarksdale is the hub of the Delta blues – when the blues was bursting out, it was said that "if you could make it in Clarksdale, you could make it in Memphis or Chicago."

Muddy Waters to Greenville

North of Vicksburg on Highway 61 where it intersects with Highway 1, a sign may appear at the roadside saying, "Rolling Fork, home of McKinley (Muddy Waters) Morganfield." Or it may not, folks are apt to poach them. Muddy Waters was born in **Rolling Fork** ⑩ on April 14, 1915, as a memorial on the south side of the **Courthouse Square** attests. Father of the Chicago electric blues style, Muddy learned to play around Stovall, Mississippi, where he was sent to live with his grandmother at an early age, and in nearby Clarksdale. On the first Saturday in May in Courthouse Square is the **Deep Delta Festival** (tel: 888-494-8582).

Head north on Highway 61, and turn left on Highway 82 to **Greenville** ⑪, the largest city in the Delta. Greenville plays host to the biggest and oldest festival, the Mississippi Delta Blues Festival, each September. The first stop should be at the intersection of Highway 82 and Reed Road. The intersection is easy to spot, as it has a pristine replica of a stern-wheel riverboat. This is the **River Road Queen Welcome Center** (tel: 662-332-2378). The interior maintains the theme, and the upper floor houses a Mississippi river road exhibit.

Like much of the state, Greenville has deep literary traditions, to which the **Greenville Writers Exhibit** pays tribute in the library (341 Main Street). Main Street dead-ends at the **Mississippi Levee**. Completed in 1912, this was an engineering feat taller and longer than the Great Wall of China.

The Nelson Street area is probably as close an evocation as there is to the 1920s atmosphere of Memphis's Beale Street. There are bars with bands, singers and records, and people hustling through the night. Plus juke, or "jook" joints, simple rooms with space for dancing and the place to hear the most authentic music (the word "jook" is thought to be a contraction of "juice," with something of a sexual context.) Ike and Tina Turner played at **Perry's Flowing Fountain**, also thought to be the original *Anna Mae's Café*

LEFT AND BELOW:
Highway 61, the
best blues tour
in the world.

from the 1985 Little Milton song. (Nelson) aficionados rate this among the top juke joints. Juke streets are often worked by drug dealers and pimps, catering to a mostly white clientele; politely declining offers of trade will usually suffice. Nelson Street's **Doe's Eat Place** has porterhouse steak described by *Men's Journal* as "the best thing to eat in America." At the opposite end of the dining scale is **Bud's Cafe** on Old Leland Road, off Highway 1 north of Highway 82. Real soul food at real soul prices, it's got a gem of a jukebox.

On the way to Indianola, back on Highway 82, the town of **Leland ⑫** has **three murals** depicting some of the local blues greats. Johnny Winter and his brother Edgar were both born here, and their father was once the mayor. They feature with Jimmie Reed and many others on the painting at Main Street and 4th. A block along at Main Street and 3rd is a brash, graphic mural honoring five decades of B.B. King's blues testimony. Leland also honors local animator Jim Henson with much Muppet memorabilia in the **Birthplace of the Frog** (South Deer Creek Drive, tel: 662-686-2687).

BELOW: if Robert Johnson really did sell his soul at a crossroads in Clarksdale, it was likely to be this one, about half a mile west of the current, glossy crossroads sign photographed by most tourists.

Mississippi mojo

Head east on Highway 82 to **Indianola ⑬**. Albert King was born here on April 25, 1923, and B.B. King (no relation) was born just outside it on September 16, 1925. Riley (Blues Boy) King, as he was known in the early days, or "the Beale Street Blues Boy,'" transformed the electric blues with guitar, bass, drums and piano or mouthorgan, into a massive traveling revue, later known as the B.B. King Orchestra. B.B. plays a free outdoor concert in **B.B. King Park** on Roosevelt Street, plus a paying gig at **Club Ebony** (404 Hannah Street, tel: 662-887-9915), every year. Indianola was also where Charley Patton died on April 28,

CROSSROADS

Robert Johnson was taking a little time to build a reputation as a bluesman – a good one, anyway. He was playing on Dockery Plantation one night when Charley Patton told him to "Quit that noise before all the peoples leave." Son House held a similarly meager opinon of Johnson's efforts.

It all changed one night in Stovall, north of Clarksdale, when Johnson played in front of House and Willie Brown. Son House said later, "When he finished, all our mouths were standing open. I said, 'Well, ain't that fast. Man, he's gone now'."

House is believed to have started the rumor that Johnson acquired his astonishing prowess in a deal struck with the Devil. It was thought that the Devil could be met, and would be available for bargaining, if a player took his guitar to a crossroads at midnight and began to pick the strings. The Devil would appear in the form of a black man, take the instrument and tune it. Fluid licks of unheard splendor would then drip from the player's fingers, in exchange for the ownership of his soul.

The publishers of this book in no way advocate any form of dealing with Satan, as he is well-known to be untrustworthy. Tuning, however, can be a help.

1934, and his grave can be seen in the New Jerusalem Church in **Holly Ridge**. Like so many bluesmen, Patton's grave went unmarked for some time, the marker provided by his record company having been purloined. The present headstone was furnished with help from musician John Fogerty.

The area around **Greenwood** offers no fewer than three graves for Robert Johnson *(see panel on facing page)*, two at Morgan City, and in Quito south of Highway 82. Past Ita Bena, fittingly between Quito and Morgan City where his two gravestones are, is a **Robert Johnson Monument**.

The third grave is a few miles north of Greenwood at Little Zion Church. The neat white church has no sign, but an address marker reading 63530. Unlike the other two, the grave here is unmarked, in keeping with most of the Johnson lore. This is, however, the site credited by blues scholars including John Hammond, Steve LaVere, and Steve Cheseborough. The (free) **Blues Heritage Museum and Gallery** (closed Mon), is dedicated to the elusive musician.

The first blues heard by W.C. Handy was the spot "where the Southern Cross the Dog," and **Moorhead** is where that is. The Southern and the Dog are, or were, the railway lines that made a perfectly perpendicular intersection. Tutwiler station was where he was snoozing when the Clarksdale train was nine hours late. He was awoken by "a lean, loose-jointed negro" singing *Where the Southern Cross the Dog* and playing a guitar with a slide, a sound he described as "the weirdest music I had ever heard." Handy researched and developed the sound, becoming known as the Father of the Blues. The Tutwiler Arts Project has commissioned a number of **blues murals,** and the **commemorative plaque** at the station gives the date of Handy's meeting as 1895, but the event is well documented as having been in 1903. Be sure to stop by the **Yellow Dog Café**. If it's on the menu, order catfish; this one-street town is enriched by catfish farming in the surrounding lakes.

Just outside Tutwiler, by the foundation stones of the Whitfield M.B. church, is the marker that Lillian McMurray of Trumpet Records in Jackson *(see page 169)* erected for **Sonny Boy Williamson's grave**.

Rosedale evokes the Robert Johnson line "Going Down to Rosedale/Take my rider by my side," which the rock group Cream appropriated into the song *Crossroads*; nearby **Beulah** was the location for the crossroads in the 1986 movie of the same name. As a tribute, Rosedale is starting to develop a **Crossroads Blues Festival** (tel: 662-759-6800).

Take MS 8 to **Dockery Plantation,** 25 miles (40 km) away. Charley Patton lived and worked here, as did Pops Staples, patriarch of the Staples Singers. Sometimes known as the "King of the Delta Blues" and certainly one of the early innovators, Patton was a source of inspiration to Howlin' Wolf, Son House, and John Lee Hooker. This is where he told Robert Johnson to "quit that noise before all the peoples leave."

Clarksdale

In early August, the **Clarksdale Sunflower Festival** is in distinguished company by featuring Mississippi musicians playing authentic Delta blues. Slide guitars, mouthharps and thumping rhythm sections drive the beats, and gravelly throats still wail the good-time

Map on page 156

Muddy Waters with Les Paul Gold top, exhibit in the Delta Blues Museum.

BELOW: merchandise bought here benefits the museum.

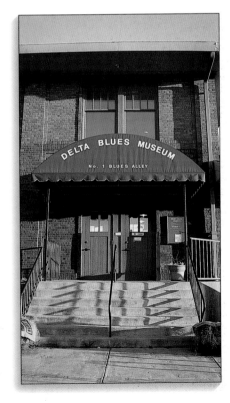

BELOW: the Riverside Hotel, where Bessie Smith died in 1937.

songs in juke joints and bars all year round. As well as being the home of the blues, **Clarksdale** 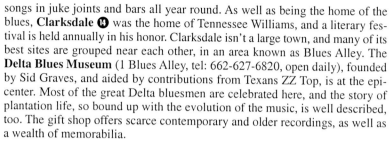 was the home of Tennessee Williams, and a literary festival is held annually in his honor. Clarksdale isn't a large town, and many of its best sites are grouped near each other, in an area known as Blues Alley. The **Delta Blues Museum** (1 Blues Alley, tel: 662-627-6820, open daily), founded by Sid Graves, and aided by contributions from Texans ZZ Top, is at the epicenter. Most of the great Delta bluesmen are celebrated here, and the story of plantation life, so bound up with the evolution of the music, is well described, too. The gift shop offers scarce contemporary and older recordings, as well as a wealth of memorabilia.

The actor Morgan Freeman, a local resident, operates two establishments in Clarksdale. One is the relaxed, bare-wood furnished club, **Ground Zero**, which features local as well as traveling acts. The other is the upscale **Madidi** restaurant, offering French cuisine; reservations are recommended (tel: 662-627-7770). Freeman is often to be seen at both venues.

The **Delta Amusement & Cafe**, across the street from Ground Zero, is excellent for diner-style Southern cooking. **Cathead Delta Blues Arts** on Delta Avenue promotes Mississippi, and particularly Delta artists of all kinds; paintings, photography, recordings and sculptures display much of the creativity of the area. Just a block away on Sunflower, good food is to be had – often with live music – at **Sarah's Kitchen**. Nearby, **Stackhouse Records** still occupies the building resembling a riverboat. The Rooster record label has decamped, alas, but still a huge selection of vinyl and CDs are available, along with rare posters, in this atmospheric store.

Wade Walton's Barbershop on Issaquena Avenue was where W.C. Handy,

Sonny Boy Williamson and John Lee Hooker got their hair cut and swapped tales and licks. Farther along the same road, a plaque marks the location of **W.C. Handy's home**. Across the street is the **Greyhound station** that was the starting point for many bluesmen's journeys to Memphis and Chicago. The original location of the local radio station **WROX** (257 Delta Avenue) was where Early Wright became Mississippi's first black DJ in 1947. Ike Turner started as a janitor and was later a DJ at WROX. The station still broadcasts on 1450 AM.

Just across the railroad tracks is the New World District, where numerous jukes such as **Smitty's Red Top Lounge** and **Margaret's Blue Diamond Lounge** operate. This, being the "wrong side of the tracks," is where visitors are apt to be advised not to go, but good manners and discretion should be an adequate guide. Just across the tracks (under the bridge, in fact), a block along and a block to the left, is where old Highway 61 crossed with old Highway 49. If there was a Robert Johnson crossroads, and if it was in Clarksdale (both unlikely), this is where it would have been.

The **Riverside Hotel** (615 Sunflower Avenue, tel: 601-624-9163) is rich in blues history. The local black hospital was in the right-hand side of the building, and when Bessie Smith met with a ghastly automobile accident in 1937, it was here that she was brought, and later died. Ike Turner claims to have resided in every room in the hotel. John F Kennedy, Jr also stayed here when hiding from the press. **Abe's Bar-B-Q** is a popular pork joint, just below the three blue guitars of the modern, much photographed but inaccurate **Crossroads sign**.

On the **Hopson Plantation** (tel: 662-624-8329) was America's first mechanized planting, picking and baling operation, and the Commissary is now a great place for a late drink or two, often with impromptu music supplied by guests from **Hopson's B&B (Bed & Beer) Shack Up Inn**. The inn offers unique accommodation in restored sharecropper cabins, complete with air-conditioning, and a couple of shacks even have pianos. If you want to meet musicians, this is the place to stay. To reach Hopson's from the Delta Blues Museum, take Sunflower Avenue and turn left onto US 61, then travel south onto US 49 a couple of miles until you see the sign.

Tunica and Robinsonville

US 61 leads to the town of **Tunica** ⓯. In 1992, there were 20 hotel rooms in Tunica County. Little over a decade later there were more than 6,000, such is the impact of legalized gambling. Tunica's **Blue and White Café** has been serving authentic Mississippi cooking since 1937; Elvis was a regular, as are ZZ Top and other fans of turnip greens, grits, and red-eye gravy. The café is by the corner of US 61 and MS 4 and open from 5am. **Robinsonville** ⓰ is little more than a strip of casinos just north of Tunica, but the **Horseshoe** has an interesting **Blues and Legends Hall of Fame** museum, and a concert venue called **Bluesville**. Although it hosts mostly big-draw mainstream acts, Bluesville does run an annual blues festival (tel: 870-338-5301) to benefit the Sonny Boy Blues Society in Helena, Arkansas. ❑

Map on page 156

BELOW: Hopson's B&B (Bed & Beer) Shack Up Inn.

THE GULF COAST

A silver thread meandering along the Florida Panhandle, Alabama and Mississippi, the Gulf Coast is the sunshine playground of the South

his magical silver strip of America's southern Gulf shore stretches from Florida through Alabama and Mississippi, all the way to Louisiana. Soft sea breezes caress the palms and grasses, long spits of sugar-white sands slip gently into the bright emerald waters of the Gulf of Mexico and the network of bays and lagoons that form the Intracoastal Waterway.

These sunshine playgrounds of the South hide from invading Yankees behind the discouraging nickname of "the Redneck Riviera." Although cowboy hats and beery country & western bars are not too hard to find in the popular resorts of Florida's Pensacola Beach and Destin, there are also beautiful quiet spots like Navarre Beach, as well as fabulous nature reserves in the Gulf Islands National Seashore. The 160 miles (257 km) of barrier islands from Santa Rosa Island, Florida, to Cat Island in Mississippi fall under the administration of the National Parks Service. These represent only 20 percent of the reserve, the other 80 percent being underwater. They provide campgrounds, nature trails, picnic and hiking areas, and also maintain several Civil War forts.

For the more cultivated and formal expressions of nature, the subtropical splendor of Bellingrath Gardens is almost unrivaled. More modern man-made recreation, especially of the adult-oriented kind, is taken to its extremes in the mini-Las Vegas neon nirvanas of Biloxi and Gulfport in Mississippi. The gaming rooms and lavish shows glitter and sizzle in front of the seaside backdrop.

Southern hospitality is particularly fine in the B&Bs of Mississippi and Alabama, welcomes in Florida are warm, and the accents of Southern cooking are at their very best with the wealth of fresh fish and seafood generously provided by the Gulf. As Bobby Mahoney, proprietor of Mary Mahoney's Old French House in Biloxi, Mississippi, said, "How can you explain the incredible amount of crawfish and lobster coming out of the muddy waters round here? There's a lot of loving going on in the dark of that mud."

Florida Panhandle

The 24-mile (37-km) spits of soft sand along I-98 from Carillon Beach to Okaloosa Island are collectively known as the Emerald Coast, or **Fort Walton Beaches**. There are beaches on both sides of the strip; on the north facing into tranquil Choctawatchee Bay, and looking south into the Gulf of Mexico.

Beginning the continuous dash of white sands that sweeps all the way to Pensacola is **Panama City Beach ❶**. Lining the seafront Miracle Mile, Panama City Beach is a family resort, the Redneck Riviera in full cry. Desolate like a ghost town in the winter chill, when the summer sun warms up, the bars twang with both kinds of music; country *and* western. Thrill rides

PRECEDING PAGES: Bay St Louis, Mississippi. **LEFT:** Navarre Beach, Florida. **BELOW:** landmark of Pensacola Beach.

clatter by the miniature golf courses, and the paraphernalia of beach vacations like boat trips and jet-skis dart through the salt spray, the aroma of fried crawfish wafting on the air. Panama City Beach is also known for golf, voted third best "Little Golf Town in the US" by *Golf Digest*. Try **Lagoon Legend** (tel: 850-235-6397) and **Club Meadows** (tel: 850-253-6950), or the **Hombre Golf Club** (tel: 850-234-3673), which hosts PGA qualifying schools.

Seaside

All-U-Can-Eat plate lunches and po-boy sandwiches here.

About 44 miles (71 km) west on the coastal highway is the town of **Seaside**, a remarkably, almost eerily pretty, meticulously planned community, a pioneer of what it calls "the new urbanism." J.S. Smolian bought 80 acres (32 hectares) of land on a family holiday near Seagrove in 1946, but it was his grandson, Robert Davis, who dreamed up this little fantasy land. Bike rentals are available from **The Seaside Bike Shop** in Central Square (tel: 850-231-2314), where there are numerous cute eateries, and **Cabana Man** in George's Gorge (tel: 850-231-5046) rents beach chairs, umbrellas, kayaks, and other beachy needs. A short way up the coast, **Grayton** is like a less planned version of Seaside; a little less kempt, a little more lived in. Trees overhang the small road, driveways are blown across with unbelievably white sand. On **Grayton Beach**, vegetarians particularly follow the neon to Pandora's Café. Adjacent to the beach is a state park with cabins to rent (tel: 800-326-3521 for reservations).

Back on I-98, about 26 miles (42 km) of soft, silvery white sand and deep green sea passes **Santa Rosa Beach**, a quiet, attractive little seafront town, to **Silver Sands Factory Stores**, which claims to be the US's largest concentration of designer outlets, with dozens of stellar names from Mallville.

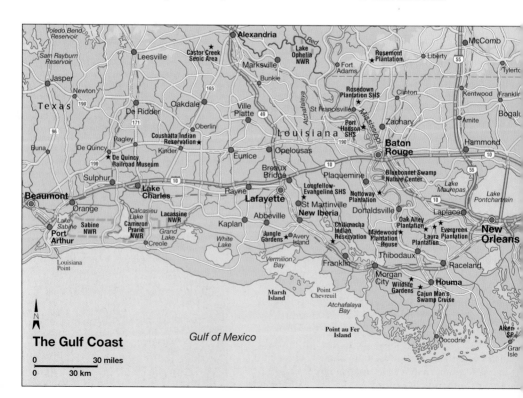

The Gulf Coast

Another 8 miles (13 km) farther on is the town of **Destin ❷**. Offering an up-market version of the beach resort, Destin has large hotels, golf courses, and beach-town shops that proffer everything from beach-wear and scuba kits to yachts. The nearby Eglin Air Force Base and test site is the world's largest, and Destin provides opportunities for the crew's recreation.

The busy but pretty marina gives harbor to well-maintained catamarans and fishing boats, and fishing is popular among tourists and off-duty Eglin jet-jockeys alike. Visitors who are not Florida residents require a license for fresh-water and seawater fishing, and they are available for three days, seven days or annually. Call 850-265-3676 for freshwater, or 850-595-8978 for sea fishing. Deep sea fishing trips are available from *Destin Princess* (tel: 850-837-5088) and Moody's Deep-Sea Fishing (tel: 850-837-1293). One of the local jet-jock-eys said, "If you want to know about the weather, just ask a pilot or a fisherman. What they get in Mobile today, we're going to eat tomorrow."

Turn inland, left, off I-98 at Benning Drive for the huge **Gulfarium** (1010 Miracle Strip Parkway, tel: 850-243-9046, open daily) which has sea-life shows with dolphins, seals, sharks, moray eels, stingrays and other water-dwellers.

Rejoin the Miracle Strip Parkway (I-98) to the right and cross over the tall bridge. The hump in the middle allows sailboats out to the Okaloosa Expanse, and gives excellent views. A few miles farther along, I-98 crosses the Intra-coastal Waterway inland to **Fort Walton Beach**.

In a shady garden off Highway 98 and built around a 223 by 178 ft (68 by 54 meter) temple mound is the interesting **Indian Temple Mound Museum** (139 Miracle Strip Parkway, tel: 850-833-9595, closed Sun, Mon). The mound itself was raised by Indians between AD 800 and 1400, and is the only surviving

Map on pages 184–85

The Emerald Coast of Florida has silver sands and clear green water.

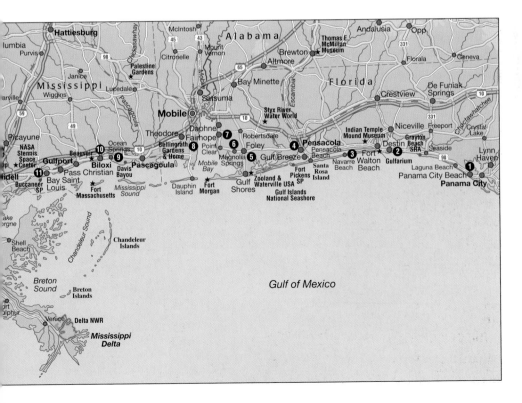

mound on the Gulf Coast. Indian technology, crafts, and artifacts are displayed with hands-on exhibits that kids love.

After Fort Walton Beach, I-98 continues on the north side of Santa Rosa Sound until Navarre, where a left turn will cross the sound again to **Navarre Beach ❸**. A few high-rise condos are beginning to huddle at each end of this otherwise unspoiled spot. Still popular with pelicans, and hardly more than a quarter of a mile long, Navarre Beach is quiet, slow, and laid-back. One diner said of the key lime pie at **Sailor's Grill**, "I swear, this is the best. So good it's sinful." Visitors to the grill are some connoisseurs of key lime pie. From here, the barrier island gets even slimmer – with the sugar-white sands of both coasts making for a pleasant drive – and buildings become more sparse. A few miles along is a picnic area with spots for swimming, and a park ranger's station. Sea oats and grasses fan the dunes, and sea birds skim the water.

Fort Pickens

Pensacola Beach claims the longest pier on the Gulf Coast at 1471 ft (448 meters). There's fishing off the pier for snapper and redfish. The more popular chain hotels like Ramada and Comfort Inn are well represented.

Reached through **Fort Pickens State Park**, a 6½-mile (11-km) spit of white sand with the Gulf close by on either side, is Fort Pickens. A museum describes the part that the fort played holding Mobile Bay for the Union during the Civil War. This area of national park land has campgrounds and endless space for picnics or beach relaxation, hiking, and birdwatching. Returning from Fort Pickens, turn left and cross the toll bridge at Navarre Beach to **Gulf Breeze**. To the left are beach and fishing areas, and, to the right on I-98, the **Naval Live Oaks**

BELOW: Blue Angels exhibit at the National Museum of Naval Aviation, Pensacola.

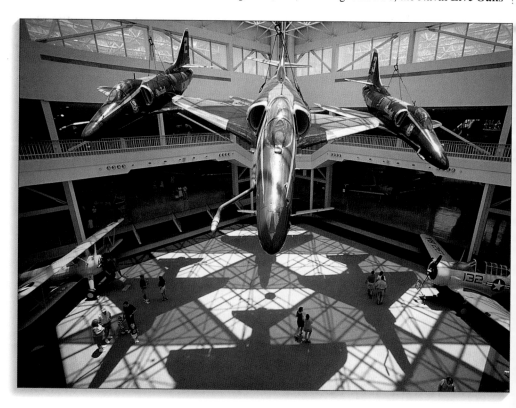

park headquarters. The visitor center presents exhibits celebrating the distinctive live oak, so much a feature of the Southern states, and is the starting point for some of the hiking trails through the magical 1,378-acre (558-hectare) wooded park area. Among the woods are trails and remnants from the Indian cultures that resided here for at least 10,000 years.

Map on pages 184–85

Pensacola

Immediately over the spectacular 3-mile (5-km) bridge to **Pensacola ❹**, and immediately off to the right, the **Visitor Center** (open daily) is well-stocked with information on accommodation and local attractions, as well as the rich history of this significant Southern coastal city. Internet access is available, too. The surrounding area is good for picnics, with fine views of Pensacola Bay.

Pensacola's main historic districts – Palafox, Seville, and the North Hill Preservation district – offer numerous examples of Southern architectural and cultural influence, from modest colonial homes to mansions with wrought-iron filigree, as well as many museums.

From the visitor center, take the Bayfront Parkway and turn right on Adams Street to the large green square, and the handsome **Old Christ Church**, a white wooden church with brown shutters, high, arched windows, and stained glass at the rear. This is the heart of the **Seville Historic District**, the oldest part of Pensacola. Historic house museums are dotted along **Government, Church**, and **Zaragosa streets**. The town's administration passed between states no fewer than 17 times in 300 years of history, as celebrated in the annual Fiesta of Five Flags around **Seville Square**.

The **Palafox Historic District** congregates around Palafox Street and Plaza

BELOW: white sands and solitude on the Azalea Coast, Alabama.

Ferdinand. At one end of the tranquil plaza is a fountain, at the other, a bust of General Andrew Jackson to mark his receiving West Florida from Spain in 1817. The castellated honey-brick **TT Wentworth Jr Museum** fronts the square with neoclassical detail. At Palafox and Romana is the **Civil War Soldier's Museum**. Farther along Palafox, the **North Hill Preservation District** has more than 400 private historic homes, and a fascinating mix of architecture.

One of the world's finest collections of aircraft is kept at the **National Museum of Naval Aviation** (tel: 850-453-2389) on Blue Angel Parkway. This passes **Fort Barrancas**, first established by the British in 1763 and now operated as a museum as part of the National Seashore.

With 32 miles (51 km) of white sand coastline between Mobile Bay and Perdido Bay, and the Gulf of Mexico on the south shore, the creation of the Intracoastal Waterway in 1933 made **Gulf Shores** into an island. To reach **Perdido Key** on the island, follow SR 282 for about 9½ miles (15 km). "Pleasure Islands" as the Key is now branded, offers the usual Redneck Riviera resort diversions, alongside the outdoor beauty of Gulf Islands National Seashore, excellent for deep-sea fishers and golfers.

Alabama coast

Continue on the coastal highway across the border into Alabama. Here the island communities of **Orange Beach** and **Gulf Shores** have fabulous broad stretches of sugar-white sand, backed by low-key resorts with pleasant hotels, beach houses, and great restaurants. Alternatively, take I-98 for about 20 miles (32 km) to where the cute, old-style appearance of the town of **Foley** ❺ belies a little shopper's mecca. Antique stores abound, as well as the **Riviera Center Factory Stores** (2601 South McKenzie Street, tel: 251-943-8888) which houses scores of outlet stores from American Outpost and Banana Republic to Zales.

BELOW: Magnolia Springs has the last water-borne mail delivery in the US.

Magnolia Springs ❻ has the last water-borne mail delivery in the US, which gives a clue to the nature of this quiet community. The pace is unhurried, manners are gentle and old-fashioned, and it is a lovely base from which to explore the beautiful Azalea Coast.

Home and birthplace to a number of authors including Winston Groom who wrote *Forrest Gump*, Fannie Flagg, author of *Fried Green Tomatoes*, a community of writers and artists is thriving and growing in the shade of the live oaks.

One block left of where Highway 49 crosses I-98 is **Magnificent Magnolia** (tel: 251-965-6232), an art gallery that stimulates the muses of the locality, providing a nurturing retreat for writers and artists. In **Jesse's Restaurant** (14770 Oak Street, tel: 251-965-3826) try a pecan-encrusted catfish Caesar salad or the excellent whiskey steak. David Worthington at **The Magnolia Inn** (14469 Oak Street, tel: 800-965-7321) offers Southern B&B hospitality as gracefully as anyone could hope for, in a home that is on the National Register of Historic Places.

At the north edge of town, on the right of I-98, the **Inspiration Oak** is the oldest oak in Alabama, but its fate is imperilled since it got caught up in local social-political crossfire.

Continue on I-98 and turn left onto Alternate-98 along the lovely wooded coastline of Mobile Bay to **Punta Clara** – also known by the English translation, "Point Clear." On the left is the **Punta Clara Kitchen** (tel: 251-928-8477). A lovely candy-colored deck with a swinging sofa wraps around the rooms of cutesy antiques, from glasses to furniture, packed like *The Old Curiosity Shop*. The Candy Kitchen sells jams, local honey, fudge, peanut-butter crunch – lots of old-style American favorite treats, and novelty candies like blue crabs – that you can watch being made. Behind the Punta Clara Kitchen, the **Wash House Restaurant** serves crab cakes, swamp quail appetisers, tuna, snapper and steak entrées with Southern accents, on white linen settings with silver cutlery.

A short way farther on Alternate-98 is the Marriott **Grand Hotel**. Despite the ravages of fire and hurricanes, a Grand Hotel has stood here since the Civil War, when it was used as a hospital for Confederates wounded at Vicksburg.

North about 2½ miles (4 km), **Fairhope ❼** is a little nest of prim, often pretty streets, with pastel facades. Litter bins have white wooden surrounds topped with flowers, and antique parlors sell vintage linen. Art galleries and bookstores abound. The sleepy residential community rolls down a steep bluff, with Creole-style cottages overlooking the bay. Nice walks by the sparkling bay meander through palms and live oak trees. Wooden piers jut in a line into the water. The bay communities celebrate Mardi Gras with parades and floats, and Fairhope sprinkles a little visual class along the processions of floats with lights in the trees, giving the town the look of a magical fairy-palace when glimpsed from the Scenic I-98 after dark.

Take the Scenic-98 north anyway. The views of Mobile Bay are easily worth the detour. About 5 miles (9 km) along, **Daphne** seems like a one-street town,

Map on pages 184–85

TIP

Many people insist the best bar in Mobile Bay, if not the entire South, is Judge Roy Bean's in the town of Daphne, famed for its Thursday night crawfish feasts.

BELOW:
Bellingrath Gardens, Alabama, grows 200 varieties of azaleas.

more workaday than Fairhope, but the highway is shaded by trees, and there are also a good number of eateries, handy in Mardi Gras season when Fairhope is mobbed. Off the highway to the west are a beach, little shops, and **Judge Roy Bean's** (508 Main Street, tel: 251-990-3663), famed for its Thursday night crawfish feast, and hailed as one of the finest bars in the South. Go back on I-98 for about 4 miles (7 km) and make a right turn on I-90 to **Malbis** to see a stunning Greek Orthodox replica of a Byzantine Athenean church (28300 Highway 27, tel: 251-626-6739, open daily). Then return along I-90 and join I-10 across the bay, past Mobile *(see page 151).*

Bellingrath Gardens and Home ❽ (tel: 800-247-8420, open daily) is one of the Deep South's most beautiful gardens and more than worth the 20-mile (32-km) excursion south to Theodore. Take I-10 west to exit 15-A and follow the signs to turn south on Bellingrath Road. Bring comfortable walking shoes, buy plenty of film, and plan to stay two to three hours. The flowers are best photographed in early morning or late afternoon.

When you leave the reception area, visit the Rose Garden and the Oriental area with teahouses and bright red bridges over a tranquil lake. Follow the path to Mirror Lake. The view across the lake toward the home is one of the most photographed. Bellingrath Gardens is legendary for the 200 varieties of 250,000 azalea shrubs, 90,000 daffodils, countless tulips, and dogwood trees that bloom in the spring. Thousands of rosebushes fill the grounds with color into winter. Some 70,000 chrysanthemums provide a blaze of color in the fall. Yellow, white, bronze, red and pink mums cascade over the sides of bridges, walls and planters and from the balconies of the home.

The tour of the 15-room home the Bellingraths built in 1937 is well worth the additional time to see their collection of Persian rugs, silver, and furniture. The Chippendale dining table and chairs once belonged to Sir Thomas Lipton, the English shipping magnate.

Mississippi coast

Off to the left on I-90, just before Ocean Springs, is the park entrance for the **Davis Bayou.** Follow Park Road about 4 miles (7 km) to the attractive and spacious visitor center. As well as information about camping, hiking and biking trails, birdwatching and boating on the bayou, the center has a lovely exhibition of wildlife paintings from local artist Walter Anderson.

Take I-90 another few miles to **Ocean Springs** ❾. Just a short bridge away from the extravagant pleasure palaces of Biloxi, Ocean Springs is a quiet, relaxed and beautiful bayside home to an artistic and boating community. The atmosphere and desirable homes make it popular as a residence for the casino staff from the brash bay-front neighbor.

Start from the far end of town at the **Ocean Springs Visitor Center**, prettily housed in the old railroad station and adorned outside with intriguing sculptures. The **Walter Anderson Museum of Art** (510 Washington Ave, tel: 601-872-3164, open daily) showcases Anderson's prolific artistic passions, by turns naive, psychedelic and beautiful. Much of this reclusive artist's work was discovered only after his demise.

BELOW: the pretty Biloxi lighthouse sits in the middle of the road.

Biloxi

Along the **Biloxi** ❿ shoreline, a long stretch of mega-casinos, smaller versions of the Las Vegas hotel resorts, lean back on their pontoons, extending a willing and eager welcome. Among the bay-front casinos, **Casino Magic** is a class act. The barkeepers at the elegant lounge by the casino entrance shake up superb top-shelf cocktails, and the Margueritas are particularly fine. Several mini-suites have large Jacuzzis in the rooms. The gaming rooms are pitched squarely at the value end of the market, offering friendly bar areas and competitive odds.

Beau Rivage is a sister hotel to Steve Wynn's spectacular Las Vegas creation, Bellagio. There are glitters of similarity, and Beau Rivage doesn't want for luxurious appointments. The walls are hung with works of art, the spa and health center are beautifully designed and equipped, and the Coast Brewing Company bar has Thursday night parties that even the locals cram in for.

In Biloxi's **Historic District**, called Vieux Marché (so near to Louisiana, a smattering of French is not uncommon) is a charming antiques market. Although known as 'The Mad Potter of Biloxi" in his lifetime, George Ohr's ceramics have been much admired by luminaries of the art world, including Andy Warhol. He is now known as "America's most innovative potter." A museum dedicated to his work and that of painter Georgia O'Keeffe is in progress, designed by no less an architect than Frank Gehry, the sculptural innovator of Guggenheim museums in New York and Bilbao. The present **Ohr-O'Keeffe Museum** is at 136 GE Ohr Street (tel: 228-374-5547, closed Sun).

Spanish Trail Books is remarkable for appearing in one of the books regularly featured on its shelves; a scene in John Grisham's *The Runaway Jury* takes place around the iron spiral staircase. Books range from Charles Dickens to

Biloxi extends a friendly welcome to visitors with time on their hands or money in their pockets.

BELOW: where Mississippi dreams are made or lost.

Map
on pages
184–85

Danielle Steele, Hammet to Updike and Simenon to Star Wars. Rare, antiquarian and plain old musty second-hand titles pack the shelves, along with vintage postcards, photographs and other publishing rarities. Outside, a pretty courtyard offers a perfect spot for coffee.

Farther along Vieux Marché, the 1954 Taylor Building and its lovely neighbor, the Kreb Building, are an attractive pairing of Art Deco and Art Nouveau.

The pretty **Biloxi Lighthouse** is unusual for standing in the middle of a major road. There are restrooms at the foot of the lighthouse.

Beauvoir

A graceful and charming raised single-story antebellum home, with a presidential library in a more federal style, **Beauvoir** is set back from the road and faces the sandy beach of the Gulf shore. This is the home of Jefferson Davis, referred to as the first president of the Confederacy, signaling that there may remain fond hopes for another.

Tours are about every 20 minutes, and waiting is on the gracious porch with half-a-dozen Southern-style rocking chairs. A small Museum of the Confederacy (open daily) features memorabilia like cannon, muskets, and uniforms. There are pictures from Davis's funeral featuring the horse-drawn hearse draped in black, with crossed rifles guarding the casket.

BELOW: interior of Beauvoir, Jefferson Davis's home.
RIGHT: sunset in the New South.

West along I-10, the unusual sight of cranes and silos on the gulf shows that **Gulfport** is a working town. Opportunities for recreation are available from a number of water-front casinos, and relaxed dining at the attractive **Long Beach Lookout** restaurant – sitting on stilts overlooking the marina – can provide consolation after a stint at the gaming tables.

The houses along the coast begin to stand taller and flex a little wider around **Pass Christian**; they settle back behind decorative gates and neat lawns. The comfy residences are set back from the road by a meridian of greenery and live oak trees. A large, elegant and modern Catholic church with exposed bells adjoins the **Inn at the Pass**. Follow I-90 and turn off after the long bridge to **Bay Saint Louis ⑪**, where the calm water turns silver. There are cute shoppes and a gorgeous **Amtrak station** in palm-shaded grounds. Houses are braced to the elements with frilly white latticework and large screened porches, many of the newer houses are raised on stilts. The **Buccaneer State Park** has a campground near the water, in a wonderful wooded setting.

Leave I-10 at Exit 2 for the **John C. Stennis Space Center** (a photo ID is required to tour the facility). This massive site is where the main engines for the space shuttle are tested. A lunar module stands on stilts by the welcome center, and inside is a scale model of the space shuttle on a complete booster pack. Nearby are picnic grounds in a pretty wooded area. Shuttle buses leave every 15 minutes for the narrated tours of Stennis, which take in the huge acoustical buffer zone to America's largest rocket test complex. There are many fascinating exhibits, including a scale model of a complete *Saturn 5–Apollo* rocket stack, as well as some real rocket engines. ❑

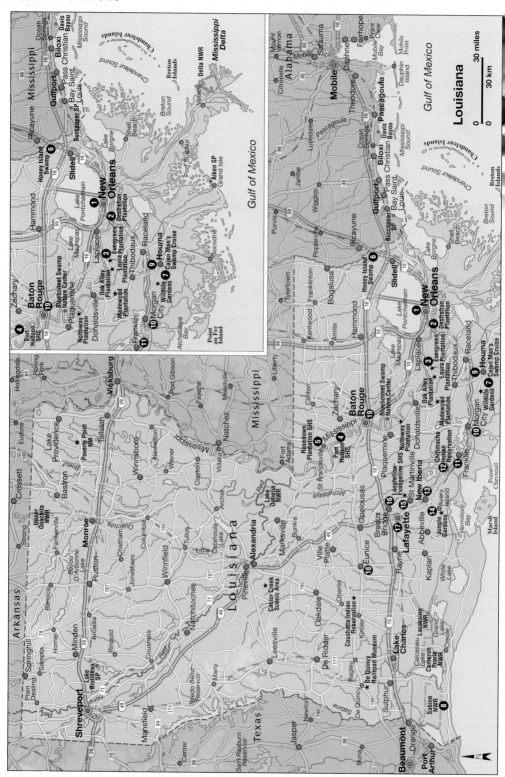

LOUISIANA

*A detailed guide to the entire state, with principal sites
cross-referenced by number to the maps*

The fertile bowl of Louisiana teems between the Gulf of Mexico
and the mighty Mississippi River, drizzled with swamps and
bayous. Alligators, egrets, and turtles bask in the steaming
marsh grass, languishing in the mist. Bald cypress, palmetto and
black gum trees simmer in the swamplands under the tropical sun.
Meanwhile, this vast natural hothouse has propogated equally lush
human cultures. The diversity and spice of culinary creativity gives
a taste of how rich a cultural feast Louisiana has to offer, with French
sauces, Creole and Cajun slow cooking.

The three main cities of the Cajun capital Lafayette, the state capital Baton Rouge, and the Big Easy itself, New Orleans, all have their
own distinct and unique ambience. The large Acadian Cultural Center in Lafayette, and the Acadian Memorial to *le grand dérangement*
in St Martinville tell of how French-Canadians transplanted to make
the bayous their home, but in the towns around the River Teche, those
stories have grown into a living modern reality. Cajun accordians and
two-steps to lilting French lyrics are still at the heart of an exuberant
social life. It's easy to find, with gumbo and *etoufée* on the side, especially in places like Breaux Bridge, Eunice, and New Iberia. As they
say: *laissez les bontemps roulez* ("let the good times roll").

Brash and beautiful Baton Rouge is an aggressive, modern city, but
with a laid-back Louisiana drawl. Baton Rouge also exemplifies a
relaxed approach to political propriety, nowhere more so than in the
Capitol building, itself a monument to the uncontested Kingfish, the
notorious governor Huey Long.

New Orleans is the town that most of the world's musicians either
wish they were from, or wish they could live in. You can stroll along
just about any street and be seduced in about five paces by a beat, a
riff, or the moan of a saxophone. Sample the simmering and sizzling
delights of the French Quarter and, whatever the time of year, somewhere there is bound to be a festival going on in what must surely be
America's favorite party town. Most notably of course is Mardi Gras,
which for some is just too much party, as well as, in April or May,
perhaps the world's finest music festival, JazzFest.

For an immersion of history, take a trip through the splendor and
grace of the antebellum and plantation homes along the Great River
Road, up to the jewel-box town of Saint Francisville. These are
places where vast acres of cotton fields with hundreds of slaves were
ruled by either a kindly ole marse or a mean-eyed monster, long the
popular stuff of novels and screenplays.

That hot, hot air, all that water, and the fecund black soil; the joy
and sheer lust for life in Louisiana is irrepressible.   ❑

PRECEDING PAGES: majestic Mysticks and general tom-foolery at one of New
Orleans' Mardi Gras parades.

NEW ORLEANS

*America's favorite party town is the birthplace of jazz,
while Creole cooking, Spanish moss and the French Quarter
spice the Big Easy's magic gumbo*

Map
on page
200

T he "City that Care Forgot" feels more like a Caribbean dominion than an American town. The almost constant festivals, the predominantly black population, the exotic culture with an undercurrent of voodoo in the air, and the sound of music creeping and seeping out of every window and doorway, are all part of an atmosphere unique in the USA. Not for nothing is this America's favorite party town.

The Big Easy's most famous attraction is the **French Quarter**, the original colony of La Nouvelle Orleans, and its centerpiece is **Jackson Square**. Also called the Vieux Carré (Old Square), Jackson Square's buildings are small and colorful, with steep gables, sloping roofs, dormer windows, and graceful fanlight windows. Jackson Square was known to the French Creoles as *Place d'Armes* and to the Spanish Colonials as *Plaza de Armas*.

Stately **St Louis Cathedral ⓐ** (tel: 504-525-9585, tours daily, except during services, www.saintlouiscathedral.org) is the square's most imposing building. The first church on this site was a small wooden structure, designed in 1724 by Adrien de Pauger, the French engineer who surveyed the original colony. It was named for Louis IX, the 13th-century saint-king of France who fought in two Crusades. The present cathedral dates from 1851.

LEFT: Jackson Square, as seen from Washington Artillery Park.
BELOW: go for the easy option in the Big Easy.

Spanish treasures

The two historic buildings flanking St Louis Cathedral are the Cabildo and the Presbytère. Both buildings date from the Spanish Colonial period and are now part of the Louisiana State Museum complex. The **Presbytère** (tel: 504-568-6968, closed Mon), on the right as you face the cathedral, was begun in 1795. The Casa Curial, as it was called by the Spanish, or Presbytère to the French, was intended as a home for the priests who served the church, but was never used for that purpose. A part of the museum complex since the early 20th century, the Presbytère houses an extensive **Mardi Gras exhibit**.

One of the most important structures in the city is the **Cabildo** (tel: 504-568-6968, closed Mon). Work began in 1795, but it wasn't fully completed until after the Americans took control of the city in 1803. Archaeologists discovered part of a wall from a 1750s police guardhouse that had been incorporated into the building, and it was in the room on the second floor called the *Sala Capitular* that transfer papers for the Louisiana Purchase were signed in 1803.

The buildings lining St Peter and St Ann streets are the **Pontalba Buildings ⓑ**, identical structures which were constructed in 1849 and 1850 and named for the colorful woman who financed and saw to their completion. Each building consists of 16 rowhouses: 12

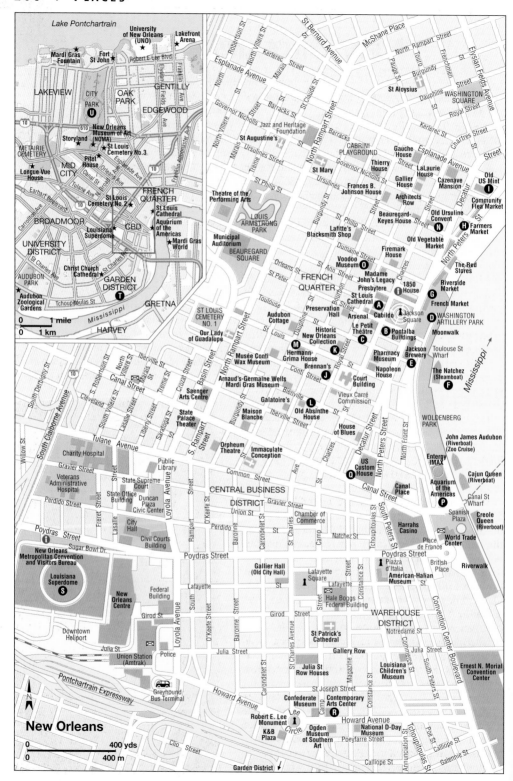

New Orleans

units facing Jackson Square, two facing Decatur Street, and two facing Chartres Street. The "lower" Pontalbas, on St Ann Street, are the property of the state of Louisiana, and the "upper" Pontalbas on St Peter Street belong to the city of New Orleans. ("Lower" and "upper" refer to the downriver and upriver sides of Jackson Square.) In the lower Pontalbas, the Louisiana State Museum maintains the **1850 House**. Adjacent to the 1850 House is the **New Orleans Welcome Center** (529 St Ann Street, tel: 504-566-5031, open daily), with a wealth of free information, including maps, brochures, and advice. The **Louisiana Office of Tourism** (tel: 504-568-5661) shares space with the Welcome Center and provides information to visitors who plan to explore other parts of the state. Across St Peter Street from the Cabildo is **Le Petit Théâtre du Vieux Carré ☉**, the oldest continually operating community theater in America, performing on this site since 1919. At 632 St Peter Street, a plaque declares that Tennessee Williams wrote *A Streetcar Named Desire* in an apartment in the building. Williams scholars claim that the playwright was inspired by the streetcar that used to rattle down Royal Street.

Map on page 200

Carnival colors of purple and green appear everywhere during Mardi Gras.

Riverfront to the French Market

Just across Decatur Street is **Washington Artillery Park ☉**. This is a wonderful place to get a picture-postcard overview of Jackson Square and the Mississippi River. Street performers are often out in full force, and the mournful sound of a jazz trumpet is never far away. From here you can walk across the riverfront streetcar tracks to **Moonwalk**, a wooden walkway smack on the river. This is one of the finest places in town to watch the ever-changing parade of tugs, fanciful riverboats, and serious cargo ships and tankers on the river, especially at sunset. Unfortunately, this is also a pretty good place to be harassed by panhandlers.

The large building nearby is the **Jackson** (or Jax) **Brewery ☉**. The restored structure dates back to 1891, and for many years the popular Jax Beer was brewed on these premises. Two other sister properties house similar shops and eateries, many with views of the Mississippi River.

The ever-colorful steamboat *Natchez* ☉ (tel: 504-586-8777, twice daily harbor/jazz cruises, nightly dinner/jazz cruises) docks behind the Jax Brewery at the Toulouse Street Wharf. An authentic paddle wheeler, this great floating white wedding cake offers delightful calliope concerts to passengers who take the sightseeing cruises. Nearby is **Café du Monde**. Open all day and all night, the café is a New Orleans legend; it has been on this spot for more than a hundred years and is the place for *café au lait* and *beignets*, little doughnuts with messy powdered sugar on top. Café du Monde is the anchor of the **French Market ☉**, a shopping complex with colonnades, arcades, and specialty shops.

Open-air cafés such as the Gazebo are great places to sample the sounds of Dixieland, and free concerts are regularly held in Dutch Alley. Concert schedules are available at the **Dutch Alley information kiosk** at the foot of St Philip Street. Park rangers at the Jean Lafitte National Historical Park Service's Folklife &

BELOW: the Presbytère dates from 1795.

Visitors Center in Dutch Alley offer free tours of the French Quarter and the Garden District, and supply information about the city and the region. Farmers have been bringing fresh produce to the **farmer's market** (open 24 hours) for more than 160 years. Sightseers and locals cram the aisles of the open-air shed, picking through bins of fresh fruits, vegetables, garlic, and pecans. There are also booths piled with wallets, jewelry, and other nonedible market goods. On weekends, a well-attended open-air flea market takes place at the rear of the farmer's market.

The **Old US Mint** (tel: 504-568-6968, closed Mon), which fronts onto Esplanade Avenue, has a fine jazz exhibit, including one of Loui Armstrong's first trumpets. The building houses an excellent jazz archive, which is available free to bona fide researchers. The mint, a massive three-story Greek-Revival structure, was constructed in 1835 on the site of an old Spanish fort. One of the first regional branches of the United States Mint, it produced about $5 million a month in coins. However, it was in operation for less than 30 years; the mint was closed in 1862 when Union forces occupied New Orleans during the War Between the States.

The word "Dixie" originated in New Orleans. It came from the French word for "ten" (dix) on $10 bank notes. These notes were called "dixies."

Royal Street

In the 19th century, the intersection of Conti and Royal streets was the banking center of the French Quarter. Money is the keynote here, and enjoyment of its pleasures is enhanced if you happen to have a lot of it, for this is the place to find upscale boutiques and fine restaurants.

World-famous **Brennan's Restaurant** (tel: 504-525-9711) is located at 417 Royal. The building was constructed around the turn of the 19th century as a residence for the maternal grandfather of French Impressionist painter Edgar Degas. Shortly thereafter it was bought by the Banque de la Louisiane, as can be seen in the initials "BL" that were worked into the fancy wrought-iron balcony. Across the street from Brennan's is a white marble building. This handsome structure, built between 1907 and 1909, now houses the **Louisiana Supreme Court**. It featured strongly in Oliver Stone's 1991 film *JFK*.

BELOW: beer and bare flesh on Bourbon Street.

Across the street and down the block from the TV station WDSU, the excellent **Historic New Orleans Collection** (tel: 504-523-4662, closed Sun, Mon) is pretty much what the name says it is: a collection of maps, documents, and memorabilia exhibiting the long and lively history of New Orleans. The Williams Gallery on the ground floor has changing exhibits of regional art, and there is an excellent research library here, while the building itself has connections with the Emperor Napoleon Bonaparte.

The corner of St Peter and Royal is said to be the most photographed place in New Orleans. **The Royal Café** is housed in one of the **LaBranche Buildings**, which were built around 1840 and are notable for their exquisite cast-iron galleries. There are actually 11 LaBranche Buildings lacing down the 600 block of St Peter Street to Cabildo Alley. Cast iron was introduced in New Orleans in 1850; these buildings originally were undoubtedly festooned with simpler wrought (handworked) iron. At 915 Royal is another well-known and much photographed landmark, the **Cornstalk Fence**, behind which sits the fine Cornstalk Hotel. One of the quarter's many house-museums is the **Gallier House** at 1118–1132 Royal, tel: 504-525-5661, closed Sun). It was built in 1857 by the well-known architect James Gallier, Jr, as a home for himself and his family. Gallier's father, James Gallier, Sr, was also a famous architect whose work can be seen all over town. Open for tours, the house is a fine example of how well-heeled Creoles of the 19th century lived.

Map on page 200

Bourbon Street blues

It's possible to hear **Bourbon Street** before you set foot in it. Within a six-block stretch you can hear hard rock, rhythm & blues, Dixieland, honky-tonk piano, Irish music, gutbucket (lowdown mean blues), Cajun and zydeco, can-cans, karaoke, and occasionally a bagpiper in full regalia.

It isn't even necessary to go inside to be entertained. Doors of clubs are flung wide open all year round, and the music pours out. Almost any place that serves mixed drinks has "go-cups," so you can take your libation along as you stroll. Aside from the bars, a tour of Bourbon Street proper begins at the **Old Absinthe House ⓛ**, a well-established institute of higher imbibing. The building was constructed in 1806 as a commercial-cum-residential structure, and is typical of an *entresol* house. Entresol is a French word meaning mezzanine, and in this context it meant a half-story between the upper and lower floors. Sophisticated **Galatoire's** (tel: 504-525-2021, closed Mon, no reservations), one of the city's old-line French Creole restaurants, has been on Bourbon since its founding in the early 20th century and has been run by the same family ever since.

Just off Bourbon Street, at 820 St Louis Street, lies the **Hermann-Grima House ⓜ** (tel: 504-525-5661, closed Sun), another beautiful house-museum. The mansion itself is handsome, but of particular note are the restored outbuildings that surround pretty ornamental gardens. There is a 19th-century kitchen, where, during the winter months, Creole cooking demonstrations take place.

Antoine's (tel: 504-581-4422), one of the city's most famous restaurants, is located on St Louis Street, between Bourbon and Royal streets. In 1840, Antoine Alciatore founded this restaurant, and it's still operated by his descendants. Antoine's is housed in a lovely old building dating from 1868 that's lavishly decorated with pale-green ironwork. At Bourbon and St Philip streets, the musty old **Lafitte's Blacksmith Shop** is a little cottage that looks like it's about to collapse. Ownership records of this neighborhood bar date back to 1772, but it may be even older.

Upper and lower French Quarter

Locals refer to the lower quarter and the upper quarter, because directions follow the flow of the river. The lower quarter is the area from Jackson Square to Esplanade Avenue, which is vaguely "east" on a map; the upper quarter lies between Canal Street and Jackson Square. Local historians still argue over which is the oldest structure in the city's Vieux Carré, but it is

BELOW: Gallier House, French Quarter.

true that the sole building to survive the devastating fire of 1788 intact is the fine **Old Ursuline Convent**  (1100 Chartres Street, tel: 504-529-3040, tours daily, www.accesscom.net/ursuline). The convent is the only remaining example in the city of pure French Creole architecture and one of the oldest buildings in the Mississippi Valley. The large structure was designed in 1745 by Ignance François Broutin for the Ursuline nuns who arrived here from France in 1727. The nuns prayed in the convent chapel during the 1815 Battle of New Orleans. Andrew Jackson, the hero of the battle, came to the convent afterwards to thank them for their prayers. Across the street from the convent, the **Beauregard-Keyes House** (tel: 504-523-7527, closed Sun) is a house-museum with a lovely walled garden. The garden is included in the tour.

An only-in-New Orleans phenomenon is the spooky **Voodoo Museum** . As well as palm-readings and voodoo tours, the museum offers night-time visits to "voodoo rituals." The museum itself features a creepy cornucopia of dolls, *gris-gris* and other mojo-stimulating specimens.

Some historians insist that the house known as **Madame John's Legacy** (632 Dumaine Street, tel: 504-568-6968, closed Mon) predates the Old Ursuline Convent and should be crowned "oldest in New Orleans." The 700 block of St Peter Street has two establishments worth mentioning. Grungy, world-famous **Preservation Hall** at No. 726 is in a former stable and presents some of the best trad jazz in the world (tel: 504-522-2841 in the daytime, 504-523-8939 at night, www.preservationhall.com). There's no bar, but you can get a "go-cup" next door from **Pat O'Brien's**, another well-known bar. Pat's is in an historic structure constructed around a stunning courtyard. It was built in 1791 and was used by the first Spanish Theatre to be founded in the United States.

Beyond the French Quarter

For any visitors with time to spend, the leafy streets beyond the French Quarter offer unparalleled delights, from overground cemeteries and fine garden homes, to a city park and a lake. However, two fascinating attractions within sight of the French Quarter should be approached with some caution.

The stretch of **Rampart Street** between St Peter and Canal streets is fairly safe during daylight hours, but visitors should avoid walking alone on any section of Rampart after dark. Unfortunately, **Armstrong Park** should be avoided entirely except during big events held in the Mahalia Jackson Theatre for the Performing Arts or the nearby Municipal Auditorium. This is a shame, because from the French Quarter the lit-up entrance is very welcming.

Old Congo Square, which many historians believe was the birthplace of jazz, is situated in front of the Municipal Auditorium. Also called Beauregard Square, this is where 18th- and 19th-century slaves gathered each Sunday afternoon to chant and dance to the accompaniment of tam-tams. **Basin Street**, of song and legend, parallels Rampart Street. This, too, is an extremely unsavory, unsafe thoroughfare.

St Louis Cemetery No. 1, the city's oldest extant cemetery, is located on Basin Street behind Our Lady of Guadalupe Church.

BELOW:
the popular graffitti-adorned tomb of voodoo queen Marie Laveau, in St Louis Cemetery No. 1.

Cities of the Dead

New Orleans' unique burial grounds are among the top sightseeing attractions in the city, but for personal safety, visitors should always visit the graveyards in the company of an organized group.

Called Cities of the Dead, the cemeteries look like small towns with tiny windowless houses and buildings whose front doors are stark white marble slabs. In 1789, **St Louis Cemetery No. 1** was established on the site of a previous one on St Peter Street, between Burgundy and Rampart streets. Its most famous inhabitant is Marie Laveau, the city's infamous voodoo queen, whose tomb is usually adorned with voodoo charms and brick-dust crosses.

St Louis Cemetery No. 2, which stretches between Iberville and St Louis streets along North Claiborne, was consecrated in 1823. It contains the tomb of pirate captain Dominique You, who fought with Andrew Jackson in the Battle of New Orleans. **St Louis Cemetery No. 3** is on Esplanade Avenue near the entrance to City Park. It opened in 1854. The entrance is through a broad, ornate iron gate, and the paved roads are wide enough for cars. There are several esquisite "society" tombs here, including the ornate mausoleum of the Hellenic Orthodox Community.

Canal Street

Canal Street, one of the widest shopping streets in America, leads all the way from the Mississippi River to City Park Avenue, near City Park. A broad, tree-lined street with tall, graceful lampposts, it serves as a gateway to the river, a signpost toward the Central Business District, and the dividing line between Uptown and Downtown.

Portrait of Marie Laveau from the Voodoo Museum; voodoo has been practiced since the early 1800s.

BELOW: the Old Ursuline Convent, one of the few buildings left after the 1788 fire.

At the foot of Canal Street – that is, the riverside end of the street – the **Canal Street Wharf** and the **Poydras Street Wharf** along Spanish Plaza are the departure points for sightseeing riverboats. The structure anchored on Canal Street across from the wharf is the $40 million **Aquarium of the Americas**  (tel: 504-581-4629, open daily, www.auduboninstitute.org). The 1 million-gallon (3.75 million-liter) aquarium houses over 10,000 fish, reptiles, birds, and foliage indigenous to North, Central, and South America. Within the aquarium complex is an **IMAX Theatre**. Farther along, at 423 Canal Street is the gray, granite **US Custom House** ⊙. Despite its austere exterior, the Custom House is worth a visit to see the Great Marble Hall, hailed as one of the finest examples of Greek-Revival architecture in the US. The Custom House is also the home of the Audubon Institute's **Insectarium**.

The trendy Warehouse District is New Orleans' center for the visual arts.

The Warehouse and Central Business Districts

At the upper end of Convention Center Boulevard and Riverwalk, in the area surrounding Julia Street, is the trendy **Warehouse District**, the leading center for visual arts in New Orleans. The revitalization of this district began in 1976, with the opening of the **Contemporary Arts Center** ⊙ at 900 Camp Street. As well as showcasing local artists, the center hosts drama, dance, and performance art shows. There's a flourishing style scene around the CAC, the nearby galleries and watering holes. In 2000, the **National D-Day Museum** opened (945 Magazine Street, tel: 504-527-6012, open daily, www.ddaymuseum.org), following three days of hoopla, including re-enactments, flotillas, and celebrity appearances by, among others, Tom Hanks and Steven Spielberg. Housed in a vast former warehouse, the museum displays a wealth of exhibits, including memorabilia from the Normandy invasions of World War II.

Across the street is the wonderful **Ogden Museum of Southern Art** (925 Camp Street, tel: 504-539-9600). Affiliated with the Smithsonian Institute, this one-of-a-kind museum traces the story of the visual arts in the American South, and showcases the best of the past, present and future of Southern culture.

Culture vultures can also visit two other museums. At 929 Camp Street, housed in a brooding Romanesque building, the **Confederate Museum** (tel: 504-523-4522, closed Sun) contains Civil War memorabilia, including personal effects of Jefferson Davis and Robert E. Lee.

The **Louisiana Children's Museum** at 420 Julia Street (tel: 504-523-1357, closed Mon) is a first-class facility offering hands-on exhibits that are both educational and fun.

In the earliest days, a vast plantation owned by the Jesuits extended upriver from what is now the French Quarter. This area comprises much of today's modern **Central Business District** (which locals call the CBD). Hunkering like a giant spaceship on Poydras Street among the skyscrapers is the **Superdome** ⊙ (Sugar Bowl Drive, tours daily). The dome is home to the New Orleans Saints football team and host of the famous annual Sugar Bowl college football game, as well as big-ticket events like Britney Spears and Rolling Stones concerts.

The Garden District

The **Garden District** ❼ is bordered by Magazine Street, and Jackson, Louisiana, and St Charles avenues. It's possible to get a tempting taste of this sweet-smelling area by driving along the main thoroughfare, Prytania Street, which is lined with handsome 19th-century homes.

Much better is to take the **St Charles streetcar**, the oldest continuously operating street railway system in the world, get off at Jackson Avenue, and simply wander around. Although there are too many fine structures to mention individually, not to be missed are the Pontchartrain Hotel, Colonel Short's Villa, and Commander's Palace restaurant. Architecture buffs should arrange to take one of the organized tours.

City Park and Lake Pontchartrain

City Park ❽ is the fifth-largest urban park in the nation. Lying on the site of the old Louis Allard plantation, which accounts for its dreamy Old South appearance, the park contains the **New Orleans Museum of Art** (tel: 504-488-2631, closed Mon), botanical gardens, an amusement park with an antique carousel, and lazy lagoons for fishing and boating. It also has more than 2,000 stately oak trees, dressed with frilly Spanish moss, which are among the loveliest in the South. The easiest way to reach City Park from the French Quarter is on Esplanade Avenue, which leads right to the entrance.

Cutting a wide swathe across the northern border of New Orleans is sparkling **Lake Pontchartrain**. Accessible from Downtown, via Elysian Fields Avenue or Canal Boulevard (an extension of Canal Street), Lakeshore Drive breezes along the lake for more than 5 miles (9 km). ❑

Map on page 200

TIP

For more information about the South's most fascinating town, pick up a copy of the *Insight Guide to New Orleans*, written and photographed by local residents.

BELOW: the Aquarium of the Americas, with streetcar.

AROUND LOUISIANA

*Antebellum plantations, Cajun music
and alligators in the soup, Let the Good Times Roll
down by the riverside and in the bayous of Acadia*

Map on page 196

The Southern plantation, with its vast acres of cotton fields and hundreds of slaves, ruled by a kindly ole marse or a mean-eyed monster, is the stuff of novelists and scriptwriters. The massive white-columned mansion shaded by moss-draped trees and sweetened with the scent of honeysuckle. Sweet (or sultry) young belles with milk-white skin, tiny waistlines and teasing eyes, gotten up in hoops and crinolines. Handsome, though sometimes sinister, cavaliers dashing off wherever they must, in order to fight for love, honor, or preferably both. **New Orleans ❶** is surrounded by plantations, some with wistful names like Rosedown, some old and crumbling, some dolled up and fit for overnight guests. All, however, offer the requisite degree of romance, and a few even add in a mystery or two. Plantations are generally open every day.

Plantation Row

Louisiana's premier plantation country follows the Mississippi River from above Baton Rouge, and ends around 23 miles (37 km) west of New Orleans. Pre-Civil War homes were built on the Great River Road to escape the dripping summer heat, and several offer bed & breakfast.

The closest plantation to New Orleans is **Destrehan ❷** (13034 River Road, Destrehan, tel: 985-764-9315). Drive west on US 61 or I-10, take exit 310, and follow the signs. The oldest plantation in the Lower Mississippi Valley, this two-story house was built in 1787 by a free man of color. About 5 miles (8 km) west of Destrehan is gorgeous **San Francisco,** built in 1856 by Edmond Bozonier Marmillion (LA 44, tel: 985-535-2341). Frances Parkinson Keyes used San Francisco as the setting for her novel *Steamboat Gothic*.

The next three plantations – Evergreen, Laura, and Oak Alley – are on the west bank. On weekends you can take the Veterans Memorial Bridge across the river, but weekdays, enjoy a delightful ferry ride from Reserve over the waters to Edgard. Then head upriver on the **Great River Road** (LA 18) about 5 miles (8 km) to **Evergreen Plantation ❸** (4677 LA 18, tel: 888-858-6877). The most intact Louisiana sugar plantation, Evergreen has 37 buildings on the National Register of Historic Places.

Upriver a little ways on LA 18 is **Laura Plantation** (2247 LA 18, tel: 225-265-7690). Laura was built in 1805, and was for many years managed by women. It was to this plantation that Senegalese slaves brought the Br'er Rabbit stories. **Oak Alley** (3645 LA 18, tel: 225-265-2151 or 800-44ALLEY), just 3 miles (5 km) upriver of Laura, is perhaps the most photographed Louisiana plantation, and a frequent movie set. The white-columned house, built in 1837 behind a stately

LEFT: sugar mill in Abbeville, Cajun Country.
BELOW: Nottoway, Plantation Row.

Many plantations and their outbuildings have been converted into B&Bs or sweet-smelling restaurants. For a list, go to the state website: www. louisianatravel.com

avenue of 28 oaks, has B&B rooms in small cabins, and a lovely restaurant.

A beautifully restored Greek Revival mansion lies 20 miles (32 km) southeast of **Houmas House**, on the west bank, via the Sunshine Bridge, LA 70, and LA 308. **Madewood** (4250 LA 308, tel: 985-369-7151), too, is open for B&B guests. Painted a pristine white, the house dates from 1846. On the west bank, 33 miles (53 km) northwest of Madewood via LA 1 is **Nottoway** (30907 LA 405, near White Castle, tel: 225-545-2730). Nottoway is, quite simply, a knockout. Completed in 1859, and resembling a gigantic wedding cake, B&B accommodation is available, as is an excellent restaurant.

North of Baton Rouge on US 61, about 15 miles (24 km) is the **Port Hudson State Historic Site** ❹ (756 W. Plains-Port Hudson Rd, tel: 225-654-3775, open daily). The 643-acre (260-hectare) site commemorates an 1863 battle, when 6,800 Rebs held off 30,000 Yankees for 48 days and nights – one of the longest sieges in US history. A boardwalk winds through an area that saw some of the fiercest fighting, and there are 6 miles (10 km) of trails. About 35 miles (56 km) north of Baton Rouge on US 61 is **St Francisville**. This charming little town with magnificent oak trees has been described as 2 miles long and 2 yards wide.

One of the most impressive mansions in the state is near the center of St Francisville. **Rosedown Plantation State Historic Site** ❺ (12501 LA 10, tel: 225-635-3332) is a stunning house-museum, where the extensive grounds include centuries-old camellias and azaleas.

Several elegant homes line US 61 north of St Francisville, most among huge oaks, magnolias, and subtropical greenery, perfect for strolling in. **The Myrtles** (7747 US 61, tel: 225-635-6277) is said to be "America's Most Haunted House," and on the site of an Indian burial ground. As well as daily tours, mystery tours of the house are conducted on weekends.

Touring the swamps

New Orleans is an island in a wetlands laping northward through salt, brackish and freshwater marsh. For almost 300 years, the Crescent City has fought the Mississippi with levees, while exploiting the Delta's rich resources of food, fur and oil, as well as its convenience for water transportation. Recently, environmental tourism has spawned numerous swamp tours. Most focus on wildlife and wetland ecology. All tourists want to see alligators, and most times they do, especially in the hot months that dominate the southern Louisiana calendar. Many operators can arrange transportation from New Orleans hotels.

The bayous meander and merge past alligators and walls of cypress, reaching through webs of twisted limbs and Spanish moss. Snakes, feral hogs, otters, deer and raccoons are spotted, as well as herons and egrets. Birds love the temperature, the canopy of cover, and the abundant food in Louisiana. The swamps are a feral wonderland, an adventure into the wilds of the earth's past.

Crawford Landing sits at the edge of **Honey Island Swamp** ❻, near Slidell on the north shore of Lake Pontchartrain, a 45-minute drive northeast of New Orleans. Dr Paul Wagner, a wetland ecologist and environmental consultant who has lived all his life at the edge of the swamp, founded his tour operation in 1982. He is the preserve manager in the White Kitchen Natural Area, a part of Honey Island Swamp, the premier cypress-tupelo gum swamp in Louisiana. **Honey Island Swamp Tours** (Crawford Landing at West Pearl River, Slidell, tel: 504-242-5877 (New Orleans), tel: 985-641-1769 (Slidell), hotel pick up: 504-242-5877), are operated by Dr Paul and Sue Wagner.

Map on page 196

A Cajun Man

Black Guidry plays Cajun tunes on his home-made accordion and guides the **Cajun Man's Swamp Cruise ❼** (Highway 182, Houma, tel: 985-868-4625) from deep-water **Bayou Black** marina, a 90-minute drive from New Orleans near Houma. Guidry often takes visitors to a little side bay where the long nose and intense eyes of a huge alligator pierce the green layer of duckweed. Guidry summons the alligator with a guttural call.

After stabbing a big chunk of chicken, Guidry holds a long, baited stick over the side, just above the water. The tranquil alligator busts the surface and opens its jaws to display a jagged array of teeth. Snapping its prey between huge molars, it slips back into the water.

The **Creole Nature Trail** (Sabine National Wildlife Refuge, 3000 Main Street; tel: 337-762-3816) begins at **Sulphur**, 10 miles (16 km) west of Lake Charles, over three hours' drive west from New Orleans, and provides a magnificent trip through vast wetlands. Its highlight is the **Sabine National Wildlife Refuge ❽**, 125,000 acres (50,000 hectares) of salt and freshwater marsh. In the fall, the refuge is full of migratory birds. In hotter months, alligators appear. The refuge takes in the "Cajun Riviera" at Holly Beach where, in the second week

BELOW: San Francisco Plantation, with azaleas.

of August, the annual Cajun Riviera Festival features a rodeo and carnival, and popular Cajun and zydeco bands. **Marsh Trail**, an elevated boardwalk, offers excellent views of waterfowl and wildlife. A pamphlet at the Sabine visitor's center lists 250 species of birds, from the common moorhen to the rare roseate spoonbill. The spoonbill is a large, pink bird, hunted relentlessly for its stunning plumage. In 1915 there were a mere 20 birds left in Cameron Parish. Numbers have increased, although sightings are still scarce.

From Canada to Cajun Country

New Orleans was founded by French Creoles – the descendants of French people born "in the colonies" – and the area west of the Crescent City was also settled by the French. However, the French of Cajun Country (which is also called Acadiana, or French Louisiana) have a different heritage from the Creoles.

In the early 17th century, the French had colonized the parts of Canada now called New Brunswick and Nova Scotia, then known as Acadia. In the mid-18th century, under British control, the *Acadiens* or "Cajuns" were expelled for refusing to forsake their Catholic faith and swear allegiance to the British crown. The expulsion, known as *le grand dérangement,* was romantically told by Henry Wadsworth Longfellow. His epic poem *Evangeline* tells of star-crossed lovers, parted by the *dérangement*, who were reunited under a gigantic oak tree in St Martinville – but, tragically, too late.

The swiftest route from New Orleans into the heart of Cajun Country is via Interstate-10. The proud "capital" of French Louisiana is Lafayette *(see page 215)*, 128 miles (205 km) west of New Orleans, but it's fun to take a longer, more scenic route, to savor the Acadian flavor.

BELOW: cypress trees, lifeblood of Louisiana's swamps.

For the scenic route, drive south on US 90, which dips down to **Houma** ❾, 57 miles (92 km) below New Orleans. Named for the Houmas Indians, Houma is a lazy little town among marshlands and bayous, an excellent departure point for swamp tours, and even a wetlands airplane tour. The Houma/Terrebonne Tourist Commission (114 Tourist Drive, tel: 800-688-2732, open daily) has a wealth of information about the area. Among the nearby attractions is the **Bayou Terrebonne Waterlife Museum** where the colorful interactive exhibits explore the wetlands, flora and fauna of this region.

Fourteen miles (22 km) west of Houma, via US 90, the **Wildlife Gardens** offer walking and boat tours through the swamp, as well as simple cabins for overnight guests, right there in the middle of the swamp. Strange dreams are guaranteed. Sprawled on the banks of the Atchafalaya River, 37 miles (60 km) northwest of Houma via US 90, **Morgan City** ❿ served as the set for the first *Tarzan* movie, filmed in 1917. **Moonwalk**, atop the Great Wall – a flood wall that runs 22 miles (35 km) alongside Front Street – is an observation deck for viewing the Atchafalaya, and gives historical displays of the environs.

Both US 90 and LA 182 lead to the pretty little town of **Franklin** ⓫, approached from the east beneath an arch of handsome live oak trees. Unique in this part of the Gallic *bois*, Franklin was settled not by

Frenchmen, but by the English. The town has a wealth of beautiful white mansions – several open for tours and some offering B&B. Among Franklin's "must-sees" is **Grevemberg House** (tel: 337-828-2092), an 1851 Greek Revival townhouse furnished with period antiques. The house displays Civil War artifacts, and charming antique toys. Take a few minutes to stroll around the **Franklin Historic District**. Franklin is a Main Street USA-type of town, and designated by the National Trust for Historic Preservation.

Three miles (5 km) north of Franklin, in the town of Charenton, via LA 326 is the **Chitimacha Indian Reservation**  (tel: 337-923-4830, open daily). The first tribe in Louisiana to be federally recognized, the reservation was established in 1925 after the tribe, which had numbered thousands, dwindled to just 50 people. The Chitimacha were famed for woven baskets, still made on the reservation, but the biggest attraction is the ever-expanding **Cypress Bayou Casino** (832 Martin Luther King Rd, tel: 800-284-4386). Open 24 hours, seven days a week, and invariably packed, gaming tables vie with video poker and slot machines, ever eager to relieve you of your dollars.

Shadows on the Tech

The Spaniards who founded **New Iberia** ⓭, 25 miles (40 km) northwest of Franklin, named it for the Iberian Peninsula of their homeland, but you'll see much more Acadian influence than Spanish. New Iberia is an attractive little town on the banks of the Teche. Information and advice is available at the Iberia Parish Tourist Commission (tel: 337-365-1540, open daily).

New Iberia's outstanding attraction is **Shadows on the Teche** (317 E. Main St, tel: 337-369-6446, open daily), Louisiana's only National Trust Historic

Map on page 196

Alligators are almost guaranteed on a swamp tour.

BELOW: swamp life: egrets and great blue herons.

House Museum & Gardens. With Bayou Teche in its backyard, and giant live oaks to shade it, Shadows was built in 1834 for sugar planter David Weeks. The furnishings are 19th-century Louisiana and European antiques. New Iberia is also home to America's oldest rice mill. Tours are conducted of the **Conrad Rice Mill** (307 Ann St, tel: 337-364-7242, closed Sun), while the on-site **Konriko Country Store** sells Cajun food baskets, crafts, and other collectible gifts.

New Iberia is just a short detour from one of South Louisiana's stellar attractions, Avery Island, about 7 miles (11 km) southwest of town. Go north on US 90 from New Iberia, take the LA 14 exit and turn left, then turn right on LA 329. There are no bridges or pontoons on the approach, and were it not for the signs, you would not even know that you'd reached an island.

A hot little island

Avery Island is synonymous with Tabasco sauce, the hot-hot condiment in kitchens and cafés the world over. Edmund McIlhenny concocted the sauce in the 1880s, and a fourth generation of McIlhennys now runs free tours of the **Tabasco Factory** (tel: 800-634-9599, closed Sun). Another relation, Edward Avery McIlhenny developed the 200-acre (80-hectare) **Jungle Gardens**, Avery Island's most spectacular attraction. The gardens blaze with camellias, azaleas, and tropical plants – there is something in bloom all year round. In spring and summer, the bird sanctuary is aflutter with white egrets and herons, while in wintertime hordes of ducks come quacking from the chilly North.

Lovely **St Martinville** , the heart and soul of the *Evangeline* legend, lies 10 miles (16 km) north of New Iberia. The St Martinville Tourist Information Center (tel: 337-394-2233, open daily) sits on the banks of the Teche, in the shadow of the fabled Evangeline Oak. A few steps from the oak, the **Acadian Memorial** commemorates *le grand dérangement* of the Acadians with a huge mural. Massive bronze plaques are engraved with 3,000 refugees names, while an eternal flame burns in a peaceful garden on the riverbank. Adjacent is the vibrant **African-American Museum**.

A block away, on the square, is **St Martin de Tours**, mother church of the Acadians; a statue of Evangeline stands in the churchyard. The neighboring **Petit Paris Museum** is small, but packed with artifacts and memorabilia from the area. Just outside the city limits, on LA 31, the star-crossed Acadian exile is remembered in the **Longfellow/Evangeline State Park**. Within the park is an interpretative center in a raised cottage, picnic grounds and barbecue grills, a craft shop, and a boat launch.

Continuing on LA 31 toward Breaux Bridge, after 2 miles (3 km) is Cypress Island Road. Follow the signs to one of the state's best-kept secrets: **Lake Martin**, home to roseate spoonbills, blue herons, 'gators, nutria, and all kinds of exotic critters. **Breaux Bridge** , 5 miles (8 km) farther along US 31, is famed for its Crawfish Festival held on the first weekend in May, when the population of less than 7,000 swells with over 100,000 hungry visitors. Breaux Bridge is also home to **Mulate's** (tel: 337-332-4648), a family restaurant-cum-dance hall that swings all

BELOW: Cajun Mardi Gras masks – the scarier the better.

year round. Mulate's can get overrun with tours from New Orleans or Baton Rouge, but if that's the case, another legendary Cajun dance hall is **La Poussiere** (1712 Grand Point Rd, tel: 337-332-1721).

Courir de Mardi Gras

Lafayette , 10 miles (16 km) west of Breaux Bridge on LA 94, is the big cheese in Cajun Country, with the region's greatest concentration of sites, sights, museums, restaurants, nightclubs, and lodging. It is also party central for the exhuberant Cajun Mardi Gras. In the surrounding countryside, the *Courir de Mardi Gras*, or Mardi Gras Run, is a wild affair with masked riders thundering on horseback to farmhouses, gathering food for a big fete in the town square.

The logical first stop is the Lafayette Convention & Visitors Bureau (1400 N.W. Evangeline Thruway, tel: 337-232-3808, open daily). Next, the **Acadian Cultural Center** presents fun and informative exhibits on Cajun culture. Across the street from the Acadian Cultural Center is **Vermilionville** (1600 Surrey St, tel: 337-233-4077, open daily), a huge Creole and Cajun living history experience with arts, crafts, cooking and live Cajun music. The **Acadian Village** (200 Green Leaf Drive, tel: 337-981-2364, open daily) is a smaller and more user-friendly folk-life museum on the banks of a lazy bayou.

Just 35 miles (56 km) northwest of Lafayette is **Eunice** ⑱, a typical Cajun town and home to the **Prairie Acadian Cultural Center** (tel: 337-262-6862, closed Sun, Mon). *Rendez-Vous des Cajuns* is a radio show broadcast from the **Liberty Center** on Saturday nights, and is a great way to meet the local people. Much music and dancing, story-telling and bonhomie makes for great entertainment, especially over Mardi Gras. ❑

Map on page 196

TIP

If you're in Eunice on a Saturday night, stop by the Liberty Center, where *Rendez-Vous des Cajuns*, a rowdy two-hour radio show, is broadcast, mostly in French. Trust us, you don't have to know the language.

LEFT AND BELOW: St Martinville.

BATON ROUGE

Only a few minutes' drive from glamorous plantations and eco-swamps, the cosmopolitan state capital makes it own modern mark on the banks of the Mississippi

Baton Rouge **⑲**, the busy, modern capital of Louisiana, opens out like the flavors of a rich gumbo, flavors of the cultures spicing this Southern state. The muddy Mississippi flows along the banks of the city's Downtown area and through a history of nations vying for control of the port's river trade route. Today, as America's fifth-largest tonnage port, Baton Rouge is still a queen of transportation and a diverse hub of commerce touting everything from Old South plantations and tasty Cajun food to the lush green landscape that makes it a "city of trees." Named by an early French explorer for a red stick marking Indian territorial boundaries, colonial Baton Rouge drew settlers from many European countries. It is now best known for the festivals, customs, and hospitality that so pleasingly coexist in this cultural melting pot.

A bird's-eye view

The heart of Baton Rouge is around the historic Downtown area and the towering **State Capitol** (tel: 225-342-7317, tours available). The 1932 Art Deco building was designed for (he might even have said "designed by") Huey P. Long, Louisiana's most flamboyant politician *(see page 47)*. Entrance is by wonderfully grand, almost bombastic sweeping stone steps. The view from the 350-ft

BELOW: Huey P. Long's 1932 State Capitol building.

(170-meter) high 27th-floor observation deck lays out the port, the petro-chemical industries along the river, and the homes and businesses of a sprawling nine-parish metropolitan area with 650,000 people. Winged allegorical figures on a 22nd-floor cutaway refer to Baton Rouge's hallmarks of Law, Science, Philosophy, and Art.

Inside the capitol's echoing marble lobby are visitors' desks dedicated to the city and Louisiana. Racks of brochures and informative guides direct visitors to the nearby oak-shaded plantation homes, and the rustic, rollicking Cajun country of the French Acadians. Browse the racks, and then slip into a guided tour of the ornate, intricately decorated capitol, and the myths and legends of Louisiana's raucous political history.

Take a walking tour

The Capitol's green, rolling grounds, rose garden, and glassy lakes preside over the city's center and its two historic neighborhoods. Adjacent to the front lawn is the 1805 **Spanish Town**, which features antebellum homes, charming cottages, and bungalows. Eight blocks south begin the gracious mansions and brightly painted houses of **Beauregard Town**. Enjoy a walking tour, or stop by the **Baton Rouge Convention and Visitors Bureau** (730 North Boulevard, tel: 225-383-1825, closed Sat, Sun) for maps of Downtown points of interest, and directions for catching the weekday trolley.

Between the two neighborhoods are the bustles of businesses, state buildings, cafés and restaurants in the **Central Business District**, where friendly ethnic eateries welcome visitors with hearty plates of food. The CBD is bordered on the west by the river and two waterfront casinos, Casino Rouge (tel: 225-709-8779)

Map on page 196

TIP

Baton Rouge is near to both plantations and swampland. Nature lovers spend hours at Alligator Bayou (tel: 225-642-8297), just off the Highland Road exit of Interstate 10. Its conservationist-minded owners give great ecotours.

LEFT AND BELOW: Old State Capitol wrought-iron stairs and rotunda, 1882.

Map on page 196

and the Belle of Baton Rouge (tel: 225-378-6070). Both offer splashy, high-end entertainment and delicious, low-cost Sunday jazz buffets.

One of the best views of the river's traffic of passing ships and barges, and the illuminated bridge at night, is from **Red Stick Plaza**. This is a promenade with sidewalks, lamplit benches, commemorative sculptures, and a dock projecting out over the water. Just below the plaza is the fine **Louisiana Arts and Science Museum** (tel: 225-344-5272, closed Mon). Located in an historic railroad depot, the museum hosts traveling exhibits, hands-on arts and space centers to entertain younger people, and a 60-ft (18-meter) domed planetarium featuring a Space Theater with IMAX-type films and laser sky shows.

Next door to the museum is the war hero, the *USS Kidd* (tel: 225-342-1942), a floating destroyer restored to its glory days of 1942. The Kidd complex includes a **Veterans Memorial Museum** with two fighter planes, a large collection of model ships, and a black granite courtyard dedicated to the honor of Louisiana veterans.

Across River Road and up oak-lined North Boulevard is the graceful white neo-Gothic castle of the **Old State Capitol** (tel: 225-342-0500, closed Mon). The 1882 spiral staircase climbs to a beautiful stained-glass dome. The **Center for Political and Governmental History** is the state's official repository of film and video archives, and has a number of interactive exhibits. The vintage footage of Louisiana politicians, sometimes singing, sometimes ranting, is both instructive and entertaining. Two blocks down North Boulevard is the **Old Governor's Mansion** (502 North Boulevard, tel: 225-387-2464, closed Sat–Mon), with tours of the period bedrooms of four Louisiana governors, plus many amusing stories of the notorious Huey and Earl Long.

Plantations and swamps

Beyond the city's center and 3 miles (5 km) down the Mississippi is **Magnolia Mound Plantation** (2161 Nicholson Drive, tel: 225-343-4955). This 1791 French Creole plantation has costumed tour guides and factual exhibits on slavery and old-time plantation medicines.

The **Rural Life Museum** (4650 Essen Lane, tel: 225-765-2437) is located along Interstate 10, 8 miles (13 km) from Downtown, past major shopping areas and cinemas. The museum is a replica of a working plantation, with a commissary, a blacksmith's shop, sugarhouse, gristmill, schoolhouse, overseer's house, and 25 acres (10 hectares) of formal gardens with statuary, winding paths, lakes, and plants indigenous to 19th-century Louisiana.

While the "patriots" owned the city's plantations and mansions, the Cajun "pioneers" of the low-lying swamps have long been Louisiana's backbone. See some of the beauty in this way of life by driving 2 miles (3 km) farther along I-10 to the Bluebonnet exit and bearing right (south) 3 miles (5 km) to the **Bluebonnet Swamp Nature Center** (tel: 225-757-8905, closed Mon). In this natural history park, a couple of miles of walkways meander through rich, green cypress-tupelo swamplands. There are turtles, alligators, and exotic birds to share the enjoyment with. ❑

BELOW: easy tranquility at the Rural Life Museum.

Literary South

Taking his nom-de-plume from the state of Tennessee, born in Columbus, Mississippi, and writing in New Orleans in 1938, Tennessee Williams is the complete Southern writer. Born Thomas Lanier Williams in 1911, although he set *A Streetcar Named Desire* in New Orleans, the character of Blanche Dubois closely resembles Precious, the daughter of the Clark family in Clarksdale, Mississippi, where Williams spent much of his boyhood. *The Glass Menagerie* may have been inspired by the ornaments collected by another Clarksdale resident.

His tales turned on the fragilities and contradictions of his tortured eccentrics, and those puzzles may give a clue to the perplexing question of why the South gushes such a flood of literary prodigy. Truman Capote, Harper Lee, Eudora Welty, Richard Wright, and Donna Tartt are just a few from the long line of Southern literary luminaries.

The Southern voice has always found eager readers the world over, from Margaret Mitchell's Civil War plantation epic *Gone with the Wind*, to Anne Rice's tales of the vampire Lestadt, John Grisham's legal twists and torts, and the North Carolina landscape of Charles Frazier's *Cold Mountain*.

The story of the modern Southern novel, and even the modern American novel, traces up a wooded gravel drive in Oxford, Mississippi, to the white timber house where William Faulkner declared himself "sole owner and proprietor" of his ficticious Yoknapatawpha county. In *As I Lay Dying* he detailed the inhabitants' thoughts and daily minutiae, in a manner often compared with James Joyce.

Tom Wolfe, a native of Richmond, Virginia, pioneered a form called The New Journalism, honed during his writing for *Rolling Stone* magazine. His essays on the wives of test pilots in the space program, later collected into *The Right Stuff*, used a stream-of-consciousness narrative with a documentary descriptive style. Owing more to Faulkner than to news reporting, he later developed his voice in his landmark entanglements of Wall Street traders, *The Bonfire of the Vanities*.

New Orleanian John Kennedy Toole committed suicide in 1969 in Biloxi, Mississippi, in desperate frustration at not being able to publish *The Confederacy of Dunces*. Convinced of the merit in his work, his mother pursued publishers until the Louisiana University Press took it up in 1980, gaining Toole posthumous critical acclaim and the 1981 Pulitzer Prize for literature. His second novel, *The Neon Bible*, considered the finer by some, followed.

"Southern Gothic" literature, examining the sublime and the grotesque in reality, is exemplified by Savannah-born writer Flannery O'Connor. One of the few writers to cross the chasm between "literary fiction" and horror, her 1952 story *Wise Blood*, later filmed by John Huston, is of a preacher offering a doctrine, "where the blind don't see and the lame don't walk and what's dead stays that way."

Southern novels are often run through with a black vein. Even *The Confederacy of Dunces* is a comedy with dark, sometimes hollow laughs. But the stories and words of the South continue to chime with a poetry that still resonates far abroad. ❏

RIGHT: Tennessee Williams won the Putlizer Prize in 1948 for *A Streetcar Named Desire*.

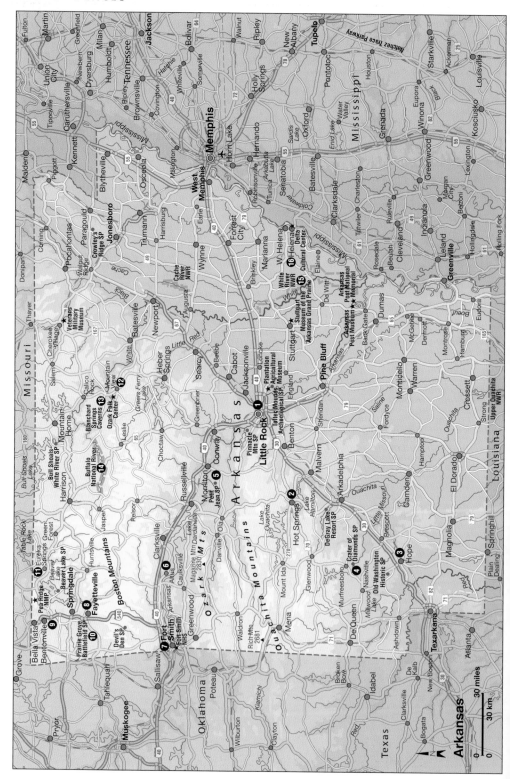

Arkansas

ARKANSAS

A detailed guide to the entire state, with principal sites cross-referenced by number to the maps

Arkansas, the home of former president Bill Clinton, is known as The Natural State, but was once nicknamed The Land of Opportunity – a name that still fits the state well. From the capital city of Little Rock, visitors can explore history and art museums, golf at award-winning courses, or fish for trophy bass in the Arkansas River. In the evenings there are live musical or theatrical performances and fine dining to enjoy. With a vehicle, it's easy to reach a state park with hiking trails, stunning river valley views, sailboats to rent, or fishing at a nearby lake. A 30-minute drive would put those with a love of the outdoors on a hiking trail in a national forest.

Even near Little Rock, outdoor opportunities abound. Within a two-hour drive are seven major lakes to choose between, including the crystal-clear Lake Ouachita, and Greers Ferry Lake. Flowing from Greers Ferry, the Little Red River boasts big rainbow trout and the world-record German brown trout. And several rivers that offer canoeing and kayaking are within a relatively short drive.

Day trips from Little Rock, though, can easily turn into overnight trips. Cities like Hot Springs, which is home to a national park, spas, thoroughbred racing, a botanical garden, and a theme park, have lodging options ranging from luxury downtown hotels to quaint bed & breakfast inns. A drive to western Arkansas leads past the state's wine country and to Fort Smith, a city with a history closely following that of the Wild West. In the eastern part of the state, visitors can learn how bottomland forests were transformed into some of the most productive farmlands in the nation, or how the area cultivated a rich tradition of blues music.

Arkansas is also home to 51 state parks, offering a variety of recreational and educational opportunities. Three state parks have lodges, and several have hiking trails, campsites, cabins, or marinas with rental boats. Some preserve Civil War battlefields or folk music and crafts, while others are dedicated to interpreting the lives of the Native Americans who first inhabited the land. And, because Arkansas has more than 600,000 surface acres (240,000 hectares) of lakes and 9,700 miles (15,600 km) of streams, several of the parks are on the water and offer accommodations with awe-inspiring views.

What may be most appealing about Arkansas, though, is that just when travelers think they've seen it all, there's always something else just waiting to be discovered. It could be a pristine waterfall, or a quirky shop in a mountain hamlet. It might even be a gem at the only diamond mine in the world open to the public. But that's to be expected in The Land of Opportunity. ❏

PRECEDING PAGES: Bathhouse Row in beautiful Hot Springs.

LITTLE ROCK

*Named for a small outcropping in the Arkansas River,
Little Rock has grown into a forward-looking
city of the 21st century*

Map on page 226

Traveling up the Arkansas River, French explorer Rene-Robert Cavalier de LaSalle spied towering bluffs near the first rock outcrop he had seen since departing the Mississippi River. He called the bluffs the "Big Rock" and the outcropping the "Little Rock." What LaSalle encountered in 1682, is the place where the Arkansas River Valley rises from the Delta and meets the Ouachita Mountains to the south and the Ozark Mountains to the north – and the geographic center of what was to become, in 1836, the state of Arkansas.

Little Rock (pop. 183,133) reached the world's attention when then-Arkansas governor Bill Clinton became president in 1992 – and again in 1996. Much of the world focused again on Little Rock when the **Clinton Presidential Center and Park Ⓐ** (tel: 866-PRES-LIB, www.clintonpresidentialcenter.com) opened in November 2004 on the banks of the Arkansas River. The library center, which is situated in a 30-acre (12-hectare) park and houses a 20,000-sq ft (1,860 sq meter) museum, epitomizes Little Rock's Downtown revitalization efforts. Once dominated by dilapidated warehouses, the **River Market District** has been transformed into a vibrant area with shops, art galleries, restaurants, and bars featuring live music – all within walking distance of the presidental library.

LEFT: Little Rock at twilight.
BELOW: Arkansas State Capitol.

Historical center

It's no surprise that much of the state's history is centered around Little Rock. Downtown, and peculiarly situated near skyscrapers, the **Historic Arkansas Museum Ⓑ** (200 East Third Street, tel: 501-324-9351, open daily) comprises five pre-Civil War buildings, including the city's oldest – the Hinderliter Grog Shop (*circa* 1827). Guides in period attire provide tours of the grounds. The attraction's recently renovated museum features exhibits including native art and furniture. A few blocks away, the **Old State House Ⓒ** (300 West Markham, tel: 501-324-9685, open daily) served as Arkansas's capitol from 1836 to 1911. The building, which is the oldest capitol west of the Mississippi River, is where Clinton made his presidential acceptance speeches. Housed in the museum are exhibits on the state's role in the Civil War and Clinton's rise to the presidency, as well as dresses worn by Arkansas' first ladies.

Not far from the Old State House, guided tours are available at the **Arkansas State Capitol**, which is modeled after the nation's Capitol building. Also Downtown, the **Arkansas Arts Center Ⓓ** (tel: 501-372-4000, open daily), which has internationally recognized collections, and the **Repertory Theatre Ⓔ** (tel: 501-378-0405), which has produced more than 30 world theatrical premieres, are but two reasons Little Rock is often considered the center of the arts in

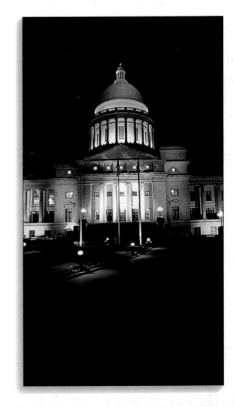

Arkansas. **Robinson Auditorium** hosts performances by the Arkansas Symphony Orchestra as well as concerts by top performers. The River Market's **Museum of Discovery ⑤** is a fun place for children and adults to learn about the sciences and see anthropological artifacts and exhibits – many of which deal with the state. Across the river is the **ALLTELL Arena ⑥** (tel: 501-340-5660), where Elton John, Britney Spears, and other big-name performers have entertained, and which hosts major sporting events.

In west Little Rock, **Wildwood Park for the Performing Arts ⑥** (20919 Denny Road, tel: 501-821-7275) includes six gardens and is the largest park in the Southeast dedicated to the performing arts. The Wildwood Music Festival every June showcases renowned and up-and-coming talents in opera and performing arts.

Central High School

In 1957, the national media descended on Little Rock as nine young men and women became the first black students to attend **Central High School ⑥** at 14th and Park streets. At the time, Arkansas, which had integrated Little Rock's public transportation system years before, was considered moderate on civil rights issues in comparison to its Southern counterparts. But when "The Little Rock Nine" attempted to enter the school, Arkansas's governor – responding to protests among whites – enlisted the Arkansas National Guard to block the students' efforts, before President Eisenhower sent in federal troops to enforce the desegregation, prompting international headlines around the globe.

Across the street from the school, which is now a National Historic Site, is a helpful **Visitors' Center** (tel: 501-374-1957, open daily) located in a renovated

BELOW: snack time in a Little Rock city park.

Mobil Service Station that features exhibits, including original newsreels, about the landmark crisis.

Map on page 226

Interesting local history, though, began long, long before. About 10 miles (16 km) southeast on US 165, then 400 yards south on Highway 386, Native Americans left their mark at what is now the **Toltec Mounds Archeological State Park** (tel: 501-961-9442, closed Mon), where they built, from AD 600 to 1500, mounds rising from the flat, fertile land they had found and farmed. Toltec is near the **Plantation Agriculture Museum**, which interprets the state's long history of cotton farming.

Parks and the outdoors

At **Riverfront Park ❶** (1 Riverfront Drive) walkers enjoying views of the Arkansas River can also learn about and see the "Little Rock." The park's Riverfest Amphitheatre regularly hosts concerts, and the entire park bustles with festivity and music during Riverfest, held each Memorial Day weekend. Farther upstream, bicyclists and runners enjoy the paved trails at **Rebsamen Park ❸**, where golfers can take a swing at its 18-hole public golf course just across the river from the "Big Rock." North Little Rock's **Burns Park ❹**, one of the largest municipal parks in the US, has among its outdoor offerings a paved trail along the river, hiking trails, campsites, picnicking areas, and two 18-hole golf courses. Just west of Little Rock, **Pinnacle Mountain** dominates the landscape and is home to a state park that has a visitor center (tel: 501-868-5806) with exhibits on the area's geology and flora and fauna. The park also has hiking trails, including one that climbs the park's namesake peak and one that affords panoramic views of the Arkansas River. ❑

The Empress of Little Rock, a gracious and good-looking B&B.

BELOW: Bill Clinton celebrates his presidential triumph on the steps of the Old State House.

AROUND ARKANSAS

Map on page 222

With gems like Hot Springs and Eureka Springs,
and real diamonds for the taking, there's a lot to enjoy
between the Ozark Mountains and the Mississippi Delta

As the Ozark and Ouachita mountains rise from the vast Mississippi Delta, so stories, songs, tales, and towns have risen with them as tall, proud, and diverse as the landscape. Arkansas is, in parts, both Old South and Wild West. Some of the early innovators of the blues drew their influences here, while immigrants, isolated among the hills of the Ozarks, nurtured and developed a tradition of folk music that is still alive. The land itself earned Arkansas the nickname of "The Natural State," as it has lush and varied landscapes of hills, lakes, and trails for outdoor adventure. **Little Rock's ❶** central location makes a perfect base for exploring the crags and corners of the state.

Hot Springs and beyond

Visitors to **Hot Springs ❷** (pop. 35,750), 55 miles (86 km) southwest of Little Rock via Interstate 30 and US 270, are amply and agreeably rewarded. Since 1904, Oaklawn Park has held thoroughbred races from late-January to mid-April, and simulcast racing through the rest of the year. The city also has award-winning golf courses, some of the state's best festivals, the Mid-America Science Museum, Magic Springs Theme Park, and Garvan Woodland Gardens on the shores of a sparkling lake. Fishing and water sports are available, as Hot Springs borders Lake Hamilton and is near one of the largest reservoirs in Arkansas, Lake Ouachita. Both lakes have resorts and marinas with rental boats and fishing-guide services.

The main draw for this attractive resort town, though, is the hot springs themselves, which have attracted the good, the glitterati, and the notorious over the decades, including gangster Al Capone, who took to the waters and conducted business from the still lovely **Arlington Hotel** (239 Central Avenue, tel: 501-623-7771). In 1832, Congress declared the land around the 47 natural springs a national preserve. Today, the visitor center at **Hot Springs National Park** (tel: 501-624-2701, open daily) is housed in the **Fordyce**, one of eight opulent bathhouses along what is known as **Bathhouse Row**. The Fordyce looks much as it did when it was completed in 1915 and has exhibits on the history of Hot Springs and the bathing experience. The staff can offer information on the park's campsites, picnic areas, and hiking trails. Also on the row, the elegant **Buckstaff** still offers traditional baths and massages.

The town's distinctive atmosphere and Art Deco architecture has attracted an arty crowd. Boutiques, art galleries and restaurants are located on and near magnolia-lined Bathhouse Row, while a 1950s cinema is the headquarters for a nationally-attended documentary film festival. South of Hot Springs, 20 miles

LEFT: tranquil Thorncrown Chapel near Eureka Springs. **BELOW:** interior of the Fordyce Bathhouse, Hot Springs.

At pretty Crater of Diamonds State Park, visiting prospectors can keep gems they find.

(32 km) on Highway 7, **DeGray Lake** is a fishing and water-sports resort, with cabins and campgrounds, plus a state park with a 96-room lodge, 18-hole golf course, campsites, horseback riding and a marina with rental boats.

Farther south, along I-30 at **Hope ❸**, the "Bill Clinton Trail" from Little Rock and Hot Springs (Clinton's boyhood home) offers tours of his birthplace as well as, in August, the Hope Watermelon Festival. Nearby, **Old Washington Historic State Park** (tel: 870-983-2684) has 25 pre-Civil War buildings and was the state's Confederate capital from 1863 – after Union troops captured Little Rock – until 1865. Interpreters in period dress greet guests at the 1836 courthouse and homes with 19th-century furniture. The park's restaurant serves traditional Southern fare in the tavern, dating from 1832.

The only diamond mine in the world where visitors may keep gems they find is the **Crater of Diamonds State Park ❹** (tel: 870-285-3113, open daily). Since the first diamond was discovered in 1906, more than 75,000 have been unearthed, including the 40.23-carat "Uncle Sam" diamond. Exhibits and films at the park describe the area's geology and showcase diamonds, and interpreters give tips for prospecting. Diamond seekers be warned, though – summertime temperatures on the park's open field can be extreme. The park is just off of Highway 26 near **Murfreesboro**, 43 miles (69 km) from I-30.

From Little Rock west and north

Arkansas' varied landscape gives wonderful views traveling west all the way from the edge of the Delta along the Arkansas River Valley, where Arkansas's first state park (1932) tops Petit Jean Mountain. Off I-40 on Highway 154 about 69 miles (111 km) from Little Rock, many of the stone structures at **Petit Jean State Park ❺** – a 24-room lodge, cabins, and bridges – were built by the Depression-era Civilian Conservation Corps *(see page 46)*. At Petit Jean are campsites, hiking trails, and scenic overlooks.

Swiss-German immigrants found the rich soil around the small town of **Altus ❻** ideal for winegrowing. The oldest of the wineries here, **Wiederkehr Wine Cellars**, has been family owned since 1880, and offers free tastings, guided tours and bottles for sale in the gift shop. German fare is served at a restaurant in the original 1880 cellar. Three other wineries offer similar services in Altus, 116 miles (187 km) from Little Rock, and a few miles south of I-40.

In 1817, the US military built Fort Smith on the western frontier to keep peace between the Cherokee and Osage Native American tribes, after their relocation to Indian Territory just west over the Arkansas River. In 1851, a federal court with jurisdiction over half of Arkansas and the entire Indian Territory, a vast area, was established at the fort. Today, the museum at the **Fort Smith National Historic Site** (tel: 479-783-3961, open daily) interprets the fort's history and tells stories of outlaws drawn to the frontier and the US marshals who upheld the law. The most notorious lawman, "Hangin' Judge" Isaac Parker, sentenced 160 criminals to death. The site has a recreation of Parker's courtroom and the original "Hell on the Border" jail. There's a real Wild West feel.

BELOW: canoeing on the Buffalo River.

As a busy river port, the city of **Fort Smith** ❼ attracted a varied clientele. **Miss Laura's** in the Belle Grove Historic District is reportedly the only former house of prostitution on the National Register of Historic Places, and now serves as the city's **visitor center**. Inside, travelers can pick up maps and information, as well as learn about its rowdy past. Across the river are the antique shops in historic Van Buren and, on the **Arkansas and Missouri Railroad** (tel: 479-750-7291), restored vintage passenger cars take half- or full-day round-trips through the Ozark Mountains.

Map on page 222

Fayetteville

With bridges towering above deep valleys, I-540 makes a swift and pleasant 58-mile (93-km) drive from Fort Smith to **Fayetteville** ❽, home to the University of Arkansas. Fayetteville, along with three neighboring cities, is one of the fastest-growing metropolitan areas in the nation. Behind much of this growth is the world's largest retailer, Wal-Mart, headquartered 27 miles (43 km) north in **Bentonville** ❾. The cute museum, located in one of the company's original "five and dime" stores on the square in downtown Bentonville, provides insights into the phenomenal rise of Sam Walton's family-owned business. The square also offers a couple of good places for a down-home lunch.

Arts, culture, and nightlife are anchored in Fayetteville by Dickson Street. On and around Dickson are art galleries, boutiques, restaurants, bars with live music and the Walton Arts Center, where symphony orchestra and other performances take place. **Devil's Den State Park**, which has campsites, cabins, trails and vistas revered by outdoor enthusiasts, is just 25 miles (40 km) from Fayetteville, while huge and deep **Beaver Lake** is only a few miles away. Just west

BELOW: visitors can get tips on prospecting at Crater of Diamonds State Park.

of Fayetteville on US 62, **Prairie Grove Battlefield State Park** ❿ encompasses 500 acres (200 hectares) and is known as one of the nation's best-preserved Civil War battlefields. The largest Civil War battle west of the Mississippi River took place at **Pea Ridge**, now a national military park *(see page 95).* A drive-through tour with recorded messages gives both the Yankee and Confederate perspective. The battlefield is located on US 62, 34 miles (55 km) east of Fayetteville.

Thirty-two miles (51 km) east of Pea Ridge via US 62, lovely **Eureka Springs** ⓫ began to flourish in the late 1800s as people were drawn by the purported healing powers of the resort town's natural springs. The town, with winding streets lined with unusual shops, eateries and art galleries, has embraced its Victorian heritage so successfully that the National Trust for Historic Preservation named Eureka one of its "Dozen Distinct Destinations."

Carrying on a heritage of different sorts, the **Ozark Folk Center** (tel: 870-269-3851) at **Mountain View** ⓬ is the only park in the US dedicated to preserving Southern folk ways of life. Folk music concerts (in season) are held in its auditorium, and the park has a gift shop, a restaurant, lodge rooms, and a crafts village where country skills are demonstrated. During warmer months, folk musicians converge on the courthouse lawn on Mountain View's town square for impromptu sessions. Mountain View is located on Ark. 9, 122 miles (196 km) from Eureka Springs or 105 miles (169 km) from Little Rock.

Just 15 miles (24 km) north, **Blanchard Springs Caverns** ⓭ (tel: 479-968-2354, open daily) is ranked among the top 10 caves in the country. Famed for its trout-filled waters, the White River also flows near the town. Water released from the massive dam at **Bull Shoals Lake** – some 64 miles (103 km) north near the Missouri border – is cold and teems with German brown, rainbow and cutthroat trout. As is true with Arkansas's other popular trout streams, resorts and outfitters are located along the White River. North of Little Rock near **Heber Springs**, the Little Red River boasts the world-record German brown trout. It flows from Greers Ferry Lake, is popular for water sports, and is home to the hybrid-striped bass and walleye.

The main natural asset of the Ozark Mountains is the **Buffalo National River** ⓮, America's first federally protected stream. The Buffalo, the most popular of more than a dozen float streams in Arkansas, is known for its campgrounds and hiking trails skirting the river. Numerous outfitters along the Buffalo provide canoe and cabin rentals.

The Arkansas Delta

In stark contrast to Arkansas's mountain ranges is its Delta region, which covers roughly the eastern third of the state. Here, two national scenic byways run north and south and provide insight into the history and slower-paced life of the region. **Crowley's Ridge Parkway** is named for the only "highlands" in the Arkansas Delta it follows. The 200-mile (320-km) route begins in northeast Arkansas and ends at the Mississippi River at the town of Helena, passing by or near five state parks, the St Francis National Forest, and several museums. On Arkansas' eastern border, the **Great River Road** skirts the Mississippi and some

BELOW:
Ozark Folk Center,
Mountain View.

of the most productive farmland in the nation. The route also passes near **Arkansas Post National Memorial**, which commemorates the first permanent European settlement in the lower Mississippi River Valley (tel: 870-548-2207), and passes through the **White River National Wildlife Refuge** ⑮, where a **visitor center** at St Charles houses exhibits on the river, Native Americans, and wildlife. Near the Great River Road, **Stuttgart's Museum of the Arkansas Grand Prairie** tells how the area became the nation's most productive rice-growing region, and how duck-hunting earned national recognition.

Map on page 222

King Biscuit Time

While cotton is king in the Delta, more than just soybeans and rice have been cultivated in this rich land. Blues music is deep-rooted in the southern Mississippi River Valley. The best place to learn about the Arkansans who've contributed to the genre is in **Helena** ⑯, 119 miles (192 km) from Little Rock and less than an hour's drive from Memphis; Mississippi's legendary Highway 61 (*see page 175*) is just over the river. Helena's **Delta Cultural Center** (141 Cherry Street, tel: 870-338-4350, closed Sun, Mon) contains exhibits on the Civil War, agriculture, slavery, and the Mississippi River, as well as features on local bluesmen like Louis Jordan, Howlin' Wolf, and Sonny Boy Williamson, original DJ for the influential radio show, "King Biscuit Time."

The town of Hope, where Bill Clinton was born, holds a watermelon festival every August.

The show made the names of many blues pioneers, and broadcasts to this day. The King Biscuit Show is the longest-running blues radio program in the world, and visitors can watch as it's aired live each weekday at 12.15pm. The station, KFFA, also hosts the King Biscuit Blues Festival. Held every October since 1986, it is the largest free outdoors blues festival in the nation. ❑

BELOW: the Victorian spa town of Eureka Springs.

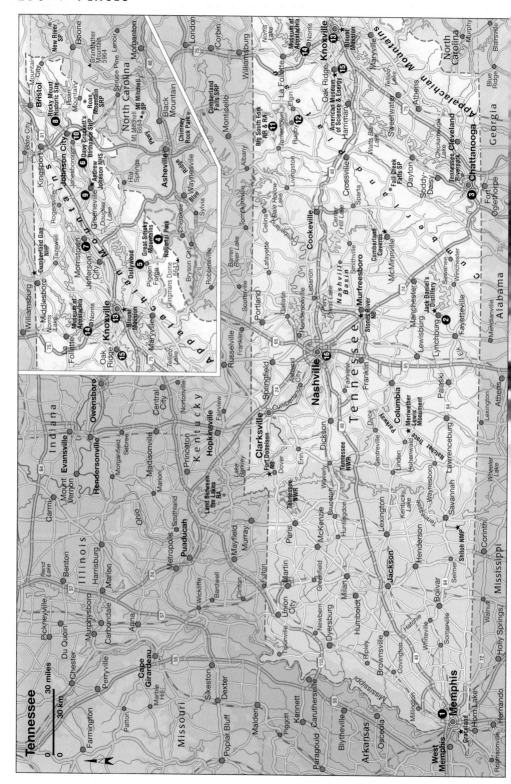

TENNESSEE

A detailed guide to the entire state, with principal sites
cross-referenced by number to the maps

Admitted into the Union in 1796, Tennessee was an early destination for frontiersmen. Davy Crockett began life and exploration near Jonesborough. Andrew Johnson, a Greeneville
native, kept his Senate seat even though Tennessee seceded from the
Union, and became president after Lincoln's assassination. Seventh
president Andrew Jackson's "rough and ready" reputation is con-
founded by the elegance of his Nashville home, The Hermitage.

Among the mountains of Tennessee, the Great Smokies rise majes-
tically. The half-million acre (200,000-hectare) national park is a
terrain practically unchanged since the Indians roamed here. The
hills are steep and rugged, the forests dense, sheer cliffs offer magnificent scenery, and lush vegetation is everywhere, with an extraordinary variety of birds, reptiles, and mammals.

A joy to explore, Tennessee is only 520 miles wide and 120 miles
(840 by 190 km) deep. Distances are short, and major cities are only
a few hours' drive apart. Fast highways cross the state, and the Tennessee Scenic Parkway System gives 2,300 miles (3,700 km) of well-
marked, mostly two-lane roads, with historic sites and excellent
recreational areas, plus the wonderful Natchez Trace Parkway.

Tennessee is not only for the "great outdoors" though. This New
South state offers modern man-made diversions: Memphis, world-
famous as the home of rock 'n' roll and the King himself, has a glass
pyramid for its namesake, and the splendid, sobering National Civil
Rights Museum. Nashville, sparkling capital of country music, was
known as the Athens of the South, and boasts a Parthenon from the
1896 state centennial, an exact replica of the Greek original.

From the mountainous east to the Mississippi River, Tennessee,
"the Volunteer State," presents visitors with an alphabet of attractions and activities: The American Museum of Science and Energy,
Beale Street in Memphis, Chickamauga Civil War battlefield, Dol-
lywood, Elvis, Fort Donelson, Graceland, The Hermitage, Iron
Mountain Stoneware, Jack Daniel's Bourbon Distillery, kayaking on
wild rivers, Lookout Mountain, the Museum of Appalachia, the
National Civil Rights Museum, Opryland, a Parthenon *and* a Pyra-
mid, quiet mountain trails, Rocky Mount, the Sunsphere, Knoxville,
Tennessee Walking Horses, the Union Soldiers' monument at
Greeneville, Victorian houses, James White's Fort, xylophones in
Nashville's Symphony Orchestra, the Sgt Alvin York Monument,
Zoo Choo at the Knoxville Zoo.

Music, mountains, heritage, history, National Scenic Byways, and
Elvis Presley, too. With all this in just one state, who could fail to be
charmed by the magic of Tennessee?   ❏

PRECEDING PAGES: rhinestones turned into silver, gold and platinum at
Nashville's Country Music Hall of Fame.

BLACK DIAMOND
IT'S TONE COOL
MemPhis
Records.Tapes & Souvenirs
BB
KING'S
BLUES
CLUB
FOOD

MEMPHIS

*With the birthplace of rock 'n' roll, the mansion of The King,
and a pyramid by the river, the home of the
World Barbecue Championship is still "Soulsville, USA"*

Map
on page
240

Memphis is a town deep in the American cultural flow. Since the completion of the railroad in 1857, when the port became the South's link to the Atlantic Ocean, Memphis has been a place where people, ideas and cultures met and mixed. In the last two centuries, emancipation from slavery, some of the great American musical movements both black and white, and a meeting point in the unstoppable currents of the civil rights movement, all burst through Memphis. Still a major trading region, Memphis is home to FedEx and the global freight company, and the Memphis Cotton Exchange remains the largest spot cotton market in the US. Also America's largest trading and processing center for hardwoods, agribusiness and distribution through the ports are vital components in Memphis's thriving economy.

A proud echo from Egypt, where Memphis's name was inspired, is a spectacular indoor stadium in the shape of a Pyramid. Downtown there are trolleys to ride, ducks to watch waddling in one of the great landmark hotels, and good Southern cooking to be nourished and comforted by, in the town that hosts the world barbecue championships, what *USA Today* calls, "one of America's friendliest cities.'"

LEFT: the bright, bright lights of Beale Street.
BELOW: a street storyteller makes a new friend.

Revitalization

The **Main Street Trolley** has revitalized Memphis' public transportation. The Memphis Area Transit Authority expanded this efficient service through Main Street and Downtown using vintage and historic carriages, giving atmosphere to this agreeable way to shake across town. Trolleys run between Central Station in the south of town, along Riverside Drive past the Pyramid in the north of the city, and along Front, Main, Second and Third streets. Call 901-274-6282 for more information.

For the major musical sites, Sun Studio *(see page 240)* operates a free shuttle, calling at the Rock 'n' Soul Museum, Beale Street, the Stax museum, Heartbreak Hotel and Graceland Plaza. The bus departs hourly from 11.15am until 6.15pm.

Memphis presently has the unusual distinction of having neither a Major League baseball team nor an NFL football team, so the 21,000 seater **Pyramid Ⓐ** stadium (1 Auction Avenue, tel: 901-521-9675) hosts basketball tournaments as well as concerts in its distinctive 32-story blue landmark arena. **Mud Island River Park Ⓑ** (125 North Front Street,, tel: 800-507-6507, open daily) is across a short bridge. The five-block **River Walk** is a model of the Mississippi's 1,000-mile (1,600-km) journey from Cairo, Illinois to its mouth at New Orleans. Outdoor events and concerts are also staged in the park. Within the park is

the **Mississippi River Museum,** which further describes the natural and cultural history of the Lower Mississippi River Valley. From Mud Island, riverboat tours are available on the *Memphis Queen*. Drive to Auction Avenue, and then turn left at North Second Street to **SlaveHaven/Burke Estate Museum** 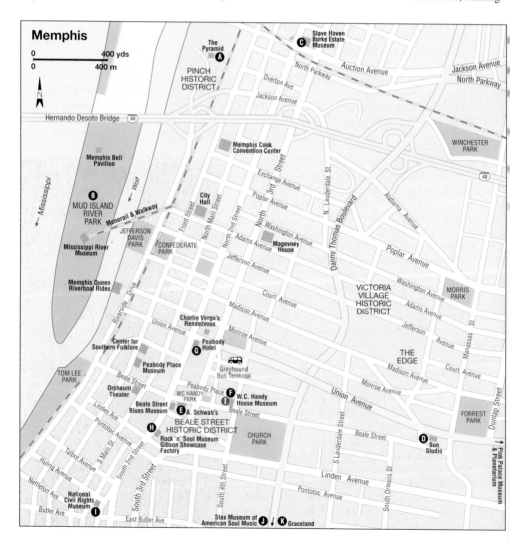 (826 North Second Street, tel: 901-527-3427, open Wed–Sun). On display are the trap doors and secret tunnels used by slaves who took refuge at this plantation, one of the stations of the Underground Railroad.

South along Second Street and left onto Union Avenue leads to the yellow logo and green blind of **Sun Studio** (706 Union Avenue, tel: 901-521-0664, open daily, tours every half-hour), legendary producer Sam Phillips's cradle of rock 'n' roll *(see page 79)*. Tours pass displays of vintage recording equipment and memorabilia from the tiny studio, which has been open for business for over 50 years. The studio is small and functional, but the echoes of Ike Turner, Jerry Lee Lewis, Roy Orbison, Johnny Cash, Carl Perkins, and The King are almost audible. Tour guides are enthusiasts and/or musicians themselves, making this one of the more enjoyable tours in Memphis, maybe in the entire South.

If you're in a car, go a short distance on Myrtle Street, turn right on Beale Street, then drive for five minutes to reach the entertainment district of **Beale Street**, which has been welcoming music lovers and party people since the 1800s. The street is a tourist attraction, but it only got that way because it drew players like Muddy Waters, John Lee Hooker, and Memphis Minnie up from the Mississippi Delta.

These few blocks of Beale Street are lined with clubs, bars, and restaurants. Most of the clubs offer a $10 wristband, which gives admission to the street's other clubs. **B.B. King's Blues Club** features both local and headline acts, and B.B. himself makes regular appearances. The **Blues City Café and Band Box** is acclaimed for its hot tamales, Southern fried catfish, and over-broiled steaks, favored by President Clinton when he was in town. The **Rum Boogie Café** features a red-hot house-band, and the stage has seen action from Stevie Ray Vaughan and Aerosmith, to name but two. The main criterion for bar selection is "who's playing tonight?"

A visit to Beale Street would be incomplete without seeing the **A. Schwab** ❸ store, definitely one of the world's more unusual souvenir opportunities. Here since 1876, Schwab offers clothing and hats, as well as a useful selection of voodoo requisites. On the corner of Beale and 4th streets, the **W. C. Handy House Museum** ❻ is a shotgun shack where this acknowledged father of the blues raised six children. Nearby, Handy is also honored in the **W. C. Handy performing arts park**. The park is a popular venue for outdoor events, festivals, and spontaneous jam sessions. Like any place where tourists throng, take a measure of street-savvy along to Beale Street, day or night.

Ducks deluxe

A block north of Beale Street is Memphis's most famous landmark, the **Peabody Hotel** ❻ (149 Union Avenue, tel: 901-529-4000; pronounce it HO-tel). The two-story colonnaded open lobby is tiled with marble, surrounded by polished statues of elephants, and has an Italian marble fountain as its centerpiece, by the cocktail bar. The fountain pool is the daytime playground for five of the hotel's most pampered guests – the Peabody ducks. Arriving in procession across a red carpet from the elevator at 11am every morning, at 5pm they waddle back again for the ride up to their penthouse on the roof. Among the stores in the lobby is **Lansky's**, the men's outfitter to The King (Elvis, that is), formerly located on Beale Street.

Grown out of the side of the hotel, **Peabody Place** is a gleaming 300,000 sq ft (28,000 sq meter) super-mall developed by the Belz Corporation, who reputedly own more real estate in Memphis than the state of Tennessee. Isaac Hayes – the celebrity chef from the TV show *South Park* – has a restaurant here that also features live music.

A short walk south along Second Street leads to the Smithsonian's **Rock 'n' Soul Museum** ❼ (145 George W. Lee Street, tel: 901-543-0800, open daily). Highly interactive displays draw out the story of the blues emerging from the cotton gins, via the radio,

Map on page 240

The birthplace of rock 'n' roll, where Ike Turner recorded "Rocket 88."

BELOW: the most pampered of all the Peabody Hotel guests.

into the emerging teenage consciousness of the 1940s and 1950s. The Killer, Jerry Lee Lewis, is quoted as saying, "without the co-operation of total resentment on the part of parents, rock & roll would never have survived." Music plays from jukebox selections around the museum cases all the way from Memphis Minnie through James Brown to Gil Scott Heron, so allow several hours to enjoy the extravaganza.

At the same address, the **Gibson Showcase Factory** is a showroom for many of the popular guitar manufacturer's more exotic offerings. Since their founding over 100 years ago by mandolin maker Orville Gibson, the brand has played an important role in popular music. Informative guided tours of the Memphis factory are available, and showcase instruments are on display in the store. The adjacent **Gibson Lounge** (tel: 901-944-7998) is a venue for visiting top-line performers of blues, jazz, country, rock, and rock 'n' roll. Tickets are normally only available at the door, on the night. Across the street from the Gibson facility, a new **sports stadium** is under construction, where the Rock 'n' Soul Museum might ultimately relocate.

Somber site

About half a mile south along Second Street, turn right at Huling Avenue to the **National Civil Rights Museum** ❶ (450 Mulberry Street, tel: 901-521-9699, open daily, www.civilrightsmuseum.org). It is built around the courtyard of the Lorraine Motel, and specifically the balcony where Martin Luther King, Jr was assassinated by a rifle-shot from the building opposite on Monday, April 4, 1968. The shot was, as with most of the 1960s political assassinations, alleged to have come from a lone gunman, James Earl Ray in this case.

BELOW: site of Martin Luther King, Jr's assassination.

The clear and moving exhibits eloquently chronicle the civil rights struggle in the US, beginning in 1619. The 1955 Montgomery bus boycott is described aboard an actual bus, where the seat occupied by Rosa Parks, and its significance, is illustrated. Some of the terrifying violence from the early 1960s in Birmingham, Alabama, is displayed in newsreel footage.

Room 306 of the Lorraine Motel, the room Dr King occupied on that April morning, is preserved intact, the bed unmade, a desk set with breakfast things, just as it was on that day, seen through a glass wall from the adjacent room. Heard in the background is a recording of Mahalia Jackson singing *Precious Lord, Take my Hand.* King had heard a choir rehearsing the song for that evening's meeting, and called down to them to "Sing the song real good tonight," shortly before the fatal shooting. Mahalia Jackson sang the song at King's funeral.

The **Stax Museum of American Soul Music** ❷ (926 East McLemore Avenue, tel: 901-942-7685, open daily) is southeast of Downtown, on the site of the original Capitol Theater cinema. One of the most influential recording stables of the soul era is celebrated here. The history of "Soulsville, USA" shows more than 2,000 exhibits, including copies of all of the Stax recordings, and much memorabilia from this explosive talent pool. Albert King's famous purple "Flying V" guitar is on show, along with one of his more extravagantly frilly shirts, as is Isaac Hayes's peacock-blue Cadillac Eldorado, trimmed in gold and named *Superfly*, naturally.

The Sun Studio shuttle, or a 10-minute drive south of Downtown, leads to **Graceland** (Elvis Presley Boulevard, tel: 901-332-3322, open daily, www.elvis.com). With around 700,000 visitors each year, Graceland is second only to the White House as the most visited private residence in the US; prepare to wait in long lines to enter, often next to Japanese impersonators in leather jackets and quiffs. For such a megastar, and in comparison to the opulence of today's celebrities, the 23-room Graceland seems surprisingly modest. As soon as Elvis had made enough money in 1957, he bought the mansionette for $102,500 as a home for himself and his parents. He kept the name, which came from the niece of the original owner, but added the musically-themed gates the same year. The interior style is unrestrained, over-the-top, distinctly 1970s, and generally eye-popping. More somberly, Elvis, and his parents Gladys and Vernon, are buried in the small, quiet Meditation Garden at the rear of the house, alongside a marker for Jessie Garron Presley, Elvis's still-born twin brother.

Hound Dog

Across the road is The King's impressive auto museum, showcasing a Stutz Bearcat and a Blackhawk, and more Cadillac fins than you could shake a hip at. A little farther along, Elvis's two aircraft, the *Lisa Marie* and *Hound Dog II,* are also open for inspection. For devoted Elvis fans, or broken-hearted lovers, down at the end of Lonely Street are the 128 rooms of **Heartbreak Hotel** (tel: 901-332-3322). With suites and lounges themed after the rooms in Graceland itself, you'll be so lonely, you could die. ❑

TIP

Down a small alley near the Peabody Hotel is Charlie Vergo's Rendezvous (tel: 901-523-2746). Charlie dishes up barbeque so delicious that a number of presidents have had ribs FedExed to the White House.

BELOW: the temple of taste, Graceland.

AROUND TENNESSEE

*Sample the cellars of the Jack Daniel's Distillery,
choo-choo into Chattanooga, or wander the
pine-scented hills to Pigeon Forge and Dollywood*

Map
on page
236

A fter the bright lights of Memphis, the rolling mountains of Tennessee are waiting to be explored. Civil War history is presented with New South panache along this route, which begins with a long straight drive down I-64 from Memphis to East Tennessee, loops through mountain roads, and ends at Knoxville – just a short drive from Nashville.

Lynchburg

The 100-mile (60-km) drive from **Memphis ❶** to Lynchburg is quicker than it seems, as the road is well maintained. Still, the **Natchez Trace Parkway**, once one of the most heavily traveled – and dangerous – roads in the Southwest frontier, offers a pleasing change of pace *(see pages 168 and 246)*. These Indian trails wound their way from the middle of the state towards Natchez, Mississippi, a distance of around 400 miles (640 km). The trail fell into disuse after riverways replaced overland travel as the primary means of transportation. At milepost 385.9, the **Meriwether Lewis Monument** marks the gravesite of the famous explorer who did so much to chart these frontiers.

The first stop is **Lynchburg ❷**, but considering the town's primary export, it may be as well to park the car, stay the night, and prepare to sleep it off. The **Jack Daniel's Distillery** (tel: 931-759-6180, open daily) makes sour-mash whiskey in this tiny town (pop. 361, according to the label on the bottle). Jack Daniel's calls itself America's oldest registered distillery; charcoal mellowing with hard sugar maple is why Tennessee whiskey differs from most Kentucky bourbons. Free tours include a stop at Mister Jack's original office, which contains "the safe that killed him." Your tour guide will be happy to explain how this event came about.

Chattanooga ❸ is a short way south on SR 50. The city's Downtown revival was thanks to an abundant but formerly neglected resource. Looping through the city, the Tennessee River had few recreational opportunities, but now the **Tennessee Riverpark** is a 22-mile (35-km) greenbelt highlighting the city's stunning natural beauty. Beginning at the Chickamauga Dam, it extends through Downtown to the scenic Tennessee River Gorge, and includes mini-parks, hiking trails, historical sites, playgrounds, and fishing piers. Walkways provide access to the Tennessee Aquarium, the Hunter Museum of Art, and other attractions.

The **Tennessee Aquarium** (tel: 800-262-0695, open daily) is built around a spectacular 60-ft (18-meter) canyon and contains two living forests and 22 tanks. Visitors follow the Tennessee River's course from its source in the Appalachian Mountains to the Gulf of Mexico. At the aquarium, river otters and

LEFT: give us a "Pee" – cheering for the Pee-Wee football league. **BELOW:** long before the riverboat era, the Natchez Trace was the highway of the South.

alligators inhabit the river areas; stingrays, sharks, and colorful ocean fish patrol the Gulf of Mexico. Next door, the **Creative Discovery Museum** (tel: 423-756-2738, open daily, closed Wed in winter) offers hands-on educational fun for kids and adults. This interactive museum includes an Artist's Studio, a Musician's Workshop, and a Field Scientist's Laboratory, where visitors can excavate for dinosaur bones.

The **Hunter Museum of Art** (tel: 423-267-0968, closed Mon) is as renowned for its setting on a 90-ft (30-meter) limestone bluff above the river as for its outstanding collection of American art. The museum is split between a 1904 Classical-Revival mansion, and a contemporary building with large windows overlooking the river. The buildings connect by an interior elliptical staircase and a rooftop sculpture garden. Artists include Mary Cassatt, Childe Hassam, Thomas Hart Benton, Ansel Adams, and Albert Bierstadt, plus many international touring exhibitions. Across from the Hunter, the **Houston Museum of Decorative Arts** (tel: 423-267-7176, closed Sun) displays Anna Safely Houston's 10,000 pieces of antique glass, china, and furniture.

Chattanooga choo choos

Glenn Miller made the song *Chattanooga Choo Choo* an international hit in the 1941 movie *Sun Valley Serenade*. It celebrated Chattanooga's railroad heritage, which centered around the grand, Beaux Arts-style **Terminal Station**, built in the early 1900s. Nowadays, the station is the busy hub of the 30-acre (12-hectare) **Chattanooga Choo Choo** complex that features vintage sleeping cars turned into unique accommodation, restaurants, shops, tennis courts, gardens, a model railroad, and a 1915 steam locomotive that served the Chattanooga & Southern Railroad.

BELOW: the world's steepest incline railway, on Lookout Mountain.

THE NATCHEZ TRACE

This 8,000-year-old trail wanders from Nashville south through Tennessee, clips the corner of Alabama, and snakes by Tupelo, Mississippi all the way to Natchez.

First a series of trails tramped by buffalo between feeding grounds, in the late 18th and early 19th centuries as many as 10,000 "Kaintucks" – boatmen from anywhere north of Natchez – regularly braved the Trace.

Delivering cargo in New Orleans and often selling their boats in Natchez, they took a rifle, a bottle of whiskey, and a pack of cards, and rode or hiked the trail back north. In the other direction, pioneers bound for Mississippi came south, and by 1800 a mail service followed the paths.

The remoteness of the trail deep in forest and undergrowth, and ferocious wild animals in the woodland made the Trace harsh and unforgiving territory, where a slight injury could easily become life-threatening. There were also the hazards of murderous predatory bandits, and two nations of hostile Indians. As a result, the Trace earned itself the nickname of "the Devil's Backbone." In the 1820s, trade developed on the Mississippi and use of the Trace declined. The woods and brush began to reclaim it, until its restoration by the National Park Service, along with a scenic drive called the Natchez Trace Parkway.

Train enthusiasts shouldn't miss the **Tennessee Valley Railroad Museum** (tel: 800-397-5544, hours vary). The 40-acre (16-hectare) outdoor museum, just outside the city, is a railroader's dream, with a marvelous collection of classic locomotives, Pullman sleeping cars, dining cars, and cabooses. Chattanooga's key role in the outcome of the Civil War is commemorated in the moving **Chickamauga and Chattanooga National Military Park** *(see page 98)*.

At **Rock City Gardens** (tel: 800-854-0675, hours vary) on Lookout Mountain, Lover's Leap claims a view over seven states. A trail pinches through Fat Man's Squeeze and over the Swing-Along Bridge, across a yawning canyon. At nearby Ruby Falls, an underground passageway leads to a soaring, illuminated waterfall. A ride on the **Lookout Mountain Incline Railway** (tel: 423-821-4224) is the scary but scenic way to reach the mountaintop. The world's oldest and steepest incline railway – opened in 1895 – scales a steep 72.7 percent grade and affords panoramic views of the city through glass-roofed rail cars.

There are also uncrowded places for fishing, boating, swimming, and water-sports on southeast Tennessee's Hiawassee Scenic River, Tellico River, and Tellico Lake, created by the Tennessee Valley Authority.

The Great Smoky Mountains

To the northeast is the main attraction of east Tennessee. Not Dollywood, although that's here too – it's the Great Smoky Mountains. Everyone who comes here has a favorite trail: waterfall, flower, or view. These comforting old mountains, beginning in Tennessee and ending in North Carolina, straddle the state boundaries as they go, and inspire very strong attachments. The fantastic **Great Smoky Mountains National Park ❹** was carved out of 500,000 acres (200,000

Map on page 236

...and I don't care who knowed it.

BELOW: won't you choo-choo me home?

hectares) of private land only about 75 years ago. People return to their old homes to reunite with families, fill a jug with clear spring water, or lay flowers on the grave of a loved one. When the first white settlers entered the region in the late 1700s, the Smokies were inhabited by the Cherokee Indians, who named the mountains Shaconage, "place of the blue smoke." The Cherokee built homes from logs and settled in villages along the Oconaluftee River and Deep Creek. Their famous chief, Sequoyah, devised a written alphabet, and the Cherokee published their own newspaper.

The town of Gatlinburg is a mini "Las Vegas of the Mountains." With wedding chapels on almost every street corner, more than 10,000 couples tie the knot each year.

Early settlers

The arrival of Europeans, mostly of Scots-Irish heritage, in the 18th century spelled the demise of Cherokee society. Between 1783 and 1819, frontiersmen flooded through the gaps in the mountains, Revolutionary War veterans received land grants in the Smokies, and treaties were signed that left the Cherokee with only a scant remnant of their ancient homeland.

Visitors are attracted to the wild streams and waterfalls, excellent trails, including a 70-mile (112-km) stretch of the **Appalachian Trail**; and the black bears, bobcats, red wolves, white-tailed deer, and other wildlife that use the Smokies both as refuge and as nursery ground. From the Smokies' windswept crest, Newfound Gap Road winds down the north face of the mountains, following the tumbling water of the West Prong of the Little Pigeon River as it flows into Sugarlands Valley.

BELOW: tire rides at Dollywood.

After gathering information from **Sugarlands Visitor Center** (tel: 865-436-1200, open daily), follow Little River Road for an excursion to **Cades Cove**, which has one of the country's best collections of pioneer homes and farm-

steads in an "open-air museum." Farmers in Cades Cove took most of their wheat and corn to be ground at the **John Cable Mill**, powered by a large wooden water wheel near the **Cades Cove Visitor Center**. John Cable's daughter, known as "Aunt" Becky, lived most of her life in the nearby two-story frame house built in 1879.

Other houses on or near the 11-mile (18-km) Cades Cove loop are open to the public, including the **John Oliver Place**, **Elijah Oliver Place**, **Tipton Place,** and **Carter Shields Cabin**. These houses make it easy to imagine just what life was like a century ago. The walls still carry a strong smell of kerosene and the faint odor of apples.

Cades Cove is so popular that bumper-to-bumper traffic is a perpetual problem on the loop road. The best solution is to detour onto gravel country roads, like Sparks Lane, park the car and take a picnic basket into the green pastures. Early morning is a magical time to see the cove; the sun burns swirling mist off the surrounding mountains, and spider webs sparkle with dew among the grass. Bluebirds perch on fenceposts, and the horses, cattle and deer graze, oblivious to human presence.

The highest peak in the Smokies is **Clingmans Dome**, towering high at 6,643 ft (2,025 meters) and straddling the Tennessee/North Carolina border. At Newfound Gap, a mile above sea level, take the 7-mile (11-km) spur road west to the Clingmans Dome parking lot, where a half-mile trail leads to a concrete observation tower. Be prepared: at these heights, fog is common, and long vistas may be obscured. On a clear day, however, the great ramparts of the Smokies spread out with blue ridge after blue ridge, separated by deep ravines. Their softness is deceptive; this is rough country.

After a hike in the Great Smoky Mountains you may need **Gatlinburg's** creature comforts. The town has dozens of hotels and motels; stores on The Parkway, its crowded main drag, sell everything from finely made mountain handicrafts and musical instruments to tacky souvenirs, T-shirts, fudge, and taffy. Popular restaurants specialize in hearty meals of freshly caught trout, or bountiful breakfasts to get you off on a solid footing. An aerial tramway transports visitors 2½ miles (4 km) to **Ober Gatlinburg** (tel: 865-436-5423, Snow Report 800-251-9202), a mountaintop amusement complex with a skating rink, craft shops, cafés, live entertainment, and winter skiing.

Some of the best quality mountain crafts are created by members of the **Great Smoky Mountains Arts and Crafts Community** (tel: 865-436-5423, open daily). Their studios and shops are on an 8-mile (13-km) loop of Glades and Buckhorn roads, 4 miles (6 km) from downtown Gatlinburg.

Dollywood

Dolly Parton's **Dollywood** ❺ also features handicrafts (tel: 800-365-5996, hours vary) at the theme park, nearby in **Pigeon Forge**. Dollywood's several stages set the countryside a-hummin' with live country & western, bluegrass, gospel, and pop music, with special appearances by big-name stars. The park is also brimming with rides and restaurants.

Map on page 236

BELOW: apple-headed Dollywood.

Tennessee's historic northeastern tip

Another early American legend – David "Davy" Crockett – was born in 1786 in a log cabin on Limestone Creek, between Greeneville and Johnson City. Humorist, explorer, and martyr at the Texas Alamo, Crockett once described himself as "common as bear spoor in a barley patch." His one-room, dirt-floor cabin has been reconstructed in the **Davy Crockett State Historic Park ❻** (tel: 423-257-2167), where there are bounteous picnic spots by the creek and lots of places to camp.

Crockett fans can follow his trail to **Morristown ❼**, where coonskin caps, buckskins and a likeness of "Ole Betsy," his favorite "shootin' iron," are on the walls of his father's reconstructed tavern, now open as the **Crockett Tavern and Pioneer Museum** (tel: 423-587-9900, open daily May–Sep).

At the **Rocky Mount Museum ❽**, Crockett and the frontier are very much alive (tel: 888-538-1791) at Piney Flats, north of Johnson City. The two-story main house was constructed in the 1770s as the first capitol of the Territory of the US south of the Ohio River. Guides in colonial dress weave flax into yarn, cook on an open hearth, and lead you back in time.

In **Greeneville ❾**, instead of the Confederate Johnny Reb usually stationed at Southern courthouses, a Union army man stands guard on the pedestal. He symbolizes east Tennessee's strong Union sentiments during the Civil War. The region's Union loyalties are also personified by Greeneville's most famous son, Andrew Johnson. When the war began, Johnson was the only Southerner to remain in the US Senate. He became Abraham Lincoln's vice president in 1864, and after Lincoln's assassination in 1865, the 17th president. The **Andrew Johnson National Historic Site** (tel: 423-638-3551, open daily) includes his log-cabin tailor shop, two homes, and his tomb.

Founded in 1779 and cradled in the Blue Ridge Mountain foothills, **Jonesborough ❿** is Tennessee's oldest town. After the Revolution, it was briefly capital of the would-be-state of Franklin. For the first weekend of October, its beautifully preserved homes, churches, and public buildings are the backdrop for the National Storytelling Festival.

Big South Fork

In east Tennessee, 10 million people come every year to Great Smoky Mountains National Park, but less than a tenth of them discover the peace and seclusion on offer in the wilds of the **Big South Fork National River and Recreation Area ⓫**.

Big South Fork sprawls over 10,000 acres (4,000 hectares) of rugged grandeur that belongs to the Cumberland Mountains of northern Tennessee and southern Kentucky. Most of its wooded ravines, rocky gorges, and white-water rivers are well away from paved roads, on trails accessible only by foot, horseback, and four-wheel drive. Operated by the US Park Service, the useful **Bandy Creek Recreation Area** has campsites, picnic pavilions, showers, and rest rooms. Train buffs shouldn't miss the **Big South Fork Scenic Railway**, a two-hour journey through a deep tunnel and beautiful gorge, and along the picturesque banks of Roaring Paunch Creek.

BELOW: the lacy cascades of Fall Creek Falls.

It is possible to go even further back in time to the Victorian English village of **Rugby** ⓬. In 1880, Thomas Hughes, a social reformer, established Rugby as a haven for younger sons of English gentry. Under Victorian primogeniture tradition, firstborn sons usually inherited their fathers' estates, compelling siblings to enter "respectable" professions such as medicine or law. Rugby allowed the disinherited to take up farming and other trades without social stigma. Victorian homes, shops, an Anglican church, a 7,000-book library, and a schoolhouse were built for the 450 villagers. The experiment failed, but the village endured. More than 20 original structures re-create the age of Dickens and Queen Victoria. The colony's rise and fall is chronicled at the Rugby schoolhouse **visitor center**.

Map on page 236

Highland wines

The lacy cascades of **Fall Creek Falls** are among the joys of roving the Cumberlands, the eastern USA's second-highest waterfall. **Jamestown** has a surprising taste of Tennessee at the **Highland Manor Winery** (tel: 931-879-9519, open daily), with entertainment at the Cumberland County Playhouse.

East of the Cumberlands, the Appalachian Mountains jut up to southwestern Virginia and southeastern Kentucky. In the late 1700s and early 1800s, Upper East Tennessee, as the area is known, was the new nation's western frontier. In 1775, Daniel Boone expanded the frontier by opening the Wilderness Road through **Cumberland Gap**. Wagon trains followed, then late last century Boone's trail was asphalted for the heavy traffic on what had become part of US 25. In a happy turnabout, in 1996, the Cumberland Gap Tunnel was opened to divert the highway away from the historic trail. The National Park Service plans to remove the asphalt and replant the trail to how it was in Boone's era. Threaded

Tennessee Walking Horse on a high-stepping stroll.

BELOW: white-water thrills.

with hiking trails, it is set to become part of the 21,000-acre (8,500-hectare) **Cumberland Gap National Historical Park** (tel: 606-248-2817). Gift shops, restaurants, and an on-the-spot wedding chapel can be found in the little town of **Cumberland Gap**, which borders the park.

Knoxville

Knoxville ⑱, with a metro population of more than 300,000, is the urban gateway to the Smokies. Students on the University of Tennessee's (UT) main campus give the city a youthful flavor. The city especially comes alive on Saturdays in the fall, when 96,000 fans, dressed in bright "UT orange," cheer on the Volunteers football team. Those in search of intellectual stimulation can enjoy the university's films, lecture series, or concerts. UT's **Frank H. McClung Museum** (tel: 865-974-2144, open daily) is a field day for curious minds of all ages. Its well-displayed collections illuminate Tennessee's past through anthropology, archaeology, and natural history.

The town of Knoxville also has many cultural and recreational amenities. **Blount Mansion** (tel: 888-654-0016, closed Sun, open Sat in summer only), almost hidden among downtown Knoxville's modern buildings, is one of Tennessee's most revered historic shrines. Here in 1796, Territorial Governor William Blount, assisted by Andrew Jackson and other prominent minds, drafted the constitution that made Tennessee America's 16th state.

James White's Fort (tel: 865-525-6514, open Mon–Fri), within musket range of Blount Mansion, was the area's first settlement. General James White built the sturdy log stockade in 1786. The fort's seven buildings bring the history to life with exhibits of pioneer weapons and furnishings.

BELOW: Tennessee mountain home.

The city has also revived some of its more recent past. After the Civil War, merchants, wholesalers, and industrialists made their fortunes behind the ornate brick facades around Jackson Avenue and Central Street. Forgotten for decades, the **Old City** has come back to life with restaurants, cafés, music clubs, artists' lofts, antique stores, art galleries, trendy apparel boutiques, and what-not shops that attract fun-seekers day and night.

World's Fair Park (tel: 800-727-8045, closed Sun) is a legacy of the 1982 event that brought visitors from near and far. It's pretty easy to find – just look for the 26-story **Sunsphere**, crowned by a golden glass ball. Stop at the Knoxville Convention and Visitors Bureau at the entrance, then ride the elevator to the observation deck for a panoramic view of the city and the lazy, hazy Smoky Mountains.

The **Knoxville Museum of Art** (tel: 865-525-6101, closed Sun, Mon), has permanent collections of art by regional and international artists. The museum has a sculpture garden, gift shop, and café. At the **South's Finest Chocolate Factory** (tel: 800-522-0874), choose from the luscious temptations created before widening eyes in the factory itself, or browse the arts and crafts shops.

The natural habitats of the **Knoxville Zoo** (tel: 865-637-5331, hours vary) contain more than 1,000 exotic birds and animals. Exhibits include Gorilla Valley,

Cheetah Savannah, and a river habitat for playful otters. Youngsters will particularly enjoy the Zoo Choo Train and Bird Show, or the rare chance to ride on an elephant or camel.

Map on page 236

A better mousetrap

The **Museum of Appalachia** ⓮ (tel: 865-494-7680, open daily) keeps the cultural heritage of the Southern Appalachians alive in the town of **Norris**, north of Knoxville. Amongst the 250,000 artifacts featured are some unusual inventions like the self-resetting mousetrap. Fiddlers, guitarists, and maestros of the dulcimer, harmonica, and washtub bass are usually in fine form on the porch of the 1840s **Great House**.

Oak Ridge ⓯, west of Knoxville, was the birthplace of the Atomic Age. During World War II, this "secret city" was created as part of the Manhattan Project to develop the atomic bomb. Now the modern city of 28,000 people welcomes visitors to the energy-related museums and other attractions. There is also a 38-mile (60-km) Oak Ridge Self-Guided Motor Tour. Pick up maps and information from the Oak Ridge Convention and Visitors' Bureau, and begin the tour next door at the **American Museum of Science and Energy** (tel: 865-576-3200, closed Mon).

The museum's 200 exhibits include quizzes, computer games, and do-it-yourself experiments relating to everything from fossil fuels to nuclear fission. Other attractions include the **Children's Museum** (tel: 865-482-1074); a hands-on Southern Appalachians heritage center; the **Oak Ridge Art Center** (tel: 865-482-1441, open daily), with permanent and touring collections; and the University of Tennessee's bright, sweet-smelling **Arboretum**. ❑

BELOW: Great Smoky Mountains.

NASHVILLE

Called the Athens of the South for its academia,
and Music City USA for its recording studios,
Nashville has a twang that tickles the head and the feet

Map
on page
236

Nashville is a blend of New South progress with Old South charm, 21st-century attractions, and a history rich in the music that has brought worldwide fame to the capital of Tennessee. The city has art galleries, museums, and entertainment venues of all kinds, from large outdoor amphitheaters and high-capacity indoor concert venues, to small, out-of-the-way places where famous entertainers are often gigging or just sitting in. Aspiring singers and songwriters come to master their craft, and strive for recognition too.

The settlement which was to become the city of Nashville was founded on Christmas Day, 1779, when James Robertson crossed the Cumberland River with a small group of men, and made camp on the overlooking bluffs. Here they built Fort Nashborough. Less than a year later, a larger group of settlers arrived by the Cumberland River. On May 1, 1780, Tennessee's first government was established with a document known as the Cumberland Compact, a set of rules created and agreed by the 200 settlers who called the area home.

What had formerly been a part of North Carolina became Tennessee, the 16th state in the new Union on June 1, 1796. Nashville became the state capital of Tennessee 47 years later, in 1843.

Nashville ⑯ was a frontier town from the beginning, a small outpost of rugged pioneers in a decidedly hostile environment, under frequent assault from Indian tribes who had banded together, determined to destroy the small settlement. Winters were harsh, with constant food shortages, sickness, and little help from outside. Despite these hardships, the town grew quickly, with Davidson Academy established in 1785, Blount College in 1794, and Nashville's first newspaper, the *Tennessee Gazette*, started in 1797.

Nashville's early growth came from the westward expansion of the original colonies, and its key position on the Cumberland River. The river served as a highway, bringing goods and new residents, and transforming small Fort Nashborough into a full-scale city with rail service, schools, a hospital, and merchants.

Nashville has been nicknamed alternately "the Athens of the South," for its institutions of higher learning, and "Music City, USA," for the many recording studios, the headquarters of Gibson and Epiphone guitars, and the Grand Ole Opry.

LEFT: President Andrew Jackson doffs on the famous Foxtrot Carousel. **BELOW:** Tootsie's Orchard Lounge is the city's premier honky-tonk.

On Broadway

Nashville was designed, like many river cities, with a main street running east to west, ending at the river bank. In Nashville, this street is **Broadway**. Streets beginning at the river and leading off either side of Broadway start as 1st Avenue, 2nd Avenue, and so on. They are designated either 1st Avenue North, or

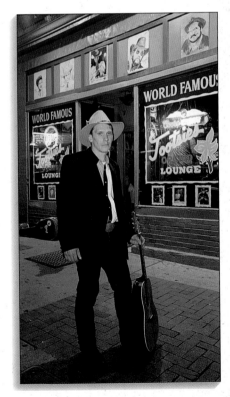

1st Avenue South, depending on whether they are north or south of Broadway. As a result, it's easy to orient yourself in the area, and much of downtown Nashville is within a comfortable seven-block walking distance. Broadway between 1st and 7th Avenue will serve as a good point of reference, as the street is always an easy place to orient from.

The Cumberland River bank is a good place to start. **Riverfront Park** is at the river bank where Broadway intersects 1st Avenue. It has parking for those who prefer to leave their cars and walk around Downtown, but there are also parking lots throughout the area. There's an excellent view across the river of the football stadium, home of Nashville's NFL team, the Tennessee Titans. Facing the river to the right is the **Shelby Street Bridge**, now a pedestrian walkway to the east bank (accessible at 4th Avenue South and McGavock Street). Also at Riverfront Park (although there is talk of moving it elsewhere in the future) is the **Tennessee Foxtrot Carousel**, designed by Nashville native and international artist Red Grooms. The vivid, working carousel features stylized horses with caricatured images of Tennesseans like Andrew Jackson and Minnie Pearl.

Wild Horse Saloon

Fort Nashborough (open daily) is less than a block from Riverfront Park up 1st Avenue North. The 1930s wood re-creation of the original fort provides a depiction of rugged pioneer life on the Cumberland. Back at Riverfront Park, it's a brief walk up Broadway to 2nd Avenue North, literally the next block. Nashville's **Hard Rock Café** is on the right. Turning right off Broadway onto 2nd Avenue North is the epicenter of Nashville's **Historic District**, the main tourist center for the city. Here are many familiar restaurants, including the popular **Old Spaghetti Factory**, as well as souvenir shops and entertainment venues. Also on 2nd Avenue North is the famous **Wild Horse Saloon** (tel: 615-902-8200, www.wildhorsesaloon.com). Nashville's premier country music club is also a great spot for lunch or dinner. On the same side of the street is **B.B. King's nightclub** (tel: 615-256-2727), another place for great food, drinks, and entertainment.

At the summit of 2nd Avenue North is **Public Square**, the former site of the original Nashville courthouse and once the heart of the city. Returning to Broadway there are restaurants, nightclubs, and souvenir shops lining both sides of the street.

At 316 Broadway, between 3rd and 4th Avenue North, is **Hatch Show Print** (tel: 615-256-2805, closed Sun), America's oldest continuously operating letterpress shop, and a perfect place to shop for reproductions of music and show posters. At the corner of 4th Avenue North and Broadway is **Gruhn Guitars**, one of the world's most esteemed vintage guitar stores. There's guaranteed good pickin' here.

Just beyond Gruhn Guitars, at 422 Broadway, is **Tootsie's Orchid Lounge** (tel: 615-726-0463). Tootsie's is Music City's premier honky-tonk, a traditional watering hole for Opry performers between shows. Ahead on the right is 5th Avenue North. Turn right, and the 1892 **Ryman Auditorium** immediately appears. It was the second but most famous home of

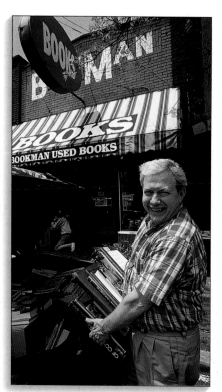

BELOW: heavy reading material.

the Grand Ole Opry (from 1943 to 1974). Two blocks up 5th Avenue North on the right, at the corner with Church Street, is the **Downtown Presbyterian Church**. Designed by William Strickland, also the architect of the State Capitol, this church is one of the best examples of Egyptian Revival architecture in America. This is also where Andrew Jackson was honored after his victory at the Battle of New Orleans in 1815. Further up 5th Avenue at Deaderick Street is the **Tennessee State Museum** (tel: 615-741-2692, closed Mon).

Tennessee marble

Up the hill to the left is **Legislative Plaza**, a vast open area. Up the steps is the Greek Revival **War Memorial Building** with an auditorium, and the **Military Museum** (closed Mon). To the right at the top of the hill is the Tennessee **State Capitol** (closed weekends), completed in 1859. Its architect, William Strickland, died before the building's completion and is buried in its walls. The building is a highly notable American example of Greek Revival architecture, and is constructed of Tennessee marble with iron roof braces. The lush grounds of the Capitol building are populated with statues, and the tombs of President James K. Polk and his First Lady wife are also here.

Across Broadway at 5th Avenue is the **Gaylord Entertainment Center**, Nashville's largest concert arena. Inside on the ground level are the **Visitors Information Center** (tel: 615-259-4747, open daily), and the **Tennessee Sports Hall of Fame and Museum** (tel: 615-782-8183, open daily). The museum comprehensively illustrates the history of local sports and sports figures from the 1800s to the present, and features lots of memorabilia. The Visitors Information Center has books, T-shirts, and other souvenirs for sale.

Map on page 236

Completed after his death, architect William Strickland is buried in the northeast corner of the State Capitol.

BELOW: gone fishin'.

Most importantly, the lobby has a kiosk stuffed with informative pamphlets and brochures covering many of the historic, cultural, and educational attractions that the city has to offer. These brochures provide directions, hours of operation and admission costs. Continuing along 5th Avenue South, you will immediately see the architecturally bold **Country Music Hall of Fame** (tel: 615-416-2096, open daily). Highly recommended for music fans, even those who might not be afficionados of country or country & western, there are displays of costumes, instruments and automobiles, as well as films, photographs, and ephemera documenting the lives and lifestyles of famous country, blues, bluegrass, folk, rockabilly and gospel artists. There is also a restaurant and a souvenir store on the premises, with an extensive selection of related books and recorded music. Parking is available adjacent to the museum.

On Broadway beyond 7th Avenue, some kind of transportation is recommended. First up on the left side of Broadway at 901 is the 24,000-sq-f t (2,230-sq-meter) **Frist Center for the Visual Arts**, Nashville's prime gallery for touring exhibitions. Continuing along Broadway away from the river, the next building on the left is the massive stone **Union Station**. Now a landmark hotel, the lobby and mezzanine level are certainly worth a peek. In another mile, Broadway forks and there are sites to see to the right and the left.

Music Row

For **Music Row**, take a left off Broadway onto 17th Avenue South. At the top of the hill a mile further, is Wedgewood Avenue. Directly across Wedgewood is **Belmont University** campus. One of the South's most significant antebellum mansions, the 150-year-old **Belmont Mansion** (tel: 615-460-5459, open daily, www.belmontmansion.com) is on the campus. Its owner, Adelicia Acklen, was one of America's richest women before, during, and after the Civil War. She managed to keep both Union and Confederate forces from appropriating her wealth, bore 10 children, outlived her three husbands (she is buried with all three of them), and died shopping in New York. She must surely have been one of the more colorful figures from American history.

Turn left at Wedgewood Avenue, then back down 16th Avenue South to the other half of Music Row. You will dead-end into a roundabout graced in the center with *Musica*, a 40-ft (12-meter) statue of dancing nudes. Around the roundabout and down the hill on Demonbreun Street are a number of sidewalk cafés and coffee shops. Otherwise, follow the roundabout 180 degrees and return to Broadway. Also on Broadway, at 1925, is **The Great Escape** (tel: 615-327-0646), a famous vintage record store.

If you take the right fork, Broadway becomes West End Avenue, then Harding Road, and eventually Highway 100, but it's all the same road. **Vanderbilt University** is on the left, at 21st Avenue. Then comes pretty, tranquil **Centennial Park** with its life-size replica of **The Parthenon**, now an art gallery (closed Mon) on the right. At 3205 West End Avenue is **Chamber's Guitars**, another mecca for vintage and modern guitar fans. West End Avenue becomes Harding Road in about 3 miles (5 km). On the left at 5025 Harding Road is the **Belle Meade Plantation** (tel: 615-356-0501, www.bellemeadeplantation.com), a Greek Revival mansion with a fine old barn where championship horses were bred in the 19th century. Along Highway 100, turn left on Cheek for the sweet-smelling **Cheekwood Botanical Gardens and Museum of Art** (closed Mon).

Music city

Printer's Alley, located off Church Street between 3rd and 4th avenues north, was once the center of Nashville's nightlife. Today, it still houses nightclubs and restaurants descended from the venues of the 1940s and 1950s. **The Exit/In** (tel: 615-321-3340) at 2208 Elliston Place, is known as Nashville's "Music Forum." Nearly every famous act in pop, rock, country and blues has played it at one time or another. **The Bluebird Cafe** (tel: 615-383-1461) is a small but respected room, mainly for acoustic music. It is located at 4104 Hillsboro Road in the Green Hills Area (reservations suggested).

Back Downtown, the **Tennessee Performing Arts Center** (tel: 615-782-4060, www.tpac.org) at 505 Deaderick Street is likely to stage anything from plays to headline vocalists. **Gibson Bluegrass Showcase** (tel: 615-514-2200, www.gibsonshowcase.com), located at Opry Mills, Briley Parkway at Exit 11, is a terrific concert venue which also houses a retail guitar store showcasing Gibson and Epiphone stringed instruments.

The Hermitage (tel: 615-889-2941, www.thehermitage.com), home of the seventh president, Andrew Jackson, is a sumptuous mansion with original furnishings, slave cabins, church, gardens, and Andrew Jackson's tomb. It's just 15 minutes from Downtown. Take I-40 east to Exit 221. ❏

Map on page 236

BELOW: Frist Center for the Visual Arts.

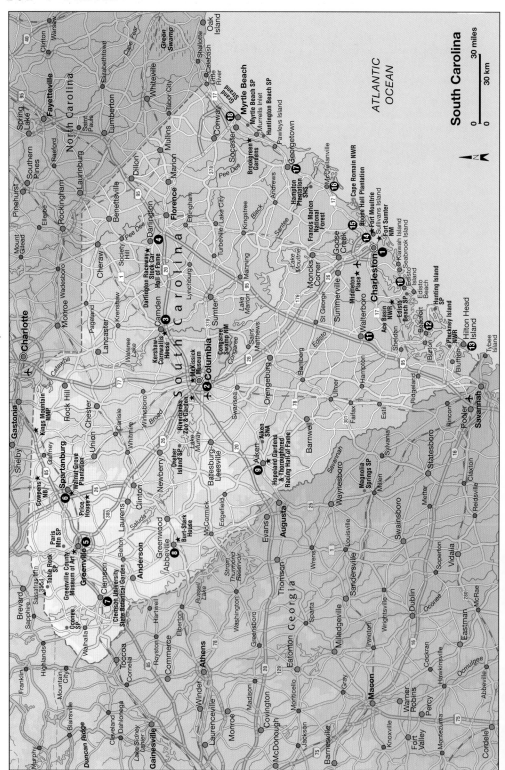

SOUTH CAROLINA

A detailed guide to the entire state, with principal sites cross-referenced by number to the maps

South Carolina is making an appropriately leisurely and graceful transition from Old to New South. In Charleston, the South Carolina Aquarium is already the biggest tourist draw in the "palmetto state," and the revitalized waterfront has sprouted an IMAX theater among its attractions. Also big attractions are a number of green championship golf courses, including Jack Nicklaus's Turtle Point, Tom Fazzio's Osprey Point, and the world-famous Ocean Ryder Cup Course.

South Carolina is home to the USA's first master-planned resort and residential community, bordered by loblolly pine, palmetto trees, and oak; Sea Pines cut the path that towns like Seaside and Disney's Celebration in Florida have followed. The Spoleto Festival, a 17-day event as modern as they come, has been described by the *Washington Post* as "America's most comprehensive arts festival."

Charleston – which played a key role in both the American Revolution and the Civil War – has spearheaded this revitalization, but the city still tends to the historical roots that run so deep in South Carolinan soil. South Carolina was the first state to secede from the Union in 1860, and the first to fire a shot in the conflict called, in these parts, "The War of Northern Aggression." Wealthy South Carolina planters had much to lose by continued association with the North and its fierce opposition to the large plantation way of life. Several members of Jefferson Davis's cabinet and staff came from South Carolina.

Founded by the British in 1670, the original settlement of Charles Towne governed territory including what is now North Carolina, South Carolina, Georgia, and upper Florida. Ten years later it moved to its present location, now the city of Charleston. South Carolina saw much military action during the Revolutionary War, and relics are scattered throughout the state. But it suffered more during that "other war," and was a particular target for revenge.

The Southern signatures of leafy, climbing kudzu and romantic, ethereal canopies of Spanish moss still shade the white-columned mansions. Moist breezes even now are best relieved by tall glasses of lemonade, and the accent still wraps soft, soothing and charming around the ears like cotton. Even the old Afro-English Gullah dialect persists among some black communities in Charleston, as it does on the island of St Helena.

So, the more it changes, the more it stays the same, and what Johannn David Schoepf wrote of South Carolina in 1783 still holds true: "There prevails here a finer manner of life, and on the whole there are more evidences of courtesy than in the northern cities." ❏

PRECEDING PAGES: beautiful Boone Hall – the driveway is said to have inspired the road to Tara in *Gone with the Wind*.

CHARLESTON

Hidden within an intricate system of deep-water creeks and salt marshes is a town as constant as the tides that have driven its fortune for 300 years – a study in preservation and progress

Map on page 266

Pirate attacks, wars, fires, earthquakes, tornadoes, and hurricanes have ravaged this lovely city for centuries, but Charlestonians have always picked up the pieces, and in great style. Often recognized as one of the most desirable places in which to live in America, the clop of horses crossing cobbled streets or the rustling of a summer breeze through palmetto trees instantly conjures a hint of the reasons why.

In 1670, a ship-load of English colonists arrived and founded Charles Towne (now open to the public – *see page 272*) on the Ashley River, 5 miles (8 km) upstream from Charleston's present location. Named after Charles II, Charles Towne endured 10 hard years of battling malaria, heat, flooding, and the Kiawah Indians. The colonists packed their bags and headed for the hills, moving to the peninsula we now know as Charleston.

The **Charleston Visitor Center Ⓐ** (375 Meeting Street, tel: 843-853-8000, open daily) is a useful first stop on any tour of the town. Built in 1856 as a South Carolina Railroad freight depot, the center is one of the oldest railroad structures in the US. Here are opportunities to find the answers to questions, take advantage of the public restroom facilities (rare in the Historic District), and enjoy a 20-minute orientation film about the city. Then, leave the car here and hop aboard one of the many transportation options.

Across Meeting Street from the Visitor Center is the first and the oldest museum in the US, the **Charleston Museum Ⓑ** (tel: 843-722-2996, closed Sun). It features permanent and occasional exhibits focusing on Charleston, the Low Country, and the state. The museum-owned **Joseph Manigault House** next door offers tours of its restored interior and exterior. Built in 1803, the house is considered one of the finest examples of Federal-style architecture in the world and is a National Historic Landmark.

The Swamp Fox

Parallel to Meeting and on the other side of the Visitor Center is King Street, the city's central business artery. Traveling south on Upper King toward Calhoun Street, **Marion Square Park** is on the left. The park takes its name from American Revolutionary hero Francis Marion, the "Swamp Fox," known for eluding British officers in the Low Country swamps where he had hunted since childhood.

Facing the park stands the **Old Citadel Ⓖ** – original site of one of the oldest military colleges in the nation, constructed in 1842. Now at a newer location farther north on the peninsula, the Citadel lost its battle to preserve single-gender education in the name of tradition, and in 1996 reluctantly admitted women cadets. Located at 171 Moultrie Street by the 65-acre

LEFT: church at Dock and Broad streets.
BELOW: some of Charleston's historical and maritime heritage.

(26-hectare), Victorian-style **Hampton Park**, the Citadel has a free on-campus museum of its own. It also presents a Dress Parade by the South Carolina Corps of Cadets most Friday afternoons throughout the academic year.

Festivals

A city of festivals, Charleston's biggest is Spoleto Festival USA. During the Spoleto and Piccolo Spoleto arts festivals each year, usually held at the end of May and early June, all the city's a stage, and there's absolutely no telling what delights there will be to see and hear: dance, experimental theater, opera, chamber music, performance art, crafts, and visual-arts shows. This is certainly the best time to experience Charleston, but keep in mind that there will be huge crowds, and hotels and airplane reservations need to be made well in advance.

Calhoun Street was named for John C. Calhoun, an important statesman before the Civil War and vice-president of the United States under Andrew Jackson, and whose statue keeps watch from a pedestal in the park. Calhoun is

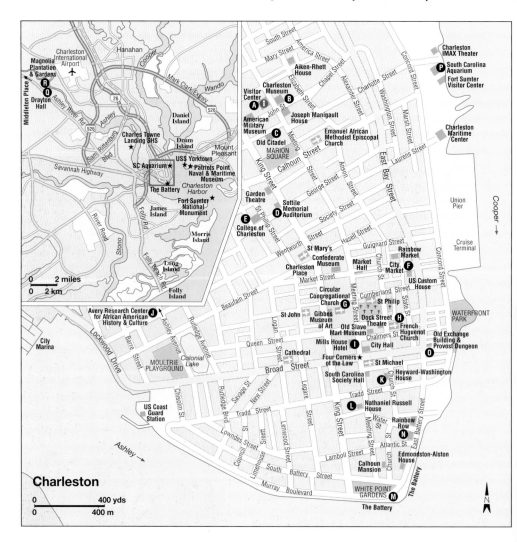

Charleston

the entrance to **Middle King Street**. An area heavily populated by College of Charleston (CofC) students, the student-oriented businesses – record shops, coffee houses, bars, and inexpensive restaurants – make it a perfect spot for browsing, grazing, and other forms of generally creative loafing.

From its earliest days, Charleston has been a city known for tolerance and the appreciation of life's little pleasures, and some of its larger pleasures too. By the early- to mid-18th century, Charleston was one of the wealthiest ports in the Southeast. Exporting cotton, rice, and indigo from its "golden coast," Charleston imported in return the riches of Europe and the West Indies. Lured by a lavish lifestyle, grand homes, exquisite taste, and religious freedom not found in other colonies – hence its nickname the Holy City – artists and immigrants, seamen and merchants, rich and poor flocked here for profit and a good time. That was how it earned its other nickname – the Unholy City.

The college of Charleston

Taking a right off King Street into George Street leads past the classical-style **Sottile Memorial Auditorium** . Owned by CofC and opened as the Gloria Theater, one of the many local movie houses operating in Charleston in the 1920s, it's where *Gone with the Wind* had its local premiere.

On the next block, the herring-bone brick pattern of the walkway reveals that this is the midst of the **College of Charleston** ❺ campus. Founded in 1770, CofC was the first municipal college in the country. Crossing St Philip Street to the entrance and core of the college, the **Old Main Campus**, a National Historic Landmark, appears on the right. It includes the **Porter's Lodge**, which for many years was the residence of the college janitor whose goats roamed the College

Map on page 266

Charlestonians declared their independence from the British at the Old Exchange; many battles followed.

BELOW:
Meeting Street.

BELOW: the "flying" staircase of the Nathaniel Russell House spirals unsupported for three floors.

Green behind, until a student riot over the animals put an end to the affair in the 1850s. It now houses faculty offices. Through the triple arches and Doric columns is the two-story stuccoed brick **Towell Library**; **Randolph Hall**, where the first classes took place; and **The Cistern**, where CofC graduates, clad in white evening dress, receive their diplomas each May.

Back on King Street, interesting and unusual specialty shops lead down to **Market Street**. Straight ahead is **Lower King Street**, Charleston's Antique District. Market is also the location of the well-known **Charleston Grill**. The Grill's acclaimed former chef, Louis Osteen, has now moved on and operates his own restaurant, **Louis's** (tel: 843-237-8757) on Pawley's Island *(see page 284)*.

After a block, Market Street encounters Meeting Street where the 1841 Roman Revival-style **Market Hall** stands, across the way from the entrance to the **City Market** ❻. The market has been in operation since just shortly after the Revolutionary War.

Open-air market

The market trails for a few blocks behind Market Hall and contains open-air sheds in which craftsmen, collectors, artisans, and others peddle everything from jewelry and clothes, to sweetgrass baskets, artwork, T-shirts, and 13 Bean Soup mix. (This is a traditional Low Country favorite, along with Hoppin' John, black beans and rice, and shrimp and grits). They say there's a two-year waiting list for a spot to sell goods at the market.

The Gibbes Museum of Art (tel: 843-720-1682, closed Sun) houses one of the finest collections of American art in the Southeast, and includes an outdoor sculpture garden. Across the street is the **Circular Congregational Church** ❼, which dates from 1681. The original church, made of white brick, was called White Meeting House, and gave its name to Meeting Street. This church features some of the most interesting tombstones in the city.

The local fascination with cemeteries may seem odd, but Charleston has some of the best, and considering how locals love a bit of ancestor worship, it isn't so very strange. Embossed with lounging skeletons atop gray slate, the stones in this cemetery rival those of the adjoining **St Philip Church** on Church Street.

The Dock Street Theatre, at 135 Church Street, was the first formal theater in the country. It has its own gallery inside and a courtyard out back, which often features the Sundown Poetry Series during the Piccolo Spoleto Festival.

Across from the theater is the dominating Gothic Revival **French Huguenot Church** ❽, set up in 1681 by French Protestant refugees. At one time, the church services were scheduled according to the tides, so that plantation owners, who traveled to the church mainly by boat, were able to arrive safely at the service in time for the opening hymn.

Up along Queen Street from the Dock Street Theater is the **Footlight Players Theatre**, home to South Carolina's longest running theater company. Commanding the corner of Queen and Meeting streets is the magnificent **Mills House Hotel** ❶ (tel: 843-577-2400). The original structure dates back to 1853, and it is one of the most elegant hotels Downtown. Robert E. Lee stayed here during his visit to Charleston in 1861. From the balcony, Lee watched as the most devastating fire in the town's history burst out of the Ansonborough neighborhood and raged through the city, devouring more than 500 buildings in its path.

Beside the Mills House on Meeting Street is the Greek Revival **Hibernian Society Hall**. Built in 1840 and one of the oldest Irish fraternal societies in America, this is the venue for the famous St Cecelia Society Ball.

Chalmers Street on the left along Meeting, near Broad Street, is the longest of the numerous cobblestone streets in the city. Along it stands the **Fireproof Building**, home to the South Carolina Historic Society, and **Washington Square Park**, which was once lined with houses of ill repute. Also on Chalmers Street, in what is now the **Old Slave Mart Museum,** horses, steamships, and, regrettably, slaves were auctioned until 1863.

Gullah

Many of the African-Americans in today's Charleston are direct descendants of the first enslaved Africans, brought to the city for their expertise in rice cultivation; rice became essential to the Charleston plantation system. Hired out as blacksmiths, masons, and artisans when they were not needed on the plantations, these slaves helped build the Charleston we know today, and their influence still permeates the city.

This is easily seen in the growing number of African-American galleries; at the **Avery Research Center for African-American History and Culture ❿** at 125 Bull Street; in piazza ceilings painted "haint blue" to ward off evil spirits; in the tight coils of the sweetgrass baskets that have been woven by the

Map on page 266

BELOW: cadets on parade, the Old Citadel.

female descendants of slaves at the market and at Broad Street for the past 300 years; in the wrought-iron gates of the **Philip Simmons Garden** from craftsman Philip Simmons, honored by the Smithsonian; and during the MOJA arts festival held each October. The Avery Center has established an excellent website linking the city's African-American sites and culture, where more information is available from: www.charlestonblackheritage.com.

Traces of the heritage are also evident in the conversations of the local people. Called Gullah, this distinctive Creole language has developed from a blend of dialects, and was spoken on many plantations. West African intonations pepper the English-derived language, and its idiomatic expressions make it sometimes difficult to understand. Pure Gullah is dying out now, but its presence is still heard in the streets of *Chaa'stun*, as they say. Tours of many of the town's Gullah-spired sites can be arranged; for information in advance, go to www.gullahtours.com.

At the intersection of Meeting and Broad streets rests the **Charleston County Courthouse**, **City Hall**, the **US Post Office** and **St Michael's Episcopal Church**, the oldest church building in the city. George Washington and Robert E. Lee worshipped here, and two signatories of the US Constitution are buried in the churchyard.

Named by Ripley's

The intersection continues to be called **The Four Corners of Law** after the *Ripley's Believe It or Not* strip coined the term because each corner represented a different legal branch – city, state, federal, and God's law. It's the only place where you can get married, divorced, pay your taxes, and pick up the mail, all in the same place, or at least reputedly so. Broad Street is known as the "Wall Street of Charleston" because of the city being originally walled and surrounded by a moat, with Broad Street as its northernmost boundary.

BELOW: East Battery is also known as High Battery.

Broad Street, lined with palmettos, flagstone sidewalks, and Charleston's real estate, law, and banking offices, comprises the city's financial center. Taking a left off Meeting Street, then a right off Broad onto Church Street, earthquake bolts are apparent on the sides of many of the buildings. Installed after the disastrous earthquake of August 31, 1886, each bolt stabilizes a metal rod running the length of the house between floors. Many Charlestonians employed this method to reinforce their homes after the 7.5 Richter Scale quake destroyed more than 100 buildings and damaged 90 percent of the city.

Along this portion of Church Street is **Cabbage Row**, on which DuBose Heyward based a fictional Catfish Row in his novel *Porgy*, which George Gershwin later turned into the wildly successful opera *Porgy and Bess*. The pre-Revolutionary string of double tenements were home to nearly 100 African-Americans, who frequently offered cabbages for sale from their window sills. Heyward based his character Porgy on Sammy Smalls, a crippled tenant. Today, the buildings are mainly occupied by gift shops.

Next door is the **Heyward-Washington House** , owned by the Charleston Museum and a National Historic Landmark. This was the 18th-century home of local prominent rice planter Daniel Heyward. His son Thomas, who also lived here, was one of the 56 esteemed gentlemen who lent their signatures to the American Declaration of Independence. Back on Meeting Street is the Federal-style **Nathaniel Russell House** at No. 51. Owned and operated by the Historic Charleston Foundation, this is one of America's most important neoclassical houses. Built in 1808, it features handsome oval rooms, an impressive free-flying staircase spiraling unsupported for three floors, elaborate plasterwork ornamentation, and the kind of genteel period furnishings favored at the time by the merchant elite.

This is just one of the many museum-houses in the city which have been bought, restored, and maintained by local preservation groups. Lists of places that are open to visit are available from the visitor center *(see page 265)*.

The Battery

Continuing along Meeting or King streets towards the water leads to **The Battery** and **White Point Gardens**. Shaded by massive live oak trees, with a large white gazebo at the center, the gardens are often used for weddings. White Point Gardens got its name from the mounds of oyster shells that once covered this southernmost tip of the peninsula. Stede Bonnet was hung for piracy not far from this park, and Anne Bonny, the first pistol-wielding woman pirate – a Charleston debutante and subject of great local scandal still discussed at dinner parties today – often enjoyed a good Cooper River skinny dip in the chilly water just over the Battery wall.

The Charleston area is known for gardens and gracious living.

BELOW: The Battery at twilight.

The cannons and statues in the park commemorate city and state heroes and the many wars in which Charleston has fought. The **South Battery** grand homes that face the park catch the harbor breezes from their two-story piazzas. Walk along the promenade lining the Battery wall and stop at the brass marker laid in the curve of the sidewalk.

One of the most signifiant sites from the Civil War can be seen from this vantage point. The target of the opening shots of the war, now maintained in the **Fort Sumter National Monument**, is way out over the water at the mouth of the harbor *(see page 93, and below for boat information)*. **East Battery**, also called High Battery, is a picturesque street lined with grand mansions and the Regency-style **Edmondston-Alston House**, which is open to the public. Farther along the street is **Rainbow Row** , the longest stretch of pre-Revolutionary houses sharing the same wall in the US. It contains 14 residences, and is the most photographed scene in Charleston.

At the foot of Broad, the street turns into East Bay Street at the **Old Exchange and Provost Dungeon** . The building was constructed by the British during the Golden Age of Charles Towne, and was used to hold imprisoned pirates and Indians in the lower level. In March 1776, South Carolina declared its independence from colonial rule on the Exchange steps.

East Bay Street past the Old Exchange is definitely a place to go prepared with an appetite; it's one of the central dining spots in the city, and thronged with popular and well-known eateries.

Down East Bay from **Waterfront Park**, with its pineapple-shaped fountain, is the **US Custom House**, where the Provincial Congress met in 1775 to set up the first independent government established in America.

A few blocks north on East Bay and heading toward the water leads to the corner of Calhoun and Concord, where the state's most visited attraction, the **South Carolina Aquarium** (tel: 843-720-1990, open daily) is situated. When the aquarium opened in 2000, it spearheaded a revitalization of this part of the waterfront, now known as **Aquarium Wharf**.

As well as an **IMAX Theatre**, there's the National Park Service's **Fort Sumter Visitor Center**, a mainland reference point for information about the fort's historic role in the "late unpleasantness" as Charlestonians refer to the conflict, and from where boats depart for trips to the site.

Plantation paradise

A Low Country tradition was for planters to pack up their bags and retreat to their townhouses in the city in order to escape the heat of sweltering Southern summers. Today, these plantations, located anywhere from 10 to 30 miles (16 to 48 km) from Charleston, are open to the public everyday and offer a glimpse into a different world.

Three plantations or gardens are located off Highway 61, northwest of the city by the Ashley River. An interesting first stop, however, is the original settlement of Charleston, the **Charles Towne Landing State Historic Site** (1500 Old Town Road, Highway 171, tel: 843-852-4200, open daily). Benefitting from

Charleston street names have eccentric pronunciations: Legare Street is pronounced Le-gree, Huger Street is Yougee; Hasell Street is pronounced Hazel; and Vanderhorst Street is Vandrost.

BELOW: joggling board, a Charleston tradition, at Magnolia Gardens.

Map
on page
266

extensive and on-going renovation, this site and nature preserve has a repro-duction 17th-century sailing vessel, an animal forest, and lovely Low Country vistas. Two of South Carolina's most beautiful plantations were built by a single family, the Draytons. Over four years, between 1738 and 1742, John Drayton built **Drayton Hall ❹** (tel: 843-769-2600), one of the finest examples of colonial architecture in America, and the only one of the plantation houses on the Ashley River to survive the Civil War intact.

The house remained in the family until 1974, when it was purchased by the National Trust. The house's style is characterized by the classical hallmarks of symmetry and bold detail, and the two-story portico is believed to be the first of its kind built in America. The National Trust has made a point of leaving the house unfurnished, which provides the perfect opportunity to study the fine architectural details.

Magnolia Plantation

Nearby **Magnolia Plantation and Gardens ❻** (tel: 843-571-1266) has been owned for over 10 generations by the Drayton family, and has one of the country's oldest and loveliest gardens (*circa* 1680). The year-round blooms include America's largest display of azaleas and camellias. More than a century ago, tourists were clambering aboard steamboats and chugging up the river just for a visit to the magnificent grounds.

Middleton Place (tel: 843-556-6020) is America's oldest landscaped garden (*circa* 1740). Although the house was burned during the "late unpleasantness," certain parts have been rebuilt. The stableyard often features craftsmen practicing old plantation trades. ❑

BELOW:
John Drayton
built Drayton
Hall between
1738 and 1742.

AROUND SOUTH CAROLINA

Map on page 262

*Home of thoroughbred champions and
little towns in a time-warp of American history,
South Carolina is a Revolutionary rural idyll*

Well away from the narow cobbled streets and fine plantation homes of Charleston ❶, South Carolina is a pleasant patchwork of orchards and farms, hills, and rugged mountain foothills. The Chattooga River, where Burt Reynolds and Jon Voight battled whitewater rapids in John Boorman's 1972 movie *Deliverance*, rips along the state's northwestern border with Georgia. Around the state, hospitable rivers and streams, and mammoth lakes welcome fishermen, swimmers, and sailors. Football is king at Clemson University and the University of South Carolina; stock-car racing rules at Darlington. Thoroughbred steeplechases and fox hunts are the favored sports in Aiken and Camden. Some of the towns are older than the state itself and were battlegrounds of the Revolution and the Civil War.

Columbia

South Carolina's state capital is the town of **Columbia** ❷, lying on the Congaree River in the heart of the state, and with a metropolitan population of over 150,000. The University of South Carolina's main campus lends vitality to this old and new city. Founded in 1786, Columbia has many historical landmarks, museums, one of the nation's best zoos, and a 50,000-acre (20,000-hectare) lake right on its doorstep.

The **Columbia Metropolitan Visitor Center** (tel: 803-545-0000, closed Sun), Downtown at 1012 Gervais Street, is a good place to start. Watch the orientation film and pick up information on attractions, hotels, restaurants, and tours, then walk across the street to the Capitol.

The Italian Renaissance **State House** (tel: 803-734-2430, closed Sun) was still under construction when it was shelled by Sherman's Union troops in May 1865. Bronze stars cover the cannonball scars. The **African-American Historical Monument** was the first of its kind on any state house grounds in the US. Dedicated in 2001, it traces the history of African-Americans from the Middle Passage, to the fight for freedom in the Civil War, and the more recent struggles for civil rights.

Civil War enthusiasts are bound to enjoy the flags, uniforms, weapons, and soliders' personal effects in the **Confederate Relic Room and Museum** (tel: 803-898-8095, closed Sun, some Sats) in the War Memorial Building on the neighboring University of South Carolina campus. The museum also exhibits 18th- and 19th-century women's fashions, old money, stamps, and everyday domestic items. The **McKissick Museum** (tel: 803-777-7251, closed Sat, Sun), in the university's early 1800s Horseshoe complex, highlights Southern folk arts, culture, and natural history. The museum's

LEFT: just in time for dinner.
BELOW: pretty Camden is one of the oldest inland towns in the state.

historical artifacts include the Howard Gemstone Collection and the Bernard Baruch Silver Collection. In the same area, the **Robert Mills Historic House and Park** (tel: 803-252-1770, closed Mon), built in 1823, commemorates the Columbia-bred architect of the Washington Monument in Washington, DC.

At the **Columbia Museum of Art** (tel: 803-799-2810, closed Mon) you can see contemporary, medieval, Baroque and Renaissance paintings, sculpture and decorative arts, and a children's gallery. Also Downtown, the **South Carolina State Museum** (tel: 803-898-4921, closed Mon) makes an interesting use of an 1890s textile plant. Four floors of the old Columbia Mills – one of the world's first totally electrified textile mills – are filled with historical displays and hands-on exhibits. You can touch the 30-million-year-old tooth of a great white shark, see a laser show, or study a replica of the world's first submarine – a Confederate vessel that sank on its maiden voyage from Charleston.

Riverbanks Zoo and Garden (tel: 803-779-8717, open daily) takes a safari through rainforests and deserts, goes under the seas and then through a Southern farm. Ranked among the nation's best zoos, Riverbanks' natural habitats are home to more than 2,000 birds, reptiles, and animals – many of them high on endangered species lists. Across the Saluda River from the zoo, the gardens have 70 acres (28 hectares) of woodlands, historic ruins, and plant collections to explore.

After a busy day of sightseeing, the restaurants, nightclubs, and unusual shops in the Five Points neighborhood, near Downtown and the university, offer a good evening out. When Columbians want to unwind on water, they take a short drive west to **Lake Murray**. Around the lake's 540-mile (870-km) shoreline are marinas, fishing docks, full-service campgrounds, playgrounds, swimming, and water-skiing. Many recreational facilities and lodgings are in **Dreher Island State Park** (tel: 803-364-4152, open daily), which is connected to the mainland by a causeway and bridges. Nature lovers may also enjoy an outing at **Congaree Swamp National Monument** (tel: 803-776-4396, open daily), east of Columbia. The 22,000-acre (9,000-hectare) sanctuary teems with wildlife and has two boardwalks for viewing. Fishing, hiking, canoeing, and camping are available, too.

BELOW: hand-carved wooden dolls are a rural Southern craft.

Camden

In 1732, **Camden ❸**, a half-hour east of Columbia, was chartered by King George II as the first official permanent settlement in South Carolina's interior. When the American Revolution broke out, Camdenites renounced their allegiance to the Crown, and in August, 1780, His Majesty's Commander in Chief in the Colonies, Lord General Charles Cornwallis, was sent to subdue the rebellious patriots. For nearly a year after winning the Battle of Camden, Cornwallis enjoyed the amenities of Camden's finest residence, the three-story Georgian Colonial mansion built by wealthy merchant Joseph Kershaw. Scarred and burned during the Civil War, the **Kershaw-Cornwallis House** has been recreated with furnishings donated by Kershaw's descendants. The house is part of the 92-acre (37-hectare) **Historic Camden Revolutionary War Site** (tel: 803-432-9841, open Tues–Sun), which includes a powder magazine, log cabins, picnic areas, and a crafts shop.

The **Camden Historic District** includes more than 60 homes, churches, and buildings dotted around the picturesque town of 6,900 people. There are self-guided walking and driving tours, or guided tours can be arranged through the Kershaw County Chamber of Commerce (tel: 803-432-2525). The fascinating **Bonds Conway House** (tel: 803-425-1123, open Thur) at 811 Fair Street was the home of Bonds Conway, the first African-American in Camden to purchase his freedom and that of his family. He was an accomplished architect and his house is now home of the Kershaw County Historical Society.

After the Civil War, Camden's mild climate attracted Northern horse breeders who built beautiful in-town estates and fostered the passion for equestrian sports. The year's two big steeplechases are the Carolina Cup in late March, and the Colonial Cup in late November. Both attract legions of horsefolk and floods of partying tailgaters, who arrange their finest tea-service, silver and china around the **Springdale Race Course** (tel: 803-432-6513, closed Sat, Sun, Sep–May) to enjoy lavish picnics. Don't miss the National Steeplechase Museum at the race course, which exhibits items from the cup championships.

For races of a different stripe, come to **Darlington ❹**, east of Camden and north of Florence, when stock cars roar around the **Darlington Raceway**. If a race isn't running, there are champion cars in the Joe Weatherly **Stock Car Hall of Fame** (tel: 843-395-8821, open daily).

Upcountry

Greenville and Spartanburg are two dynamic cities in the state's northwestern Upcountry. **Greenville ❺** (pop. about 60,000) is proud of its city parks (more than 60) and excellent zoo. Several blocks of Main Street are pedestrianized and

Map on page 262

Riverbanks Zoo and Garden in Columbia has animals, historic ruins and rare plants.

BELOW: the Kershaw-Cornwallis House, Camden.

Founded in 1790 by affluent coastal planters, Pendleton seems like a page from an early American album. Around the grassy village green, weathered brick buildings house antique shops and an eclectic mix of restaurants.

lined with antique, apparel, and gift shops. A short drive from the city, Paris Mountain, Caesars Head, and Table Rock state parks have recreational lakes, picnic areas, and campgrounds in the wooded Blue Ridge Mountain foothills. **Table Rock State Park** (tel: 864-878-9813) gets its name from the distinctive round dome of Table Rock Mountain, one of the Upcountry's best-known landmarks. The two-lane, 130-mile (210-km) **Cherokee Foothills Scenic Highway** (SC 11), is a picture-postcard route to those and other state parks, historic sites, and woodland hiking trails. The Scenic Highway loops north across the state from I-85 at the Georgia border to I-85 at Gaffney.

Greenville proposes several options for art lovers. The **Greenville County Museum of Art** (tel: 864-271-7570, closed Mon) displays fine collections of Southern and American paintings, sculpture, photography, and fabric art. The **Bob Jones Museum and Gallery** (tel: 864-776-1306, closed Mon) exhibits more than 400 religious paintings by Rembrandt, Titian, Rubens, Van Dyck, and other European artists from the 13th to the 19th centuries.

Walnut Grove Plantation (tel: 864-576-6546, closed Mon) has graced the countryside near **Spartanburg ❻** since 1765. The elegant main house is restored and furnished with period antiques. Also in the grounds are a doctor's office, smokehouse, gristmill, and a family burial ground. Spartanburg's other historic shrines open to the public include the 1795 **Price House** (tel: 864-576-6546) and the 1790 **Jammie Seay House** (tel: 864-596-3501), which is open by appointment only.

At **Clemson University ❼**, 3 miles (5 km) from **Pendleton**, stop at Tilman Hall Visitor Center for maps to help explore the museums, gardens, and historic buildings on the wooded, 1,500-acre (600-hectare) campus. Or stroll among the 2,200 varieties of ornamental plants in the sweet-smelling **State Botanical Garden** (tel: 864-656-3405, open daily). Walkways lead by a Chinese pagoda, an arboretum, gristmill, and lakeside teahouse, and a number of the trails are adapted for the blind.

Fort Hill (tel: 864-656-2475, hours vary), on the campus, was the antebellum home of John C. Calhoun, US vice-president under Andrew Jackson and John Quincy Adams, and one of the South's most notable 19th-century statesmen. The mansion was part of plantation land donated by Calhoun's heirs to the state for its agricultural university.

Abbeville

Abbeville ❽, southeast of Pendleton and Clemson, is a charming town in a time warp, where sitting on a bench in the public square evokes 240 years of American history. Designed in oblong, 18th-century style by a homesick Frenchman who named the town after his home town, the square is attractively planted with seasonal flowers. Its most imposing monument is a Confederate memorial obelisk. "Old Bob" is a cast-iron bell that has, over the years, summoned Abbevillians to all manner of happy and sad observances. Old Bob probably pealed joyously in 1860, when South Carolina's first organized pro-secession rally was held here, but must have tolled mournfully

Map
on page
262

in May, 1865 – three weeks after the surrender at Appomattox – when Confederate president Jefferson Davis convened his war cabinet for the last time at the **Burt-Stark Mansion** (tel: 864-459-4297, hours vary), now a museum.

A stroll around the square takes you through a raft of antique shops, the 1842 Trinity Episcopal Church, the handsomely restored 1880s Belmont Inn, and the turn-of-the-19th-century **Opera House** (tel: 864-459-2157, open seasonally). Once a forum for traveling vaudeville troupes – Fanny Brice, Al Jolson, and Jimmy Durante graced its stage – the Opera House now hosts theatrical productions most weekends. One of the best collections of Native American art outside the Southwest is held at the **Dr Samuel R. Poliakoff Collection of Western Art** (tel: 864-459-4009, closed Sun).

Aiken

Aiken ❾, like Camden, is enamored of horses. Thoroughbreds have been training in Aiken's mild, pine-scented climate since the mid-19th century. Outstanding "graduates" include Kelso, Horse of the Year five years running in the 1960s; the 1981 Kentucky Derby winner, Pleasant Colony; and 1993 Derby champion Sea Hero. The **Thoroughbred Racing Hall of Fame** (tel: 803-642-7758, closed Mon) honors these and other Aiken-trained blue bloods. Located in a former carriage house at **Hopeland Gardens**, the hall salutes the champions with racing silks, photos, paintings, trophies, and other memorabilia. After visiting, you can enjoy Hopeland's native trees and flowers, wetlands, and outdoor sculptures. On certain summer evenings from May through August, the air trills with jazz, bluegrass, classical, and other musical charms.

The city's horse mania reaches a fever pitch during three weekends in March when the Aiken Triple Crown fills historic Aiken Mile Track with harness, steeplechase, and flat races. Needless to say, the "Triple" also puts Aiken's high society into high gear. Champagne brunches, teas, lunches, suppers, and balls go on practically non-stop throughout the month. Even if you don't get an invitation to one of the gala events, be sure to take a driving tour through the **Aiken Winter Colony Historic Districts**, where "cottages" routinely have 50 to 90 rooms, and, of course, stables. As you drive Whiskey Road, Easy Street, and other paved roads and bridle paths, you'll pass many training farms and polo fields. These are especially active from November to April.

DuPont Planetarium (tel: 803-641-3313, call for times), in the Ruth Patrick Science Education Center on the campus of USC Aiken, produces programs in its tilted dome. The **Aiken County Historical Museum** (tel: 803-642-2015, closed Mon), housed in a 1930s Winter Colony mansion called Banksia, exhibits Indian artifacts, an old-timey drugstore, and rooms furnished in period style. At **Aiken State Natural Area** (tel: 803-649-2857), 16 miles (26 km) east of the city, it's easy to relax on any of the four lakes and enjoy camping, swimming, boating, and nature trails. There's also plentiful recreation to be had at the big lakes created by impoundments of the Savannah River on the border between South Carolina and Georgia. ❑

BELOW: Aiken, South Carolina, is horse country.

SOUTH CAROLINA COAST

*Shell-covered shores by sleepy coastal towns in no hurry
to catch up, industry here means casting a net
or catering to world-class golfers*

Map
on page
262

If you listen to the accounts of those who grew up along South Carolina's coast, you'll discover a place rich in simplicity and close to the earth. Weather-worn cottages face a shell-covered shore, and shrimp boats head out to sea. Riverside plantations anchor avenues of oak, and sea-island blacks keep alive the spirituals and Gullah language of their enslaved ancestors. The coast is a golden ribbon of tidal creeks and marshes separated by waves of green-and-gold spartina grass. It is a geography formed by earthquakes, hurricanes, tidal pools, wars, and a people too proud to give up. Secluded beaches and islands remain, but the modern world is catching up. Development may raise the standard of living for some lucky few, but for the rest of us a plot of soil, a cast net, and the peace to roam an island without walls is more than enough to make life full and enriching.

South of Charleston

Taking US 17 south from Charleston and down SC 20 through **Johns Island**, you pass the Stono River Marina (once home of the Stono Indians); Fenwick Hall (whose proprietor once entertained pirates); Wadmalaw Island, famous for the **Charleston Tea Plantation** (tel: 803-377-3049, call for times) – the only one in the United States; and **Rockville** (known as Wadmalaw Island's "Little Nantucket"). Once on **Kiawah Island**, head for Beachwalker Park. Its wide boardwalk winds through a tangle of oaks, pines, palmettos, and yucca plants before reaching a 10-mile (16-km) beach bordered by private condos.

As for golf, test your skills at Jack Nicklaus's Turtle Point; Tom Fazzio's Osprey Point; or the famed Ocean Course (tel: 800-845-2471) – site for Ryder Cup matches. If that isn't enough, move to **Seabrook Island** (tel: 843-768-1000) next door with 3 miles (5 km) of beaches, two championship courses, and 200 villas.

Follow US 17 south about 15 miles (24 km) to SC 174, which leads through a moss-covered archway of oak trees to **Edisto Island ⑩**, one of the oldest settlements in South Carolina. Once home to the Edistow Indians and prosperous sea-island cotton planters, Edisto Island still preserves remnants of the past. Visitors can find broken arrowheads, pottery, and sharks' teeth at an Indian shell mound on the beach (please leave what you find). The privately owned, **Windsor Plantation** (*circa* 1857), stands as a typical representation of a sea-island home built up on piers to catch the cooling breeze and to avoid tempestuous tides.

Where US 17 intersects with the Atlantic, **Edisto Beach State Park** offers a mile of prime, seashell-covered beach and 1,255 acres (505 hectares) of oak forest and salt marsh.

LEFT: classy Hilton Head Island.
BELOW: the Gullah Festival is held near Beaufort.

Low Country folk art

Back on US 17, head inland on SC 64 to the town of **Walterboro** . Its main street is typical of many small, Southern towns, complete with a jail, courthouse, post office, pharmacy, barbershop, and a few specialty shops. Settled in 1784, its prosperity as the largest railroad depot on the Savannah-to-Charleston line in the mid-1890s can still be seen in its luxurious, antebellum and Victorian homes shaded by plentiful hickory trees. Thee are several churches dating back before the 18th century. The **Colleton Museum** (tel: 843-549-2303, closed Sun) and the **South Carolina Artisans Center** (tel: 843-549-0011, open daily) are both great places to view Low Country folk art. The 133-ft (41-meter) landmark tower slit with narrow windows at the edge of town is not, as some may suggest, a former prison, but rather a 100,000-gallon (380,000-liter) water tower.

Beaufort

Take SC 303 back to US 17 and head south toward Beaufort through the ACE Basin, where the Ashepoo, Combahee, and Edisto rivers form one of the largest estuarine systems on the east coast. Travel down US 21 past the horse farms, marshlands, and vegetable farms of Port Royal Island. When you reach Beaufort itself, head down Boundary Street until you reach Henry C. Chambers Waterfront Park and nearby historic Bay Street lined with specialty shops and boasting the town's favorite eateries and night-time hang-outs.

Established in 1711, **Beaufort**  (pronounced Bew-fort) is the second-oldest town in South Carolina. Its pre-Revolutionary homes are constructed of tabby and oyster shells, limestone, wooden pegs, and home-made nails. Its grand, antebellum homes point to a time of prosperity during the American Revolution.

BELOW: Rhett House Inn, near Beaufort.

Most of Beaufort's historic homes are privately owned, with the exception of the Federal-style **Verdier House**, built by a wealthy merchant in 1790. Along with Beaufort's historic churches (including the Old Sheldon Church ruins north of town), **The Beaufort Museum** (tel: 843-524-6334, closed Sun) is worth a visit for its history as home of the Beaufort Voluntary Artillery – one of the oldest military units in the nation. The sea islands surrounding Beaufort feature semi-tropical wildland and carry overtones of a Gullah heritage still alive today *(see page 281)*. The 19th-century lighthouse on Hunting Island offers a sweeping view of the coastline and state park below.

Hilton Head

Take SC 170 out of Beaufort heading south until you reach SC 278. Travel down this highway past the historic town of Bluffton, the scenic Pinckney Island National Wildlife Refuge until you reach **Hilton Head Island** ⓭, 30 miles (48 km) south of Beaufort.

Until the 1956 construction of a bridge linking the island to the mainland, Hilton Head resembled many of the other sea islands – isolated, rural, and poor with a population descended from slaves. In a region where change comes slowly, Hilton Head startled Low Country residents – and Hilton natives – with its sudden economic boon, and the many changes that prosperity brought.

Hilton Head has the nation's first master-planned resort and residential community, **Sea Pines**. Just one of the island's many resort "plantations" featuring golf, tennis, and water sports, Sea Pines also encompasses a forest preserve. The resort's **Harbour Town Yacht Basin and Marina** is a luxurious affair with its numerous specialty shops.

Bordered by loblolly pine, palmetto trees, and oak, Hilton Head's beaches shelter endangered, 200-lb (90-kg) loggerhead turtles, who bury their eggs in the soft sand on summer nights. Bottle-nosed dolphins are easy to spot, away from the public-access beaches. The **Coastal Discovery Museum** (tel: 843-689-6767, open daily) has hands-on nature exhibits, tours, and cruises exploring the local wildlife.

North of Charleston

North on US 17 from Charleston, take North SC 703 to **Sullivans Island** ⓮. The drive winds by waves of whistling spartina grass and over the Intracoastal Waterway right onto the island's Middle Street. All establishments are as rough-and-tumble as the island itself, so don't worry about tracking in the sand.

At the tip of the island facing Fort Sumter (where the first shots of the Civil War were fired, *see pages 93 and 272*) in Charleston Harbor, **Fort Moultrie** (tel: 843-883-3123, open daily) is on the site of the 1776 fort that withstood the British in the American Revolution, thanks to bullet-absorbing palmetto-logs – hence the palmetto emblem on the state flag.

Head back in the opposite direction on Middle Street for the **Isle of Palms**, with activities including biking, watersports, shrimping, and crabbing. On the northeast end of the island, the **Wild Dunes Resort** offers extensive golf and tennis facilities.

Map on page 262

South Carolina is known throughout the world for its championship golf courses.

BELOW: Port Royal.

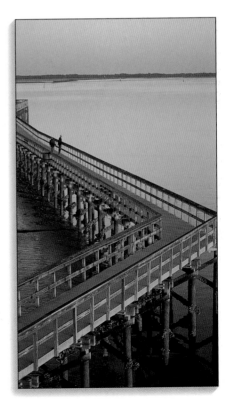

Back on US 17 just north of Charleston, **Mount Pleasant** (with a string of dockside seafood restaurants on Shem Creek) is the next town. Along the way, wooden roadside stands sell the area's famous hand-woven sweetgrass baskets, a Gullah tradition. Unlike the austere plantations farther north, **Boone Hall** (tel: 843-571-3123, open daily) is most people's idea of a genuine antebellum residence. The hall's breathtaking avenue of live oaks draped with Spanish moss is said to have inspired the plantation entrance for the movie *Gone with the Wind*. The present house was rebuilt in 1935, but the surrounding buildings are much older, dating to around the mid-1700s, and include a smokehouse and a gin house. Of particular note are the nine original slave cabins considered to be one of the best-preserved "slave streets" remaining.

Driving on US 17 toward McClellanville, pass through **Francis Marion National Forest**, which covers over 250,000 acres (100,000 hectares). Logging companies fight with environmentalists over the area, but don't get the wrong idea – thousands of acres have been preserved for endangered plants and animals, and hiking, camping, and canoeing facilities are reserved for lovers of the outdoors.

To experience more wilderness, venture out on SC 584 to **Moore's Landing**, where you can take an easy boat ride to **Cape Romain National Wildlife Refuge** (tel: 843-928-3368, closed Mon). A 22-mile (35-km) stretch of barrier islands, Cape Romain encompasses 90 million acres (36 million hectares) of land and water populated only by dolphins, egrets, pelicans, herons, and other wildlife viewed by boat, nature trail, and walking along the beach.

Bordered by the Francis Marion National Forest and the Cape Romain National Wildlife Refuge, is the small fishing village of **McClellanville** . Its history dates back to a hurricane-torn 1822 settlement. The shrimp boats, clam dredges, and oyster boats moving in and out of the local shrimp docks hark back to 1900 when McClellanville was the United States's largest exporter of oysters.

BELOW: sorting shrimp near Beaufort.

Ghost capital of the South

Georgetown is the third-oldest city in the state. This historic seaport's revitalized Downtown area features a Harborwalk on the Sampit River, and the town's Historic District keeps alive a vibrant past. Many residents think of it as a "little Charleston," complete with historic homes, sea-going vessels, and numerous B&B inns located Downtown and on Winyah Bay. It's also the ghost capital of the South – nearly every historic home has stories to tell of a resident spirit or two.

With the exception of the **Kaminski House Museum** (tel: 843-546-7706, open daily), which has a fine collection of 18th-century antiques, many homes are not open to the public but could be noted on any walking or driving tour. The **Rice Museum**, Prince George-Winyah Episcopal Church, and the Georgetown County Courthouse do allow visitors inside.

Famous for its handcrafted hammocks, **Pawley's Island** was used by 1800s plantation owners to escape the threat of malaria during the summer months. Although the hurricane of 1822 destroyed many of the earlier buildings, Pawley's remains the epitome of South Carolina beach towns, with its paint-peeled cottages standing watch over Myrtle Avenue. **Murrells Inlet** is the oldest fishing village in the state as well as the owner of the title "the seafood capital of South Carolina." Don't even think about leaving without sampling some of the seafood from one of the restaurants along this stretch of US 17. The catch is so fresh it practically swims into your plate.

Map
on page
262

Golf Coast

Myrtle Beach ⑱ visitors, young and old, whirl on the dance floors of the popular **Myrtle Beach Pavilion Amusement Park** (tel: 843-448-6456, hours vary), while thrill seekers race through the air on the famed Corkscrew. The most important ride, though, is a vintage Herschel-Spillman Merry-Go-Round. Built in 1912, it is one of fewer than 100 hand-carved carousels in the US.

On Ocean Boulevard, **Ripley's Believe It or Not Museum** (tel: 843-448-2331, open daily), the **Aquarium** (tel: 843-916-0888), and the **Moving Theater** (tel: 843-626-0069) offer different kinds of thrills. And the **Dixie Stampede** (tel: 843-497-9700, open Feb–Dec) gives an Old South spark to dinner-theater.

Myrtle Beach is just one stop along the 60-mile (100-km) stretch of beach called the **Grand Strand** that runs from the northern tip of South Carolina down to Georgetown. This strip has been called the "golf coast," with more than 75 championship golf courses and resorts.

Only 3 miles (5 km) to the south, the 312-acre (126-hectare) **Myrtle Beach State Park** is South Carolina's most popular state park. No surprise, really, with around 350 campsites, a 730-ft (220-meter) fishing pier, and the popular Sculptured Oak Nature Trail to divert and entertain all who stop by. ❏

BELOW: Harbour Town marina on Hilton Head Island.

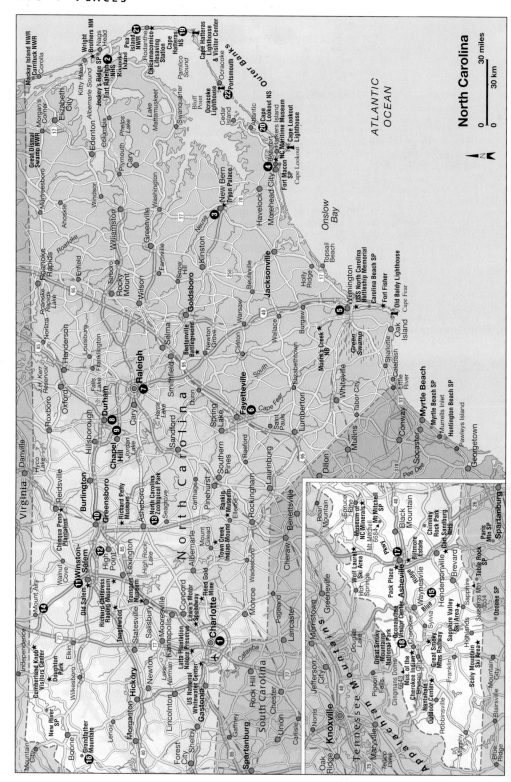

North Carolina

NORTH CAROLINA

A detailed guide to the entire state, with principal sites cross-referenced by number to the maps

Standing at the four corners of Trade and Tryon in Charlotte are huge sculptures entitled *Transportation, Commerce, Industry,* and *the Future*. Transportation is personified by a railroad worker, and Commerce by a gold miner spilling money on the head of a banker. A woman of the mills represents Industry, a child peeking from her skirts hinting at past child labor. A mother holding a child represents the Future of the city. The New South is proclaiming itself in North Carolina fresh, rejuvenated, and mindful of the homage that is due to its past. The International Civil Rights Center and Museum in Greensboro, and the Stagville Center in Durham are among the many living tributes to the black history of the South, and the evidence of the colonial South survives in forts and mansions throughout the state.

But North Carolina's eyes fix firmly on the prizes of the future. Textiles, tobacco, and tourism have been North Carolina's main industries until late, but banking and the clean-room high-tech industries have become a larger presence in recent years. Pure quartz crystals mined near Spruce Pine become key components in many of the world's computer chips, and Raleigh-Durham's Research Triangle Park leads the world with biotech innovation. Charlotte has grown to become one of the nerve centers of the world's banking.

For visitors, North Carolina is blessed with wild and wonderful coastal regions, romantically rolling hills, and the Blue Ridge Mountains that provided inspiration for Charles Frazier's *Cold Mountain*. The moderate four-season climate makes visits beautiful. Five interstate highways (26, 40, 77, 85, and 95) offer easy access to the state, and five airports (Charlotte, Raleigh-Durham, Greensboro, Asheville, and Wilmington) connect North Carolina to the rest of the world. Stretching westward over 500 miles (800 km) from Manteo to Murphy, the state has an abundance of scenic byways, designated by easy-to-follow highway markers, and out-of-the-way places perfect for exploring. The rugged Atlantic coastline is marked by the barrier islands that have wrecked thousands of ships, and offers spectacular views and walks near a wistful line of lighthouses, erected to guide and guard the shipping lanes.

Asheville has adopted the forward-looking nickname of "The Land of the Sky," of late, and the state is still known to many as "the Tar-Heel State." The origins of the Tar-Heel moniker are unclear, but may be derived from how the defending forces resolutely stuck their heels down in front of the British during the Revolutionary War. Still, whatever it chooses to call itself, North Carolina is a beautiful and very friendly place to visit. ❏

PRECEDING PAGES: Biltmore, near Asheville, is a 250-room French Renaissance chateau built by George Vanderbilt in 1895.

CHARLOTTE

*North Carolina's Queen City has grown
from a sleepy little backwater
into an international banking monarch*

Map
on page
292

C harlotte, North Carolina, the newest star in the New South firmament, grew from a regional sales center to one of the world's top banking capitals in the last few decades. Headquarters of the internationally prominent Bank of America, Charlotte sprouted a crown of skyscrapers befitting its nickname, "the Queen City." Between its soaring skyline and its shady canopy of willow oaks, the city deserves a reputation as one of the South's most beautiful modern cities. Named the "Best City to Live In" by the National Council of Mayors, Charlotte is in one of the US's fastest-growing urban areas. Over 500,000 people live within the city limits, with 1.6 million in the metro areas.

Industry and The Future

The Square, where Trade and Tryon streets cross, marks the heart of the city. Here the county's first courthouse reared on long pilings from the mud in 1768. Even before that, the crossroads figured significantly in the area's history. An ancient buffalo trail used by Native Americans crossed the Great Wagon Road from Pennsylvania here. Four statues ring The Square, representing Charlotte's history and heritage on a grand scale. Crafted by Raymond Kaskey, the monumental bronzes are representations of Transportation, Commerce, Industry and The Future, the city's bywords, both of yesterday and of today. The majority of Charlotte's cultural and entertainment offerings occupy the 12 blocks surrounding The Square. Restaurants, hotels, nightclubs, museums, and galleries line the streets in every direction. Although the **Center City** is easy and pleasant to walk around, with wide, well-lit sidewalks, free Gold Rush trolley buses can also take you within a block of most attractions.

On the southeast corner of the Square stands the 60-story **Bank of America Corporate Center Ⓐ** (100 North Tryon Sreet), world headquarters of the nation's largest consumer bank, and Charlotte's tallest skyscraper. Walk through the marble lobby (open daily), dominated by three fresco panels by local artist Ben Long to **Founders Hall**, a lofty atrium lined with shops and restaurants. On the second-floor balcony is the box-office of the **North Carolina Blumenthal Performing Arts Center** (tel: 704-372-1000, closed Sun), the city's premier performance venue and home stage of the acclaimed North Carolina Dance Theatre.

The Bank of America lobby is just one of several public buildings and churches around the city with frescos by North Carolina artist Ben Long. Charlotte has more frescos – an artform nearly forgotten since the Renaissance – than any other city outside of Italy.

At the entrance of **Transamerica Square** in the 400 block of North Tryon Street, Long created a

LEFT: public art in front of the Carillon Building. **BELOW:** sculpture on The Square.

frescoed dome, depicting North Carolina places and people, including former Bank of America CEO Hugh McColl. More frescoes are in the **First Presbyterian Church** (200 West Trade Street, tel: 704-331-0608, open weekdays), and the lobby of the **Charlotte-Mecklenburg Law Enforcement Center** (601 East Trade Street, tel: 704-336-2338, closed Sun).

A stroll down Tryon

Heading south on Tryon Street from The Square passes some of the newest and oldest buildings in the city. **Thomas Polk Park**, named for Charlotte's founder, is a good place to start on The Square's southwest corner. The tiny park's waterfall makes a refreshing stop on Charlotte's steamy summer days.

Three blocks south, look for the modest entrance to the **Latta Arcade** (316 South Tryon Street), one of Center City's few remaining commercial buildings from the early 20th century. The elegant glass-roofed arcade leads to narrow, pedestrian-only **Brevard Court**, lined with shops and restaurants, a scene

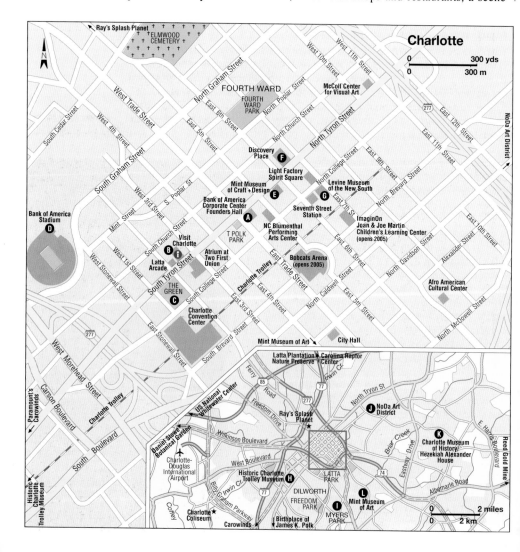

straight out of Charles Dickens. Next door, **Visit Charlotte at Main Street** ❸ (330 South Tryon, tel: 704-331-2700, closed Sun), the city's official visitor center, offers stacks of information on the city. Maps of historic Fourth Ward and the city's many works of public art, and guided tours are available from here. The tall buildings dominating the area here make up the headquarters of the third-largest consumer bank in the US, the **Wachovia Center**. Locals joke that the south end of Tryon belongs to Wachovia, while Bank of America holds sway north of The Square.

The Green

The Green ❸, Wachovia's most ambitious effort to date, is a park that stretches across the block from South Tryon to the entrance of the **Charlotte Convention Center** (500 South College Street, tel: 704-339-6000). On the park's south side, a fun fountain of spouting fish leads to an unusual and entertaining audio path, with motion-activated sounds.

The magnificent Radcliffe condominiums, million-dollar pieds-à-terre for Charlotte's glitterati, line the north side of the Green. This is the lair of sport celebs such as Bob Johnson, founder of the BET network and owner of the NBA Charlotte Bobcats, and NASCAR star Jeff Gordon. The historic 1920s shop, **Radcliffe Flowers** (435 South Tryon), that gave the project its name, today is a charming restaurant. The **Bank of America Stadium** ❸ (800 South Mint Street, tel: 704-358-7407) is a couple of blocks to the west, home of the NFL Carolina Panthers and dominating the landscape. Pairs of snarling black panthers with bronze fangs flank the stylish sports facility's entrances. Stop by the Team Store (open daily) for Panther gear, or for tours of the stadium.

Map on page 292

Charlotte is a center for the arts in the South.

BELOW: nightlife in a New South town.

The North End

In the blocks north of The Square, NationsBank, now Bank of America, changed the face of Charlotte's Downtown area. Most of its museums, and a cluster of galleries, dining, and nightlife are near **Bobcats Arena** (East Trade and North 5th Streets, tel: 704-262-2287), home of Charlotte's new NBA expansion team.

At the **Mint Museum of Craft + Design** 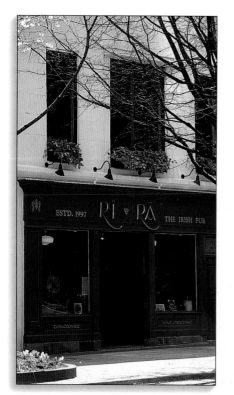 (220 North Tryon, tel: 704-337-2000, closed Mon), a Dale Chihuly-designed chandelier graces the lobby of one of the country's premier showcases of wood, ceramic, glass, and fiber art objects. The museum anchors an ever-expanding string of galleries and museums at Tryon's north end. Next door, in the Art Deco-inspired Hearst Building, the **Bank of America Gallery** (tel: 704-338-3104, closed Sun) exhibits selections from the country's largest corporate collection of art.

The **McColl Center for Visual Art** (721 North Tryon Street, tel: 704-332-5535, closed Sun); the **Light Factory** in Spirit Square (345 North College Street, tel: 704-333-9755, open daily), and the fine **Afro-American Cultural Center** (401 North Myers Street, tel: 704-374-1565, closed Mon), with a notable collection by black artists, are all within a few blocks. A new modern art museum and a new Center City location for the Mint Museum of Art will place Charlotte among the South's foremost art destinations.

The blocks to the west of North Tryon are Charlotte's oldest residential neighborhood, the **Fourth Ward**. Ornate Victorian homes restored to their original splendor line the shady sidewalks, making for a wonderful stroll, as long as it's not too hot. An IMAX theater and exhibits from dinosaurs to space exploration make learning fun at **Discovery Place** (301 North Tryon, tel: 704-372-6261, open daily), one of the top 10 hands-on science museums in the country.

BELOW: work hard, play hard.

The **Levine Museum of the New South** (200 East 7th Street, tel: 704-333-1887, closed Mon) presents a multimedia journey through the South and the city's heritage, from its days as a textile capital to its current status as a banking superpower. Special exhibits follow the career of native son, the preacher Billy Graham, and the rise of the motorsports industry. Behind the museum stands one of Charlotte's unique mixed-use buildings, **Seventh Street Station** (225 East 6th Street). A gourmet grocery and restaurants occupy the street level; above, a parking garage offers complimentary parking. Colorful panels decorate the outside of the building. Touch them and they respond with a chime… or a giggle.

The Station is one of the major stops on the Charlotte Trolley line. Across the tracks lies Charlotte's newest attraction for children, **ImaginOn, The Joan and Joe Martin Children's Learning Center** (East Seventh and Brevard streets, tel: 704-336-6204, call for opening times). A joint project of the local Children's Theatre and the Charlotte/Mecklenburg Public Library, the new center brings stories to life in a rich and entertaining setting.

Other attractions in the area especially attractive to younger visitors include an indoor waterpark, **Ray's Splash Planet** (215 North Sycamore Street, tel: 704-432-4729, open daily), and **Paramount's Carowinds** (tel: 704-588-2600, closed Nov–Apr), located 14 miles

(25 km) south of the Center City on I-77. The theme park thrills all ages with rides and coasters themed on Paramount movies. The extensive waterpark keeps the family cool on Carolina's hot summer days.

Older athletes enjoy a day at the **US National Whitewater Center** (tel: 704-372-9695, open daily). The US Olympic kayak team come for their training to the artificial rapids at this state-of-the-art facility on the Catawba River, 10 miles (16 km) west of Charlotte.

A trolley runs through it

Riding Charlotte's newly restored electric trolley is a highlight of any city visit. The trolley parallels Church Street through the Center City beginning at North 9th Street, then plunges through the Charlotte Convention Center, before passing over I-277 into **Historic South End**. Running daily into the evening hours, the trolley is a favorite way for visitors and locals to see the sights.

Once the heart of Charlotte's textile industry, the renovated mills and warehouses of South End house numerous dining and entertainment options. Hop aboard an antique trolley car for a do-it-yourself pub crawl or ride to the end of the line, where the **Historic Charlotte Trolley Museum ⓗ** (2104 South Boulevard, tel: 704-375-0850) tells the story of the city's early streetcar suburbs.

The spring blooming season (March to April) finds Charlotte residents and visitors alike cruising the streets of historic neighborhoods close to the Center City. **Myers Park ❶**, where most streets seem to be named Queens Road, has some of the city's most spectacular mansions. Beyond lies **South Park**, the area's top destination for upscale shopping.

East Boulevard, stretching from South Boulevard to Queens Road West, runs

Map on page 292

The Levine Museum of the New South, 200 East 7th Street, presents a multimedia journey through Charlotte's, and the South's, distinctive heritage. Tel: 704-333-1887.

BELOW: the Mint Museum of Craft + Design.

through the heart of historic **Dilworth** past restored Queen Anne mansions and a row of restaurants. At **Freedom Park** (1900 East Boulevard, tel: 704-336-2884), a favorite spot for strolling, paved paths circle a lake, passing groves of cherry trees and a children's nature museum. To experience more of Carolina's fabulous flora, visit **Daniel Stowe Botanical Garden** (Belmont, tel: 704-825-4490, open daily), one of the South's must-see horticultural showcases.

NoDa Arts District

Artists in search of inexpensive studio space redeemed a run-down mill village just north of Downtown, turning it into a bohemian community of studios and galleries they dubbed **NoDa ❶**. Upscale condominiums followed, and today a dynamic art scene centers around North Davidson and 36th streets. Coffee shops, theaters, and some of the city's best art galleries teem with an eclectic mixture of locals during the Gallery Crawls, which are held on the first and third Friday of every month.

Long before this current renaissance, there was another Charlotte, with an historical story dating back to colonial times. Citizens adopted the Mecklenburg Declaration of Independence on May 20, 1775, a year before the Continental Congress signed their more famous Declaration. Charlotte witnessed the country's first gold rush after Conrad Reed found a huge gold nugget on his family's farm. So much gold came out of the area's mines that the first branch of the US Mint was established here.

Explore the region's early history at the **Charlotte Museum of History ⓚ** (3500 Shamrock Road, tel: 704-568-1774, closed Mon). On the museum grounds is the **Hezekiah Alexander House**, the oldest stone building in the

THE LAND OF NASCAR

For stock-car racing fans, Charlotte is a pilgrimage. With 90 percent of all active NASCAR race teams based in the area, and Lowe's Motor Speedway, home of two important Nextel Cup races, on Charlotte's northeast border, the region offers race fans more sights per mile than any other. At the Speedway, take a narrated tour of Lowe's famous tri-oval, offered daily. Learn to drive a real racecar at the Richard Petty Driving Experience. For a lesser investment, pilot a miniature car at the NASCAR SpeedPark in nearby Concord Mills Mall (I-85, exit 49).

Near the Speedway, the Sam Bass Illustration & Design Museum, the Hendrick Motorsports Museum, and Roush Racing recall the stars and cars that made racing history.

Just 23 miles (37 km) north on I-77, the town of Mooresville (pop. 19,000) bills itself as "Race City USA." Make your first stop the North Carolina Auto Racing Hall of Fame to pick up a map of the many race shops that welcome visitors. One site not to be missed is Dale Earnhardt, Inc., the Taj Mahal of garages.

About an hour north on I-85 lie two other landmarks: the Richard Petty Museum in Randleman and the Richard Childress Racing Museum in Welcome, dedicated to the memory of driver Dale Earnhardt.

county and home of one of the signers of the "Meck Dec." The interior, open for guided tours, contains many period furnishings. At **Reed Gold Mine** (Stanfield, tel: 704-721-4653, open daily) in Cabarras County, now a state historic site, you can learn how gold was prospected and processed, tour the tunnels, and pan for gold yourself.

The **Mint Museum of Art** ❶ (2730 Randolph Road, tel: 704-337-2000, closed Mon) is housed in the original Mint building. This branch of the Mint hosts important traveling exhibitions as well its own massive collections of European porcelain, South American Pre-Columbian and Spanish Baroque art.

Billy Graham territory

One of Charlotte's most famous sons returns to his roots with the opening of the **Billy Graham Center for World Evangelism** (tel: 704-401-2432) off the Billy Graham Parkway in southwest Charlotte. The campus features the evangelist's childhood home, as well as a museum documenting his many crusades and the official archive of his writings.

For a sampler of the region's charms, **Latta Plantation Nature Preserve** (Huntersville, tel: 704-875-2312, open daily), 12 miles (19 km) north of town, makes an excellent destination. This star of the Mecklenburg County Park and Recreation system includes a historic plantation house (tel: 704-875-2312, closed Mon), the **Carolina Raptor Center** (tel: 704-875-6521, open daily), home to injured birds of prey, and the **Latta Equestrian Center** (tel: 704-875-0808, open daily), offering trail rides year-round. Nature trails stretch down to the shores of Mountain Island Lake, where you can rent a canoe or kayak. It's the perfect place to spend another North Carolina day. ❑

Map on page 292

BELOW: the best place for movies in the NoDa neighborhood.

AROUND NORTH CAROLINA

The flourishing fortunes of Pepsi-Cola and the biotech Research Triangle Park bring a touch of modernity to a region known in the past mainly for tobacco and the Smoky Mountains

Map on page 288

From the wild dunes of the Outer Banks to the highest mountains in the east, North Carolina offers some of the most varied, and most scenic, vistas in the South. Its history is equally varied, stretching from the site of the first British colony on the continent to research laboratories where today's biotech breakthroughs are made. This chapter follows the development of the state, beginning by the sea and then moving westwards. From centrally located **Charlotte ❶**, Interstate 85 runs toward Greensboro *(see page 303)*, then tours east towards the sea and west to the mountains.

The Roanoke Mystery

Twenty years before Jamestown and 43 years before the Pilgrims landed on Plymouth Rock, British settlers chose Roanoke Island, between the mainland and the Outer Banks, as the site of the first English colony in the New World. They named their settlement after their patron, the adventurer Sir Walter Raleigh, and began to build. But the colony came to a mysterious end. When Governor John White returned after a three-year absence, he found the fort abandoned, and the colonists gone. The word "Croatoan" carved on a post provided the only clue to their disappearance.

Controversy has raged ever since about the fate of the colonists, but the mystery remains. During the summer months, the state's original outdoor drama, *The Lost Colony* (tel: 252-473-3414, Jun–Aug), recounts the history of the Roanoke settlement and speculates on its fate. The play has fared better than the colony itself. Written by Pulitzer Prize-winner Paul Green, it has run every summer since 1937 at the Waterside Theater, on the grounds of **Fort Raleigh National Historic Site ❷** (tel: 252-473-5772, open daily), itself a reconstruction of the 1585 palisade.

From Roanoke Island, continue to the Outer Banks *(see page 310)*, just minutes away, or turn inland and wander through the state's eastern counties, an intricate maze of inlets and tidal rivers. The abundance of marshes makes this one of the best bird-watching areas on the East Coast. Huge flocks of snow geese and swans winter in these wetlands, also inhabited by alligator, deer, red wolves, and black bear.

Early settlers established towns along the rivers of eastern Carolina, and some of the most interesting lie along US 17, the highway through eastern Carolina, running 285 miles (459 km) from Virginia to South Carolina. Throughout the region are scenic harbors and waterfronts that captivate photographers.

Towns worth a visit include **Elizabeth City**, a seaport at the edge of the Great Dismal Swamp, 20 miles (32 km) from the Virginia border, and **Edenton**, said

LEFT: the Smokies and the bears. **BELOW:** the play *The Lost Colony* is performed every summer.

The ocean town of Calabash, near the border with South Carolina, has given its name to a style of seafood, lightly breaded and fried.

BELOW: North Carolina flag in Wilmington.

to be one of the prettiest towns in the South. **Bath**, the colony's first incorporated town (1705), retains many of its original buildings. In **New Bern ❸** (pop. 24,000), costumed guides re-create the gracious life of North Carolina's royal governors at **Tryon Palace** (tel: 252-514-4900, open daily). The magnificent Georgian mansion, rebuilt from the original plans, was one of the finest buildings in the colonies. New Bern also gave Pepsi-Cola to the world; you can sip a bit of history at the re-created soda fountain (256 Middle Street, tel: 252-636-5898, closed Sun) where the formula was invented in 1898. From New Bern, it's 37 miles (60 km) down US 70 to Morehead City and **Beaufort ❹** (pronounced in North Carolina "*BO-furt*"), once the colony's largest seaport. The area rings with tales of the pirate Blackbeard, who ran his ship, the *Queen Anne's Revenge*, ashore near Beaufort. The **North Carolina Maritime Museum** (tel: 252-728-7317, open daily) displays items from the wreck.

The Cape Fear Coast

Along the coast south about 90 miles (145 km) is **Wilmington ❺** (pop. 90,000), North Carolina's largest port, founded in 1739. Wilmington celebrates its history in one of the nation's largest historic commercial districts, extending 200 blocks along the Cape Fear River. Lovingly restored shops, restaurants, galleries, inns, and museums, make for one of the most vibrant scenes in the state.

The **Battleship *USS North Carolina*** (tel: 910-251-5797, open daily), veteran of many World War II Pacific engagements, dominates the shore on the far side, and a vintage navy launch taxis visitors across. The Battleship is the site of a spectacular 4th of July party with a huge fireworks display.

During the Civil War, Wilmington was the last port remaining open to the Confederacy. Blockade-runners supplied Richmond and the Confederate armies until the 1865 fall of **Fort Fisher** (Kure Beach, tel: 910-458-5538, closed Sun, Mon in winter). Wilmington today is North Carolina's film capital, with over 400 film-related projects produced. Weekend tours of the **EUE/Screen Gems Studios** are available during the summer months (tel: 910-343-3433).

A string of North Carolina's most popular beaches, including Carolina, Wrightsville, and Kure, lie just minutes from Wilmington. At **Carolina Beach State Park** (tel: 910-458-8206, open daily), the Flytrap Trail leads past beds of carnivorous plants, native only to the Cape Fear watershed. One further stop along US 17 is a particular delight for foodies. **Calabash** (pop. 1,500), just before the South Carolina border, lends its name to a famous lightly breaded and fried seafood. Steamed oysters are another local specialty.

Interstate 40 runs 420 miles (676 km) across North Carolina, from Wilmington to the Tennessee border. Passing through four of the state's major cities, it is a handy corridor for exploration, but for all that North Carolina offers, consider some side trips, too.

The "Old North" state is noted for its natural beauty, so branch off the beaten path by land or sea. Paddling a canoe or kayak or rafting are inviting options. Even novices enjoy the easy paddling in eastern North Carolina's blackwater rivers, where paddle trails lead through stands of cypress trees hundreds of years old, hung with Spanish moss. Further west, paddles become more challenging, culminating with some of the best whitewater runs in the country on the Nantahala, New, French Broad and other mountain rivers. The **Nantahala Outdoor Center** (tel: 800-232-7238) organizes trips for every ability. Hiking is also a lovely way to see the sights, especially in western North Carolina, where thousands of miles of footpaths, including the **Appalachian Trail**, wind over the mountains.

Map on page 288

The Sandhills to the center of the state

Ancient sand dunes form a unique ecosystem in southeast North Carolina. Home of the longleaf pine and the endangered red-cockaded woodpecker, the area is also a famous golfing destination. For dedicated golfers, a pilgrimage to the **Pinehurst Resort** (tel: 910-235-8553, open daily) to play the legendary Number 2 is a must. Designed by Donald Ross in 1907, this course consistently ranks among the country's top 10.

A military history detour beckons through nearby **Fayetteville** ❻ (pop. 125,000) and **Fort Bragg**, where museums detail the history of America's fighting forces, including the state-of-the-art **Airborne and Special Operations Museum** (tel: 910-483-3003, closed Mon).

Raleigh, Durham, and Chapel Hill form a rough triangle bounded by I-85, I-40, and I-95 about 90 miles (145 km) west of Wilmington. This is the heartland and favorite jumping ground of the legendary Atlantic Athletic Conference of basketball fame. The North Carolina State Wolfpack of Raleigh, the Carolina Tarheels of Chapel Hill, and the Duke Blue Devils of Durham are some of the winningest teams in college hoops.

BELOW: be here on the 4th of July for a fantastic fireworks display.

Raleigh-Durham

This area has an abundance of excellent state- and university-sponsored museums, gardens, and other attractions, all of which charge no admission, making this a teriffic destination for travelers on a budget. **Raleigh ❼** (pop. 300,000), is North Carolina's capital city, with an active arts and entertainment scene. The **North Carolina Museum of Art** (tel: 919-839-6262, closed Mon, Tues); the **North Carolina Museum of Natural Sciences** (tel: 919-733-7450, open daily) and its neighbor, the **North Carolina Museum of History** (tel: 919-715-0200, closed Mon), are some of the the highlights of over a dozen free museums, tours and gardens in Raleigh.

Durham ❽ (pop. 200,000), once a thriving tobacco capital, today grabs headlines as the home of **Duke University** and its famous medical center, endowed by the immense Duke tobacco fortune. A stroll through the magnolia trees that line the neo-gothic West Campus reveals many treasures, including **Duke Chapel** (tel: 919-684-2572, open daily) where patriarch Washington Duke lies in marble state; the extensive **Sarah P. Duke Gardens** (tel: 919-684-3698, open daily); and the new **Nasher Museum of Art** (tel: 919-684-5135, closed Mon).

Chapel Hill ❾ (pop. 50,000) remains the quintessential college town. The University of North Carolina, founded here in 1789, is the nation's oldest state-supported college. Stroll down Franklin Street to soak up the student vibe. Notable sights on campus include the **North Carolina Botanical Garden** (tel: 919-962-0522, open daily), the office of Chapel Hill alum Charles Kuralt (tel: 919-962-1204, open Tues and Thur); and the Memorabilia Room at the **Dean E. Smith Center** (tel: 919-962-6000, open weekdays), where athlete supremo

Durham, known as the City of Medicine USA, has a physician-to-patient ratio four times the national average.

BELOW:
State Capitol
building, Raleigh.

Michael Jordan's jersey holds center court. There's another important triangle within the Triangle, the world-famous **Research Triangle Park** (RTP). This special business park, set aside for high-tech companies, hothouses some of the top biotech research facilities in the nation. Pick up a driving-tour brochure at the Durham Visitor Center (tel: 919-687-0288, closed Sun).

Map on page 288

The Triad Heartland

About an hour's drive to the west of the Triangle, the combined interstates I-40 and I-85 bring you to Greensboro, Winston-Salem, and High Point, the major towns of the Triad. Early settlers of these rolling Piedmont hills came from sects seeking religious freedom, an influence that continues today.

Sports Illustrated named Chapel Hill the "Number One College Town in America."

Quakers founded **Greensboro** ❿ (pop. 225,000), named after the "Quaker General" Nathanael Greene, who inflicted a costly victory on British general Cornwallis during the American Revolution. **Guilford Courthouse National Military Park** (tel: 336-288-1776, open daily) presents a compelling re-creation of the hotly contested battle. In 1960, the city made a landmark contribution to the civil rights movement when the "Greensboro Four" staged the first sit-in at the local Woolworth's, now maintained as the **International Civil Rights Center and Museum** (tel: 336-274-9199, open weekdays).

Moravians settled the Wachovia tract, now the city of **Winston-Salem** ⓫ (pop. 190,000), in the mid-1700s, and presentations in the historic part of the city, at **Old Salem** (tel: 336-721-7300, open daily) re-create their culture, led by docents in period attire. From the present-day Czech Republic, the Moravians first put down roots in Bethlehem, Pennsylvania, and later moved to North Carolina at the invitation of a lord proprietor who wanted industrious people who

BELOW:
Duke University chapel, Durham.

Stop for a pot of tea and tasty Moravian cookies in Old Salem

could make a contribution to the area. On the grounds are a Toy Museum, and a museum of early Southern decor. Sample the famous Moravian cookies at Winkler Bakery, or dine on authentic dishes at the Old Salem Tavern.

High Point  (pop. 90,000) has over 120 furniture factories, including the 15 largest in the world, and proudly calls itself the "Home Furnishings Capital of the World." Unbelievable discounts on furnishings attract shoppers from near and far. Many also enjoy a souvenir photograph at a local landmark, the **World's Largest Chest of Drawers,** at 508 Hamilton Street. A half-hour drive down I-73/74 from the Triad leads to one of the state's most popular destinations – the **North Carolina Zoo** (tel: 336-879-7001, open daily) in **Asheboro.** The nation's largest natural-habitat zoo exhibits animals from Africa and North America. The polar bears, seen entertainingly through an underwater window, are a local favorite.

Fans of fine pots will want to continue a further 12 miles (19 km) down I-73 to **Seagrove,** the pottery capital of the South. More than 100 potteries in the area fire pieces from North Carolina's distinctive red clay. Seagrove's busy **North Carolina Pottery Center** (tel: 336-873-8430, closed Sun, Mon) provides maps to area potteries, and exhibits some of the finest examples of North Carolina clay art, including the popular "face jugs."

US 64 west from Asheboro leads to **Lexington** (pop. 20,000), a major capital of barbecue. Come hungry. Nearly two dozen specialty restaurants here serve "chopped pig" cooked over a hickory fire and topped with a secret sauce.

The little town of **Mount Airy** (pop. 8,500), 35 miles (56 km) north of Winston-Salem on I-74, came to fame when native son Andy Griffith used it as the model for Mayberry, the fictional town of his romantically rural TV series.

BELOW:
Old Salem was
settled in 1766.

OPEN

Fans today find the town largely unspoiled. You can savor a pork-chop sandwich at **Snappy Lunch**, or have a haircut at **Floyd's City Barber Shop**. The **Andy Griffith Museum** in the Mount Airy Visitor Center (tel: 336-789-4636, open daily) displays a wealth of Andy's personal memorabilia. Mount Airy is also a noted center for bluegrass and old-time music. Shows and jam sessions feature the region's top fiddlers and banjo pickers, and take place every week, year-round. Admission is usually free.

Map on page 288

Blue Ridge Parkway

The **Blue Ridge Parkway** ⓰ runs through 469 miles (755 km) of dramatic mountain scenery, joining Shenandoah National Park in Virginia with Great Smoky Mountains National Park on the North Carolina/Tennessee border. Although the parkway is open year-round, some sections may be closed in winter due to snow. Check with the National Park Service (tel: 828-298-0398) for up-to-the-minute weather conditions.

Traffic backups often tie up the 252 miles (405 km) of the parkway in North Carolina, especially during the autumn foliage season. The two-lane roadway is winding and often narrow, with low speed limits and steep grades. If possible, allow several days to tour. Also, bring a sweater, even in summer; temperatures are often 10 degrees or more cooler than in the Carolina lowlands. If you plan on hiking in the mountains, pack foul-weather gear, water, and high-energy snacks. Concrete mileposts – marked "MP" – announce distances along the parkway. NC 89, running 20 miles (32 km) west from Mount Airy, enters at MP 217, close to the Virginia border, near **Cumberland Knob Visitor Center**. Fabulous overlooks, trails, and campgrounds encourage frequent stops to

BELOW: the nation's largest natural-habitat zoo is in Asheboro.

THE BLACK SOUTH

For generations, the South ignored, and even belittled, its African-American heritage. Now, memorials to black history have become important stops for visitors of all colors. The black South is the foundation of the region's very existence. In the early years, it was mainly the black population who paved the streets, built the buildings, and toiled in the fields that brought wealth to the region.

There are over 500 historic sites of African-American significance throughout the South. Some represent the shameful legacy of slavery and the struggle for civil rights; others pay tribute to the black South's uplifting music and art. They evoke mythic figures such as Casey Jones, Mr Bojangles, Kunta Kinte, Porgy and Bess. As a collection, they represent the substantial contribution Southern blacks have made to the United States. Many regional tourist boards now provide brochures of important sites of black heritage, and African-American walking trails.

Important black sites are detailed throughout this book, but of particular significance are the Martin Luther King National Historic Site, Atlanta (see page 113), the National Civil Rights Museum, Memphis (see page 242), and the artful Gullah Tours around Charleston (see page 270). See also the feature on civil rights in Alabama, page 141.

explore and learn more about the cultural and natural history of the Southern Appalachians, and also to savor the stupendous views. Although wildflowers bloom along the parkway throughout the summer, the mountain laurel, rhododendron, and flame azaleas are most magnificent in June and July. Some of the best places to see them are **Doughton Park** at MP 238 and **Craggy Gardens** at MP 364, where acres of purple and pink blossoms delight the eye.

The Southern Highlands Craft Guild displays traditional mountain handicrafts at a number of attractive stops along the parkway, including **Flat Top Manor** (tel: 828-295-7938, closed winter) in Moses Cone Park, MP 294 near Blowing Rock; and the **Folk Art Center** (tel: 828-298-7928, open daily) just outside Asheville at MP 382.

The High Country

The Boone/Blowing Rock area (MP 291) makes a good overnight stop near the parkway's north end. An outdoor drama, *Horn in the West* (tel: 828-264-2120, Jun–Aug), recounts the life of pioneer and local hero Daniel Boone.

Charles Kuralt, a state native and host of over 600 *On the Road* TV travel shows, loved this area. Follow his footsteps to **Grandfather Mountain** ⑯ (tel: 828-733-4337, open daily), a United Nations Biosphere Preserve noted for families of black bears and a mile-high hanging bridge. Kuralt liked to hang out by the pot-bellied stove at **Mast General Store** (tel: 828-963-6511, open daily) in Valle Crucis. Virgin stands of white pine and hemlock and groves of flowering rhododendron line the short trail to spectacular **Linville Falls** (tel: 828-652-1103, open daily).

The **Museum of North Carolina Minerals** (tel: 828-765-9483, open daily) at MP 331 displays minerals and gemstones, including emeralds, diamonds, and rubies, mined in the Carolina mountains. NC 128 branches off at MP 355 to **Mount Mitchell State Park** (tel: 828-675-4611) where a paved road leads to the top of the highest peak in the eastern United States at 6,684 ft (2 km). An exhibit hall (open May-Oct) near the summit explores the mountain's geology, history and weather.

Mountain Crossroads

Asheville ⑰ (pop. 70,000), located at the intersection of I-40, I-26, and the Blue Ridge Parkway (MP 380), provides an excellent staging area for journeys into the surrounding mountains. It is also the home of one of North Carolina's most famous attractions, the magnificent **Biltmore Estate** (tel: 828-225-1333, open daily). The 250-room French Renaissance chateau built by George Vanderbilt in 1895 is considered by many to be the United States' grandest castle. Plan to spend a full day exploring the house and extensive gardens, and sampling wines at the popular Biltmore Winery.

Cosmopolitan Asheville's renovated Art Deco Downtown area is awash with boutiques, coffee houses, craft shops, galleries, and a variety of dining options. There is definitely a scene here, with more artists and young professionals moving in each month. Asheville's city centerpiece, **Pack Place Education,**

BELOW: mile-high swinging bridge on Grandfather Mountain.

Arts and Science Center (tel: 828-257-4500, closed Mon), houses a complex of museums including the Asheville Museum of Art and the Colburn Gem and Mineral Museum. Out front, in Pack Square, look for a replica of the winged statue immortalized in Thomas Wolfe's classic *Look Homeward, Angel.* Wolfe, a native, evoked many of the city's locations in his autobiographical novel. His mother's boarding house, where much of the story takes place, is preserved as a part of the **Thomas Wolfe Memorial** (tel: 828-253-8304, closed Mon).

Less than an hour's drive outside Asheville, **Chimney Rock Park** (tel: 828-625-9281, open daily) offers a stunning view of the Carolina Piedmont and Lake Lure, selected by *National Geographic* as one of the 10 most beautiful artificial lakes. Walk up or take the 26-story elevator to the top of the natural granite tower.

The Southern Highlands

Beyond Asheville, the Blue Ridge Parkway continues for 90 more winding miles (145 km) through the Pisgah and Nantahala National Forests, a journey that can take most of a day, before reaching the final milepost, 469, just outside Cherokee and Great Smoky Mountains National Park. Travelers on a schedule may prefer the more direct route via I-40, US 23/74 and US 19 (50 miles, 80 km), which reaches Cherokee in less than two hours.

The home of the eastern branch of the Cherokee Nation has a story to tell. The Native Americans here descend from the remnant of the tribe who avoided forced removal to Oklahoma in 1838. An outdoor drama presentation, *Unto These Hills* (tel: 828-497-2111, Jun–Aug), recounts the history of the Cherokee, from the arrival of the Spanish in 1540 to the tragic "Trail of Tears" that took thousands of lives on the long, forced march west.

Map on page 288

There are over 100 potteries in the area around Seagrove.

BELOW: skyline view of Asheville from the mountains.

Map
on page
288

The hotel at Harrah's Cherokee Casino exhibits the world's largest collection of contemporary Cherokee art.

BELOW: Cherokee, North Carolina.

There are more heartbreaking tales about the Trail of Tears at the **Museum of the Cherokee Indian** (tel: 828-497-3481, open daily). **Oconaluftee Indian Village** (tel: 828-497-2315, closed Nov–Apr) re-creates the daily life of the tribe in the 1750s. The deluxe-but money-draining **Harrah's Cherokee Casino** (tel: 828-497-7777), on the reservation, offers blackjack, slots, and stage shows. Fortunately, profits benefit the tribe.

Behind Cherokee rise the Great Smokies, the largest untamed wilderness remaining in the eastern United States, also the most visited of all the national parks, with 9 million visitors annually. The 33-mile (53-km) road over Newfound Gap to Gatlinburg, Tennessee, the main route through the park, often backs up with traffic, especially when one of the resident black bears puts in an appearance. Stop at **Oconaluftee Visitor Center ⑱** (tel: 423-436-1200, open daily), 2 miles (3 km) north of Cherokee, for maps and information.

The roof of the South

West of Cherokee, the North Carolina mountains stretch for many more miles through a country of waterfalls, ruby mines, and villages full of summer visitors and antique shops. Scenic byways invite you to roam, or you can take the **Great Smoky Mountains Railroad** (tel: 828-586-8811, open year-round) from Dillsboro for a spine-tingling trip through steep gorges.

Here on the roof of the South, the borders of Georgia, Tennessee, North and South Carolina lie close together. The scenery is wild, and cultural roots run deep. Festivals of music and dance, and schools that teach traditional crafts, along with luxurious resorts and historic inns, all preserve the unique heritage of North Carolina's Southern Highlands. ❑

Hollywood's View

The rich landscapes of the South, from the Appalachian Mountains through the South Carolina swamps across the Mississippi Delta all the way to darkly exotic New Orleans, have for years offered movie-makers backdrops for romance and adventure.

Played by Gregory Peck, small-town lawyer Atticus Finch brought Southern issues vividly to a head in the 1962 movie of Harper Lee's Alabama story, *To Kill A Mockingbird*. The tender tale is believed to be drawn from that most reclusive of author's childhood in Monroeville. A childhood she shared, incidentally, with the rather less reclusive Truman Capote, screenwriter of *Breakfast at Tiffany's* and a collaborator on a deeply sinister adaptation of Henry James's 1898 story *The Turn of the Screw*, filmed in 1961 as *The Innocents*.

The contradictions, rivalries, and bitter ironies of the Civil War in Georgia combined for the 1939 classic that's still thought of as the quintessential Southern romance; the film of Margaret Mitchell's *Gone with the Wind* tallied up eight Oscars in Hollywood.

"The War" continues to provide a thought-provoking context, and as the majority of the battles were fought on Confederate land, the South is always the cinema setting. Robert F. Maxwell's 2002 four-hour behemoth *Gods and Generals* made a serious attempt to get inside Rebel hero Stonewall Jackson's camp. With its terrific length, and a point-of-view that may have unsettled some audiences, even Robert Duvall's meticulous portrayal of the general couldn't win large audiences.

The 2003 adaptation of *Cold Mountain* may have suffered a similar fate; movie-goers seem a little reluctant to stand in line for re-appraisals of the war. Using only a few shots of the Blue Ridge Mountains, the film crew decamped to the chilly, less-expensive hills of Romania to use as a substitute for evocative North Carolina. The film was better received in Europe than in America.

Successful modern films with Southern themes continue to emphasize the romantic, tragic, comedic, and Gothic elements that are so much a part of the image of Dixie. The South Carolina swamplands lent a terrifying "parallel universe" reality to John Boorman's 1972 fear-fest, *Deliverance*. In 1989, Bruce Beresford scooped up three Oscars for *Driving Miss Daisy*, the amiable comedy of a Jewish woman (Jessica Tandy) and her relationship with her black chauffeur.

The Southern gift of storytelling was highlighted in 1991 with Fannie Flagg's tale of reminiscence, *Fried Green Tomatoes at the Whistle Stop Café*, fetching another Southern Oscar statuette nomination for Miss Tandy. John Grisham's legal pot-boilers have also met with considerable success, with *The Firm*, *The Pelican Brief*, *The Client,* and *The Runaway Jury* all set against Southern backdrops like Memphis and New Orleans.

Plots turning on Southern manners and mores have seduced cinemagoers since the silver screen first flickered alight, and Southern sentiments, accents and manners will no doubt go on providing screenwriters with inexhaustable creative inspiration. ❏

RIGHT: it wasn't until after *Gone with the Wind* had started shooting that a 25-year-old English actress, Vivien Leigh, was cast as the heroine.

THE OUTER BANKS

*With wide, water-thrashed beaches and sea oats along low
sand dunes, the islands of the Outer Banks retain
a certain wildness despite encroaching development*

A string of narrow islands and peninsulas along the far eastern shore, the Outer Banks emerge like the head of a whale breaching into the Atlantic. Two coastlines, **Cape Hatteras National Seashore ⑲** and **Cape Lookout National Seashore ⑳**, preserve 120 miles (190 km) of these beaches on Bodie, Hatteras and Ocracoke islands, and Core and Shackleford banks. While most coastal islands lie within 10 miles (16 km) of shore, the Outer Banks belong to the realm of the sea. In places, 30 miles (48 km) of water separate Hatteras Island from the mainland. The Outer Banks are perfect for peace, isolation, national parks, watersports, fishing, hang-gliding, and getting away from it all. Lodging and other visitor amenties are available in the areas not designated as National Seashores; for details of these, contact the Outer Banks Visitors Bureau, tel: 877-BY-THE-SEE, www.outerbanks.org.

National Seashores

The National Seashores of the Outer Banks have their own personalities, distinct from the rest of the state. The islands have wide, water-thrashed beaches. Scattered patches of sea oats and beach grasses bind low dunes behind them. Clumps of shrubby marsh elder and bayberry dot the swales. Most trees lean away from

BELOW:
Bodie Lighthouse.

the sea, a feature formed by the relentless salt spray that stunts the branches on windward sides.

Two strong navigational currents pass off the Outer Banks. The Gulf Stream flows north from Florida at a speed of about 4 knots. It swings east near **Cape Hatteras**, providing a perfect send-off for ships bound for Europe. The cooler Virginia Coastal Drift flows closer to shore. Near the crook in **Hatteras Island**, navigational hazards in the form of submerged and shifting sandbars reach 8 to 10 miles (13 to 16 km) out to sea. Early ship captains dreaded this passage; the islands are so low that, to read natural landmarks, they had to remain close to shore. But they dared not venture near Diamond Shoals, the "graveyard of the Atlantic." Over the centuries, more than 600 ships ended their journeys disastrously here.

To warn ships of hazardous waters, the construction of lighthouses was a high priority during colonial times. Cape Hatteras got its first lighthouse, a 90-ft (27-meter) sandstone tower, in 1803. The present one was completed in 1870. With 1¼ million bricks, it towers 208 ft (63 meters) above the beach and the seagulls, the tallest lighthouse in the United States.

When it was built, the **Cape Hatteras Lighthouse** stood 1,500 ft (450 meters) from shore. Decades of erosion have brought waves within 200 ft (60 meters) of its base. The keeper's quarters house a museum and a visitor center (tel: 252-995-4474, open daily).

Map on page 288

Lighthouses mark other portions of the Outer Banks. All have distinctive exterior patterns and flash for different time periods at night so that navigators can identify them. The squat, whitewashed **Ocracoke Lighthouse** was built in 1823, the oldest still operating in North Carolina. Diamond-patterned **Cape Lookout Lighthouse**, completed in 1859, warns sailors of the low-lying Core Banks. The horizontally striped **Bodie Island Lighthouse**, in service since 1872, guards Oregon Inlet. During the late 19th century, the US Life-Saving Service established guard stations at 8-mile (13-km) intervals along the banks. Patrolmen paced the beaches, scouting for ships in distress. When a vessel grounded, they rushed to its aid with a lifeboat and rescue equipment. Two of the original life-saving stations, **Chicamacomico** (at Rodanthe) and **Little Kinnakeet** (near Avon) remain. At Chicamacomico, park interpreters re-enact life-saving drills on some afternoons in summer.

Cape Hatteras's islands are linked by Route 12. The **Bodie Island** and Hatteras Island sections of the seashore surround **Pea Island National Wildlife Refuge ㉑**. Observation platforms and several short trails lead from the highway to excellent viewpoints for watching the Canada and snow geese, whistling swans, and migratory ducks that spend the winter at the refuge. Pull-offs along Route 12 offer access to the beach, while long piers at **Rodanthe, Avon,** and **Frisco** give anglers a rare opportunity to cast for deep-water fish, which are not normally caught in the surf.

December 2003 marked the 100th anniversary of the Wright Brothers' powered flight. This was celebrated locally with vintage aircraft shows and military fly-overs.

First in flight

Near **Kitty Hawk** is **Kill Devil Hills** – named, some say, for drink that would kill even the Devil – and the granite **Wright Brothers National Memorial** (tel: 252-441-7132, open daily), which commemorates the first powered airplane flight by brothers Orville and Wilbur Wright on December 17, 1903. At **Nags Head**, many visitors stop for a walk on **Jockeys Ridge**, a towering and unstabilized sand dune that migrates with the prevailing winds. Access to **Ocracoke Island**, at the southern end of Cape Hatteras, is via ferry from Hatteras; for information on ferry schedules, telephone: 800-BY-FERRY.

Ocracoke is also the departure point for the historic village of **Portsmouth ㉒**, at the north end of Cape Lookout. Early residents of Portsmouth made their living "lightering" (transferring) cargo from ocean-going vessels to boats that served Core and Pamlico sounds. The town is quiet now. A self-guiding trail winds among remaining structures, providing a glimpse into its former life.

Except for the visitor center on **Harkers Island**, **Cape Lookout** is waterbound. Visitors can take excursion boats from Harkers Island to the lighthouse on **Core Banks**, or from Beaufort to the west end of Shackleford Banks. As off-road vehicles are allowed only on certain beaches, Cape Lookout's islands beckon backcountry hikers and campers. Take all necessary supplies and plenty of water along, and be sure to arrange a return pick-up time with the ferry operator beforehand, since you will be all alone in uninhabited areas where the sun, sea, and wind prevail. ❑

BELOW:
Jockeys Ridge.

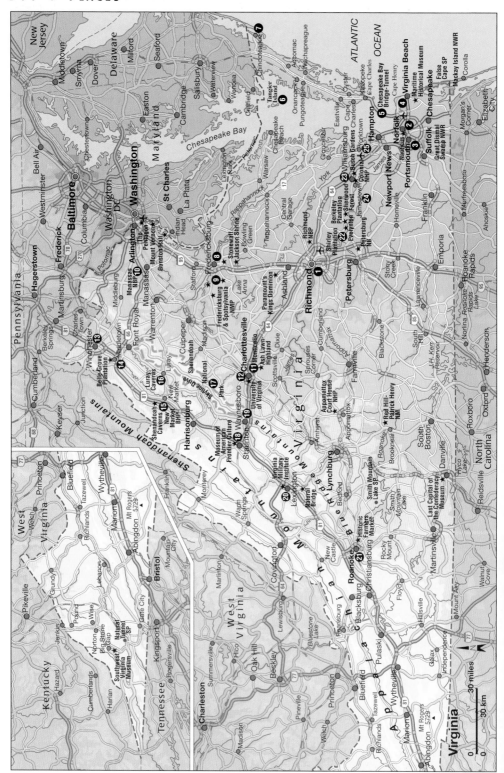

VIRGINA

*A detailed guide to the entire state, with principal sites
clearly cross-referenced by number to the maps*

Thomas Jefferson, third president of the United States, wrote in a letter in 1791: "On the whole, I find nothing anywhere else… which Virginia need envy to any part of the world." He was referring, in this instance, to the weather, but since he was an acknowledged master-builder, ardent gardener, and architect of several of his state's most elegant buildings, we hold his truths on Virginia to be self-evident.

An emerald jewel in the crown of the New South, the northern hills of Virginia are rapidly becoming a garden suburb for the nation's Capitol, Washington, DC. Escapees from the "company town" travel to weekend homes near Richmond, Fredericksburg, and even sleepy little Luray. The 17½-mile (28-km) Chesapeake Bay Bridge-Tunnel is one of the engineering wonders of the modern world, and the rising sweep of the bridge makes for a truly memorable drive.

Although one of the last Southern states to secede from the Union, in many ways Virginia was the worst affected. As many historians point out, over half the battles fought in the war took place in its green rolling hills. George Washington, the young country's first president, was born here. Jefferson, elected in 1801, ushered in an era commonly known as the Virginia Dynasty, and for the next 25 years the leader of the nation would be elected from the ranks of Virginia gentlemen. Another leader of a different nation felt so strongly about the land that he gave up a career to follow a cause: Robert E. Lee was offered the command of the Union forces in the War Between The States. He could not bear to take up arms against his Virginia kinsmen, however. History books the world over record the heavy consequences that followed his decision.

So what is it about Virginia that so stirred these men of distinction and now motivates the movers and shakers who toil in DC? The very things that any visitor cannot fail to appreciate: blue hazy mountains with trickling waterfalls, and deer so unafraid that they wander right up to strangers; small towns where, even today, children use rubber inner tubes to float on the clear mountain creeks, and a sea with fine shell-laden golden sands, stretching for miles along the coast.

In this state of great beauty and great men, the last word could best be left to another of them. The poet Walt Whitman was moved to write in 1865: "Dilapidated, fenceless, and trodden with war as Virginia is, wherever I move across her surface, I find myself roused to surprise and admiration." ❑

PRECEDING PAGES: Monticello, an hour's drive west of Richmond, was designed and built by Thomas Jefferson between 1768 and 1809.

RICHMOND

It was once the capital of the Confederacy, and later the home of Mr Bojangles. Now the movers and shakers of the nation's capital are equally at home in Richmond

Map on page 318

Richmond is at the heart of the New South, and still embodies all the best of the Old South. More than a billion dollars of shiny new buildings grace the Downtown skyline, while on the back streets and leafy neighborhoods are graceful, restored mansions, new museums, and rejuvenated warehouses, now reborn as art galleries and Downtown apartments. Bestriding the James River, the city has spread south, but most of the interesting sites are located on the north side, following the city's colonial layout of 1737.

Situated less than an hour's drive from Williamsburg *(see page 334)* to the east and Jefferson's Monticello to the west *(see page 326)*, Richmond makes a perfect base for exploring central Virginia. The city's importance cannot be overestimated, as it is both the former capital of the old Confederacy and a hub of the northern New South. All of which can be savored at an agreeable Southern gentleman's (or gentlewoman's) pace.

Downtown delights

In many ways, **Franklin Street** could be called the "Gateway to Downtown Richmond." Landmarks such as the Commonwealth Club provide the perfect prelude to how the old blends so well with the new. All along Franklin Street, historic houses saved from the wrecking ball now serve as private residences or as offices for organizations like the Garden Club of Virginia, the Junior League of Richmond, and the Woman's Club. Notable among them is the **Jefferson Hotel Ⓐ** (101 W. Franklin Street, tel: 800-424-8014), a Downtown landmark since 1895 and still dispensing old-world hospitality. **Main Street** is where Richmond means business, for all along this road are industrial, business, financial, government, and legal offices.

The historical district around **Broad Street** features 19th- and 20th-century commercial buildings that have become fine stores and apartments. This section has also been dubbed "President's Row" because of the presidential streets running across it, names that ring throughout the colonial history of America: Adams, Jefferson, Madison, and Monroe.

Broad Street itself presents a mini-history of architecture, from Romanesque to Art Deco, and leads Downtown to **Capitol Square**. This area has seen the arrival of ventures like the **Richmond Coliseum** and a busy convention center.

Just a few blocks from the Coliseum is the historical district known as **Jackson Ward**, a quintessential urban neighborhood with wonderful cast-iron architecture that shouldn't be missed, but should be approached with caution late at night. Jackson Ward had its heyday in the 1900s, and the area was home to

LEFT: interior of Old City Hall.
BELOW: the old Tredegar Ironworks is now a Civil War Visitors Center.

many prominent Richmond black people. The fine **Maggie L. Walker National Historic Site** **B** (600 N. 2nd Street, tel: 804-771-2017, closed Sun) is a memorial to one of the most successful black businesswomen in the post-Civil War South, with four previously derelict buildings undergoing restoration by the National Park Service.

Not far away is the **Bill "Bojangles" Robinson Monument** **C**. This commemorates "Bojangles," the fast-as-lightening tap dancer who grew up in Jackson Ward before finding fame with his feet. He is caught in a typical pose, dancing down a flight of steps. The **Black History Museum and Cultural Center** on E. Clay Street (tel: 804-698-1788) details African-American experiences in the Old Dominion.

Court End

Within an eight-block section of the Downtown area is **Court End**, containing National Historic Landmarks, excellent museums, and many buildings on the National Register of Historic Places.

The focal point of Court End's past is the **Capitol of Virginia** **D** at 9th and Grace streets, the second-oldest working capitol in the United States (Maryland is the first). Designed by Thomas Jefferson and modeled after a Roman temple in Nimes, France, it was later used as the model for the nation's Capitol building in Washington, DC. Free guided tours are available.

Other buildings of interest surround the Capitol. The **Executive Mansion** is the home of Virginia's governor. Richmond's **Old City Hall** on Capitol Square is in the Gothic Revival style and houses the courtroom from which the area derives its name. **Morton's Row** along Governor Street provides a look at the

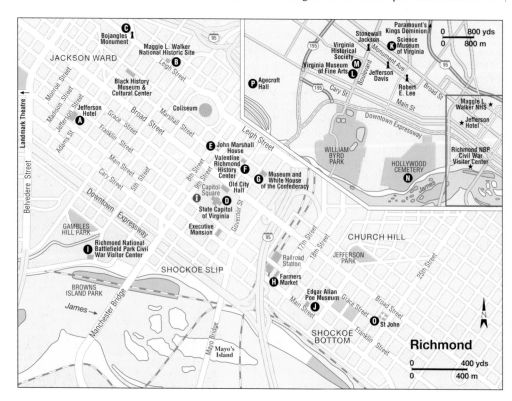

Italianate residences that used to surround Capitol Square (these are now state offices). Farther along on the Court End tour is the **John Marshall House** ❺ at 9th and Marshall streets. This was Marshall's residence for the 45 years during which he served as Secretary of State, Ambassador to France, and Chief Justice of the Supreme Court of the United States.

The **Wickham House** on Clay Street provides a glimpse into the life of John Wickham, Richmond's wealthiest citizen when he built the house in 1812. It is maintained by the **Valentine Richmond History Center** ❻, which relates Richmond's varied history through excellent exhibits and slides. At 1201 E. Clay Street is the **Museum and White House of the Confederacy** ❼ (tel: 804-649-1861, open daily), providing further insight into Richmond's unparalled role during the Civil War. The home served as the residence of Jefferson Davis, president of the Confederacy from 1861 to 1865, and the museum houses the largest Confederate collection in the nation. Most of the exhibits from the war were contributed by local veterans, and in the early days of the museum, they, or their descendants, often worked as guides.

Rafting past down-town Richmond.

Shockoe

South of Capitol Square and down by the riverside is **Shockoe Slip.** No other area in town better displays Richmond's integration of the past and present to produce an enjoyable future. In the 19th century, Shockoe Slip was a lively area full of stores and tobacco warehouses, but fell into decay as commerce along the James River slowed. Today, the Slip is active again, but now it's full of diners, shoppers, and strollers taking full advantage of the revitalization. This is also the scene in **Shockoe Bottom**, a warehouse district southeast along the river that saw a renewed growth after the completion of new a flood wall to protect the area from the danger of high waters.

Trendy restaurants, offices, and residences are housed in renovated red-brick buildings from the earlier commercial boom. For example, the old **Belle Bossieux Building** (now a popular restaurant) on 18th Street, was built as a row of shops with residences above. It was designed by Edmund Bossieux, a New Orleans native who obviously liked the city's architectural style. The **Farmers Market** ❽, one of the oldest continuously operating in the country, is held by the intersection of 17th and Main streets. Virginian farmers have been bringing fresh farm produce to market here for more than 200 years. Be sure to stock up before leaving town.

The **Richmond National Battlefield Park Civil War Visitor Center** ❾ (Tredegar and 5th streets, tel: 804-771-2145) is along the James River and near Canal Walk. Housed in the 19th-century building formerly owned by **Tredegar Ironworks** – the central armament suppliers during the Civil War – the center has an excellent stock of information about local attractions and hotels, as well as the battlefields surrounding Richmond. The poignant and historic military sites, including Richmond, Petersburg, and Appomattox, are among the most important of the Southern campaign (*see pages 94 and 100*).

BELOW:
St John's Church, where Patrick Henry made the speech that galvanized a nation.

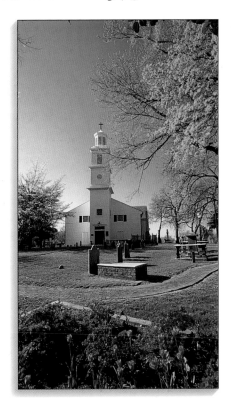

An eerie contrast to the lively Shockoe Bottom commercial scene is provided by the **Edgar Allan Poe Museum** at 1914-16 E. Main Street (tel: 804-648-5523, closed Mon). Richmond's oldest structure is now a fascinating memorial to one of America's finest writers. It presents the life and career of this strange, but talented, local author.

TIP

The Virginia Museum of Fine Arts recently announced major expansion plans, to be completed by 2007. Key features will be more gallery space, a new atrium, a new entrance plaza, a parking garage, and a sculpture garden.

Metropolitan Richmond

If time allows, there are many attractions that are also worth seeing farther away from the city center. Head northwest up Broad Street for two striking museums. Housed in the former Broad Street Railroad Station is the **Science Museum of Virginia** (2500 W. Broad Street, tel: 804-864-1400, open daily). With an engaging and informative presentation of science, this is a venue that the whole family can appreciate. There are very few "Do Not Touch" signs here; instead, visitors are encouraged to observe, interact, and experience the impact of science on life. The museum is best known for its IMAX dome. Adjacent to the Science Museum is the **Children's Museum of Richmond** (tel: 804-474-CMOR), perfect for visitors from six months to 12 years old.

On the statue-laced **Monument Avenue** are many tributes to the South, including General Robert E. Lee astride his horse *Traveller*, erected in 1890. Also along the avenue are some of Richmond's most beautiful metropolitan homes, a testament to the city's former gentle and gracious beauty. Nearby, the **Fan District**, so-called because of the shape of its streets, also has some lovely renovated Victorian homes, plus lots of local restaurants. The **Virginia Museum of Fine Arts** (2800 Grove Avenue, tel: 804-340-1400, hours vary) is by the broad and spacious avenue appropriately called **The Boulevard**. In addition to

BELOW: aerial view of Virginia's capital.

its modern art, the collection of Fabergé jeweled Easter eggs and "objects of fantasy" is one of the largest in the country. One block away on North Boulevard is the **Virginia Historical Society** Ⓜ, which has an excellent museum.

South of the Fan District is the **Hollywood Cemetery** Ⓝ. Rolling hills, and bluffs overlooking the James River afford the serene and forested cemetery with the perfect setting for a sobering walk through history. The site provides the resting places for more than 18,000 Confederate soldiers, including Confederate president Jefferson Davis, and US presidents James Monroe and John Tyler.

Give me liberty or give me death!

On the other side of Downtown, **St John's Church** Ⓞ (2401 E. Broad Street) stands on historic **Church Hill**, overlooking the city skyline. Here Patrick Henry made his famous "Give me liberty or give me death!" speech. Guided tours allow visitors to stand where Patrick Henry spoke to an audience including George Washington, Thomas Jefferson, and Benjamin Harrison on that day in 1775. The speech is often re-created on Sundays.

There's more to Richmond a little farther afield. The **West End** takes in both the west side of the city and part of Henrico County. The highlight is **Agecroft Hall** Ⓟ (4305 Sulgrave Road, tel: 804-353-4241, closed Mon), a restored 15th-century English manor house and gardens. It's perfect for a day excursion out of town, as is a cruise aboard a 20th-century paddlewheeler. The scenic trip along the James River offers dining and entertainment opportunities. Alternatively, the whole family might enjoy **Paramount's Kings Dominion**, 20 miles (32 km) north of Richmond on I-95, an amusement park with 12 roller coasters and the tallest Drop Ride in North America. ❑

Map on page 318

BELOW: Court End contains many historic landmarks.

AROUND VIRGINIA

A modern naval center, swimming ponies, beautiful homes and natural beauty – there's history and culture unsurpassed in the shade of the Blue Ridge Mountains

Map on page 314

Virginia begins at the ocean, and ends in the Blue Ridge Mountains, and its development has mirrored its topography. In the 1600s, colonial settlers founded Jamestown, and later Williamsburg, on the far eastern shore. Slowly, as the state prospered, they spread themselves with their families westward. Our route around the state follows this pioneering trail, and commences, as the colonists did, by the ocean. Fortunately for travelers, the state capital, **Richmond ❶** *(see page 317),* is convenient to both the mountains and the sea.

Sea breezes

For more than 300 years, the ocean has sustained and romanced the **Tidewater** area, the region in southeastern Virginia along the inlets and river coves to the sea. The busy town of **Norfolk ❷** is right at the heart of the region and serves as a good base for exploration. **Waterside** is a marketplace with shops that stretch along the waterfront; from the promenade a selection of harbor tours are available on a number of vessels. **Nauticus** (tel: 757-664-1000, closed Mon) is a three-level maritime museum featuring one-of-a-kind interactive exhibits, which take visitors on an adventure of marine discovery.

The **Norfolk Naval Base** opened in 1917 on a tiny site, and has extended to 5,200 sprawling acres (2,100 hectares), playing a major role in the history of the military, and growing to become the capital base for the United States Navy.

The salty tang of the sea is never far away in these parts. Across the river in **Portsmouth ❸**, more military history awaits. The **Portsmouth Naval Shipyard Museum** was established in 1949 in the shipyard itself, and later moved to its current waterfront site. Just around the corner from the shipyards is the bright red **Lightship Museum**.

On a peninsula, the towns of **Newport News** and **Hampton** have been military bases, huge shipbuilding facilities, and a port of embarkation and debarkation for troops through American history. In keeping with its strategic importance, there are a number of museums devoted to the military, and some dedicated to transportation. The **Hampton History Museum** (tel: 757-727-1610, closed Sun) has displays telling of the arrival of Captain John Smith and the demise of Blackbeard the Pirate.

Jutting out into the ocean, **Virginia Beach ❹** is the Atlantic coast's longest resort beach, stretching along a golden 28 miles (45 km). The sand and surf are, of course, Virginia Beach's major attractions, and the ever-popular hot-dog stands, huge amphitheater, razzle-dazzle nightlife, and general bonhomie are never far way. But there's more to this resort; the Virginia Beach **Maritime Historical Museum**, for

LEFT: Virginia's Eastern Shore.
BELOW: tubing it.

instance. The building was originally a US Life-Saving/Coast Guard Station, and now houses nautical artifacts, scrimshaw, ship models, photographs, marine memorabilia, and a great little gift shop for coastal souvenirs.

The Eastern Shore

The Eastern Shore is a distinctive part of Virginia.; the people, places, and food make this land between Chesapeake Bay and the Atlantic Ocean a very separate place. Coming from Virginia's Tidewater area, a typical drive starts with the **Chesapeake Bay Bridge-Tunnel ❺** and heads north. The Bridge-Tunnel is one of the engineering wonders of the world, running 17½ miles (28 km) across the wide-sweeping bay. On reaching the area, use US 13 to explore until something appeals, then turn off the main road into another way of life.

The pretty upscale town of **Cape Charles** provides a quick introduction to the Eastern Shore, while little fishing towns like **Oyster** and **Cherrystone** give a perfect glimpse of life as it has been lived for decades. Historic **Eastville** features beautiful homes, government buildings, and churches, all within an easy stroll or drive off attractive Courthouse Green. Quiet **Pungoteague**, which means "Place of Fine Sand," is the location of several stately old homes and the oldest church on the Eastern Shore, **St George's Episcopal Church**, which dates from 1738.

The busier **Wachapreague** ("Little City by the Sea") waterfront is popular with both fishermen and tourists. **Onancock**, "Foggy Place," is great for an hour or so of exploration. Market Street has attractive shops and leads to the wharf where the **Hopkins & Brothers** store has been a Virginia landmark since it first opened in 1842.

BELOW: swim with the ponies.

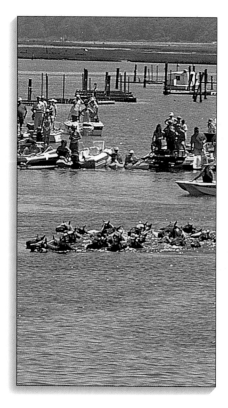

THE CHINCOTEAGUE PONY SWIM

Tangier Island's most famous event takes place during the summer in the town of Chincoteague. The wild ponies of neighboring Assateague Island are thought to be the descendants of Spanish ponies, whose owners were shipwrecked on the way to Peru.

Some may have bred with runaway horses from the camps of the early colonialists. Roaming freely all year round, the animals achieved national fame with the publication of Marguerite Henry's book *Misty of Chincoteague*, and tourists have been flocking to see the ponies ever since, most of which are owned by members of the Chincoteague fire department.

In the last week of July, firemen herd the excess foals across the narrow channel to Chincoteague in an event that causes much mirth and even a spot of betting among the spectators as they speculate on which pony will swim the fastest. The following day, the ponies are driven along Chincoteague's Main Street for the annual animal auction, which is held as a fundraiser for the (volunteer) fire department.

To witness this unusual spectacle, a hotel room needs to be booked months – or even years – in advance, as the event has become extremely popular.

The wharf is also an embarkation point for boat trips to **Tangier Island ❻**, one of the state's most unusual tourist destinations. The island was first sighted by Captain John Smith in 1608 and has remained relatively unchanged for decades (some say centuries). Local fishermen and their families speak with an accent that has persisted in the community since their Elizabethan ancestors arrived from Cornwall, in southwestern England.

Up by the Maryland border, the town of **Chincoteague ❼** is an island community that has made its living on the water and, now, from tourism. **Main Street** has an old-fashioned feel to it, and side streets provide good dining, shopping, rooms to rent, and hugely popular annual events (see panel opposite).

Map on page 314

Richmond towards Washington, DC

Thanks to the proximity of Washington, DC, Northern Virginia is distinct from the rest of the state. The political machinery, businesses, and people make this region a great deal busier than the outlying areas.

Heading toward Washington, DC, from **Richmond** on busy I-95, is the pretty, historic city of **Fredericksburg ❽**. Once considered part of Central Virginia, the suburbs and commuter zeal of the nation's capital have spread so far from the city limits that Fredericksburg, 50 miles (80 km) away, has been annexed by Northern Virginia. Still, it's easy to understand why upscale Washingtonians would want to live here.

The town was founded on the banks of the Rappahannock River in 1728. Historic sites are on every street corner: the **Rising Sun Tavern**; the **Mercer Apothecary Shop** with its shelves filled with Dr Mercer's medicine bottles; and the **Mary Washington House**, purchased by George for his mother. Many of

Mount Vernon, George Washington's home. For other sites in the DC area, see Insight Guide: Washington, DC.

BELOW: Fredericksburg Civil War site.

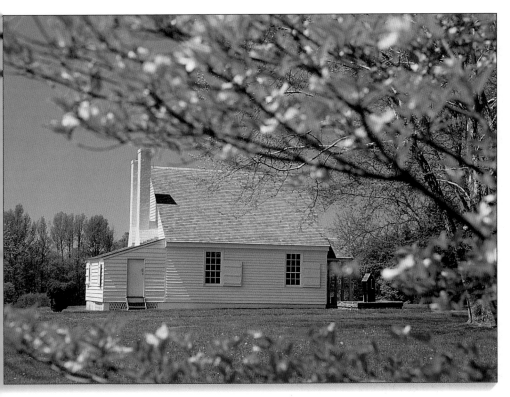

BELOW:
Middleburg is in Virginia's Hunt Country.

Mrs Washington's belongings remain, as well as a beautiful English garden in the back. George's only sister, Betty, lived in nearby **Kenmore**, an elegant 18th-century plantation home. The **Fredericksburg and Spotsylvania National Military Park** ❾ is made up of no fewer than four battlefields, 17 miles (27 km) from town. The Civil War hit Northern Virginia perhaps harder than any other part of the South – or the North, for that matter. Up to 60 percent of all the military encounters took place in the border state of Virginia, and poignant reminders of the conflict are everywhere. Casualties here, combined with those at **Manassas**, southwest of Washington, were heartwrenching: more than 37,000 young men were killed or wounded in the fighting *(see page 93)*.

Both Manassas ❿ and **Middleburg**, 45 miles (70 km) west of Washington, DC, lie in the region referred to by some as Hunt Country. Anyone interested in horses or fox-hunting will feel right at home in the pleasant pasture land and well-heeled, equestrian atmosphere surrounding this pretty town. The old-fashioned streets are best explored on foot (if not on horseback) and many of its restaurants serve Virginia wine from local vineyards.

Richmond to Monticello

Thomas Jefferson's home, **Monticello** ⓫ (tel: 434-984-9800, open daily, www.monticello.org) lies about an hour's drive west of Richmond off busy Interstate 64. Designed and built by the architect and statesman between 1768 and 1809, Jefferson saw to it that Monticello (Italian for "little mountain") was unlike any other American house of its day. It is indisputably one of the nation's architectural masterpieces, and one of the few American homes on UNESCO's World Heritage List (along with such treasures as the Taj Mahal, the Pyramids, Versailles, and the Great Wall of China).

The neoclassical style is highlighted by the dramatic dome, which appears on the back of the US nickel. Jefferson hated the architecture of Williamsburg, and said that if the British-inspired houses had not had roofs they would be mistaken for brick kilns. Hence his penchant for domes, which he mounted on several important buildings.

The entrance hall was the president's private museum, displaying, among other artifacts, items collected by Lewis and Clark during their expedition to the West. A tour of the house and grounds reveals much about the man, his home, his role as architect of several houses, and also about Virginia and US history. Jefferson is buried under the obelisk that he designed for himself.

Monticello can be seen from James Monroe's lovely home, **Ash Lawn-Highland** (tel: 434-293-9539, open daily), only 2 miles (3 km) away. Thomas Jefferson designed Ash Lawn for his great friend James Monroe, who was the fifth president.

Monticello is situated along what has come to be called the **Constitution Route**, established in 1975 to recognize its historic significance for Virginia. Four US presidents (Jefferson, Madison, Monroe, and Zachary Taylor) and 11 Virginia governors were either born or built their estates along this road. The Constitution Route runs right through the university town of **Charlottesville** ⑫. The town revolves around the **University of Virginia**, including Jefferson's renowned **Rotunda** (that dome again). Jefferson planned the university as the first secular college in America, and, at the same time laid out the university's "academical village" around graceful, languid lawns. Charlottesville itself has been discovered by Washington, DC's intelligentsia and media folk, many of whom have country retreats in the area. As a result, the town's shops and restaurants are sophisticated and expensive compared to the rest of rural Virginia.

The countryside north of Charlottesville features some of Virginia's finest vineyards set into rolling hills. From Charlottesville, it's only a short drive to the town of Waynesboro *(see page 330)*, where there is a choice to travel along the beautiful Shenandoah Valley, either to the north or the south.

Map
on page
314

The Shenandoah Valley

The country charm of the Shenandoah Valley attracts thousands of visitors annually, especially during the fall, when the leaves of the trees turn to burnt oranges and reds. The valley reaches from north to south, from West Virginia down through the state, and ends at the lovely town of Roanoke. Long famous in song and history, Shenandoah is flanked by green wooded hills and the misty Blue Ridge Mountains, which rise from 3,000 to 5,000 ft (900 to 1,500 meters). The valley runs about 200 miles (320 km) long and is from 10 to 20 miles (16 to 32 km) wide.

I-81 runs the entire length, but Route 11 is more pleasurable, ambling through small towns, past wineries and subterranean caverns, historic sites, and pretty inns that recall a more leisurely time. **Winchester** ⑬ makes a good intro-

BELOW: Jefferson's Rotunda, University of Virginia.

The pace of life here makes a change from the busy commuter belts ringing Washington, DC.

duction to the valley. Vitally important during the Civil War, Winchester changed hands 72 times during the skirmishes, and was the scene of six major battles. The Winchester-Frederick County Visitor Center is located in the **Hollingsworth Mill House**, just off I-81. It adjoins one of Winchester's three important museums, **Abrams Delight**, built in 1754 by one of the earliest settlers.

George Washington's Office Museum in the Downtown area is a small log cabin that Washington used as an office in 1755 and 1756 while he supervised the construction of Fort Loudoun as protection against Indians and the French. Just north on Braddock Street, **Stonewall Jackson's Headquarters Museum** serves as a third draw for museum and history buffs. The first weekend in May is a glorious time to visit Winchester, when the area turns into a pale blossom heaven, as petals from the clusters of fruit trees drift languidly on the breeze and float lazily to the ground. This celestial event is celebrated in an annual **Apple Blossom Festival**.

Plantations and antiques

Most visitors to **Middletown** head straight for the **Wayside Inn** for a great meal (try the peanut soup), to spend the night, or to while away the time before heading next door to the **Wayside Theatre**. Due east of Washington, DC, Middletown in recent years has begun to mirror the preoccupations of its increasingly upscale clientele.

Just south of Middletown, the **Belle Grove Plantation** (tel: 540-869-2028, open daily) is worthy of an excursion. The house, built in 1794, is significant because of Thomas Jefferson's involvement in its design. About 10 minutes' drive down the road from Belle Grove is **Strasburg**, rightfully known as "The

BELOW: the Luray Caverns were discovered in 1878.

SHENANDOAH NATIONAL PARK

Shenandoah National Park is a long, narrow corridor of ridges and valleys clothed in dense forest and laced with streams and waterfalls. Running along the backbone of the Blue Ridge Mountains is the Skyline Drive, a 105-mile (160-km) scenic highway that serves as the park's main thoroughfare. The effort to create a national park in the Blue Ridge was launched in the 1920s, and construction of the Skyline Drive began in 1931. Several of the campgrounds, picnic areas, and lodging facilities were built by the Civilian Conservation Corps *(see page 46)*. The park was dedicated in 1936.

A second major project, the Blue Ridge Parkway, was also started in the 1930s. Often described as "the most graceful road in America," the Parkway stretches 469 miles (755 km) along the backbone of the Appalachian Mountains between Shenandoah and Great Smoky Mountain national parks, crossing Virginia into North Carolina. Along the way are countless overlooks, historic sites, wayside exhibits, hiking trails, and museums. Both roads are marked by mileposts, with a speed limit that means a leisurely pace is strictly enforced. Together, these two roads form the longest and one of the most stunning drives in the United States.

Antique Capital of the Blue Ridge." The **Strasburg Emporium** and other small stores give ample opportunity to shop 'til you drop. Beyond Strasburg, the Shenandoah Valley opens out, the Blue Mountain ridges sloping up to the skies on both sides. Further south, **Shenandoah Caverns** surprise many people with their netherworld beauty and stunning lighting. Descend by elevator to Bacon Hall, where the formations here look remarkably like strips of bacon.

Map on page 314

Teenage rebels

The New Market area played a key role in the Civil War. The **New Market Battlefield Historical Park** ⓱ honors the brave charge made by teenage cadets recruited from the Virginia Military Institute to join their older brothers-in-arms on the battlefield. The cadets helped to rally the troops, and on May 15, 1864, contributed to a major Confederate victory. There are extensive background exhibits and a poignant walking tour.

Many people are lured to the small town of Luray by the **Luray Caverns** ⓰ (tel: 540-743-6551, open daily). These large, somewhat spooky caves were discovered by a local entrepreneur in 1878, and have since been the site of several subterranean weddings. Couples are serenaded by a huge "stalacpipe" organ, mentioned in the *Guinness Book of Records*, which plays notes when air is pushed through the stalactites by electronically controlled, rubber-tipped plungers. When visiting the caverns, be sure to take a sweater as it is chilly underground, even when it's blazing hot outside. An impressive car collection and a gigantic maze are also on the premises.

Luray, a gateway to the **Shenandoah National Park** ⓱, is dominated by a beautiful hotel on a hill, **The Mimslyn Inn** (tel: 540-743-5101). Despite its

BELOW: the Blue Ridge Parkway has been called the most graceful road in America.

imposing position, this hostelry with an elegant dining room and indoor roof ter-
race is cozy and welcoming. A very pleasant and fairly inexpensive country
inn, there is a relaxed, local Virginia atmosphere at the lobby bar, and around the
rocking chairs on the verandah.

After passing through the busy university city of **Harrisonburg**, the quieter
college town of **Staunton** ⑱ awaits. This hilly town has a restored train depot,
and the **Woodrow Wilson Birthplace and Museum**, which details the life and
times of the 28th president. The most popular exhibit is his Pierce-Arrow lim-
ousine. Staunton is also the home of the **Museum of American Frontier Culture**. This hugely successful undertaking features 18th- and 19th-century
working farms transplanted from England, Germany, Northern Ireland, and
America, offering insights into country life.

Southern artist

A half-hour to the east of Staunton, the town of **Waynesboro** ⑲ is known as
the home of Southern artist P. Buckley Moss. Her stick-figure paintings are collected throughout the world, and the **P. Buckley Moss Museum** in Waynesboro
displays and sells much of her work. Around Waynesboro, it's easy to pick up
I-64, the big interstate that heads east toward Charlottesville and Monticello,
then continues on towards Richmond *(see page 317)*.

History lures travelers to **Lexington** ⑳, the prettiest town in the valley, if not
in Virginia itself. A 19th-century college town, Lexington is home to both the
Virginia Military Institute (VMI) and **Washington and Lee University**.
Despite its military heritage, the town is not at all rigid or stuffy. Locals are
unfailingly pleasant and helpful, and the antique shops (including delightful

BELOW: the
Shenandoah Valley
near Front Royal.

secondhand book shops) make it a lovely place to stroll. VMI was founded in 1839 and is the oldest state-supported military college in the US, earning it the sobriquet "The West Point of the South." Stonewall Jackson taught here. Tree-shaded Washington and Lee University was founded in 1749. Tiptoe quietly into **Lee Chapel** to see the final resting place of Robert E. Lee. The visitor center, the **Stonewall Jackson House**, Jackson's pre-Civil War home, and the **Stonewall Jackson Memorial Cemetery** are all within walking distance.

Just 14 miles (22 km) south of Lexington, **Natural Bridge** is known as one of the seven natural wonders of the world. This 215-ft (65-meter) high stone arch, carved by water over the centuries, stands as one of the valley's most famous sites. Its popularity owes as much to marketing as to nature, though; there are plenty of sites as beautiful – and less commercialized – up in the mountains of Shenandoah National Park *(see page 328).*

Star City of the South

Roanoke ㉑ is the valley's largest city, the southern end of the rolling, pine-scented ravine. Known as the "Star City of the South," its emblem, a huge 88-ft (27-meter) neon star on **Mill Mountain**, overlooks the city and the valley. Roanoke is known for its historic **Farmers Market**, where growers have brought fresh fruits, vegetables, and flowers by country road for nearly 125 years. The little Downtown area around the marketplace has been spruced up a treat, and the **Center in the Square**, a multilevel arts center, throbs with life and live performances. Other attractions include the **Virginia Museum of Transportation** (big trains and other vehicles) and the **Harrison Museum of African American Culture**. A fitting end to any Shenandoah Valley visit. ❑

Map on page 314

The Hotel Roanoke, tel: 540-985-5900, was built in 1882 to celebrate the golden age of railroad travel. It's right Downtown, and impossible to miss.

BELOW:
Roanoke: Star City of the South.

COLONIAL VIRGINIA

*Just a pretty drive away from Richmond are sturdy brick plantation
homes; Williamsburg, capital of the former colony; Yorktown,
and Jamestown, which celebrates its 400th anniversary in 2007*

Map
on page
314

When many Virginia visitors think of the Old Dominion, they think of
colonial Williamsburg, which, along with its two stately companions,
Jamestown and Yorktown, form Virginia's Historic Triangle, the oldest
part of the state and among the oldest places in the US. The three sites, which
make up the **Colonial National Historical Park**, are linked by the lovely 23-
mile (35-km) **Colonial Parkway**, a road that meanders through forests and
fields. Although I-64 makes the Williamsburg area only an hour away from
Richmond, the most interesting route from the capital follows the Plantation
Road (Route 5). In a drive of less than 60 miles (95 km), the road between
Richmond and Williamsburg winds through more than 300 years of Virginian
and American history.

Plantation Road

Only 18 miles (29 km) from Richmond's soaring skyline is the finest plantation
in the area. As with many stately mansions, the road up to **Shirley Plantation**
(tel: 800-232-1613, open daily) is, fittingly, along a tree-lined drive. Shirley
was founded in 1613, just six years after the settlers arrived in Jamestown,
making it the oldest plantation in Virginia. The brick structure is one of the
nation's prime examples of Queen Anne architecture.
It has been the home of the Carter family since 1723;
Anne Hill Carter was the mother of Robert E. Lee
and was born at Shirley.

LEFT: the
Governor's Palace,
Williamsburg.
BELOW: artisans at
work, Jamestown.

Many prominent Virginians enjoyed hospitality
here, including George Washington and Thomas Jefferson. Look for the plethora of pineapples, an international symbol of hospitality, in the hand-carved
woodwork of the house and the pineapple pinial on
the peak of the rooftop. The tour is good value, and
the stroll along the river is invigorating.

Leading up to **Berkeley Plantation** (tel: 804-829-
6018, open daily) is a short dirt road that was designed
for carriages. A sign requests that motorists drive
"leisurely." Berkeley dates from 1726 and has played
host to George Washington, the succeeding nine US
presidents, and thousands of tourists. Colonial-clad
tour guides point out that the military song *Taps* was
composed here in 1862, while Union forces were
encamped at the plantation during the Civil War.
William Henry Harrison, Governor Benjamin Harrison's third son, was born at Berkeley and grew up to
become the famous Indian fighter "Tippecanoe," the
ninth president of the United States, and grandfather
of Benjamin Harrison, the 23rd president.

By taking a fork in the road from Berkeley, you'll
arrive at **Westover Gardens** (tel: 804-829-2882, open
daily). The plantation, built about 1730, is not open to

There's more to Williamsburg than just history. The Williamsburg Winery is the state's largest, and tours and tastings take place every day. Busch Gardens Williamsburg regularly wins the "Most Beautiful Theme Park" award, while Prime Outlets has 80 stores with discounted designer goods.

BELOW: earthworks mark the battlefield of Yorktown.

the public, but its grounds, on the banks of the James River, are perfect for strolling. The best view is seen by walking across the lawn instead of following the path. The small structure by the ice house has passageways leading to the river, dug in case of attack by Indians.

Next on the route is **Evelynton** (tel: 800-473-5075, open daily). Even if plantation interiors don't appeal, take the road up to the house to enjoy the outside, the greenhouse, and the gift shop. The escorted tours inform about the family's patriarch, Edmund Ruffin, who fired the first shot of the Civil War at Fort Sumter. He also earned the title, the "Father of American Agronomy," by virtually saving 19th-century Virginia from a bleak agricultural economy.

The last plantation before Williamsburg is **Sherwood Forest Plantation** (tel: 804-282-1441, open daily), former home of President John Tyler, and said to be the longest frame house in America. It has been a working plantation for almost 250 years and is still occupied by members of the Tyler family. The family's pet graveyard can be seen nearby.

Williamsburg

Williamsburg ㉓ (tel: 757-253-0192, open daily, www.visitwilliamsburg.com) was once the capital of a colony that extended, it is said, all the way to the present-day state of Minnesota. The Colonial Williamsburg Foundation now looks after around 85 percent of the 220-acre (90-hectare) town laid out by Royal Governor Francis Nicholson. Bisected by mile-long **Duke of Gloucester Street**, the Historical Area (tel: 757-229-1000, open daily) contains 88 original structures, 50 major reconstructions, and 40 exhibition buildings. There are also 90 acres (35 hectares) of gardens and greens, several museums, not to mention nearby **Carter's Grove**, which features a 1754 mansion, **Wolstenholme Towne**, with a museum, a slave quarter, and a reception center. In colonial Virginia, there's much to see, as you would imagine from a destination that has employed 3,500 archaeologists, researchers, historians, and historical interpreters.

Any visit should begin at the **visitor center** and *Williamsburg – The Story of a Patriot*, a 35-minute film. The best way to see often-crowded Williamsburg – the town gets 4 million visitors in a busy tourist year – is to arrive just before the center closes at night and buy admission tickets for the next day.

One of America's first planned cities, Williamsburg was constructed between 1698 and 1707, after the abandonment of Jamestown. It was conceived as a gentle country town, so each house on the main street was surrounded by half an acre of land to allow for the smokehouse, stable, dairy, orchard and slave quarters. It was a prosperous market town, with the **College of William and Mary** at one end, and **the Capitol** at the other end. The residence of the crown's representative in the colony of Virginia was the grand, centrally located **Governor's Palace**.

The town may look and feel something like a stylish, upmarket theme park minus the cotton candy, but it's a great place to depart from the strains and stresses of 21st-century life and become immersed into a slower, and more langorous style and pace.

Jamestown

Jamestown ㉔ (tel: 757-253-4838, open daily) was the original site of the first permanent English settlement in the New World. In 1997, archaeologists discovered the remains of the original 1607 British fort, unearthing tens of thousands of relics, including a human skeleton. The excavation, which will continue until the 400th anniversary of Jamestown in 2007, is seen as one of the most important finds in recent times. Festivities and commemorative events are planned to run concurrently with the dig. The ruins of a 1640s church tower, and the excavated site of the old capital, are also worth seeing. The settlers' story is told through film and full-size re-creations of ships and outdoor settings at **Jamestown Settlement** (tel: 757-229-1733, open daily), where costumed interpreters portray life at the beginning of the 17th century.

Yorktown

Yorktown ㉕ (tel: 757-253-4838, open daily), lying 14 miles (20 km) along the Colonial Parkway from Williamsburg, is the historic site of the last major battle of the Revolutionary War and, in 1781, the surrender of Lord Cornwallis to General George Washington. The visitor center presents a film about the history of the town, and is the place to begin a **Battlefield Tour**. From the top of the visitor center, look out over the earthworks that mark the lines of the battlefield. The Historic Area's **Main Street** has gracious homes dating from when Yorktown prospered as a tobacco port. The **Nelson Home**, where a signatory to the Declaration of Independence lived, was built in 1711. Nearby, the **Yorktown Victory Center** tells the story of the American Revolution through a film and outdoor living history exhibitions. ❏

Map on page 314

BELOW:
Revolutionary
rifles, Yorktown.

INSIGHT GUIDES
Travel Tips

✕ INSIGHT GUIDES Phonecard

One global card to keep travellers in touch. Easy. Convenient. Saves you time and money.

It's a global phonecard

Save up to 70%* on international calls from over 55 countries

Free 24 hour global customer service

Recharge your card at any time via customer service or online

It's a message service

Family and friends can send you voice messages for free.

Listen to these messages using the phone* or online

Free email service - you can even listen to your email over the phone*

It's a travel assistance service

24 hour emergency travel assistance – if and when you need it.

Store important travel documents online in your own secure vault

For more information, call rates, and all Access Numbers in over 55 countries, (check your destination is covered) go to **www.insightguides.ekit.com** or call Customer Service.

JOIN now and receive US$ 5 bonus when you join for US$ 20 or more.

Join today at

www.insightguides.ekit.com

When requested use ref code: **INSAD0103**

OR SIMPLY FREE CALL
24 HOUR CUSTOMER SERVICE

UK	0800 376 1705
USA	1800 706 1333
Canada	1800 808 5773
Australia	1800 11 44 78
South Africa	0800 997 285

THEN PRESS **0**

For all other countries please go to "Access Numbers" at **www.insightguides.ekit.com**

* Retrieval rates apply for listening to messages. Savings based on using a hotel or payphone and calling to a landline. Correct at time of printing 01.03

(INS001)

powered by ⊕ *ekit*

"The easiest way to make calls and receive messages around the world"

CONTENTS

Getting Acquainted

Time Zones

The New South spans two time zones: **Eastern** (which is Greenwich Mean Time minus five hours) and **Central** (Greenwich Mean Time minus six hours)

DAYLIGHT SAVINGS TIME

This begins each year at 2am on the first Sunday in April when clocks are advanced one hour, and ends on the first Sunday in October, hen clocks are put back.

Electricity

Standard electricity in North America is 110–115 volts, 60 cycles AC. An adapter is necessary for most appliances from overseas, with the exception of Japan.

Weights & Measures

The US operates on the imperial system of weights and measures. Metric is rarely used. Below is a conversion chart:
1 inch = 2.54 centimeters
1 foot = 30.48 centimeters
1 mile = 1.609 kilometers
1 quart = 1.136 liters
1 ounce = 28.40 grams
1 pound = 0.453 kilograms
1 yard = 0.9144 meters

Business Hours

Banks 9am–5pm, weekdays. Some stay open until 6pm and on Saturdays.
Post Offices 8am–4 or 5.30pm, weekdays, Saturday closing earlier and opening later.

Shops Shopping centers and malls are generally open 10am–9pm. Downtown area shops often close at 5–6pm. Most cities have 24-hour restaurants, convenience stores and supermarkets.

Public Holidays

As with other countries, the US has gradually shifted most of its public holidays to the Monday closest to the actual dates, creating a number of three-day weekends throughout the year. Major holidays such as Christmas and New Year's are celebrated on the actual day.

Keep in mind that during public holidays, post offices, banks, government offices and many private businesses are closed. Major holidays are:

- **January 1**
New Year's Day
- **Third Monday in January**
Martin Luther King Jr Day
- **Third Monday in February**
Presidents' Day
- **March/April**
Good Friday, Easter Monday
- **Last Monday in May**
Memorial Day
- **July 4**
Independence Day
- **First Monday in September**
Labor Day
- **Second Monday in October**
Columbus Day
- **Fourth Thursday in November**
Thanksgiving.
- **November 11**
Veteran's Day
- **December 25**
Christmas Day

Planning the Trip

Visas & Passports

A machine-readable passport, a passport-sized photograph, a visitor's visa, proof of intent to leave the US after your visit and (depending upon your country of origin) an international vaccination certificate, are required of most foreign nationals for entry into the US. Vaccination certificate requirements vary, but proof of immunization against smallpox or cholera may be necessary. Visitors from the UK staying less than 90 days do not need a visa if their passport was issued before October 26, 2004 and is machine-readable. Passports issued after this date are required to have a chip containing "biometric" data; otherwise a visa will be required.

Canadian and Mexican citizens, and British residents of Canada and Bermuda, are normally exempt from these requirements. But it is wise to check for specific regulations on international travel in your country. **Information:** Up-to-date details on entry requirements and machine-readable passports may be found on the US State Department's website: www.travel.state.gov/visa_services.html or on www.dhs.gov.

Customs

For a breakdown of customs allowances write to:
United States Customs Service
P.O. Box 7407
Washington, DC 20044
Meat or meat products, illegal drugs, firearms, seeds, plants and fruits are among the prohibited goods. Also do not bring in any duty-free goods which are worth more than

$400 (returning Americans) or $100 (foreign travelers). Visitors over 21 may bring in 200 cigarettes, 3 lbs (1.3 kg) of tobacco or 50 cigars and 34 fl. oz (1 liter) of alcohol.

Airport Security

In light of events on September 11, 2001, air travel in the US has changed drastically. Be at the airport early, expect searches and questions to be asked, and do not attempt to carry any sharp objects in your hand luggage. This includes scissors, nailclippers, pen-knives, nailfiles and other seemingly innocuous items.

Smoking Attitudes

If you're a smoker, you are probably aware that the US does not offer the friendliest welcome to your habit. The South is more relaxed than much of America, but you should still ask before lighing up in public – there are usually designated areas. And, if in a group, it is considered good manners to ask your companions' permission.

Health & Insurance

Medical services are extremely expensive. Always arrange full and comprehensive travel insurance to cover any emergencies. Check the small print – most policies exclude treatment for water, winter or mountain sports accidents unless excess cover has been included. If you need medical assistance, consult the *Yellow Pages* for the physician or pharmacist nearest to

Heat Exposure

The heat and humidity through-out the South can not only be uncomfortable, but also dangerous. If spending the day outdoors, carry water and take rest in the shade. Otherwise, mint juleps, iced tea and light clothing are the only remedies for the South's sultry summers.

you. In large cities, there is usually a physician referral service number listed. If you need immediate attention, go directly to a hospital emergency room (most are open 24 hours a day). You may be asked to produce proof of insurance cover before being treated.

Care should be taken to avoid dehydration and overexposure to the sun. This can happen rapidly even on cloudy days. A high-factor sun lotion, hat and water bottle are essential accessories.

Money Matters

American visitors

Credit cards are accepted almost everywhere, although not all cards at all places. Most hotels, restaurants and shops take the major ones such as American Express, Diners Club, MasterCard, Visa and En Route. Along with out-of-state or overseas bank cards, they can also be used to withdraw money at ATMs.
Travelers' checks are widely accepted, although you may have to provide proof of identification when cashing them at banks (this is not required at most stores).

Overseas visitors

Travelers' checks in US dollars are much more widely accepted than those in other currencies. The best rates of exchange for travelers' checks are in banks. Take along your passport.

Tax

Most states levy a sales tax. The amount varies from state to state (up to around 8 percent in some) and is invariably excluded from the marked price. You may also have to pay a local sales tax on top of this.

When looking at prices, beware of other costs that may or may not be included in the stated price such as lodging or "bed tax" and taxes on restaurant meals, drinks and car rental. These are especially hefty in tourist towns. If in doubt – ask.

Traveling with Kids

Two pieces of advice about traveling with children: first, be prepared and, second, don't expect to cover too much ground. Take everything you need: Southern towns may be small and supplies limited. If you need baby formula, special foods, diapers or medication, carry them with you along with a general first-aid kit. Games, books and crayons help kids pass time in the car.

Carry food and drinks in a day pack for snacks on the road. Give yourself plenty of time, as kids do not travel at the same pace as adults. They're a lot less interested in traveling from point A to point B than in exploring their immediate surroundings. What you find fascinating, they may find boring and vice versa.

Be sure wilderness areas and other back-country places are suitable for children. Are there wild animals, steep stairways, cliffs or other hazards? Is a lot of walking necessary? Are food, water, shelter, bathrooms and other essentials available at the site? Avoid dehydration by having children drink plenty of water before and during outdoor activities. Don't push children beyond their limits. Rest often and allow time for extra napping.

Useful Websites

- **Travel South**
  www.travelsouthusa.org
- **The Gulf Coast**
  www.southcoastusa.com
- **Alabama** www.touralabama.org
- **Arkansas** www.arkansas.com
- **Georgia** www.georgia.org
- **Louisiana**
  www.louisianatravel.com
- **Mississippi**
  www.visitmississippi.org
- **North Carolina**
  www.visitnc.com
- **South Carolina**
  www.travelsc.com
- **Tennessee** www.tnvacation.com
- **Virginia** www.virginia.org

Practical Tips

POST OFFICES

Even the most remote towns are served by the United States Postal Service. Smaller post offices are limited to business hours (Monday to Friday 9am–5pm), although central, big-city branches may have extended opening times and be open on Saturdays. Stamps are sold at all post offices, plus at some convenience stores, filling stations, hotels and transportation terminals, usually from vending machines.Be sure to have a lot of change handy.

EXPRESS MAIL

For reasonably quick delivery at a modest price, ask for priority mail. For overnight deliveries, try US Express Mail. Many people prefer to use one of several domestic and international courier services, including:
Fedex, Tel: 800-463-3339
DHL, Tel: 800-225-5345
United Parcel Service,
Tel: 800-742-5877

POSTE RESTANTE

Visitors can receive mail at Southern post offices if it is addressed to them, care of "General Delivery," followed by the city name and (very important) the zip code. You must pick up this mail in person within a week or two of its arrival and show some personal identification, like a passport, driver's license or valid credit card.

Telecommunications

TELEPHONE

Coin-operated telephones can be found in hotels, restaurants, shopping centers, gas stations and often in lighted booths on street corners. To call long-distance, dial 1+area code +local number. Have plenty of change with you to deposit on the operator's prompting.

To make a collect call in the United States, you must know the name of the recipient's telephone carrier. sPrepaid phone cards are widely available at gas stations and convenience stores; these are handy for longer calls and are generally better value.

Toll-free calls

When in the US, make use of toll-free (no-charge) numbers. They start with 800, 1-800, 888, 877 or the newer 866.

Cheaper rates

Long-distance rates are cheaper after 5pm on weekdays and throughout weekends.

TELEGRAMS & FAXES

Western Union (Tel: 800-325-6000) takes telegram and telex messages, plus orders to wire money over the phone. Faxes can be found in most hotels and copy centers.

Phone Codes

With the proliferation of fax lines, modems and cellular phones in recent years, the telephone system is seriously overloaded. To cope with these demands, the country has been forced to divide, then sub-divide its existing telephone exchanges, in some cases every six months. Although every effort has been made to keep the telephone prefixes listed here up to date, it's always a good idea to check with the operator if you're in any doubt about a number.

INTERNET AND EMAIL

Many public libraries, copy centers and hotels offer email and Internet access. Or visit a cyber café. Service providers such as Earthlink (www.i.e.w.com) and Hotmail (www.hotmail.com) offer web mail accounts that will enable access while traveling.

Embassies

Australia: 1601 Massachusetts Ave NW, Washington, DC 20036, Tel: 202-797-3000
Canada: 501 Pennsylvania Ave NW, Washington, DC 20001, Tel: 202-682-1740
Denmark: 3200 Whitehaven St NW, Washington, DC 20008, Tel: 202-234-4300
France: 4101 Reservoir Road NW, Washington, DC 20007, Tel: 202-944-6000
Germany: 4645 Reservoir Road NW, Washington, DC 20007, Tel: 202-298-4000
Great Britain: 3100 Massachusetts Ave NW, Washington, DC 20008, Tel: 202-462-1340
Ireland: 2234 Massachusetts Ave NW Washington, DC 20008, Tel: 202-462-3939
Israel: 3514 International Drive NW, Washington, DC 20008, Tel: 202-364-5500
Italy: 3000 Whitehaven St NW, Washington, DC 20008, Tel: 202-612-4000
Japan: 2520 Massachusetts Ave NW, Washington, DC 20008, Tel: 202-238-6700
Mexico: 1911 Pennsylvania Ave NW, Washington, DC 20006, Tel: 202-728-1600
New Zealand: 37 Observatory Circle NW, Washington, DC 20008, Tel: 202-328-4800
Singapore: 3501 International Place NW, Washington, DC 20008, Tel: 202-537-3100
Spain: 2375 Pennsylvania Ave NW, Washington, DC 20037, Tel: 202-452-0100

Useful Numbers

- **Emergencies** 911 (the operator will put you through to the police, ambulance or fire services)
- **Operator** 0 (dial if you are having any problems with a line from any phone)
- **Telephone information**
Local: 411
Long-distance: 1+area code
+555-1212
Toll-free directory: 800-555-1212

Security & Crime

ON THE ROAD

If you are driving, never pick up anyone you don't know. Always be wary of who is around you. If you have trouble on the road, stay in the car and lock the doors, turn on your hazard lights and/or leave the hood up to increase your visibility and alert passing police. It's well worth carrying a sign requesting help. Do not accept a rental car that is obviously labeled as such. Company decals and special license plates may attract thieves on the look-out for tourist valuables.

IN THE CITY

Most big cities have their share of crime. Common sense is your most effective weapon. Try to avoid walking alone at night – at the very least stick to livelier, more brightly lit thoroughfares and walk confidently as if you know where you are going.

Keep an eye on your belongings. Never leave your car unlocked, or small children by themselves. Avoid leaving luggage and other valuables in plain sight in a parked car; lock them safely in the trunk or take them with you. If you have any valuables, you may want to lock them in the hotel safe. Take particular care when using bank ATMS at night. If you are in doubt about which areas are safe, seek advice from hotel staff or police.

Gay Travelers

In many respects the South is a very conservative area. Public displays of affection, whether straight or gay, may attract unwanted and unpleasant attention. Gay-friendly establishments may be in short supply, but discreet couples should be able to fully enjoy the South. There will be no problem in New Orleans.

Disabled Travelers

For general information on travel for the handicapped, contact **Moss Rehabilitation Hospital Travel Information Service**, 1200 West Tabor Road, Philadelphia, PA 19141, Tel: 215-456-9600, TDD 215-456-9602, or **The Information Center for Individuals with Disabilities**, PO Box 750119, Arlington Heights, MA 62475, Fax: 781-860-0673.

Hitchhiking

Hitchhiking is ill-advised every-where. It's a dangerous method of travel. Don't do it!

Tipping

Although rarely obligatory, many service personnel in the US rely on tips for a large part of their income. General rates are:
- **waiters & bartenders**
15–20 percent
- **taxi drivers**
15 percent
- **airport/hotel baggage handlers**
around $1 per bag
- **chambermaids**
for overnight stays it is not necessary to tip, for longer stays a minimum of $1–2 per day
- **doormen**
50¢–$1 for helping unload a car or other services
- **hairdressers, manicurists and masseurs** 15 percent

Clothes Size Guide

This table gives a comparison of American, Continental and British clothing sizes. It is always best to try on any article before buying it, as sizes may vary.

Women's Dresses/Suits

American	Continental	British
8	40/36N	10/32
10	42/38N	12/34
12	44/40N	14/36
14	46/42N	16/38
16	48/44N	18/40

Women's Shoes

American	Continental	British
5½	37	4
6½	38	5
7½	39	6
8½	40	7
9½	41	8

Men's Suits

American	Continental	British
34	44	34
-	46	36
38	48	38
-	50	40
42	52	42
-	54	44
46	56	46

Men's Shirts

American	Continental	British
14	36	14
14½	37	14½
15	38	15
15½	39	15½
16	40	16
16½	41	16½
17	42	17

Men's Shoes

American	Continental	British
6½	-	6
7½	40	7
8½	41	8
9½	42	9
10½	43	10
11½	44	11

Getting Around

Airlines

If it is too impractical because of long distances to drive to the destinations listed in this book, an easy alternative is to fly. Airlines that serve the airports in the major cities included here are:
American Tel: 1-800-433-7300
 www.aa.com
Delta Tel: 1-800-221-2121
 www.delta.com
Continental Tel: 1-800-523-3237
 www.continental.com
United Tel: 1-800-864-8331
 www.united.com
US Airways 1-800-428–4322
 www.usairways.com

By Train

Although passenger services were greatly curtailed in the latter part of the 20th century, it is still possible to travel by rail. Amtrak is the major rail passenger carrier in the US. Its network links many cities, but sadly bypasses many more. However, there are still some excellent routes that glide through breathtaking scenery. Not the fastest or cheapest way of getting around America, but riding the rails can be a leisurely and highly enjoyable experience if you have the time. Many of the South's Gulf Coast cities are linked by Amtrak.

Train passes
Passes for unlimited travel on Amtrak over a fixed period of time are available only from a travel agent in a foreign country. Proof of non-US residency is required. Be sure to ask about

two- or three-stopover discounts, senior citizens and children's discounts, and also Amtrak's package tours.
Information: Details about Amtrak's train service can be obtained by calling 1-800-872-7245 or www.amtrak.com.

By Bus

The national bus line, Greyhound, as well as a number of smaller charter companies, provide an impressive network of ground travel, offering daily service to major towns and cities. Routes and schedules are subject to change, so it is a good idea to check all arrangements with local stations in advance. Most cities also have municipal bus systems.

As both Greyhound and municipal stations are often situated in somewhat squalid areas, try to stay alert and do not wander too far, particularly after dark. Plan your journey for daylight arrival if possible. On the whole, the buses themselves are safe and reasonably comfortable; choosing a seat near to the driver may discourage unwanted attention from any fellow passengers.
Information: reservations and local bus station details are available on Tel: 1-800-229-9424, www.greyhound.com

Bus passes
An Ameripass offers unlimited travel within 68 consecutive days. The pass may be purchased only outside the US. Details are available from the Greyhound bus company and most foreign travel agents.

By Car

Car rental agencies are located at all airports and in cities and large towns. In most places you must be at least 21 years old (25 at some locations) to rent a car and you must have a valid driver's license and at least one major credit card. Be sure to check insurance

provisions before signing anything. Cover is usually $15–25 per day. You may already be covered by your own auto insurance or credit card company, however, so check with them first.

CAR RENTAL COMPANIES

Alamo, Tel: (US) 800-462-5266; Web: www.goalamo.com
Avis, Tel: (US) 800-230-4898; Web: www.avis.com
Budget, Tel: (US) 800-527-0700; Web: www.budget.com
Dollar, Tel: (US) 800-800-4000; Web: www.dollar.com
Enterprise, Tel: (US) 800-736-8222; Web: www.enterprise.com
Hertz, Tel: (US) 800-654-3131; Web: www.hertz.com
National, Tel: (US) 800-227-7368; Web: www.nationalcar.com
Thrifty, Tel: (US) 800-847-4389 Web: www.thrifty.com

RV RENTALS

No special license is necessary to operate a motor home (or recreational vehicle – RV for short), but they aren't cheap. When you add up the cost of rental fees, insurance, gas and campsites, you may find that renting a car and staying in motels or camping is less expensive. Keep in mind, too, that RVs are large and slow and may be difficult to handle on narrow mountain roads. If parking space is

AAA Membership

The Automobile Association of America (AAA) can help members with personalized itineraries. Benefits of AAA membership include a 24-hour emergency breakdown service, great road maps and travel literature. Insurance is also available through the association, which has a reciprocal arrangement with some of the automobile associations in other countries. Tel: 1-800-874-7532 or visit their website: www.aaa.com

tight, driving an RV may be extremely inconvenient. Access to some roads may be limited. For additional information about RV rentals, call the **Recreational Vehicle Rental Association**, Tel: 800-336-0355

Public Transportation

Most major cities have a public bus service. However, timetable information is often difficult to come by and services are usually quite inconsistently spaced out. In addition to these basic services, the following cities have public transportation facilities that make exploring them easier.

Atlanta: Atlanta's MARTA underground rail system can take you to the city's main areas and to and from the airport.
Birmingham: The Dart circulator tram service crosses Downtown from east to west and then from north to south at the east and west edges of the former line. Trams operate every 10 to 20 minutes.
Charleston: The Dash trolley operates daily until midnight throughout the city center.
Charlotte: Free Gold Rush trolley buses serve most attractions in the city center.
Memphis: The Main Street Trolley ferries passengers around the Downtown and Main Street areas on vintage carriages. Sun Studios operates a free shuttle to take visitors to some of the city's main musical sites.
Mobile: The MODA tram loops Main street every ten minutes. And it's free.
New Orleans: Bus routes cover Downtown, the French Quarter and all major areas. Most have a five- to 10-minute interval. The St Charles streetcar runs to the Garden District, while other streetcars, mainly of interest to tourists, run alongside the Mississippi Riverbank.
Savannah: Free trolley buses.

Where to Stay

Hotels & Motels

Chain hotels and motels are reliable and convenient but tend to lack unique character. You can, however, usually depend on a clean, comfortable room for a reasonable price. In general, prices range from $50 to $150 per room depending on the location, the season and additional amenities. When making reservations, ask specifically about special weekend or corporate rates and "package deals." Reservations staff in America are notorious for quoting only the most expensive rates, but many hotels offer a variety of discounts and promotions.

Book your room by credit card and secure a guaranteed late arrival, in the foreseeable circumstance that your flight is interminably stacked up over the airport or your 40-minute limo ride from the airport turns into a two-hour nightmare of traffic jams. The telephone numbers listed below are the main numbers that should be dialed in order to make reservations once in the US.

CHAIN HOTELS

Best Western, Tel: 1-800-780-7234
Hilton, Tel: 1-800-774-1500
Holiday Inn, Tel: 1-800-465-4329
Hyatt, Tel: 1-800-633-7313
La Quinta, Tel: 1-866-725-1661
Marriott, Tel: 1-888-236-2427
Quality Inn, Tel: 1-877-424-6423
Radisson, Tel: 1-888-201-1718
Ramada, Tel: 1-800-272-6232
Sheraton, Tel: 1-888-625-5144

CHAIN MOTELS

Budget Host Inns, Tel: 1-800-283-4678
Choice Hotels International, Tel: 1-800-228-5150
Days Inn of America, Tel: 1-800-544-8313
Econolodge, Tel: 1-800-553-2666
Hampton Inns, Tel: 1-800-426-7866
Motel 6, Tel: 1-800-466-8356
Red Roof Inns, Tel: 1-800-843-7663

Hostels

Hostelling International/American Youth Hostels
8401 Colesville Road
Suite 600
Silver Spring, MD 20910
Tel: 301-495-1240
Web: www.hiayh.org.
YMCA
YMCA of the USA, Association Advancement, 101 North Wacker Drive, Chicago, IL 60606
Tel: 312-977-0031
Web: www.ymca.com
YWCA
1015 18th Street NW
Suite 1100
Washington DC 20036
Tel: 202-467-0801
Web: www.ywca.com

Southern B&Bs

If you have the time to do a little research you may find that B&Bs offer better service and more hospitality (not to mention a good breakfast, including grits, to get you going in the morning) for about the same price as a chain hotel. Often run by families with thorough local knowledge, they're likely to enhance your stay even further.
Recommended Country Inns: The South, by Carol and Dan Thalimer, Globe Pequot Press is an excellent source. On-line information is available at: www.bbonline.com; www.bnbfinder.com

Georgia

Known as: the Peach State because of the growers' reputation for producing the highest quality fruit. The peach is also the state's official fruit. There are numerous boulevards in Atlanta known as "Peachtree Street," but very few peach trees.

Motto: Wisdom, Justice, and Moderation.

Entered Union: January 2, 1788, joined as the fourth of the original 13 colonies.

Population: 8.6 million.

Area: 59,441 sq. miles (153,951 sq. km).

Time Zones: Eastern Time Zone (GMT minus 5 hours).

Capital: Atlanta

Local Dialing Codes: 678 and 404 (Atlanta), 706 (north and northeast, 478 (central), 706 (west-central), 229 (southwest), 912 (southeast).

Famous Figures: Vice-president of the Confederacy Alexander H. Stephens, author Margaret Mitchell, founder of the Girl Scouts Juliette Gordon Low, author Conrad Aiken, civil rights activist Martin Luther King Jr, author Alice Walker, baseball player Ty Cobb, baseball player and first black player in the major leagues Jackie Robinson.

Georgia tourist information
285 Peachtree Center Avenue
Suite 1000, Atlanta, GA 30303
Toll-free: 800-847-4842
Web: www.georgiaonmymind.org

Atlanta tourist information
Atlanta Convention and Visitors Bureau Center, 233 Peachtree Street, GA, 30303
Tel: 404-521-6600
Web: www.atlanta.net

Savannah tourist information
101 East Bay Street GA, 31401
Tel: 877-7282-6624
Web: www.savannah-visit.com

FROM THE AIRPORT

Hartsfield International, the second busiest in the country, is located 10 miles (16 km) from Downtown. Many hotels offer courtesy buses from the airport. Atlanta Airport Shuttle is one of several companies providing service into the city. MARTA (Metropolitan Rapid Transit Authority), a rapid-rail system comprising north–south and east–west lines intersecting at the main Five Points Station in downtown Atlanta, provides direct access to Hartsfield Airport.

WHERE TO STAY

Atlanta is a popular city for conventions, and downtown hotels are fullest – and prices highest – during such events. The city has plenty of stylish, luxury hotels in the upper price ranges, as well many chain hotels. For lower-priced accommodations and to avoid city traffic, consider staying on the outskirts and taking the MARTA underground rail line in to central attractions. For bed-and-breakfast inns in various price ranges, try B&B Atlanta, tel: 404-875-0525.

Atlanta Marriott Marquis
265 Peachtree Center Ave.
Tel: 404-521-0000
Fax: 404-586-6299
www.marriott.com
This whale of a hotel is one of local architect John Portman's beauties: the atrium lobby has a volume of 9.5 million cu. ft (269,010 cu. meters), and visitors feel they've entered the rib cage of some mythical beast. Pool, sauna, whirlpool, steam room, health club – all the perks. **$$$$**

Beverly Hills Inn
65 Sheridan Drive NE
Tel: 404-233-8520
Toll-free: 800-331-8520

Fax: 404-233-8659
www.beverlyhillsinn.com
European-style B&B in an historic building in the heart of prestigious Buckhead. Spacious, romantic rooms with hardwood floors, loveseats, flower-filled balconies and some four-poster beds. Library and garden room. **$$$**

Crowne Plaza Buckhead
3377 Peachtree Road
Tel: 404-264-1111
Fax: 404-233-7061
www.crowneplaza.com
Convenience with a bit of style in Atlanta's most fun neighborhood, the Crowne Plaza is not the cheapest place, but is good value for money. It's also within walking distance of restaurants and two of Atlanta's best shopping centers. **$$$**

Hostelling International – Atlanta
223 Ponce de Leon Ave
Tel: 404-872-1042
Email: rsvp@mindspring.com
Located in the heart of downtown Atlanta. Amenities include kitchen, parking, games and courtyard. **$**

Sheraton Buckhead
3405 Lenox Road NE
Tel: 404-261-9250
Fax: 404-848-7391
www.sheraton.com
Southern hospitality is on display here. There are 364 recently renovated rooms and suites, a health & racquet center, three dining venues; MARTA and Lenox Square are just across the street. **$$$–$$$$**

Hotels: Categories based on average cost of a double room for one night.
$ = under $65
$$ = up to $100
$$$ = up to $150
$$$$ = over $150

Restaurants: Categories based on average cost of dinner and a glass of wine, before tip.
$ = under $15
$$ = up to $30
$$$ = over $30

Westin Peachtree Plaza
210 Peachtree Street
Tel: 404-659-1400
Fax: 404-589-7424
www.starwoodhotels.com
With its 1,068 pie-shaped rooms, this 72-story, circular high-rise is an Atlanta landmark, and one of the tallest hotels in America. Designed by famed architect John Portman, the structure is a must-see for visitors, whether checking in or not. Small pets allowed. **$$$$**

WHERE TO EAT

If you were to randomly parachute into Atlanta, odds are you would land on a good restaurant. The following list is nothing if not extremely limited and idiosyncratic. You should not leave Atlanta without stopping in at that Jimmy Dean – Ford Fairlane dream of a diner on Ponce de Leon Avenue, the **Majestic**. Don't miss that other paean to junk food, on "Ponce" as well, the **Krispy Kreme** donut shop.

Anthony's
3109 Piedmont Road NE
Tel: 404-262-7379
Surely Atlanta's "Belle of the Ball," from the first cocktail on the verandah through "Roasts Carved From Our Silver Chariot," and on to a chocolate soufflé. The setting is antebellum plantation home; the service is Anglo-Atlantan. (Yes, one of the owners does have a Sheffield accent.) Reservations advised. **$$$**

Buckhead Diner
3073 Piedmont Road (at East Paces Ferry Road)
Tel: 404-262-3336
If Anthony's represents the Old South, the Buckhead Diner represents the New. See and be seen here, and enjoy the glorified pizza, hamburgers, soft-shell crabs, onion rings and tarted-up southern icons such as Banana Cream Pie. It's all "down home" – if home has a pair of BMWs parked out back. **$$**

Danté's Down the Hatch
3380 Peachtree Rd. NE, Buckhead
Tel: 404-266-1600
For around twenty-five years,

Danté Stephensen's fine fondue cuisine (using only Australian beef), 18th-century sailing-vessel decor, live jazz (and live crocodiles in the moat) have been turning heads and bringing back such patrons as Jimmy and Rosalyn Carter, Burt Reynolds and William S. Buckley. Keep your strawberry frozen daiquiri glass as a souvenir. Reservations advised. **$$**

The Dining Room
Ritz-Carlton Hotel, Buckhead
3434 Peachtree Road
Tel: 404-237-2700
This five-star, four-course gem is one of Atlanta's top restaurants. Fantastic wine list; a once-in-a-lifetime dining pleasure. **$$$**

The Varsity
61 North Avenue
Tel: 404-881-1706
One of Atlanta's most famous restaurants, a drive-in burger-and-Coke joint. Take antacid tablets before ordering the chili dogs, onion rings, fried fruit pies or fluorescent orange shakes. **$**

WHERE TO SHOP

People from all over the South flock to shop in Atlanta. Underground Atlanta, though just another of many shopping malls in the city, has the added advantage of being, well, underground. It's located in the old infrastructure of the downtown area.

If Buckhead is Atlanta's shopping mecca, then Phipps Plaza and Lenox Square are the ultimate destinations for millions of plastic-wielding pilgrims. At the corner of Lenox and Peachtree roads, Phipps Plaza, a monument in polished brass and marble, is the Taj Mahal of malls. Tiffany's, Lord & Taylor, Gucci, Versace and Saks are here, as well as a movie theater complex.

Built in 1959, Lenox Square, on East Paces Ferry Road, was Atlanta's first mall and, with continual expansion, is the largest in the Southeast. The four-level mall is home to over 250 stores, 27 of them unique to Atlanta.

Around Georgia

WHERE TO STAY

Athens

Foundry Park Inn
295 E. Dougherty Street
Tel: 706-549-7020
Toll-free: 866-928-4367
www.foundryparkinn.com
Built in classic style on one of Athen's oldest historic sites, this Downtown spa caters to your every need. Restaurants and attractions are within walking distance. **$$$**

Nicholson House Inn
6925 Jefferson Road
Tel: 706-353-2200
Fax: 706-353-7799
www.nicholsonhouseinn.com
This antebellum Georgia home was built in 1820, and has been lovingly restored. Its decor includes antiques sand Civil War artifacts. Gourmet breakfasts come with fresh fruit and bread in a lavish setting. **$$–$$$**

Macon

Atrium La Quinta Inn & Suites
3944 River Place Drive
Tel: 478-475-0206
Toll-Free: 800-531-5900
www.laquintamacon.com
Quiet rooms with rich wood furniture, large desks and spacious bright bathrooms. A pretty, landscaped courtyard surrounds the outdoor pool, sundeck and gazebo. **$$–$$$**

Best Western-Riverside
2400 Riverside Drive
Tel: 478-743-6311
Fax: 478-743-9420
www.bestwestern.com
A 125-unit motor inn with pool. **$**

Crowne Plaza
108 First Street
Tel: 478-746-1461
Toll-free: 800-227-6963
www.crowneplaza.com
Upscale hotel in the heart of historic downtown. Its many amenities include pool and sauna, exercise room, two restaurants and bars. **$$**

1842 Inn
353 College Street
Tel: 478-741-1842

Fax: 478-741-1842
www.1842.com
A historic bed-and-breakfast.
Features 19th-century ambiance
with 21st-century perks. Some of
the 21 units have fireplaces and
whirlpool baths. **$$$$**

WHERE TO EAT

Athens
The Basil Press
104 E. Washington Street
Tel: 706-227-8926
Bistro-style restaurant serving
Southern cuisine with a
Mediterranean flair. Sunday brunch
and outdoor dining in summer. **$$**
Charlie Williams' Pinecrest Lodge
Off Whitehall Road (follow signs)
Tel: 706-353-2606
Toll-free: 800-551-4267
Williams' legendary barbeque
began as sa treat for friends after
work. It's now been popular with
local residents for over 60 years **$**
Five & Ten
1653 S. Lumpkin Street
Tel: 706-546-7300
Chef/owner Hugh Acheson has
been named one of America's best
new chefs by *Food & Wine*
Magazine. His international cuisine
features seafood and pastas.
$$–$$$

Brunswick
Georgia Pig
Exit 29 off I-95
Tel: 912-264-6664
Expertly prepared barbeque dished
up in pleasant surroundings. A
mighty fine pit stop. **$**

Macon
Michael's on Mulberry
588 Mulberry St.
Tel: 478-743-3997
Dine al fresco in historic Downtown.
The menu features steak, seafood
and pastas, sushi and pistachio
chicken. **$$**
Willow on Fifth Restaurant
325 Fifth Street
Tel: 478-745-9007
Sister restaurant of the famous
Blue Willow Inn in Social Circle, in
the heart of Macon's museum
district. Bountiful buffet of

traditional Southern cooking,
featuring a seafood buffet on Friday
and Saturday nights. **$**

Madison
Ye Olde Colonial Restaurant
108 E. Washington Street
Tel: 706-342-2211
Cafeteria-style breakfasts, lunches
and dinners made from locally
grown produce when possible. The
blackberry cobbler disappears as
quickly as it's baked. And there's
barbeque of course. **$–$$**

Rutledge
The Yesterday Cafe
120 Fairplay Street
Tel: 706-557-9338
Set amid antiques stores, a rustic
meal here is the only sensible
option. At night the Southern
cooking gets fancier and it's a good
idea to dress up. **$–$$**

Social Circle
The Blue Willow Inn Restaurant
294 N. Cherokee Road
tel: 770-464-2161
A charming restaurant in a 1907
Greek Revival mansion. The
southern-style buffet stretches
around the room and includes
everything you'd expect. **$$**

St Simons Island
Dressner's Village Cafe
223 Mallory Street
Tel: 912-634-1217
A good choice for breakfast. **$**

WHERE TO SHOP

Five Points in Athens is a charming,
tree-lined shopping, dining and
residential area. Many of the shops
and boutiques are housed in
original 1920s and 30s homes,
selling fashions, jewelry, art,
antiques and gifts. Bargain hunters
should head for Tanger Outlets in
Commerce, I-85 at US 441, for
brand-name goods at outlet prices.
Macon's Colonial Mall contains 200
specialty shops and department
stores, and an authentic Venetian
carousel. The Ingleside Village
Shopping and Arts District features
galleries and specialty shops.

Savannah

FROM THE AIRPORT

Two shuttle services complement
the usual rental cars and taxis. Low
Country Adventures/Gray Line to
Hilton Head Island (tel: 1-800-845-
5582) and B & B Shuttle provides
transportation to and from the
Savannah/Hilton Head International
Airport to the Savannah area (tel:
912-964-1411).

WHERE TO STAY

East Bay Inn
225 East Bay Street
Tel: 912-238-1225
Toll-free: 800-500-1225
Fax: 912-232-2709
www.eastbayinn.com
An historic bed-and-breakfast, this
28-unit restored 1853 warehouse
features large, Georgian-style
rooms. **$$$–$$$$**
The Gastonian
220 E. Gaston Street
Tel: 912-232-2869
Toll-free: 800-322-6603
Fax: 912-232-0710
www.gastonian.com
This 16-unit historic B&B was
created from restored late-1800s
houses. Six rooms with whirlpool
baths. No pets allowed. **$$$$**
Magnolia Place Inn
503 Whitaker Street
Tel: 912-236-7674
Toll-free: 800-238-7674
Fax: 912-236-1145

Price Codes

Hotels: Categories based on
average cost of a double room
for one night.
    $ = under $65
    $$ = up to $100
    $$$ = up to $150
    $$$$ = over $150

Restaurants: Categories based
on average cost of dinner and a
glass of wine, before tip.
    $ = under $15
    $$ = up to $30
    $$$ = over $30

www.magnoliaplaceinn.com
A 12-unit restored Victorian
mansion, this historic B&B has a
hot tub in the courtyard and
whirlpool baths and fireplaces in
some rooms. No pets. **$$$**
Savannah's Bed and Breakfast Inn
117 W. Gordon Street
Tel: 912-238-0518
Historic house dating from 1853.
Home-cooked breakfasts. **$$**

WHERE TO EAT

The Chart House
202 West Bay Street
Tel: 912-234-6686
Reserve a table and order the
prime rib in this three-story
nautical-themed restored
warehouse. **$$**
Downtown Cafe at Main
1 West Broughton Street
Tel: 912-233-9666
A touch of seafood enhances this
mostly Italian menu. Good location
and a wine list straight from the
Sonoma Valley. **$$$**
The Lady & Sons
311 W. Congress Street
Tel: 912-233-2600
Specialties such as mustard-fried
catfish, complete with cornbread
and all the trimmings. Open daily for
lunch, Thur–Sat for dinner. **$–$$**
The Pirates' House
20 East Broad and Bay streets
Tel: 912-233-5757
Seafood galore at this Savannah
landmark. **$$$**

WHERE TO SHOP

City Market in the Historic District is
a fun place to browse for gifts by
local artists. The De Soto Historic
District offers more specialist
shops. River Street is lined with art
galleries and boutiques, including
The Basket Place, which sells
sweetgrass baskets, a local
specialty. Oglethorpe Mall, 7804
Abercorn Street, and Savannah
Mall, Rio Road and Abercorn Exit,
have department stores and
national chains. There are bargains
at Savannah Festival Factory Stores,
11 Gateway Boulevard South.

Alabama

Getting Acquainted

Known as: Alabama has no
"official" nickname, but "the Heart
of Dixie" has appeared on license
plates since the 1950s.
Motto: We Dare Maintain Our Rights.
Entered Union: December 14,
1819, joined as the 22nd member
of the United States. The state was
formed from land ceded by Georgia
in 1802 and originally known as the
Alabama Territory.
Population: 4.5 million.
Area: 50,766 sq. miles (131,443
sq. km).
Time Zones: Central Time Zone
(GMT minus 6 hours).
Capital: Montgomery
Local Dialing Codes: 256 (North
and Northeast), 205 (western and
central), 334 (southeast), 251
(southwest and panhandle).
Famous Figures: Educator and civil
rights activist Booker T.
Washington, country & western
musician Hank Williams, bluesman
W.C. Handy, writer Helen Keller,
baseball players Hank Aaron, Ozzie
Smith and Willie Mays, heavyweight
champion Joe Louis, football coach
Bear Bryant, football player Joe
Namath, track legends Carl Lewis
and Jesse Owens.

Useful Addresses

Alabama tourist information
Bureau of Tourism and Travel,
401 Adams Ave, Suite 126,
Montgomery, AL 36104
Toll-free: 800-252-2262
Web: www.touralabama.org
**Greater Birmingham Convention
and Visitors Bureau**
2200 Ninth Avenue North
Birmingham, AL 35203
Toll-free: 800-458-8085

Web: www.birminghamal.org
Mobile Visitors Corporation
PO Box 204
Mobile, AL 35601
US Freephone: 800-5MOBILE
Web: www.mobile.org
**Montgomery Area Chamber of
Commerce and Visitor Center**
300 Water Street
Montgomery, AL 36104
Tel: 334-262-0013
www.montgomerychamber.com

Birmingham

FROM THE AIRPORT

In addition to the usual assortment
of car rental agencies, there is an
Airport Express bus (tel: 205-591-
7770) and Birmingham Door-to-Door
Service (tel: 205-591-5550).
Otherwise, taxis are always waiting
to get you into the city.

WHERE TO STAY

Pickwick Hotel
1023 20th Street S.
Tel: 205-933-9555
Toll-free: 800-255-7304
Art-deco style and friendly service
make this small hotel something
special. In the lively Five Points
South area, near good restaurants,
nightclubs and shopping. Rooms
and suites. **$$–$$$**
Redmont (Crowne Plaza)
2101 Fifth Avenue N.
Tel: 205-324-2101
Built in 1926, the Redmont is the
oldest surviving hotel of the Magic
City era. Renovated in 2001, the
118 rooms and suites are small by
today's standards, but have a
warm, European feel to them, much
enjoyed by guests. **$$$**
Tutwiler Hotel
2021 Park Place
Tel: 205-322-2100
Toll-free: 800-WYNDHAM
Fax: 205-325-1198
Historic hotel in the business
district, built in the 1920s and
lavishly restored for the millennium.
Now part of the Wyndham chain.
Convenient for the cultural center
and Civil Rights Institute. 147
rooms. **$$$$**

Wynfrey Hotel
US 31 just off I-459, exit 13
Tel: 205-987-1600
Toll-free: 800-476-7006
Fax: 205-987-0454
www.wynfrey.com
The elegant lobby adorned with Italian marble and French chandeliers is the gateway to comfortable rooms and gracious service. It adjoins the Galleria, the state's largest mall. **$$$-$$$$**

WHERE TO EAT

Bottega
2240 Highland Avenue
Tel: 205-939-1000
Chef Frank Stitt's restaurant showcases regional foods of the Mediterranean. The main dining room has 17-foot ceilings and a second-floor dining loft. The Bottega Cafe next door serves a lighter version with such choices as andouille sausage or smoked salmon pizza. **$$$**

Highlands Bar & Grill
2011 11th Avenue S
Tel: 205-939-1400
The state's most acclaimed restaurant and chef Frank Stitt's first establishment. Southern ingredients are presented in a classic French style in the romantic dining room. Try the special house drink: watermelon Margaritas. **$$$**

Hot and Hot Fish Club
2180 11th Court South
Tel: 205-933-5474
www.hotandhotfishclub.com
The odd name comes from a 19th-century South Carolina eating society. Grab a seat at the limestone dining counter to watch the chef in the open kitchen prepare your favorite seafood, relax at a table or dine al fresco. Save room for the irresistible signature desert – chocolate souffle. **$$-$$$**

Irondale Café
1906 First Avenue N., Irondale
Tel: 205-956-5258
The cafe opened by the railroad tracks in 1928 by author Fannie Flagg's aunt was the inspiration for Fannie's bestselling *Fried Green Tomatoes at the Whistle Stop Cafe.* The current owners still serve the famous fried Southern food and steamed vegetables. **$**

Niki's West
233 Finley Avenue W.
Tel: 205-252-5751
This family-owned restaurant opposite the Farmer's Market is famous for its "meat-and-three" steam table. Go through the cafeteria line or be seated in the nautical-themed dining rooms for a steak and seafood meal. **$$**

WHERE TO SHOP

Pepper Place, on Second Avenue South between 28th and 29th, is a collection of shops and galleries housed in a former Dr Pepper bottling plant. It also has an open-air market on Saturdays for organic produce, freshly baked goods, crafts and music.

For antiques, the upscale suburb of Mountain Brook couldn't be better. Try King's House Antiques on Montevallo Road, Circa Interiors and Antiques for estate-caliber chairs, mirrors and heirlooms at 2831 Culver Road, or Hen House Antiques in English Village.

Birmingham is also the national headquarters of Books-A-Million, Inc., which began as a corner newsstand in 1917 and is now the premier book chain in the Southeast. Look for their light, airy stores throughout the South.

Around Alabama

WHERE TO STAY

Huntsville
Huntsville Marriott
I-565 exit 15
Tel: 256-830-2222
In the shadow of the rockets at the US Space and Rocket Center. Rooms on the west side overlook the space Camp Habitat next door and the full-size space shuttle. **$$$**

Monte Sano State Park Cabins
Tel: 256-534-3757
Offering sweeping views of the valleys east of downtown Huntsville, these Arts and Crafts-style cabins were built from local stone and timber in the late 1930s and have fireplaces, rustic furniture, twin beds, kitchenettes and screened porches. **$-$$**

Montgomery
The Legends at Capitol Hill
I-65 Exit 181
Toll-free: 888-250-3757
www.legendsgolfresort.com
Just outside Montgomery, this 80-room lodge is pleasantly situated on the 17th fairway of the Senator golf course. The stained wood and fieldstone of its Craftsman design adds to the relaxed, rustic feeling. Good restaurant and gift shop. **$$$$**

Red Bluff Cottage
551 Clay Street
Tel: 334-264-0056
Toll-free: 888-551-2529
Fax: 334-263-3054
www.redbluffcottage.com
A cottage with gazebo and large porch commands excellent views of the Alabama River plain and State Capitol. Pretty rooms. **$$**

Tuscaloosa
Four Points Hotel – Tuscaloosa Capstone (Sheraton)
320 Paul Bryant Dr.
Tel: 205-752-3200
Toll-free: 800-477-2262
Fax: 205-343-1138
Full-service hotel located on the University of Alabama campus. Among the thoughtful extras are fresh cookies delivered to your room for afternoon tea. **$$$**

WHERE TO EAT

Huntsville
Eunice's Country Kitchen
Andrew Jackson Way, off I-565 exit 20
Tel: 256-534-9550
Homemade biscuits, Tennessee country ham and big hugs have been Eunice Merrell's specialty since 1952. This modest café is *the* place for local color, drawing local and national patrons whose autographed photos line the walls. **$$**

G's Country Kitchen
2501 Oakwood Avenue
Tel: 256-533-3034

Price Codes

Hotels: Categories based on average cost of a double room for one night.
$ = under $65
$$ = up to $100
$$$ = up to $150
$$$$ = over $150

Restaurants: Categories based on average cost of dinner and a glass of wine, before tip.
$ = under $15
$$ = up to $30
$$$ = over $30

If you're a vegetable lover, it's worth going out of your way to find G's (for Greta) in the little shopping center below Pulaski Pike. Fried corn, yams, turnip greens and fried green tomatoes complement baked chicken that slides off the bone. **$**

Pauli's Chop House
101 Washington Street
Tel: 256-704-5555
Delicious wood-fire grilled steaks and chops are the specialty here. Cozy atmosphere in a pre-Civil War building, but the food and service are definitely upscale. **$$$**

Montgomery

City Grill
8147 Vaughn Road
Tel: 334-244-0960
Gourmet dining in an intimate atmosphere. The seasonal menu features seafood, steaks and pasta dishes. The wine list is extensive. **$$$**

Farmers Market Cafe and Pit BBQ
315 N. McDonough Street
Tel: 334-262-1970
People come in droves to this vast and clamorous cafeteria for excellent southern-style barbeque and set-you-up breakfasts. **$**

Jubilee Seafood
1057 Woodley Road
Tel: 334-256-2600
Great shrimp, crab, oysters and snapper served in a roadhouse atmosphere. **$$**

Martin's
1796 Carter Hill Road
Tel: 334-265-1767

The home cooking at this long-standing local favorite features hot golden corn muffins and meringue-topped chocolate pie. Excellent vegetables, chicken and generous meat-and-three plates. **$$**

Moses Crawford Catering
2227 E. South Boulevard
Tel: 334-281-0053
Satisfying soul food served in a laid-back atmosphere. **$**

Sinclair's
1051 E. Fairview Avenue
Tel: 334-234-7462
Set in an old Sinclair service station, this casual restaurant has an American menu of steaks, seafood and pastries. The Cajun filet is memorable. **$$–$$$**

Vintage Year
407 Cloverdale Road
Tel: 334-264-8463
An upscale restaurant of eclectic American fare with Pacific Rim spices and herbs plus a Southwest touch. Favorites are the salmon, provolone and beef tenderloin. **$$$**

Tuscaloosa

Dreamland Barbecue
5535 15th Avenue E.
Tel: 205-758-8135
www.dreamlandbbq.com
In 1958, John "Big Daddy" Bishop opened a ramshackled restaurant off Jug Factory Road to feed college students, football players and fans. Barbeque ribs are served with white bread on a paper plate and covered with sauce. On weekends, expect to wait. The menu is limited to what they do best: ribs, bread, drinks. **$–$$**

WHERE TO SHOP

Huntsville

Shopping centers include Madison Square Mall on US 72 (University Drive West) with 200 stores, and Parkway Place on South Memorial Parkway. Antiques are on offer at the Railroad Station Antique Mall on I-565 exit 19 (315 Jefferson) and Hartlex Antique Mall, 181 Hughes Road in Madison, with dozens of booths The Unclaimed Baggage Center, a short drive away in

Scottsboro, is the place for bargains on everything from clothing to sporting goods and cameras (see page 145).

Montgomery

Green Garden Gallery, 1041 E. Fairview, highlights the state's best contemporary artists. The city's antiques district is on Mulberry Avenue across I-85 from Jackson Hospital. For pecan candy head for Priester's Pecans, down I-65 at Fort Deposit, exit 142.

Mobile

FROM THE AIRPORT

Apart from the usual assortment of rental cars and taxi ranks, the Mobile Regional Airport Shuttle offers passengers transportation to and from the airport to the city (tel: 251-633-0313).

WHERE TO STAY

Adam's Mark Hotel
64 Water Street
Tel: 251-438-4000
Toll-free: 866-749-6073
Fax: 251-415-0123
www.adamsmark.com
Towering 28 stories over downtown Mobile, this cosmopolitan hotel is a stone's throw away from historic central attractions and good restaurants. Many rooms overlook the bay. **$$–$$$**

Admiral Semmes (Radisson)
251 Government Street
Tel: 251-432-8000
Toll-free: 800-233-3333
A handsome 12-story landmark built in 1940 with marble floors, crystal chandeliers and a grand staircase. It's near the museums and in the shadow of the massive Mobile Government Plaza. Enjoy cocktails in the bar where Jimmy Buffet played some of his first gigs. **$$–$$$**

Holiday Inn Express – Civic Center
255 Church Street
Tel: 251-433-6923
Fax: 251-433-8869
A great budget option Downtown, opposite the Civic Center, with

large, clean rooms, a pool and free parking. Rooms fill up fast so book ahead. **$–$$**

Kate Shepard House
1552 Monterey Place
Tel: 251-479-7048
Delightful B&B in a large Queen Anne home in Mobile's Historic District. Warm and charming hosts, a grand piano, and huge rooms lovingly and individually decorated. The house itself has 11 fireplaces and four stained-glass windows. **$$$**

Malaga Inn
357 Church Street
Tel/Fax: 251-438-4701
Toll-free: 800-531-5900
This unique Downtown inn is set in a gas-lit courtyard. The rooms are nicely decorated and many feature hardwood floors. **$$**

Towle House
1104 Montauk Avenue
Tel: 251-432-6440
Toll-free: 800-938-6953
Fax: 334-433-4381
www.towle-house.com
A handsome Victorian home situated in Mobile's historic district. Gourmet breakfast and evening cocktails are included. **$$$**

WHERE TO EAT

Justine's at The Pillars
1757 Government Street
Tel: 251-471-3411
White-tablecloth dining in a landmark house with lush surroundings. Fresh local seafood, hand-cut prime beef and specialty dishes. Plus an extensive wine list. **$$–$$$**

Wintzell's Oyster House
605 Dauphin Street
Tel: 251-432-4605
Mobile's oldest restaurant opened as a six-stool oyster bar in 1938. Relax in comfy booths, or watch the staff twist open fresh oysters at the bar. Great atmosphere. **$**

Dew Drop Inn
1808 Old Shell Road
Tel: 251-473-7872
Classic American chili dogs and chili cheeseburgers. **$**

Roussos
166 S. Royal Street
Tel: 251-433-3322
An attraction in itself, this famous seafood restaurant has been family-run for over 40 years. If they're not too busy, ask for a kitchen tour to see the chefs at work. **$$**

WHERE TO SHOP

If you've got a sweet tooth, head Downtown to Dauphin Street. Among the delectable specialty shops here are the A & M Peanut Shop, where peanuts in the shell are roasted in an old-fashioned roaster, and Three Georges & The Nuthouse, Mobile's oldest candy company, where you can watch them hand-dip chocolates and buy pralines, fudge, divinity and other Southern delights. Mrs. Wheat's Treats on South Florida Street also specializes in homemade Southern candy. Cathedral Square Art Gallery on Dauphin Street is an artists' cooperative that showcases the fine art work of local artists. No matter what time of year you visit, you can pick up some Mardis Gras kitsch at Toomey's Mardi Gras Mart, 755-A McRae Avenue.

For antiques and collectibles, try Southern Traditions Antique Mall, located off I-10 on the way to Bellingrath Gardens, or Cotton City Antique Mall on Airport Boulevard, where you'll find glassware, jewelry, pottery and Civil War artifacts. If you're willing to drive for a bargain, the Tanger Outlet Center, 40 miles southeast of Mobile at Foley, near the Gulf Coast, is one of the largest factory outlet centers in the country.

Mississippi

Getting Acquainted

Known as: the Magnolia State thanks to the abundance of its state flower – the magnolia.
Motto: By Valor and Arms.
Entered Union: December 10, 1817, joined as the 20th member of the United States.
Population: 2.8 million.
Area: 48,434 sq. miles (258.999 sq. km).
Time Zones: Central Time Zone (GMT minus 6 hours).
Capital: Jackson
Local Dialing Codes: 662 (north), 601 (south), 228 (Gulf Coast).
Famous Figures: Singer-songwriter Jimmy Buffet, guitarist gr eat Bo Diddley, football player Breat Farve, Muppets creator Jim Henson, blues artist B. B. King, the king – Elvis Presley, playwright Tennessee Williams, talk-show host Oprah Winfrey.

Useful Addresses

Mississippi tourist information
PO Box 849, Jackson, MS 39205
Tel: 601-359-3297
Toll-free: 866-733-6477
Web: www.visitmississippi.org
Vicksburg tourist information
PO Box 110, Vicksburg, MS 39181
Tel: 601-636-9421
Toll-free: 800-221-3536
Web: www.vicksburgcvb.org
Jackson Convention & Visitors Bureau
921 N. President Street, Jackson, MS 39202
Tel: 601-960-1891
Toll-free: 800-354-7695
Web: www.visitjackson.com
Natchez Convention & Visitors Bureau
640 S. Canal Street, Box C,

Natchez, MS 39120
Tel: 601.446.6345
Toll-free: 800.647.6724
www.cityofnatchez.com

Vicksburg

FROM THE AIRPORT

The nearest airport to Vicksburg is Jackson International Airport, about 45 miles away. There are no shuttle services operating between the two. The drive should take about one hour, direct on I-20.

WHERE TO STAY

As you might expect, this venerable Mississippi River town has a fine selection of historic homes and antebellum mansions that have been turned into beautiful and gracious visitor accommodations. Many are good value for money. For those on a budget, there is a good range of inexpensive inns and chain motels. Vicksburg also has several casino hotels with room rates to suit all price brackets.

Anchuca Historic Mansion and Inn
1010 First East Street
Tel: 601-661-0111
Toll-free: 888-686-0111
www.anchucamansion.com
Listed on the National Register of Historic Places, this Greek Revival mansion is named after the Choctaw word for "happy home." It was the site of Jefferson Davis's

last public address during the Civil War. Rooms are large, and historically decorated. **$$–$$$$**
Battlefield Inn
41371 I-20 N. Frontage Road
Tel: 601-638-9249
Located next to Vicksburg Military Park, a guest once described this high-spirited motel complete with karaoke, parrots and cocktails as "Gracelands in Vicksburg." There's also a pool. **$–$$**
Cedar Grove Inn
2200 Oak Street
Tel: 601-636-1000
Toll-free: 800-862-1300
Fax: 601-634-6126
www.cedargroveinn.com
Superior accommodations in an authentic plantation house with rooms named after Civil War heroes and *Gone with the Wind* characters. You can sleep in the same room (and bed!) that General Grant stayed in after Vicksburg surrendered to Union forces. There's even a cannon ball in the wall. **$$$–$$$$**
The Corners Bed and Breakfast Inn
601 Klein Street
Tel: 601-636-7421
Toll-free: 800-444-7421
Fax: 601-636-7232
www.thecorners.com
This two-story, cottage-style mansion offers impeccable service, with an excellent view of the Mississippi and Yazoo rivers. Southern charm and period antiques furnish the entire house. The candlelit gourmet breakfast lends a dash of Southern charm. **$$–$$$**
Vicksburg Inn Bed and Breakfast
6444 Old Turnpike Road
PO Box 86
Tel: 570-966-8906
www.vicksburginn.com
This brick, Victorian mansion built in 1886, retains the atmosphere of a bygone age. There are rocking chairs on the front porch and a piano parlor for evening entertainment. **$$–$$$**

WHERE TO EAT

Catfish is the Mississippi specialty, either caught in the wild or raised in

the catfish farms of the Delta. Try it fried in batter – the traditional method of cooking – but it's just as delicious grilled or blackened Cajun-style. In Vicksburg you'll find everything from fine dining in romantic and historic surroundings, to international fare, to informal local spots serving barbeque and Southern favorites.

Andre's
Cedar Grove Inn
2200 Oak Street
Tel: 601-636-100
www.cedargroveinn.com
Once voted Vicksburg's best restaurant, the elegant setting complements the sophisticated Southern cuisine of catfish, Cajun crawfish and an unmissable brandy bread pudding. **$$–$$$**
Rowdy's Family Catfish Shack
Hwy. 27 and Hwy. 80 Intersection, I-20 exit 5B
Tel: 601-638-2375
This long-time Vicksburg favorite is the place to try Mississippi pond-raised catfish – fried, grilled or blackened and served with batter fries and special dressing. **$**
Walnut Hills Restaurant and Roundtable
1214 Adams Street
Tel: 601-638-4910
Once the home of confederate president Jefferson Davis, everyone comes here today for the highly regarded round table meals, a family-style affair where a lazy Susan on the table holds all the Southern classics you can eat. **$–$$**

WHERE TO SHOP

Historic Washington Street in downtown Vicksburg has several antiques shops, such as River City Antiques, Griz Old Tyme Photography, Gifts and Collectibles, and the cleverly named Granny Had One. Vicksburg Factory Outlets, on East Clay Street at I-20, has everything from Bibles to vitamins at bargain prices. Pemberton Square Mall on Pemberton Boulevard has department and specialty stores.

WHERE TO STAY

Clarksdale
Belle Clark B&B
211 Clark Street
Tel: 662-627-1280
www.thebelleclark.com
Beautiful historic home, built in
1859 by the founders of Clarksdale.
Bedrooms and sitting rooms in the
main house are filled with antiques.
Modern rooms in house at rear.
Wonderful Southern breakfast.
$$–$$$$
The Shack Up Inn
001 Commissary Circle
Tel: 662-624-8329
www.shackupinn.com
Here B&B stands for Bed & Beer.
Six sharecropper's shacks on the
old Hopson Plantation have been
renovated with indoor plumbing,
showers and air conditioning.
Otherwise the corrugated tin roofs,
funky furniture and rockers on the
porches provide a true Delta
experience. **$–$$**

Greenwood
The Alluvian
318 Howard Street
Tel: 662-453-2114
Toll-free: 866-600-5201
Fax: 662-453-2118
This cosmopolitan boutique hotel is
a wonder in the heart of this old
Delta town. Wickedly comfortable
beds, plush decor, breakfast.
$$$–$$$$

Jackson
Millsaps Buie House
628 N. State Street
Tel: 601-352-0221
Toll-free: 800-784-0221
Fax: 601-352-0221
Over 100 years old, the house has
stayed in the Millsaps Buie family
throughout its lifetime. Eleven grand
rooms are period furnished and the
buffet-style breakfast features
Southern favorites like grits.
$$$–$$$$
Old Capitol Inn
226 North State Street
Tel: 601-359-9000
Elegant hotel in downtown Jackson.

Rooms are individually decorated
with oriental or Southern romantic
styling. Buffet breakfast. **$$$**
The Poindexter Park Inn
803 Deer Park Street
Tel: 601-944-1392
This attractive white-columned B&B
has a library of blues reference
works, and the owner herself is an
authority on local blues, history and
lore. **$$**

Natchez
The Briars
PO Box 1245
Tel: 601-446-9654
Toll-free: 800-634-1818
Fax: 601-445-6037
Jefferson Davis married Varina
Howell in 1845 at this beautiful
antebellum home, set on a
promontory with a fantastic view
over the Mississippi. Spacious,
antique-filled rooms. **$$$**
Dunleith
84 Homochitto Street
Tel: 601-448-8500
Toll-free: 800-433-2445
www.natchez-dunleith.com
This stunning plantation home
resembles a Greek temple and is
surrounded by landscaped gardens
and wooded bayous. Guests sleep
in the period furnished rooms
upstairs and enjoy breakfast in an
old poultry house. **$$$–$$$$**
Monmouth Plantation
36 Melrose Avenue
Tel: 601-442-5852
Toll-free: 800-828-4531
Fax: 601-446-7762
www.monmouthplantation.com
This luxurious 1818 mansion
contains many original pieces
belonging to its first owner, General
John A. Quitman. The romantic
rooms are surrounded by lush
gardens. Fine dining. **$$$–$$$$**

Oxford
Puddin' Place
1008 University Avenue
Tel: 601-234-1250
B&B just off the square with lovely
rooms (some are suites with living
rooms) which are wonderful value
for money. Frilly decor with rocking
chairs and fresh linen; enormous
breakfasts. **$–$$**

Port Gibson
Bernheimer House B&B
212 Walnut Street
Tel: 601-437-2843
www.bernheimerhouse.com
Rambling Queen Anne-style house
with a fantastic wrap-around porch,
antique-filled rooms and welcoming
hosts. **$$$**
Oak Square Plantation
1207 Church Street
Tel: 601-437-4350
Freephone: 800-729-0240
Fax: 601-437-5768
The elegant guest rooms in this
1850 Greek Revival-style plantation
house are filled with antiques and
have draped canopy beds. **$$–$$$**

Tupelo
Mockingbird Inn B&B
305 North Gloster
Tel: 601-841-0286
An early 20th-century home. Each
of the seven guest rooms are
sensually decorated with a different
international theme. Relax outside
in the gazebo or porch swing.
$$–$$$

WHERE TO EAT

Clarksdale
Madidi
164 Delta Avenue
Tel: 662-627-7770
www.madidires.com
Actor Morgan Freeman co-owns this
stylish restaurant, set in a *circa*
1900 building and decorated with
local artworks. Classically prepared

Price Codes

Hotels: Categories based on
average cost of a double room
for one night.
$ = under $65
$$ = up to $100
$$$ = up to $150
$$$$ = over $150

Restaurants: Categories based
on average cost of dinner and a
glass of wine, before tip.
$ = under $15
$$ = up to $30
$$$ = over $30

dishes from hybrid striped bass to veal, duck and beef. **$$–$$$**

Greenville
Doe's Eat Place
502 Nelson Street
Tel: 601-334-3315
Not a whole lot to see, inside or out, but the enormous steaks and tasty tamales attract everyone from the poorest locals to out of town politicians. **$–$$$**
Jim's Cafe
314 Washington Avenue
Tel: 601-332-5951
A down home downtown cafe that typifies Southern life. Don't miss the banana pudding. **$**

Jackson
Crechale's
3107 Highway 80 West
Tel: 601-355-1840
A cafe with its own special sauces and fried frog's legs. Don't worry if you can't eat them all. They've got a "froggy bag" to take with you and a jukebox that's free. **$–$$**
Hal & Mal's Restaurant & Brewery
200 S. Commerce Street
Tel: 601-948-0888
Great food in a casual pub atmosphere. Red beans & rice is their specialty. Live music. **$–$$**
Mayflower Cafe
123 West Capitol Street
tel: 601-355-4122
It's known for its seafood, but other cafe classics such as meatloaf and country-fried steak are excellent as well. A favorite lunch spot for local politicians. **$–$$**
Two Sisters' Kitchen
707 N. Congress Street
Tel: 601-353-1180.
Set in a two-story house, the fresh Southern fare is served in a casual buffet style with dollops of hospitality. **$**

Natchez
Mammy's Cupboard
555 Highway 61 South
Tel: 601-445-8957
Not the most politically correct building but certainly the most unusual in the South. To enter you walk under a huge sculpture of an African-American Mammy. Once

inside the true Southern cuisine is mouth watering. **$–$$**
Fat Mama's Tamales
500 S. Canal Street
Tel:601-442-4548
Located in a cheerful log cabin on Canal Street, Fat Mama's serves Mexican food with a Natchez touch, accompanied by "knock-you-naked" margaritas. **$–$$**

Oxford
Ajax Diner
Town Square
Tel: 601-232-8880
Great salads and an eight- ounce hamburger done just right. **$**
City Grocery
152 Courthouse Square
Tel: 662-232-8080
Reservations are recommended at this lively restaurant on the Square. Outstanding continental and Southern-style dishes, try the shrimp and grits. **$$–$$$**

WHERE TO SHOP

Civil War memorabilia, both genuine and reproductions, can be found throughout the state, particularly in Natchez where there are a wealth of antiques stores.

Square Books on the town square in Oxford is a goldmine of titles on everything from Faulkner to Southern cooking to blues music. There are offshoots for second-hand books and children's books nearby. Cat Head Records in Clarksdale specializes in blues music and books and has colorful artworks by local artists for sale. Artists throughout Mississippi produce a wealth of local crafts. Look for hand-stitched quilts, corn husk dolls, pine-needle baskets, pottery, wood carvings and Choctaw basket weavings made of swamp cane.The Mississippi Craftsmen's Guild has crafts centers in Ridgeland on the Natchez Trace and in Jackson at the Chimneyville Crafts Gallery at the Agriculture and Forestry Museum. The annual Chimneyville Crafts Festival, held in Jackson in late November/early December, has high-quality crafts from around the country for sale.

The Gulf Coast

Useful Addresses

SouthCoastUSA
www.southcoastusa.com
Toll-free 800-359-6299
For online reservations and links to specific destinations all along the Gulf Coast.
Florida tourist information
Visit Florida, PO Box 1100, Tallahassee, FL 32302
Tel: 850-488-5607
www.flausa.com
Pensacola Area Convention & Visitor Information Center
1401 E. Gregory Street
Pensacola, FL 32501
Tel: 850-434-1234
Toll-free: 800-874-1234
www.visitpensacola.com
Alabama tourist Information
(see page 347)
Alabama Gulf Coast Convention & Visitors Bureau
PO Drawer 457
Gulf Shores, AL 36547
Tel: 334-968-7511
Toll-free: 800-745-7263
www.gulfshores.com
Mississippi tourist Information
(see page 350)
Mississippi Gulf Coast Convention & Visitors Bureau
942 Beach Drive
Gulfport, MS 39506
Toll-free: 888-467-4853
www.gulfcoast.org

Where to Stay

FLORIDA PANHANDLE

Destin
Henderson Park Inn
2700 Scenic Highway 98E
Tel: 850-837-4853
Toll-Free: 800-336-4853
www.hendersonparkinn.com

Porch swings look out onto the Gulf of Mexico and a sandy beach. **$$**

Panama City Beach
Howard Johnson's Boardwalk Beach Resort
9450 S. Thomas Drive
Tel: 850-234-3484
Toll-free: 800-224-4853
A beachfront family-style resort with 632 units, pools, tennis, restaurants, and bars. **$**
Marriott Bay Point Resort
4200 Marriott Drive
Tel: 850-234-3483
Toll-free: 800-874-7105
www.marriottbaypoint.com
An elegant resort with antique furnishings, Asian rugs, and beautiful views. 355 rooms and suites, golf, tennis. **$$–$$$$**

Pensacola
Pensacola Victorian B&B
203 E. Gregory Street
Tel: 850-434-2818
Toll-free: 800-370-8354
www.pensacolavictorian.com
An early 20th-century station serves as the lobby of this 15-story hotel, with restaurant, bar, health club. **$$**
Seville Inn
223 E. Garden Street
Tel: 850-433-8331
Toll-free: 800-277-7275
www.sevilleinn.com
On the edge of the historic Seville district, this inn offers two pools, bar and shuttle service. **$**

Seaside
Josephine's French Country Inn
101 Seaside Avenue
Tel: 850-231-1940
Toll-free: 800-848-1840
Fax: 850-321-2446
www.josephinesfl.com
Elegant Georgian-style mansion in the quaint community of Seaside. Charming rooms decorated with antiques and lace. **$$$**

ALABAMA

Gulf Shores
The Beach House
9218 Dacus Lane
Tel: 251-540-7039
Toll-free: 800-659-6004

www.bigbeachhouse.com
B&B in a rambling wooden house atop the dunes, with large porches overlooking the sea. Rooms have pine floors, oriental rugs and kingsize feather beds. **$$$$**
Waterway Inn
2513 E. 2nd Street
Tel: 251-968-7615
Fax: 251-967-2298
www.thewaterwayinn.com
Spacious, quiet rooms, some with full kitchens, on the Intracoastal Canal minutes from the beach. Fish from the docks and cook your catch on charcoal grills. **$–$$**
Youngs by the Sea Motel
401 East Beach Blvd. (Hwy. 182)
Tel: 251-948-4181
Toll-free: 800-245-0032
www.youngsbytheseamotel.com
Comfortable waterfront rooms with full kitchens and private beach. A family favorite for decades. **$–$$**

Orange Beach
Island House Hotel
26650 Perdido Beach Boulevard
Tel: 251-981-6100
Toll Free: (800) 264-2642
www.islandhousehotel.com
Gulf-front rooms and suites with private balconies and first-class amenities. Private beach and golf packages available. **$$–$$$$**
The Original Romar House
23500 Perdido Beach Boulevard
Tel: 251-974-1625
Toll-free: 800-487-6627
www.bbonline.com/al/romarhouse/
Seaside bed-and-breakfast inn, built in 1920s in art-deco style. Five rooms, a suite and guest cottage, all furnished with period antiques. Heated pool. **$$–$$$$**
Perdido Beach Resort
27200 Perdido Beach Boulevard
Tel: 251-981-9811
Toll-free: 800-634-8001
www.perdidobeachresort.com
Mediterranean-style resort hotel on the beach. Spacious rooms and suites have private balconies with beautiful Gulf views. **$$–$$$$**

Magnolia Springs
Magnolia Springs B&B
14469 Oak Street
www.magnoliasprings.com

Built in 1897, and beautifully restored with the original pine walls, ceilings and floors. Sit on the front porch swing and unwind or stroll the oak-lined streets of this laid-back town where mail is still delivered by boat. The charming host offers real Southern hospitality. **$$$**

Point Clear
The Grand Hotel Resort & Golf Club & Spa
1 Grand Boulevard
Tel: 251-928-9201
Toll-free: 800-544-9933
www.marriottgrand.com
Possibly Alabama's best resort. The Grand Dining Room's Sunday brunch is popular, while the Bay View Room serves up fantastic seafood and the Grand Spa offers pampering to die for. **$$$$**

MISSISSIPPI

Biloxi
Balmoral Inn
120 Balmoral Avenue
Tel: 228-388-6776
Toll-free: 800-393-9131
www.gcww.com/balmoralinn.com
Only 10 rooms and a beachfront location makes advanced reservations a necessity. Pool and golf packages available. **$$**
Biloxi Beach Resort
2736 Beach Boulevard
Tel: 228-388-3310
Toll-free: 800-345-1570
www.biloxibeachresort.com
A center of activity with

entertainment for guests; golf packages available. **$$$**

Father Ryan House B&B
1196 Beach Boulevard
Tel: 228-435-1189
Toll-free: 800-295-1189
Fax: 228-436-3063
www.frryan.com
Historic home of the Confederate poet Father Abram Ryan. One of the oldest houses on the coast, opposite the beach. Rooms and suites furnished with hand-crafted beds and antiques. **$$$–$$$$**

Green Oaks
580 Beach Boulevard
Tel: 228-436-6257
Toll-free: 888-436-6257
Fax: 228-436-6225
www.gcww.com/greenoaks
Historic B&B built in 1826, surrounded by old oaks with a view of the beach and barrier islands. Rooms have antiques and four-poster beds. **$$$**

Ocean Springs
Gulf Hills Resort and Conference Center
13701 Paso Road
Tel: 228-875-4211
Fax: 228-875-4213
Toll-Free: 877-875-4211
www.gulfhillsresort.com
Full-service hotel with an outdoor pool and golf packages. **$$$**

Shadowlawn B&B
112 A Shearwater Drive
Tel: 228-875-6954
Fax: 228-875-6595
Built on the shores of Biloxi Bay in 1907, the porch affords views of the bay and moss-draped oaks. **$$**

Wilson House Inn
6312 Allen Road
Tel: 228-875-6933
Toll-free: 800-872-6933
Fax: 228-875-6933
A log home with wrap-around porch built in 1923. Six rooms and a Southern breakfast. **$$**

Where to Eat

FLORIDA PANHANDLE

Panama City Beach
Boar's Head
17290 Front Beach Road
Tel: 850-234-6628
A rustic, yet elegant, restaurant and tavern that offers juicy prime rib, shrimp bisque, escargot and blackened fish dishes. **$$**

Captain Anderson's
5551 N. Lagoon Drive
Tel: 850-234-2225
Tasty Greek and seafood specialties served amid a rustic, nautical decor. **$–$$$**

Pensacola
Barnhill's Buffet
10 S. New Warrington Road
Tel: 850-456-2760
www.barnhills.com
One of a line of Southern buffet restaurants. On top of the generous salad bar there is every variety of Southern meat, vegetable and casserole you could imagine. **$$**

Bay Breeze Restaurant
7601 Scenic Highway
Tel: 850-477-7155
www.ramadabayview.com
Fine dining on the coast. Enjoy aperitifs in the nearby piano-bar. **$$$**

Copeland's Famous New Orleans Restaurant and Bar
400 E. Chase Street
Tel: 850-432-7738
www.copelandspensacola.com
Cajun-style cuisine using the best in fresh Gulf Coast seafood. **$$**

ALABAMA

Gulf Shores
King Neptune's Seafood Restaurant
1137 Gulf Shores Parkway
Tel: 251-968-5464
www.kingneptunes.com
Unpretentious diner-style restaurant serving the freshest Gulf Coast seafood, from oysters on the half shell to Royal Red shrimp, seafood platters, sandwiches, lunch and dinner specials. A local legend. **$–$$**

Orange Beach
Bayside Grill
27842 Canal Road at Sportsman Marina
Tel: 251-981-4899
Creole and Caribbean cuisine, featuring wood-grilled fresh fish, steaks, chicken and ribs. A local favorite for seafood. **$$**

Café Grazie
27267 Perdido Beach Blvd.
Tel: 251-981-7278
Casual family restaurant serving seafood Italian style, along with pasta and pizza. In the SanRoc Cay complex. **$–$$**

Calypso Joe's Fish-Grille Market
27075 Marina Road
Tel: 251-981-1415
www.calypsomango.com
Colorful, open-air bistro serving fun food with a Caribbean flair, from conch chowder to fish in a tin. The live crab races each evening are a hoot. Below Mango's at the Orange Beach Marina. **$–$$**

Mangos on the Island
27075 Marina Road
Tel: 251-981-1416
Website: www.calypsomango.com
Fine waterfront dining at the Orange Beach Marina. Outstanding Caribbean and French Creole dishes such as pecan-encrusted tilapia and jerk shrimp in a banana leaf. Extensive wine list. **$$–$$$**

MISSISSIPPI

Biloxi
Boomtown Buffet
Boomtown Casino
676 Bayview Avenue
Tel: 228-435-7000
Toll-free: 800-627-0777
www.boomtownbiloxi.com
Buffets like this are a dime a dozen in Biloxi casinos, designed to keep the gamblers in-house. This is one of the better ones. **$$**

Mary Mahoney's
116 Rue Magnolia
Tel: 228-436-6000
www.marymahoneys.com
Fine French dining, inside and outside, in a series of small rooms shaded by old oak trees. Strong wine list to accompany the Creole menu. A local legend mentioned in John Grisham novels. **$$$**

Gulfport
Chappy's Seafood
624 E. Beach Boulevard
Tel: 228-865-9755

Popular restaurant with some interesting regional specialties. Try the frogs legs with a side order of fried green tomatoes. **$**

Ocean Springs
Aunt Jenny's Catfish Restaurant
1217 N. Washington Avenue
Tel: 601-875-9201
Located in an old waterfront house that once served riverboat visitors. The fried catfish and chicken with a side of okra can't be beat. **$$**
Fisherman's Wharf
705 Bienville Road
Tel: 228-872-6111
Wonderful fresh fish in casual surroundings. **$**

Where to Shop

Cordova Mall, the largest in the Pensacola area, features upscale department stores and more than 140 specialty stores. Quayside Art Gallery, at the corner of Zarragossa and Jefferson streets in the Historic District, is a cooperative of more than 200 artists from the Southeast. Their works are on display in a former fire engine building dating from 1873. For antiques and collectibles, don't miss the Blue Moon on Navy Boulevard, a retro mall with some 65 dealers.

The place to shop on the Alabama Gulf Coast is Tanger Outlet Center in Foley, with 120 stores offering brand name clothing, luggage and other merchandise at discount prices.

Ocean Springs, Mississippi, has a wealth of art galleries. Art & Soul (1304 Government Street) and Whistle Stop Art (714 Washington Avenue) are just two. Pewter is available at Ballard Peter (1110 Government Street) and silver at Gabbie's On the Avenue. Stop by the Candy Cottage (702 Washington Avenue) to whet your sweet tooth. The best place for antiques is a shop called Memories (1013 Government Street).

Biloxi's best bets for antiques are the Beauvoir Antique Mall (190 Beauvoir Road) and Vieux Marche Antiques (120 Lameuse Street).

Louisiana

Getting Acquainted

Known as: the Pelican State – a tribute to the official state bird.
Motto: Union, Justice and Confidence.
Entered Union: April 30, 1812 as the 18th member of the United States; had been called the Territory of Orleans.
Population: 4.5 million.
Area: 51,843 sq. miles (134.272 sq. km).
Time Zones: Central Time Zone (GMT minus 6 hours).
Capital: Baton Rouge
Local Dialing Codes: 318 (north), 337 (southwest), 225 (around Baton Rouge), 504 (around New Orleans), 985 (remainder of southeast).
Famous Figures: Jazz legend Louis Armstrong, novelist Truman Capote, musicians Fats Domino, Jerry Lee Lewis and Wynton Marsalis.

Useful Addresses

Louisiana tourist information
Louisiana Office of Tourism
P.O. Box 94291, Baton Rouge, LA 70804-9291
Tel: 225-342-8100
Web: www.louisianatravel.com
New Orleans tourist information
New Orleans Visitors Bureau
2020 St Charles Avenue, 70130
Tel: 504-566-5011
Toll-free: 800-672-6124
Web: www.neworleanscvb.com
Baton Rouge tourist information
Baton Rouge Area Visitors Bureau
730 North Boulevard, 70802
Tel: 225-383-1825
Toll-free: 800-527-6843
Fax: 225-346-1253
Web: www.batonrougetour.com

New Orleans

FROM THE AIRPORT

In addition to taxi ranks and rental car agencies, there is a shuttle to Downtown (tel: 504-522-3500), a public bus leaving every 15–20 minutes (tel: 504-367-7433) and the Coastliner/Mississippi Coast Service with transportation to several Gulf Coast destinations (tel: 800-647-3957).

WHERE TO STAY

In New Orleans you can stay in lovingly restored antebellum homes, Creole cottages, historic guest houses and inns, boutique hotels or upscale chains offering every amenity. If you want to be where the action is, choose accommodations in the French Quarter or the Central Business District, which is within walking distance. The leafy Garden District and Uptown areas are also easily accessible from Downtown on the St Charles Avenue streetcar. There are many lovely bed-and-breakfast options. For guidance try one of the reservation services, such as **Bed and Breakfast, Inc.**, tel: 504-488-4640 or 800-729-4640, www.HistoricLodging.com or **New Orleans Bed & Breakfast and Accommodations**, tel: 504-838-0071 or 888-240-0070, www.neworleansbandb.com. Wherever you're staying, make reservations well ahead, especially during Mardi Gras, JazzFest and other special events.

Bourbon Orleans–Wyndham Historic Hotel
717 Orleans Street
Tel: 504-523-2222
Toll-free: 800-521-5338
Fax: 504-525-8166
www.bourbonorleans.com
Queen Anne furnishings and marble baths grace this French Quarter hotel built around an outdoor courtyard where cabanas encircle the pool. Rooms with balconies overlook Bourbon Street, but it is quieter on the courtyard side. **$$$$**

Chateau Hotel
1001 Chartres Street
Tel: 504-524-9636
Toll-free: 800-828-1822
Fax: 504-524-2989
A small, tastefully furnished
motel with a charming courtyard,
located in the residential Lower
Quarter – a good choice for budget
travelers. **$**

**Hostelling International –
Marquette**
2253 Carondelet Street
Tel: 504-523-3014
Fax: 504-529-5933
The nation's fourth-largest
youth hostel is set in a complex
of century-old buildings one
block from St Charles Avenue.
There are dormitory rooms with
bunk beds, private rooms and
apartments. **$**

Lafayette Hotel
600 St. Charles Avenue
Tel: 504-524-4441
Toll-free: 888-221-3447
Fax: 504-523-7327
Web: www.neworleanscollection.com
A small gem, the very Gallic
Lafayette's beautiful rooms have
minibars, ottomans, easy chairs
and bookshelves. Many have four-
posters, and some on St. Charles
Avenue open onto balconies – great
during Carnival season. **$$$**

Le Richelieu
1234 Chartres Street
Tel: 504-529-2492
Toll-free: 800-535-9653
Fax: 504-524-8179
www.lerichelieuhotel.com
This lovely 88-room hotel,
considered by many the best
bargain in town, is in a restored
macaroni factory and 19th-century
row of houses in the Lower Quarter.
Large rooms are individually
decorated, with balconies, brass
ceiling fans and fridges. **$$**

New Orleans Guest House
1118 Ursulines Street
Tel: 504-566-1177
Toll-free: 800-562-1177
Brick Creole cottage built in 1848
and renovated into 14 rooms with
private bath. Free parking,
breakfast in the lush courtyard. **$$$**

Olde Victorian Inn
914 N. Rampart Street

Tel: 504-522-2446
Toll-free: 800-725-2446
www.oldevictorianinn.com
B&B in the French Quarter.
Beautifully restored 1840s home
furnished with antiques and
reproductions. Most rooms have
fireplaces and some have
balconies. **$$$–$$$$**

WHERE TO EAT

New Orleans' extraordinary range of
food includes everything from haute
cuisine and Bananas Foster to
blackened catfish and Creole soul
food. Many restaurants require men
to wear a jacket and tie. If in doubt,
dress up unless an establishment
is clearly casual.

Alex Patout's Louisiana Restaurant
221 Royal Street, French Quarter
Tel: 504-525-7788
www.patout.com
The chef-owner comes from a long
line of Cajun culinary artists. His
stylish restaurant showcases
seafoods enhanced by exotic
sauces and seasonings. Fixed-price
menus for lunch and dinner;
reservations recommended for
dinner; closed for lunch on
weekends. **$$$**

Antoine's
713 St Louis Street, French Quarter
Tel: 504-581-4422
www.antoines.com
This well-known French Creole
restaurant has been run by the
same family since 1840. Famous

dishes such as Oysters Rockefeller
originated at Antoine's. Many
dishes are sensational, especially
the Baked Alaska. **$$$**

Bon Ton Cafe
401 Magazine Street
Tel: 504-524-3386
Cajun restaurant serving Louisiana
specialties such as Redfish Bon
Ton, made from old family recipes.
Great bread pudding. **$$$**

Gumbo Shop
630 Saint Peter Street
Tel: 504-525-1486
Toll-free: 800-554-8626
www.gumboshop.com
Traditional and contemporary Creole
cuisine, served in a casually
elegant 1795 Creole cottage. Lovely
garden patio. Half a block from
Jackson Square. **$$**

**Michaul's Live Cajun Music
Restaurant**
840 St. Charles Avenue
Tel: 504-522-5517
Toll-free: 800-563-4055
www.michauls.com
A local favorite for authentic Cajun
food and music. There's free dance
lessons, so everyone can join in.
$$–$$$

Old Dog New Trick Cafe
307 Exchange Alley
Tel: 504-522-4569
www.olddognewtrick.com
One of the few places in the meat-
lvong South where you can tuck into
a wholesome vegetarian meal. Meat
dishes are spicy and everything is
homemade. Beer and wine served.
$$

**The Praline Connection Gospel and
Blues Hall**
907 S. Peters Street
Tel: 504-523-3973
www.pralineconnection.com
Ask any local where to go for soul
food and they're bound to point you
in this direction. Daily lunch buffet,
but on Sunday you get the added
attraction of a gospel brunch with
shows at 11am and 2pm. **$–$$**

WHERE TO SHOP

Royal and Magazine streets in the
French Quarter and Warehouse
District respectively are the places
for great antiques. Try Interiors

Market (2240 Magazine Street), French Antique Shop (225 Royal Street), and Royal Antiquest Ltd (309 Royal Street).

The entire town is terrific for shopping. Buy candy at Aunt Sally's Praline Shops (810 Decatur Street), Carnival souvenirs at Beads by the Dozen (1401 Edwards Avenue), Masks at Little Shop of Fantasy (523 Dumaine Street). International visitors can take advantage of Louisiana's tax-free shopping scheme and claim back tax paid on purchases, either at the airport before departure or on the return home. For details check the website: www.louisianataxfree.com

Around Louisiana

WHERE TO STAY

Breaux Bridge
Bayou Cabins
100 Mills Ave, Hwy 94
Tel: 337-332-6158
www.bayoucabins.com
Atmospheric 19th-century Cajun cabins with porches overlooking Bayou Teche. **$**
Country Oaks Cajun Cottages
1138 Lawless Tauzin Road
Tel: 337-332-3093
Toll-free: 800-318-2423
Secluded cottages on a private lake with fireplaces, fishing and wooded walking trails. **$$**
Maison Des Amis
111 Washington Street
Tel: 337-507-3399
Fax: 337-332-2227
www.cafedesamis.com
Many come to stay the night, just to get first dibs on the renowned breakfast at Cafe Des Amis. **$$**

Eunice
Howard's Inn
3789 Highway 190
Tel: 337-457-2066
Motel on the highway with plenty of parking and a huge lobby in which to lounge. **$$**
L'Acadie Inn
259 Tassso Loop
Tel: 337-457-5211
Fax: 337-550-7655
www.hotboudin.com

Lance and Kelly Pitre offer real Cajun hospitality, and hot boudin for breakfast, too. They know everyone and everything in town. **$$**
Potier's Prairie Cajun Inn
110 West Park Avenue
Tel: 337-457-0440
www.potiers.net
French-speaking inn with tasty Cajun food, located in the downtown cultural center. **$$**
The Seale Guesthouse
125 Seale Lane
Tel: 337-457-3753
Pretty guesthouse in tranquil wooded grounds with large front porch. Six rooms tastefully decorated with antiques. **$$**

Franklin
Hanson House
114 E. Main Street
Tel: 337-828-3271
Toll-free: 877-928-3271
www.hansonhouse.bigdogz.com
Antebellum guesthouse located in Franklin's historic district. Spacious rooms. **$$**

Lafayette
Bois des Chênes
338 N. Sterling Drive
Tel: 337-233-7816
Fax: 337-233-7816
Lovingly converted plantation carriage house close to the city center. Breakfast included. **$$**
Country French Bed & Breakfast
616 General Mouton
Tel: 337-234-2866
Located within a country French antiques shop and furnished as you would expect. **$$**
Lafayette Hilton and Towers
1521 Pinhook Road
Tel: 337-235-6111
Toll-free: 800-456-1612
Fax: 337-261-0311
Luxurious rooms, some with views of Vermillion Bayou. Pool, exercise facilities, spa. **$$$$**

New Iberia
Acadian Cottages
5505 Rip Van Winkle Road
Tel: 337-365-3332
Toll-free: 800-375-3332
www.ripvanwinkle.com
An historic collection of cottages

set in a semi-tropical environment and furnished with antiques. **$$**
Chez Herbert B&B
5304 Shoreline Drive
Tel: 337-367-6447
Fax: 337-364-3217
Overlooking Bayou Teche and set under a canopy of ancient oak trees. **$$**
La Maison B&B
8317 Weeks Island Road
Tel: 337-364-2970
Toll-free: 800-422-2586
A secluded country home set amid sugarcane fields. **$$**

St Martinville
Bienvenue House
421 N. Main Street
Tel: 337-394-9100
Toll-free: 888-394-9100
www.bienvenuehouse.com
Antebellum home with porch swings and gourmet breakfast, within walking distance of the town's Historic Square. **$$**
La Maison Louie B&B
517 E. Bridge Street
Tel: 337-394-1872
Open weekends only, there's a friendly welcome for guests to this French colonial house. **$$**
The Old Castillo Hotel
220 Evangeline Boulevard
Tel: 337-394-4010
Toll-free: 800-880-7050
Fax: 337-394-7983
Beautiful historic inn with excellent restaurant on Bayou Teche. **$$**

WHERE TO EAT

Breaux Bridge
Bayou Boudin and Cracklin Cafe
100 Mills Avenue
Tel: 337-332-6158
www.bayoucabins.com
Cajun specialties served in an 1869 home on Bayou Teche. **$$**
Crawfish Capital Cafe
1401 Rees Street
Tel: 337-332-4458
www.crawfishcapitalcafe.com
A fish and steak joint serving gumbo, étouffée and other Cajun classics. **$$**
Mulate's Restaurant
325 Mills Avenue

Price Codes

Hotels: Categories based on average cost of a double room for one night.
$ = under $65
$$ = up to $100
$$$ = up to $150
$$$$ = over $150

Restaurants: Categories based on average cost of dinner and a glass of wine, before tip.
$ = under $15
$$ = up to $30
$$$ = over $30

Tel: 337-332-4648
Toll-free: 800-422-2586
www.mulates.com
Wildly popular Cajun food and foot-stompin' music spot. **$$**

Eunice
Johnson's Grocery
700 E. Maple Avenue
Tel: 318-457-9314
The place to try the local boudin, or black pudding. **$**
Ruby's Cafe
221 W. Walnut Avenue
Tel: 337-457-2583
Generous portions of well-flavored Cajun food for next to nothing. **$**

Franklin
Charlie's of Franklin
1416 Northwest Boulevard
Tel: 337-828-4169
Seafood and steak joint with great atmosphere. **$$**

Lafayette
Acadiana Catfish Shack
5818 Johnston Street
Tel: 337-988-2200
www.catfishshack.com
Excellent seafood served buffet style. **$**
Poor Boy's Riverside Inn
US Highway 90 East
Tel: 337-235-8559
Cajun seafood and steaks served in a casual atmosphere overlooking a beautiful setting. Call for precise directions. **$**
Prejean's
3480 1-49 North

Tel: 337-896-3247
Famous for its live Cajun music and award-winning gumbos, but look out for tour groups. **$**

New Iberia
Cafe Jefferson at Rip Van Winkle Gardens
5505 Rip Van Winkle Road
Tel: 337-364-5111
Toll-free: 800-375-3332
www.ripvanwinkle.com
A great setting on Lake Peigneur and creatively spiced Cajun cuisine. **$$**
Clementine Dining & Spirits
113 E. Main Street
Tel: 337-560-1007
Vintage bar and restaurant featuring local artwork. **$$**
Little River Inn
833 E. Main Street
Tel: 337-367-7466
Fine Cajun cuisine in an upscale atmosphere overlooking the Trappey Oak. **$$**

St. Martinville
La Place D'Evangeline Restaurant
220 Evangeline Boulevard
Tel: 337-394-4010
Toll-free: 800-621-3017
French cuisine, located in the Historic District. **$**
Maison de Ville Restaurant
100 N. Main Street
Tel: 337-394-5700
Serves fine regional cuisine and there's an interesting bar. **$$**

WHERE TO SHOP

Floyd's Record Shop, 434 E. Main Street in Ville Platte, has a large selection of southern Louisiana music, including records by local Cajun musicians. The Jefferson Street Market in Lafayette sells local crafts and artwork, from handwoven textiles to bent-willow furniture. The Lafayette Art Gallery, 412 Travis Street, is another outlet for local artists selling pottery, paintings, glass, and jewelry. For Cajun foods to take home, try the Cajun Country Store, 401 E. Cypress in Lafayette, or Konriko Company Store, next to the Conrad

Rice Mill in New Iberia. Two good bookshops with a range of regional titles are Lilly's, 913 Harding Street in Lafayette, and Books Along the Teche, 110 E. Main Street in New Iberia. The latter gives out a map of sites mentioned in the detective novels of James Lee Burke.

Baton Rouge

FROM THE AIRPORT

Baton Rouge Metropolitan Airport only has domestic flights. Taxis and rental cars are the only ground transportation available.

WHERE TO STAY

Best Western Chateau Louisianne Suite Hotel
710 N. Lobdell Avenue
Tel: 225-927-6700
Toll-free: 800-256-6263
Quiet, romantic boutique hotel in mid-city. All rooms are suites, set around a three-story atrium, with an indoor courtyard. Outdoor pool, indoor whirlpool, steam room and fitness center. **$$–$$$**
Radisson Hotel and Conference Center
4728 Constitution Avenue
Tel: 225-925-2244
Fax: 225-930-0140
www.radisson.com/batonrougela
Attractive, comfortable rooms and suites near the LSU campus. Amenities include a health club, laundry, pool, restaurant and free airport transportation. **$$$**
Sheraton Baton Rouge Convention Center Hotel
103 France Street
Tel: 225-242-2600
A recently opened full-service hotel, located Downtown near city attractions and adjacent to the riverboat casino. 300 rooms and suites, with pool, fitness center and a Cajun restaurant. **$$–$$$**
The Stockade Bed & Breakfast
8860 Highland Road
Tel: 225-769-7358
Toll-free: 888-900-5430
www.thestockade.com
Large, Spanish hacienda-style home set inside a former Civil War

stockade on the historic Highland Road. Quaint rooms, delicious breakfast. **$$**

WHERE TO EAT

Brunet's Cajun Restaurant
135 S. Flannery Road
Tel: 225-272-6226
Cajun food and Cajun music. **$**
Drusilla Seafood Restaurant
3482 Drusilla Lane
Tel: 225-923-0896
A local favorite for seafood, steaks, and Cajun food. Good atmosphere. **$**
Mamacita's Restaurant and Cantina
7524 Bluebonnet Boulevard
Tel: 225-769-3850
They've kicked the spicy Cajun habit and wrapped up some tortillas instead to dish up Mexican food Louisiana style. **$**
Mulate's
8322 Bluebonnet Boulevard
Tel: 225-767-4794
Toll-free: 800-477-8978
www.mulates.com
Another branch of Louisiana's most famous restaurant. Live music nightly. **$$**

WHERE TO SHOP

Baton Rouge has dozens of antiques shops. Try Montage Marketplace, 3655 Perkins Road, with merchandise from over 40 dealers under one roof. The Mall of Louisiana, the largest in the area, and its rival, the Mall at Cortana, both have major department stores and specialty stores. The Tanger Outlet Center, south of Baton Rouge off I-10 at Gonzales, is Louisiana's largest outlet mall with 48 designer stores offering large discounts off the retail price.

Arkansas

Getting Acquainted

Known as: the Natural State for its natural beauty and an abundance of wildlife.
Motto: The People Rule.
Entered Union: June 15, 1836 joined as the 25th member of the United States.
Population: 2.7 million.
Area: 53,182 sq. miles (137,740 sq. km).
Time Zones: Central Time Zone (GMT minus 6 hours).
Capital: Little Rock
Local Dialing Codes: 501 (Little Rock area), 479 (northwest), 870 (remainder of state).
Famous Figures: Poet and writer Maya Angelou, singer Johnny Cash, thriller writer John Grisham, five-star general Douglas MacArthur, former president Bill Clinton.

Useful Addresses

Arkansas tourist information
Arkansas Department of Parks and Tourism, One Capitol Mall, Little Rock, AR 72201
Toll-free: 800-628-8725
Web: www.arkansas.com
Little Rock tourist information
Little Rock Visitors Bureau
Robinson Center
Markham and Broadway
Little Rock, AR 72201
Tel: 501-376-4781
Toll-free: 800-844-4781
Fax: 501-374-2255
Web: www.littlerock.com

Little Rock

FROM THE AIRPORT

Little Rock's airport only serves domestic flights, but has several shuttle services for getting to and from the airport. Hot Springs Shuttle (tel: 501-321-9911) serves Hot Springs and Little Rock; Inter Shuttle (tel: 501-376-7433) serves the entire state.

WHERE TO STAY

Capital Hotel
111 W. Markham Street
Tel: 501-374-7474
Toll-free: 800-766-7666
www.thecapitalhotel.com
Handsome Victorian hotel with a fine restaurant. **$$$**
Doubletree Hotel
424 W. Markham Street
Tel: 501 372-4371
Toll-Free: 800 222-8733
www.doubletree.com
All the amenities in this high-end hotel chain. **$$$**
The Empress of Little Rock
2120 Louisiana Street
Tel: 501-374-7966
www.TheEmpress.com
Impressive Gothic Queen Anne house featuring elegant double stairway and tower with poker room. Gourmet breakfast. **$$$**
The Legacy Hotel and Suites
625 Capitol Avenue
Tel: 501-374-0100.
This historic hotel has recently undergone a $1.3 million renovation. **$$$**
Peabody Little Rock
3 Statehouse Plaza
Tel: 501-375-5000
Toll-free: 800-375-5505
www.peabodylittlerock.com
As Downtown as you can get, this modern sister to Memphis's historic hotel has well-appointed rooms, plus the legendary Peabody ducks in the lobby fountain. **$$$**

WHERE TO EAT

Ashley's at the Capital Hotel
111 W. Markham Street
Tel: 501-374-7474
Toll-Free: 800-766-7666
One of only two four-diamond restaurants in Arkansas. Fish and beef entrees feature on the menu, but the biggest delights await on the dessert tray. **$$$**

Brave New Restaurant
2300 Cottondale Lane
Tel: 501-663-2677
www.bravenewrestaurant.com
A casual environment with good
service at a reasonable cost. **$$**

Doe's Eat Place
1023 W. Markham Street
Tel: 501-376-1195
A transplant from Greenville,
Mississippi, this casual restaurant
is famed locally for its burgers and
huge, choice-cut steaks. Funky
atmosphere. **$$**

Faded Rose Restaurant
1615 Rebsamen Park Road
Tel: 501-663-9734
Steaks, burgers and Yankee grub. **$**

Flying Fish
511 President Clinton Avenue
Tel: 501-375-3474
Fried catfish and seafood
restaurant in the River Market
District. **$$$**

Graffiti's Italian Restaurant
7811 Cantrell Road
Tel: 501-224-9079
Daily specials. Casual atmosphere.
$$

Iriana's Pizza
103 W. Markham Street
Tel: 501-374-3656
This restaurant specializes in tasty
thick-crust pizza and also makes
excellent Italian sausages. **$$**

Loca Luna
3519 Old Cantrell Road
Tel: 501-663-4666
www.localuna.com
American-style bistro that's popular
with the locals. Good bar. **$$**

WHERE TO SHOP

River Market is the anchor to the
district of the same name. It is
home to a seasonal Farmer's
Market and Art at the Market,
featuring works by local artisans.
Additionally, there are several
unusual boutiques located here.

Antiques shops are scattered
throughout the city. Some of the
best include Fabulous Finds (2905
Cantrell) in the Riverdale District
and Marshall Clements (1509
Rebsamen Park). Antiquarius (3625
Kavanaugh) carries pieces from
Europe, while the Argenta Antique

Mall (201 E. Broadway, downtown
North Little Rock) has a diverse
sampling of wares from more than
20 dealers.

Around Arkansas

WHERE TO STAY

Eureka Springs

Angel at Rose Hall B&B
46 Hillside Avenue
Tel: 479-253-5405
Toll-free: 800-828-4255
Fax: 479-253-5405
www.eurekaspringsangel.com
The atmosphere is so charming it is
often booked out for weddings. All
rooms feature elegant antiques and
king beds, but there are also
balconies and stained-glass
windows. **$$$**

Arlington Resort Hotel and Spa
239 Central Avenue
Tel: 501-623-7771
Toll-free: 800-643-1502
Fax: 501-623-2243
www.arlingtonhotel.com
A large hotel situated in the
Ouachita Mountains and home to
the Oaklawn Race Track. Spring-fed
mineral baths and massages at the
spa. Three restaurants. **$$$**

Basin Park Hotel
12 Spring Street
Toll-free: 877-643-4972
www.basinpark.com
Many of these modern rooms
include a Jacuzzi. The Serenity Spa,
located on-site, is what most people
come to these parts for. **$$$**

Price Codes

Hotels: Categories based on
average cost of a double room
for one night.
$ = under $65
$$ = up to $100
$$$ = up to $150
$$$$ = over $150

Restaurants: Categories based
on average cost of dinner and a
glass of wine, before tip.
$ = under $15
$$ = up to $30
$$$ = over $30

1886 Crescent Hotel and Spa
75 Prospect
Toll-free: 800-342-9766
www.crescent-hotel.com
The Crescent's been attracting
visitors for over 100 years. Those
who come for the adventure or
healing fresh-air qualities of the
Ozarks want to return here for its
charm. Fully modernized and lovely.
Spa treatments available. **$$$**

Rogue's Manor Sweet Spring
124 Spring Street
Toll-free: 800-250-5827
www.roguesmanor.com
Located in the Historic District, the
four, theme-decorated suites are
elegantly done. Mostly though,
Rogue's makes its name as a
restaurant serving fine steak and
lobster dinners. **$$$**

Fayetteville

The Radisson
70 N. East Avenue
Tel: 479-442-5555
Toll-free: 800-333-3333
Fax: 479-442-2105
www.radisson.com/fayettevillear
A chain establishment with clean,
spacious rooms and friendly service
at reasonable prices. **$$**

Fort Smith

Beland Manor B&B
1320 S. Albert Pike
Tel: 479-782-3300
Toll-free: 800-334-5052
www.fort-smith.net
A colonial mansion with good
service. Some room have
fireplaces. **$$**

Hot Springs

The Arlington Resort Hotel and Spa
239 Central Avenue
Tel: 501-623-7771
Fax: 501-623-6191
Web: www.arlingtonhotel.com
This full-service resort has been
pampering visitors since 1873.
Facilities include an on-premises
bath house with thermal water
baths and massages, twin
cascading heated pools, shops,
restaurant and beauty salon.
Bedrooms on certain floors have
thermal water in their private
bathtubs. **$$**

Embassy Suites
400 Convention Boulevard
Tel: 501-624-9200
www.embassysuiteshotsprings.com
A chain hotel popular with both
conventioneers and tourists. **$$**

Lookout Point Lakeside Inn
104 Lookout Circle
Tel: 501-525-6155
Toll-free: 866-525-6155
Fax: 501-52505850
www.lookoutpointinn.com
Not Downtown, but very, very nice,
especially if you want to be near the
lake. 10 rooms. **$$$**

Majestic Resort and Spa
101 Park Avenue
Tel: 501-623-5511
Toll-free: 800-643-1504
www.themajestichotel.com
An historic hotel built in 1882. The
traditional soda fountain is a hit
with kids, and there are full spa
facilities to entertain the grown-ups.
$$$

Wildwood 1884 B&B Inn
808 Park Avenue
Tel: 501-624-4267
Web: www.wildwood1884.com
Carefully restored 1884 Queen
Anne mansion with original wood-
work, antiques and stained glass.
Some rooms have porches. **$$**

WHERE TO EAT

Eureka Springs
Chez Charles
37 N. Main Street
Tel: 479-253-9509
Toll-Free: 888-253-1003

Price Codes

Hotels: Categories based on
average cost of a double room
for one night.
$ = under $65
$$ = up to $100
$$$ = up to $150
$$$$ = over $150

Restaurants: Categories based
on average cost of dinner and a
glass of wine, before tip.
$ = under $15
$$ = up to $30
$$$ = over $30

Well-prepared contemporary menu
featuring steaks. Formal setting. **$$**

DeVito's Italian Restaurant
5 Center Street
Eureka Springs
Tel: 479-253-6807
Great classics in one of the best
Italian restaurants in Arkansas.
There's a casual, family-oriented
setting. **$$**

Jim and Brent's Bistro
173 S. Main Street
Tel: 479-253-7457
Popular local hang-out. Basic menu
and ingredients, but done with
obvious attention to detail. **$$**

Mud Street Cafe
22 G South Main Street
Tel: 479-253-6732
www.mudstreetcafe.com
The best coffee in Arkansas is
served at this local hang out. Mud
Street's muffins are a must in the
morning, and there's local art on
the walls. Open for breakfast and
lunch only. **$**

Fayetteville
AQ Chicken House
Highway 71
Tel: 479-443-7555
www.aqchicken.com
Casual family restaurant serving
chicken with all the fixings. **$**

Ozark Brewing Company
430 W Dickson Street
Tel: 479-521-2739
www.ozarkbrew.com
A micro brewery that proves very
capable of cooking tasty pastas,
seafood and very hearty steak
entrees. **$$**

Powerhouse Seafood and Grill
112 N University Avenue
Tel: 479-442-8300
Fayetteville's oldest restaurant has
a dramatic setting in a disused
powerhouse. The menu features
Cajun-style seafood, chicken, pasta
and steak. **$$**

Fort Smith
The Lighthouse Inn
6000 Midland Boulevard
Tel: 479-783-9420
An occasional alligator appears on
the mainly seafood-based menu,
served with a great view of the
Arkansas River. **$$**

Taliano's Italian Restaurant
201 N. 14th Street
Tel: 501-785-2292
Fax: 501-785-2640
www.talianosrestaurant.com
A third-generation, family-run Italian
restaurant. All the recipes have
been passed down through the
Cadelli family. **$$**

Hot Springs
Brick House Grill
801 Central Avenue, Suite 24
Tel: 501-321-2926
Casual steakhouse with soups and
salads available to anyone looking
for something less hearty. **$$**

Bella Arti Ristorante
719 Central Avenue
Scenic Ark. 7
Tel: 501-624-7474
Italian cuisine classics dominate
the menu, but they still find room
for Angus steaks and fresh Maine
lobster. **$$$**

Hamilton House
Highway 7 South to Lake Hamilton
Tel: 501-525-2727
It's worth the trip to the lake to
dine in this charming house with
marvelous waterside views. Makes
a special evening even better. **$$$**

Hot Springs Brau Haus
801 Central Avenue
Scenic Ark. 7
Tel: 501-624-7866
German restaurant with a large
selection of imported beers. **$$**

McClard's
505 Albert Pike
Tel: 501-624-9586
Serving savory, well-seasoned
barbecue since 1908. One of Bill
Clinton's favorite spots. **$**

Miller's Chicken and Steak House
4723 Central Avenue
Tel: 501-525-8861
Long-standing favorite for freshly
cooked country-style food. **$$**

WHERE TO SHOP

Hot Springs and Eureka Springs are
good places for antiques and
original arts and crafts. The Ozark
Folk Center Country Store (tel: 870-
269- 3851) in the town of Mountain
View is the place for down-home
food, music CDs and cookbooks.

Tennessee

Getting Acquainted

Known as: the Volunteer State from the War of 1812 when volunteer soldiers from Tennessee under General Andrew Jackson displayed enormous valor during the Battle of New Orleans.
Motto: Agriculture and Commerce.
Entered Union: June 1, 1796 as the 16th member of the United States. The state was formed from land ceded to the federal government by North Carolina in 1784 and known as the Territory of the United States South of the River Ohio.
Population: 5.7 million.
Area: 42,244 sq. miles (109,412 sq. km).
Time Zones: Central Time Zone (GMT minus 6 hours).
Capital: Nashville
Local Dialing Codes: 901 (Memphis area) 731 (remaining western quarter of state), 615 (Nashville area), 931 (remaining central third), 865 (Knoxville area), 423 (remaining eastern third).
Famous Figures: Andrew Jackson (7th President), James K. Polk (11th President), Andrew Johnson (17th President), frontiersman Davy Crockett, Union Admiral David Farragut, Confederate Cavalry General Nathan Bedford Forrest, World War I hero Sergeant Alvin York, Nobel Peace Prize winner Cordell Hull, Pulitzer-prize winning author Alex Haley, singer Tina Turner.

Useful Addresses

Tennessee tourist information
Department of Tourist Development, Fifth Floor, Rachel Jackson Building, 320 Sixth Avenue N., Nashville, TN 37243
Tel: 615-741-9001
Web: www.state.tn.us
Memphis tourist information
Memphis Visitors Bureau
47 Union Avenue
Memphis, TN 38103
Tel: 901-543-5300
Fax: 901-543-5350
www.memphistravel.com
Nashville tourist information
Nashville Visitors Bureau
211 Commerce Street, Suite 100
Nashville, TN 37201
Tel: 615-259-4700
Toll-free: 800-657-6910
www.nashvillecvb.com

Memphis

FROM THE AIRPORT

Many hotels and motels offer complimentary shuttle services from Memphis International Airport. Otherwise MATA DASH (tel: 901-522-1677) offers a city-wide shuttle service. A public bus service also operates hourly to the city (tel: 901-274-MATA).

WHERE TO STAY

Renovations in recent years have made the downtown area an attractive place to stay, close to Beale Street and many museums. Midtown is another convenient area for sightseeing. The city is fairly spread out, so although many good hotels are located in East Memphis, be prepared to drive for some 20 miles from the center. Graceland is south, out towards the airport.

Bridgewater House B&B
7015 Raleigh La Grange Road, Cordova
Tel: 901-384-0080
Toll-free: 800-466-1001
Intimate B&B in a century-old former schoolhouse, shaded by acres of mature oaks. Rooms have ceiling fans, antiques, hardwood floors and down comforters. **$$**
East Memphis Hilton
5069 Sanderlin Avenue
Tel: 901-767-6666
Toll-free: 800-445-8667
Fax: 901-767-5428
www.hilton.com
264 rooms on eight floors. The glass-walled atrium and elevators afford fine views. Convenient for Midtown museums and restaurants. **$$$**
French Quarter Suites Hotel
2144 Madison Avenue
Tel: 901-728-4000
Toll-free: 800-843-0353
Fax: 901-278-1262
New Orleans' style with wrought-iron railings around a central atrium. Romantic features vary from half-canopied king beds to double whirlpool bathtubs and private balconies. Close to the nightlife in Midtown's Overland Square. **$$$**
Heartbreak Hotel
3734 Elvis Presley Boulevard
Tel: 901-332-3322
Toll-free: 800-238-2000
www.heartbreakhotel.net
Adjacent to Graceland, this is the place for Elvis fans, with a heart-shaped pool and in-room Elvis movies. All rooms have fridge and microwave for snacks and there are also themed suites. Packages include Graceland tours. **$$-$$$**
Holiday Inn Select Memphis East
5795 Popular Ave
Tel: 901-682-7881
Toll-free: 800-465-4329
243 rooms on ten floors. Superior Holiday Inn award winner in two consecutive years, no small feat in the city where Holiday Inn originated. **$$**
The Peabody Hotel
149 Union Avenue
Tel: 901-529-4000
Toll-free: 800-732-2639
Fax: 901-529-3600
www.peabodymemphis.com
One of the South's most elegant hotels with 458 rooms and 15 suites on 12 floors. Outstanding Downtown location one block from Beale St. The grand lobby is the place for high tea and to watch the famous Peabody ducks march from the fountain to the Duck Palace on the hotel roof. **$$$-$$$$**
Radisson Hotel Memphis
185 Union Avenue
Tel: 901-528-1800
Toll-free: 800-333-3333,
www.radisson.com
Good value in the heart of down-

town Memphis, within walking distance of Beale St. Outdoor pool, whirlpool and sauna. **$$–$$$**

Talbot Heirs Guesthouse
99 S. Second Street
Tel: 901-527-9772
Toll-free: 800-955-3956
Fax: 901-527-3700
www.talbotheirs.com
Stylish boutique hotel in the heart of Downtown. Nine large, uniquely decorated rooms, all with kitchens and contemporary art. **$$$$**

WHERE TO EAT

Memphis has a great range of restaurants, from legendary diners where Elvis was a regular to casual restaurants serving traditional Southern specialties to trendy cosmopolitan establishments serving internationally inspired fare. Above all, Memphis is famous for barbecue, particularly smoked pork ribs, served "wet" (cooked in sauce) or "dry"' (add your own).

Alfred's
197 Beale Street
Tel: 901-525-3711
Toll-free: 888-433-3711
www.alfreds-on-beale.com
Located in the heart of Beale Street's nightlife. Barbecue and pasta feature hugely on the menu and there are children's meals. **$$**

Automatic Slim's Tonga Club
83 S. Second Street
Tel: 901-525-7948
Where Memphis meets Manhattan. Southwestern and Caribbean inspired cuisine. **$$**

B.B. King's Blues Club and Restaurant
143 Beale Street
Tel: 901-524-5464
More barbecue, but lots of other good choices, too. There is memorabilia from the famous blues artist and a smokin' hot house band. Try the fried dill pickles. **$$**

Bravo! Ristorante
939 Ridge Lake Blvd (Adam's Mark Hotel)
Tel: 901-684-6664
If Memphis can have a pyramid, it can also have a bit of Italy. Professionally trained singers serve up re-

gional specialties and a serving of opera, operetta and Broadway. **$$$**

Buckley's Fine Filet Grill
Downtown
117 Union Avenue
Tel: 901-578-9001
This steakhouse is consistently recognized as one of Memphis' best. Vegetarians will struggle, carnivores will indulge. **$$**

Cafe Francisco
400 N. Main Street
Tel: 901-578-8002
www.cafefrancisco.com
They roast their own coffee beans here and serve great pastries, desserts and breads to go with. **$**

Chez Philippe
149 Union Avenue (The Peabody)
Tel: 901-529-4188
www.peabodymemphis.com
The finest Memphis has to offer according to many customers. Master Chef Jose Gutierrez has made this French-style restaurant a Four Star award winner. **$$$**

Ellen's Soul Food Restaurant
601 South Parkway East
Tel: 901-942-4888
Some of the best meatloaf going is served at this straightforward, but popular diner. All dishes served with piping hot cornmeal pancakes. **$**

Interstate Bar-B-Q
2265 S. Third Street
Tel: 901-775-2304
Okay, so Memphis is full of good barbecue joints, but this one was rated Number 2 in the United States by *People* magazine. There's more than just ribs here. BBQ spaghetti? It's on the menu. **$**

Leach Family Restaurant
694 Madison at Orleans
Tel: 901-521-0867
Get in early at lunchtime as the most popular dishes start to disappear by 1pm. Their fried chicken is especially good and their peach cobbler for dessert is delicious. **$**

Paulette's
2110 Madison Avenue
Tel: 901-726-5128
Cozy old-world ambiance, filet mignon, salmon, shrimp and European specialties, plus live music, make this a very popular Memphis dining spot. **$$$**

The Rendezvous
52 S. Second Street – Rear
Tel: 901-523-2746
Memphis's most famous barbecue joint is tucked away downstairs in a Downtown alley opposite the Peabody. Lively atmosphere and fantastic dry ribs. **$**

WHERE TO SHOP

Peabody Place is a huge, glitzy shopping mall adjoining the Peabody Hotel. Movies are shown here, too. Central Avenue has antiques shops, including Consignments (2300 Central Avenue), Market Central (2215 Central Avenue) and Palladio Antiques (2169 Central Avenue).

Main Street is the place for art. Try Bennett Stained Glass (338 S. Main Street) or the Durden Gallery (509 S. Main Street).

Around Tennessee

WHERE TO STAY

Chattanooga
Chanticleer Inn
1300 Mockingbird Lane
Lookout Mountain, Georgia
Tel: 706-820-2015
www.stayatchanticleer.com
This is the perfect romantic getaway, a group of 1930s stone cottages located at the top of Lookout Mountain, next door to Rock City. **$–$$**

Chattanooga Choo Choo
1400 Market Street
Tel: 423-756-3400
Toll-free: 1-800-Track 29
www.choochoo.com
This massive Beaux Arts train station with its soaring domed lobby has converted vintage sleeping cars into characterful accommodations. Convenient access to downtown. **$$**

Read House
827 Broad Street
Tel: 423-266-4121
Chattanooga's grand hotel is the best place to stay Downtown. Recent renovations have preserved the spacious rooms and splendid Georgian style. It's also close to restaurants and attractions. **$–$$**

Price Codes

Hotels: Categories based on average cost of a double room for one night.
$ = under $65
$$ = up to $100
$$$ = up to $150
$$$$ = over $150

Restaurants: Categories based on average cost of dinner and a glass of wine, before tip.
$ = under $15
$$ = up to $30
$$$ = over $30

Gatlinburg
Best Western Zoder's Inn
402 Parkway
Tel: 865-436-5681
www.zoders.com
Fireplaces, waterbeds and in-room hot tubs are some of the amenities which make this one of the best in this resort city.s 90 rooms
$$–$$$$
Brookside Resort
463 East Parkway
tel: 865-436-5611
www.brooksideresort.com
Wooded landscape with a mountain stream. 225 rooms, most with wood-burning fireplaces. **$$**
Gatlinburg Inn
755 Parkway
tel: 865-436-5133
One of the city's oldest resort hotels. 67 rooms. **$$–$$$$**

Knoxville
Clubhouse Inn and Suites
208 Market Place Lane
Tel: 865-531-1900
Fax: 865-531-8807
www.clubhouseinn.com
A full service hotel featuring spacious guest rooms, cable TV, an exercise room, three whirlpool rooms and a restaurant. **$$**
Holiday Inn Select Downtown
525 Henley Street
Tel: 865 522-2800
High-rise hotel with beautiful mountain views, on the site of the 1982 Knoxville World's Fair. The World's Fair Park has an enormous children's playground. **$$**

Hostelling International - Knoxville
404 E. Fourth Avenue
Tel: 865-546-8090
Hostel in the historic Fourth and Grille neighborhood. Facilities include kitchen, laundry, parking and internet. **$**
Maplehurst Inn Bed & Breakfast
800 W. Hill Avenue
Tel: 865-523-7773
www.maplehurstinn.com
Elegant rooms, and a secluded penthouse with private balcony, fireplace and Jacuzzi. Marble tubs, full breakfast. **$$–$$$**

Oak Ridge
Doubletree
215 S. Illinois Avenue
Tel: 865-481-2468
Spacious, attractive rooms with coffee makers and refrigerators. Facilities include an exercise room, indoor/outdoor pools and whirlpools, restaurant and lounge. **$$**

Pigeon Forge
Grand Resort Hotel & Convention Center
3171 Parkway
Tel: 865-453-1000
Toll-free: 800-251-4444
www.grandresorthotel.com
425 rooms. **$$**

WHERE TO EAT

Cracker Barrel is a Tennessee-based chain of restaurants located all over the South, usually on Interstate highway exits. For Southern-style cooking at this type of eatery, this is as good as it gets. **$**

Chattanooga
The Loft
328 Cherokee Boulevard
Tel: 423-266-3601
www.theloft.com
Outstanding steaks and beef. **$$$**
Mt Vernon
3509 S. Broad Street
Tel: 423-266-6591
Local specialties, steak, seafood. **$$**
Town and Country
110 N. Market Street
Tel: 423-267-8544
A Chattanooga institution for good Southern cuisine. **$$**

212 Market
212 Market Street
Tel: 423-265-1212
www.212market.com
One of Chattanooga's best restaurants serving continental cuisine with a Southern accent. **$$$**

Gatlinburg
Brass Lantern
710 Parkway
Tel: 865-436-4168
www.thebrasslanternrestaurant.com
Casual, contemporary restaurant serving steaks, burgers, salads and family fare. **$$**
The Burning Bush
Parkway at Park Entrance
Tel: 865-436-4669
The Bountiful Breakfast is of special note with such unusual delicacies as quail and Smoky Mountain trout on the menu. **$$$**
The Open Hearth
1138 Parkway
Tel: 865-436-5648
Steaks and prime ribs are the specialties and are extremely tasty. **$$**
Smoky Mountain Trout House
410 Parkway
Tel: 423-436-5416
Fresh Smoky Mountain trout is the specialty of the house, but there is more on the menu, too. **$$**

Jonesborough
The Parson's Table
102 Woodrow Avenue
Tel: 423-753-8002
The building was once a church; now it's a superlative restaurant serving refined Southern specialties with a touch of French flair. **$$$**

Knoxville
Calhoun's
400 Neyland Drive
Tel: 865-673-3355
Enjoy excellent barbecue ribs and a fine river view. **$**
Chesapeake's
500 Henley Street
Tel: 423-673-3433
Seafood, steaks and chicken. Blue crab and lobster are specialties. **$$**
Great American Steak and Buffet
4310 Chapman Highway
Tel: 865-579-6002

900 Merchants Drive
Tel: 865-687-8773
Almost anything you can imagine is
probably on one of the buffet
tables, and it's all good. **$**

The Orangery
5412 Kingston Pike
Tel: 865-588-2964
French cuisine and Old World
ambiance. Contemporary American
dishes are also served. **$$$**

Oak Ridge
Village Restaurant
123 Central Avenue
Tel: 865-483-1675
Tasty and affordable home-style
cooking. **$$**

Pigeon Forge
Santos
3270 Parkway
Tel: 865 428-5840
Fine Italian restaurant in the heart
of Southern fried country. **$$**

Nashville

FROM THE AIRPORT

In addition to a selection of rental
car agencies and taxi ranks, Gray
Line Tours operates a shuttle
service to Downtown from Nashville
International Airport (tel: 615-883-
5555, www.graylinenashville.com

WHERE TO STAY

Due to its extensive growth,
Nashville has spread into the
surrounding counties, making the
city somewhat like the center of a
clock, with a downtown district
surrounded by outlying areas,
including Franklin, Clarksville,
Ashland City, Murfreesboro,
Madison, Gallatin, Dickson and
Ashland City, all less than 60 miles
away. The best places to stay are
anywhere in the downtown-university
area if you want to see Nashville.

Fiddlers Inn North
2410 Music Valley Drive
Tel: 615-885-1440
Fax: 615-883-6477
202 rooms located in the center of
the Opryland area. **$$**

Gaylord Opryland Resort
2800 Opryland Drive
Toll-free: 877-456-OPRY
www.gaylordhotels.com
A Music City extravaganza with
Vegas-Disney overtones. Showy and
pricey. **$$$$**

Hampton Inn-West End
1919 West End
Tel: 615-329-1144
Toll-free: 888-880-5394
www.hamptoninnnashville.com
A lower-priced option close to Music
Row and the university area. **$$**

The Hancock House
2144 Nashville Park
Tel: 615-452-8431
A Colonial Revival house *circa*
1850, furnished with period
antiques, private baths and
fireplaces. There is also a well-fitted
cabin and a Jacuzzi suite. Fine
dining by reservation. **$$$**

Hermitage Hotel
Sixth Avenue N. and Union Avenue
Tel: 615-244-3121
Toll-free: 888-888-9414
www.thehermitagehotel.com
The 1910 Hermitage Hotel
Downtown is Nashville's grand
hotel, with a luxurious Beaux Arts
lobby and spacious suites. **$$$**

Hilton Suites Downtown Nashville
121 4th Avenue South
Tel: 615-620-1000
Toll-free: 800-445-8667
A newer hotel in the heart of the
Lower Broadway area, convenient to
everything Downtown. **$$**

Sheraton Music City
777 McGavock Pike
Tel: 615-885-2200
Toll-free: 800-325-3535
Fax: 615-871-0926
www.sheratonmusiccity.com
It is hard to match the ritzy elegance of Opryland, but this hotel
comes close with its Georgian
styling, smooth marble floors and
cherry-wood paneling. Near the
airport. **$$$**

Wyndham Union Station Hotel
1001 Broadway
Tel: 615-726-1001
Toll-free: 800-996-3426
Elegant hotel situated in the
magnificent former Union Station
railway terminal. Convenient
Downtown location. **$$$–$$$$**

WHERE TO EAT

Antonio's
7097 Old Harding
Tel: 615-646-9166
Nashville's best Italian restaurant is
moderately expensive but well
worth the money. Dinner only.
Reservations suggested. **$$$**

Arthur's
1001 Broadway
Tel: 615-255-1494
www.arthursrestaurant.com
Elegant four-star restaurant located
in the historic Union Station Hotel.
The continental menu changes
daily. Jacket and tie required. **$$$**

Cooker Bar and Grill
2609 West End Avenue and other
locations in the metro area
Tel: 615-327-2925
Southern and regional dishes like
meat loaf, pot roast, country fried
steak and fried okra are the special-
ties of the house. The outstanding
service also deserves a mention. **$**

Loveless Cafe
8400 Highway 100
Tel: 615-646-9700
Famous for more than 40 years for
its country ham and biscuits, this is
a place not to be missed. Open
daily for breakfast, lunch, and
dinner; reservations suggested for
weekend breakfast. **$$**

Mario's
2005 Broadway
Tel: 615-327-3232
www.mariosfinedining.xom
Exclusive restaurant serving
Northern Italian cuisine and fine
wines. Jacket and tie. **$$$**

Merchant's
401 Broadway
Tel: 615-254-1892
This former cowboy bar now serves
New Southern cuisine to the
executive set in a renovated brick
building, one block from the Second
Avenue Historic District. **$$$**

The Stockyard
901 Second Avenue N.
Tel: 615-255-6464
www.stockyardrestaurant.com
Steaks are the specialty, but there
is lots more on the menu. The Bull
Pen Lounge downstairs is one of
Nashville's top spots for live
country music and dancing. **$$$**

Valentino's Ristorante
1907 West End Avenue
Tel: 615-327-0148
Fine Northern Italian cuisine at reasonable prices. Consistently voted one of Nashville's best Italian restaurants for its good service and elegant but casual atmosphere. **$$**

The Wild Boar Restaurant
2014 Broadway
Tel: 615-329-1313
www.wboar.com
Creative French cuisine and courteous, helpful service. Excellent wine list. **$$–$$$**

WHERE TO SHOP

Much of the shopping scene in Nashville is centered on the large shopping malls in the suburbs, including the Bellevue Center, Cool Springs Galleria, and the Mall at Green Hills, which has upscale department stores and specialty shops. For discount shopping, Factory Stores of America is the city's largest outlet mall, located across from the Opryland Hotel. Music fans should head Downtown for record shops such as Ernest Tubb Records, 417 Broadway, which specializes in country music. Nashville is also a good place to shop for Western wear. Try Boot Country, 2412 Music Valley Drive, for a mind-boggling array of cowboy boots, or Trails West, 154 Second Avenue, for all the top brands of boots, hats and denim clothing.

Price Codes

Hotels: Categories based on average cost of a double room for one night.
$ = under $65
$$ = up to $100
$$$ = up to $150
$$$$ = over $150

Restaurants: Categories based on average cost of dinner and a glass of wine, before tip.
$ = under $15
$$ = up to $30
$$$ = over $30

South Carolina

Getting Acquainted

Known as: the Palmetto State for the strength of the palmetto log walls of Fort Moultrie that withstood British cannon fire and protected Charleston Harbor during the years of the American Revolution.
Motto: "*Animis Opibusque Parati*" – Prepared in Mind and Resources.
Entered Union: The 8th state entered the Union on May 23, 1788.
Population: 4 million.
Area: 1,113 sq. miles (2,882 sq. km), including 186 miles (300 km) of coastline.
Time Zone: Eastern Time Zone (GMT minus five hours).
Capital: Columbia
Local Dialing Codes: 803 (mid-state), 864 (west) 843 (east coast).
Famous Figures: Author Pat Conroy of *Prince of Tides* fame, Jim Rice of the Boston Red Sox, the Godfather of Soul James Brown, boxer Joe Frazier, jazz musician Dizzy Gillespie, United States president Andrew Jackson.

Useful Addresses

South Carolina tourist information
Department of Tourism, 1205 Pendleton Street, Room 505, Columbia, SC 29201
Tel: 803-734-1700
www.travelsc.com
Charleston Area Visitors Bureau
375 Meeting Street
Charleston, SC 29403
Toll-free: 800-774-0006
www.charlestoncvb.com

Charleston

FROM THE AIRPORT

If you're not renting a car at the airport, a pricey taxi ride is your only other option to get to downtown Charleston.

WHERE TO STAY

Ansonborough Inn
21 Hassell Street
Tel: 843-723-1655
Toll-free: 800-522-2073
Fax: 843-577-6888
www.ansonboroughinn.com
Once a stationer's warehouse, this all-suite, *circa* 1900 inn has heart-pine beams, locally fired bricks, and an impressive atrium lobby. **$$**

Battery Carriage House
20 South Battery
Tel: 843-727-3100
Toll-free: 800-775-5575
One of the most romantic of Charleston's inns, it overlooks White Point Gardens and Charleston Harbor. **$$$**

Governor's House Inn
117 Broad Street
Tel: 843-720-2070
Toll-free: 800-720-9812
www.governorshouse.com
Originally the residence of Governor Edward Rutledge, the youngest signer of the Declaration of Independence, this elegant inn retains an air of tradition with its broad verandah, chandeliers, fireplaces, spacious rooms and exceptional service. In the center of the Historic district. **$$$$**

Kings Courtyard Inn
198 King Street
Tel: 843-723-7000
Toll-free: 800-845-6119
This Greek-Revival style inn has unusual Egyptian detail. One of historic King Street's largest and oldest structures. **$$–$$$**

The Mills House Hotel
115 Meeting Street
Tel: 843-577-2400
Toll-free: 800-874-9600
In 1861, General Robert E. Lee stayed at this antebellum hotel in the Historic District. **$$$$**

Planters Inn
112 North Market Street
Tel: 843-722-2345
Toll-free: 800-845-7082
Fax: 843-577-2125
www.plantersinn.com
Antiques adorn most rooms in this upscale hotel, originally built in 1844 to house Hornick's Dry Goods. On the edge of Charleston's City Market. **$$$**

Two Meeting Street Inn
Two Meeting Street
Tel: 843-723-7322
www.twomeetingstreet.com
The distinguished sister of the Governor's House. Built in 1844, the inn originally housed a saloon and restaurant and has been lovingly restored. **$$–$$$**

WHERE TO EAT

A.W. Shuck's Seafood Restaurant
35 Market Street
Tel: 843-723-1151
Fresh seafood in a lively atmosphere draws hungry visitors to this restaurant in the heart of the historic market. **$–$$**

Blossom Cafe
171 E. Bay Street
Tel: 843-722-9200
Light, innovative Italian fare served beneath a glass atrium and in an outdoor, walled garden. **$–$$**

Carolina's
10 Exchange Street
Tel: 843-724-3800
Recommended by Charlestonians, this American bistro is set against a backdrop of historic architecture and serves regional cuisine. **$$**

82 Queen
82 Queen Street
Tel: 843-723-7591
This 18th-century landmark serves Low Country favorites and encompasses three buildings situated around a garden courtyard. **$–$$$**

Hanks Seafood
10 Hayne Street
Tel: 843-723-3474
www.hanksseafood.com
A classic fish restaurant. **$$**

Hyman's Seafood Co.
215 Meeting Street
Tel: 803-723-6000
Adjoining Aaron's Deli, this seafood restaurant and popular raw bar draws a lively crowd. **$–$$$**

Louis's Charleston Grill
224 King Street
Tel: 803-577-4522
Located at Charleston Place, this restaurant features the regional cuisine of nationally acclaimed chef Louis Osteen. **$$$**

McCrady's
2 Unity Alley
Tel: 843-577-0025
Located in the oldest tavern in the United States, McCrady's maintains a historic flavor peppered with contemporary cuisine. **$–$$**

Peninsula Grill
112 N Market Street
Tel: 843-723-0700
www.peninsulagrill.com
Regularly voted one of Charleston's best restaurants by locals. Haute cuisine and proper cocktails in a sophisticated setting. **$$$**

Pinckney Cafe and Espresso
18 Pinckney Street
Tel: 843-577-0961
The imaginative menu features fresh, well-cooked seafood. Pleasant terrace, relaxed atmosphere, fragrant coffees and irresistible desserts. **$**

Restaurant Million
2 Unity Alley
Tel: 843-577-3141
Charleston's only member of the prestigious Relais & Chateaux chain, serving a delicious array of haute cuisine. **$$$**

Saracen
141 E. Bay Street
Tel: 843-723-6242
Contemporary international fare in an elegant restaurant situated in a Moorish-style building a few blocks from historic Rainbow Row. **$$–$$$**

WHERE TO SHOP

The Old City Market on Market Street was built in 1841 and features many small shops, restaurants and an open-air market that sell everything from produce to antiques. This is a good place to buy the Gullah-inspired handmade sweetgrass baskets.

WHERE TO STAY

Abbeville
Abbewood
509 N. Main Street
Tel: 864-459-5822
This *circa* 1860s restored home features a leaded glass entrance and wrap-around veranda. **$**

The Vintage Inn
1205 N. Main Street
Tel: 864-459-4784
Toll-free: 800-890-7312
An elegantly restored 1870s Victorian home, with wicker furniture on a wrap-around porch. **$–$$**

Aiken
Annie's Inn
US 78 East
Tel: 803-649-6836
Escape to this 150-year-old farmhouse, and enjoy a stroll through its 200-year-old cemetery and expansive pecan grove. **$**

Beaufort
Rhett House
1009 Craven Street
Tel: 843-524-9030
Fax: 843-524-1310
Toll-free: 888-480-9530
www.rhetthouseinn.com
Built in 1820, this plantation house bordering the Intercoastal Waterway has stately white columns, broad verandahs, rocking chairs and period decor. Many rooms have fireplaces and private balconies. **$$$$**

TwoSuns Inn
1705 Bay Street
Tel: 843-522-1122
Toll-free: 800-532-4244
With a sunrise view of the bay, this 1917 home prides itself on antiques and collectibles. **$$**

Camden
Candlelight Inn
1904 Broad Street
Tel: 803-424-1057
Situated in Camden's Historic District and shaded by a canopy of live oaks, the Candlelight Inn

displays a variety of needlework, quilts, and antiques. **$**

Greenleaf Inn
1308 N. Broad Street
Tel: 800-437-5874
Comprised of the Reynold's House (*c.* 1805) and the McLean House (*c.* 1890), this bed and breakfast has been carefully restored to retain its traditional flavor. **$**

Columbia
Claussen's Inn
2003 Green Street
Tel: 803-765-0440
Toll-free: 800-622-3382
With 29 king-size guest rooms, this historic inn is situated in the Claussen bakery building and features a three-story atrium. **$$**

Richland Street B&B
1425 Richland Street
Tel: 803-779-7001
Toll-free: 800-779-7011
Each room here exhibits its own personality and is decorated with period antiques. In the heart of the Historic District. **$–$$**

Georgetown
Harbor House Bed and Breakfast
15 Cannon Street
Tel: 843-546-6532
Toll-free: 877-511-0101
www.harborhouse.com
Large waterfront inn with a distinctive red roof, built in 1740 as a shipping warehouse. Lovely, spacious rooms. **$$$**

1790 House B&B
630 Highmarket Street

Tel: 843-546-4821
Toll-free: 800-890-7432
In Georgetown's Historic District, this historic inn is known for its hospitality. **$–$$**

Shaw House B&B
613 Cypress Court
Tel: 843-546-9663
Overlooking miles of marsh land, the Colonial-style Shaw House offers spacious rooms and numerous activities including bird watching and biking. **$**

Greenville
Pettigru Place
302 Pettigru Street
Tel: 864-242-4529
Toll-free: 877-362-4644
This restored 1920s home offers a tranquil rest on a quiet, historic street in downtown Greenville. **$–$$**

Hilton Head Island
Westin Resort
2 Grasslawn Avene
Tel: 843-681-4000
Considered the most luxurious of the island resort hotels, Westin Resort features a touted Sunday Brunch and a five-diamond AAA rating. **$$$–$$$$**

McClellanville
Laurel Hill Plantation
8913 North Hwy 17
Tel: 843-887-3708
Toll-free: 888-887-3708
The wrap-around porches of this plantation overlook Cape Romain Wildlife Refuge's expansive salt marshes. **$**

Mrytle Beach
Brustman House
400 25th Avenue S.
Tel: (843) 448-7699
Toll-free: 800-448-3063
Set against a wooded backdrop, this bed and breakfast is only 300 yards (275 meters) from the beach. Its 10-grain buttermilk pancakes are a house breakfast specialty. **$**

Serendipity Inn
407 71st Avenue N.
Tel: 843-449-5268
Toll-free: 800-448-3063
This award-winning, Spanish mission-style inn has a heated pool,

shuffleboard, and beach access 300 yards (275 meters) away. **$–$$**

Pawley's Island
Litchfield Plantation
River Road
Tel: 843-237-9121
Toll-free: 800-869-1410
Built *circa* 1750, this fine mansion was once situated on a sweeping rice plantation. Now it's a delightful and welcoming country inn. **$$–$$$**

Pendleton
Liberty Hall Inn
621 S. Mechanic Street
Tel: 864-646-7500
Toll-free 800-643-7944
Housed in the restored *circa* 1840 Piedmont Plantation, it's also near the town square and Clemson University. **$**

WHERE TO EAT

Abbeville
The Village Grill
110 Trinity Street
Tel: 864-459-2500
Located right off the town square, this casual restaurant has something for everyone with chicken, steak and seafood dishes. **$–$$**

Aiken
Duke's Bar-B-Que
4248 Whiskey Road
Tel: 803-649-7675
Sample South Carolina barbecue at its best. **$**

No. 10 Downing Street
241 Laurens Street SW
Tel: 803-642-9062
For a special lunch or a memorable dinner, visit one of No. 10 Downing Street's four dining rooms, complete with fireplaces. **$–$$**

Beaufort
Plum's
904 and 1/2 Bay Street
Tel: 843-525-1946
A front-porch eatery on Waterfront Park, serving up hot Reubens and evening blues. **$–$$**

Sgt White's Diner
1908 Boundary Street
Tel: 843-522-2029

Price Codes

Hotels: Categories based on average cost of a double room for one night.
$ = under $65
$$ = up to $100
$$$ = up to $150
$$$$ = over $150

Restaurants: Categories based on average cost of dinner and a glass of wine, before tip.
$ = under $15
$$ = up to $30
$$$ = over $30

This diner is locally loved for its Southern cooking and down-home atmosphere. **$**

Camden
The Tavern
1308/10 N. Broad Street
Tel: 800-437-5874
Located beside the Greenleaf Inn, the Tavern serves European-style cuisine prepared by an Austrian chef. **$–$$**

Columbia
Maurice's Gourmet Bar-B-Que
1600 Charleston Hwy
Tel: 803-791-5887
With nine locations throughout the area, Maurice's is a Midland South Carolina tradition you won't want to miss. **$**
Villa Tronco
1213 Blanding Street
Tel: 803-256-7677
Columbia's oldest Italian restaurant has been serving fabulous food and old-world charm for over 50 years. **$–$$**

Georgetown
Pink Magnolia
719 Front Street
Tel: 843-527-6506
Fresh seafood salads, creole and crab cakes served at your table right on the harbor walk or indoors. The non-seafood specialty is a fried-chicken salad. **$$**
The River Room
801 Front Street
Tel: 843-527-4110

Price Codes

Hotels: Categories based on average cost of a double room for one night.
$ = under $65
$$ = up to $100
$$$ = up to $150
$$$$ = over $150

Restaurants: Categories based on average cost of dinner and a glass of wine, before tip.
$ = under $15
$$ = up to $30
$$$ = over $30

Located in an 1800s dry goods port with original brick and woodwork, this casual restaurant specializes in grilled fish. **$–$$**

Greenville
Annie's Natural Cafe
121 S. Main Street
Tel: 864-271-4872
Unique vegetarian restaurant with atmospheric European-style courtyard dining. **$–$$**
Nippon Center Yagoto
500 Congaree Road
Tel: 864-288-8471
Japanese restaurant and cultural center serving traditional cuisine with an emphasis on the artistry of presentation. **$$–$$$**

Hilton Head Island
Crazy Crab
Harbour Town
Tel: 843 363-2722
Steamed, fried, baked or broiled, Crazy Crab's seafood hits the spot in a family atmosphere. **$–$$**
The Quarterdeck
Harbour Town
Tel: 843-671-2222
Fine dining and a popular happy hour, overlooking Calibogue Sound and the 18th hole of Harbour Town Golf Links. **$–$$**

McClellanville
The Crab Pot Restaurant
Hwy 17
Tel: 843-887-3156
This casual roadside restaurant draws a crowd hungry for owner Laura McClellan's crab cakes. **$–$$**

Murrells Inlet
The Seafarer Restaurant
Hwy 17 and Hwy 707
Tel: 803-651-7666. The seafood buffet includes oyster, shrimp, crab legs, and clams. **$–$$**

Myrtle Beach
Bennett's Calabash Seafood
9701 Hwy 17, North Kings Hwy
Tel: 843-449-7865
Originating in North Carolina, Calabash-style seafood has been popular here since the 1940s when local fishermen first battered and deep-fried their catch. **$–$$**

Dixie Stampede
North Junction of Hwy 17 and 17 By-pass
Tel: 843-497-6615
Enjoy an Old South, non-alcoholic family dinner-theater experience with a four-course feast of meat and potatoes. **$$**

Pawleys Island
The Carriage House
River Road
Tel: 843-237-9322
Located at lovely Litchfield Plantation, this fine dining establishment serves fish, steak, pork and pasta. Reservations required. **$$**
Tyler's Cove
Hwy 17 North
Tel: 843-237-4848
Experience the relaxed atmosphere of Pawley's Island over a seafood, pasta, or steak dinner on the outdoor deck of this restaurant located at the Hammock Shops. **$$**

Spartanburg
Simple Simon
Pine Street
Tel: 864-582-9461
This 1950s diner is a popular spot for local students and old timers. **$**

WHERE TO SHOP

Visitors to South Carolina's capital, Columbia, should stop by the State House Gift Shop on Main Street (tel: 888-234-1622) for sterling silver pendants and crystal or pewter picture frames. Another destination could be the Aiken Mall (2441 Whiskey Road, tel: 803-641-0869) in the town of the same name, which has over 40 stores.

Lowcountry shoppers are in for a treat at the gift shop of the Lowcountry Visitors Center & Museum (I-95 and US 17, Exit 33, tel: 1-800-528-6870). As well as selling Civil War prints, Gullah music and grass baskets, the center is located in an 1868 farmhouse set in four acres (called Point South). One of the refurbished rooms is a 1900s parlor, while another features displays from 10 local Lowcountry museums.

North Carolina

Known as: the Tar Heel State because North Carolina soldiers stuck in during a fierce Civil War battle like tar sticks to heels.
Motto: "*Esse Quam Videri*" – To Be Rather Than to Seem.
Entered Union: The 12th state entered the Union on November 12, 1789.
Population: 8 million.
Area: 52,712 sq. miles (136,524 sq. km).
Time Zones: Eastern Time Zone (GMT minus five hours).
Capital: Raleigh
Local Dialing Codes: 828 (western tip), 336 (Winston-Salem area), 980 and 704 (Charlotte area), 919 (Raleigh area), 910 (south) and 252 (east coast and Outer Banks).
Famous Figures: Frontiersman Daniel Boone, evangelist Dr Billy Graham, actors Ava Gardner and Andy Griffith, sportscaster Howard Cosell, jazz pianist Thelonious Monk, stock-car racer Richard Petty, US presidents James K. Polk and Andrew Johnson.

Useful Addresses

North Carolina tourist information
North Carolina Division of Tourism
301 N. Wilmington Street
Raleigh, NC 27601
Tel: 800-847-4862
www.visitnc.com
Charlotte tourist information
Charlotte Visitors Bureau
500 S. College Street
Charlotte, NC 28202
Tel: 704-334-2282
Toll-free: 800-722-1994
www.charlottecvg.org

Charlotte

FROM THE AIRPORT

In addition to the taxi rank and an assortment of rental car companies, many hotels have a free pick-up service from the airport. The city bus service, CATS, also carries passengers to and from Downtown.

WHERE TO STAY

The Dunhill Hotel
237 N. Tryon Street
Tel: 704-332-4141
Toll-free: 800-354-4141
The city's only historic hotel caters to individuals and business travelers. 60 rooms. **$–$$**
The Homeplace
5901 Sardis Road
Tel: 704-365-1936
A delightful turn-of-the-century country home in the suburbs with congenial hosts. 3 rooms. **$**
Morehead Inn
1122 E. Morehead Street
Tel: 704-376-3357
Toll-free: 888-667-3432
www.moreheadinn.com
Formerly a private home, this Dilworth inn offers many extras. 11 rooms and 1 apartment. **$–$$**
The Park Hotel
2200 Rexford Road
Tel: 704-364-8220
Toll-free: 800-334-0331
www.theparkhotel.com
A luxury hotel near SouthPark with an impeccable reputation for food and service. 190 rooms and 4 suites. **$$$$**

WHERE TO EAT

Bravo Ristorante
Adams Mark Hotel
555 S. McDowell Street
Tel: 704-372-4100
Professional singers not only serenade you but act as your servers at this classic Italian restaurant. **$$–$$$**
The Coffee Cup
914 S. Clarkson Street
Tel: 704-375-8855
Formica-topped tables and a

battered old jukebox add charm to this local "meat and three" establishment. **$**
Dilworth Wing Ranch Grill and Bar
2200 Park Road
Tel: 704-371-8700
Once the neighborhood hardware store, now a cozy restaurant serving gourmet chicken wings, soups and salads. **$$**
Morton's of Chicago
227 W. Trade Street
Tel: 704-333-2602
Thick beefsteaks and lobsters flown in from the source, topped off with delectable desserts, are standard fare at this upscale restaurant chain. **$$$–$$$$**
Providence Cafe
110 Perrin Place
Tel: 704-376-2008
Innovative cuisine, from sandwiches on *focaccia* crust to wondrous desserts, makes this a favorite stop, even after-hours. **$$–$$$$**

WHERE TO SHOP

The Metrolina Expo Antiques and Collectible Market (7100 N. Statesville Road, www.metrolinaexpo.com) only opens on the first weekend of each month, but over 2,000 dealers flock here for this event. If you're looking for cheap fashions, go to Prime Outlets Gaffney (I-85 at Exit 90, www.primeoutlets.com). It's home to more than 80 of America's biggest designer brands.

Around North Carolina

WHERE TO STAY

Asheville
The Grove Park Inn Resort
290 Macon Avenue
Tel: 828-252-2711
Toll-free: 800-438-5800
A full-service mountain resort, dating to 1913, offering everything from afternoon tea to golf. 510 rooms. **$$–$$$**
Richmond Hill Inn
87 Richmond Hill Drive
Tel: 828-252-7313
Toll-free: 888-742-4550

Fax: 828-252-8726
Web: www.richmondhillinn.com
This romantic 19th-century
mansion commands fine
panoramic views from atop a
wooded hill. Quiet, individual
cottages and Garden Pavilion
rooms with a library, croquet
court, porch rockers and fine
dining. A peaceful haven. **$$$$**

Beaufort
Langdon House Bed & Breakfast
135 Craven Street
Tel: 252-728-5499
A well-kept Colonial house with a
charming host. 4 rooms. **$–$$**

Blowing Rock
Hillwinds Inn
Sunset Drive and Ransom Street
Tel: 828295-7660
Toll-free: 800-821-4908
www.hillwindsinn.com
An immaculate village motel that's
convenient to restaurants and
shops. **$**
Westglow Spa
Hwy 221 South
Tel: 828-295-4463
Toll-free: 800-562-0807
www.westglow.com
An artist's private mountain home
now welcomes guests, and a
European-style spa occupies his
studio site. 6 rooms and 2
cottages. **$$–$$$$**

Boone
Lovill House Inn
404 Old Bristol Road
Tel: 828-264-4204
Toll-free: 800-849-9466
www.lovillhouseinn.com
An historic mountain B&B offering
breakfast and bicycles. 5 rooms. **$**

Chapel Hill
Carolina Inn
211 Pittsboro Street
Tel: 919-933-2001
Toll-free: 800-962-8519
Fax: 919-962-3400
Web: www.carolinainn.com
This elegantly furnished historic
inn provides a good base for
exploring downtown Chapel Hill and
the shops and restaurants of
Franklin Street. **$$$$**

Durham
Carolina Duke Motor Inn
2517 Guess Road
Tel/Fax: 919-286-0771
Toll-free: 800-438-1158
Very reasonable rooms and suites.
Amenities include swimming pool
and area transportation. **$**
Washington Duke Inn & Golf Club
3001 Cameron Boulevard
Tel: 919-490-0999
Toll-free: 800-443-3853
www.washingtondukeinn.com
A luxury hotel near Duke University
that overlooks the golf course. 171
rooms. **$$**

Greensboro
The Biltmore Greensboro Hotel
111 Washington Street
Tel: 336-272-3474
Toll-free: 800 332-0303
www.biltmorehotelgreensboro.com
A Downtown luxury hotel laced with
history and charm. 29 rooms. **$–$$**
Microtel Inn
4304 Big Tree Way
Tel: 336-547-7007
Toll-free: 888-771-7171
www.microtelinn.com
Clean, comfortable, good-value. **$**

Lake Lure (near Chimney Rock)
Sunrise Hill
361 Charlotte Drive
Tel: 828-625-2789
Toll-free: 877-733-2785
www.lodgeonlakelure.com
A former state highway patrol lodge,
this lakeside B&B charms visitors
February through December. **$–$$**

Mount Airy
Mayberry Motor Inn
1001 US Hwy 52N
Tel: 336-786-4109
www.mayberrymotorinn.com
Well-kept, comfortable rooms. Very
good value. Continental breakfast.
Nearby jogging and nature trail. **$**

Nags Head
First Colony Inn
6720 S. Virginia Dare Trail
Tel: 252-441-2343
Fax: 252-441-9234
Toll-free: 800-368-9390
www.firstcolonyinn.com
Handsome older inn, carefully

restored and furnished with
antiques. Pool and Jacuzzis. **$$**

New Bern
Harmony House Inn
215 Pollock Street
Tel: 252-636-3810
Toll-free: 800-636-3113
www.harmonyhouseinn.com
This Greek Revival B&B in the heart
of the Historic District offers a
delightful breakfast. 9 rooms. **$**

Ocracoke
Berkley Manor
A block east of Cedar Island Ferry
Tel: 252-928-5911
Toll-free: 800-832-1223
www.berkleymanor.com
No phones or TVs will intrude at
this rustic B&B that's within walking
distance of the village. 9 rooms. **$**
The Island Inn and Dining Room
25 Lighthouse Road
Tel: 252-928-4351
Toll-free: 877-456-3466
Fax: 252-928-4352
www.ocracokeislandinn.com
The characterful older section
(s1901) offers rooms with antiques,
private baths and a heated outdoor
pool. The family-friendly motel-style
section also has a pool. **$$$**

Pinehurst
Pinehurst Resort & Country Club
1 Carolina Vista
Tel: 910-295-6811
Toll-free: 800-371-2545
www.pinehurst.com
A renowned resort in the heart of

Price Codes

Hotels: Categories based on
average cost of a double room
for one night.
$ = under $65
$$ = up to $100
$$$ = up to $150
$$$$ = over $150

Restaurants: Categories based
on average cost of dinner and a
glass of wine, before tip.
$ = under $15
$$ = up to $30
$$$ = over $30

Pinehurst offers golf, tennis, croquet, trap and skeet shooting, water sports, carriage rides and fine dining. 299 rooms. **$$–$$$**

Raleigh
The Oakwood Inn Bed & Breakfast
411 North Bloodworth Street
Tel: 919-832-9712
Tel: 800-267-9712
www.oakwoodinnbb.com
A restored Victorian home near the Capitol. 6 rooms. **$**
Velvet Cloak Inn
1505 Hillsborough Street
Tel: 919-828-0333
Toll-free: 800-334-4372
Close to NC State University, this is where the movers and shakers of Raleigh do business. 172 rooms. **$**

Wilmington
Best Western Carolinian
2916 Market Street
Tel: 910-763-4653
Toll-free: 800-528-1234
www.bestwestern.com
Between Downtown and the Atlantic beaches. Deluxe amenities and lovely mature gardens. **$$**
Catherine's Inn
410 Front Street
Tel: 910-251-0863
Toll-free: 800-476-0723
www.catherinesinn.com
A bed-and-breakfast home filled with antiques. 3 rooms. **$**
The Inn on Orange B&B
410 Orange Street
Tel: 910-815-0035
Toll-free: 800-381-4666
Fax: 910-762-2279
www.innonorange.com
An historic Italianate Victorian home not too far from the river and close to Downtown. Rooms have ceiling fans, fireplaces and TVs on request. **$$–$$$**

Winston-Salem
Augustus T. Zevely Inn
803 S. Main Street
Tel: 336-748-9299
Toll-free: 928-9299
B&B in the heart of Old Salem. Quaint, charming rooms with homey touches. 12 rooms. **$–$$**
The Brookstown Inn
200 Brookstown Inn

Tel: 336-725-1120
Toll-free: 800-845-4262
An old textile and flour mill dating to 1856. Includes breakfast and an afternoon wine reception. 39 rooms and 32 suites. **$–$$**

WHERE TO EAT

Asheville
Blue Moon Bakery and Cafe
60 Biltmore Avenue
Tel: 828-252-6063
A popular all-round restaurant. Above- average sandwiches, pizzas, desserts and breakfasts. **$**
Flying Frog Cafe at Haywood Park
1 Battery Park
Tel: 828-252-2522
Nouvelle cuisine served in an elegant atmosphere. **$$–$$$**

Beaufort
The Beaufort Grocery
117 Queen Street
Tel: 252-728-3899
www.beaufortgrocery.com
Popular local restaurant in a former grocery store serving seafood, beef and poultry entrées. **$**

Blowing Rock
The Blowing Rock Cafe
349 Sunset Drive
Tel: 828-295-9474
Locals and visitors love the food and ambiance of this cozy café. **$**

Chapel Hill
The Fearrington House
Fearrington Village
Tel: 919-542-2121
Gourmet cuisine, beautiful to the eye and the palate, is served in a restored farm house. **$$$**
Spanky's
101 E. Franklin Street
Tel: 919-967-2678
Buzzing restaurant serving sandwiches, seafood and pasta. Spanky's club sandwich is a favorite. **$**

Durham
Bullock's Bar-B-Que
3330 Quebec Drive
Tel: 919-383-6202
Diners queue early for chopped pork barbecue and Brunswick stew. **$**

Lake Lure
Lake Lure Inn
US 64 and 74
Tel: 828-625-2525
Fine dining every day but Monday at this refurbished lakeside inn. Brunch is served on Sunday. **$**

Lexington
Lexington Barbecue #1
10 US Highway 29 & 70 South
Tel: 336-249-9814
This 1950s-style roadside restaurant sets the benchmark for North Carolina barbecue.Eat it with red slaw and hush puppies. **$**

Mount Airy
Snappy Lunch
125 N. Main Street
Tel: 336-786-4931
Known for its hefty pork chop sandwich — a cornucopia of juicy meat, condiments and trimmings. Plenty of atmosphere too. **$**

Nags Head
Kelly's Outer Banks Restaurant & Tavern
2316 South Croatan Hwy
Tel: 252-441-4116
Fresh seafood, steaks and prime rib are served in this well-established restaurant. **$–$$**
Owens' Restaurant
7114 South Virginia Dare Trail
Tel: 252-441-7309
The freshest seafood found on the Outer Banks is served at this family-owned restaurant. **$–$$**

New Bern
The Harvey Mansion Restaurant & Lounge
216 Pollock Street
Tel: 919-638-3205
Upscale restaurant serves international cuisine in a restored historic structure dating to 1797. **$–$$**

Raleigh
The Angus Barn
9401 Glenwood Avenue
Tel: 919-787-3505
Known for its steaks and seafood, plus its extensive winelist. **$–$$**
42nd St Oyster Bar & Seafood Grill
508 W. Jones Street
Tel: 919-831-2811

www.raleigh42ndstreet.com
Located in a restored warehouse, this seafood restaurant is popular with locals and politicians. $–$$

Irregardless
901 W. Morgan Street
Tel: 919-833-8898
Vegetable dishes and other health-conscious foods are the order of the day at this bistro. $

Wilmington
Elijah's Restaurant
2 Ann Street
Tel: 910-343-1448
Award-winning seafood chowder and other tasty dishes. The adjoining oyster bar with outdoor covered patio faces onto Cape Fear. $$

The Pilot House
Chandler's Wharf, 2 Ann Street
Tel: 910-343-0200
A variety of entrees is served at this waterside restaurant. $–$$

Winston-Salem
Leon's Cafe
924 South Marshall Street
Tel: 336-725-9593
Innovative cuisine is the standard in this neighborhood restaurant close to Old Salem. $

Salem Tavern Dining Room
736 S. Main Street
Tel: 336-748-8585
Costumed servers tend to all your needs at this Colonial restaurant, known for its chicken pot pie. $

Village Tavern
221 Reynolda Village
Tel: 336-748-0221
Popular family restaurant serving pub-style food in a lively atmosphere. $$

WHERE TO SHOP

Durham
Brightleaf District (905 W. Main Street) is the west end's shopping area. Anchored by Brightleaf Square, which is on the National Register of HIstoric Places, the area is full of restaurants, jewelers, galleries and more. The Ninth Street Shopping District (www.ninthst.com) is more eclectic, with organic produce, a drugstore soda fountain and bookshops.

Virginia

Getting Acquainted

Known As: the Old Dominion.
Motto: "*Sic Semper Tyrannis*" – Thus Always to Tyrants.
Entered Union: 1788.
Population: 7.1 million (12th largest in nation).
Area: 40,815 sq. miles (105,710 sq. km).
Time Zone: Eastern Time Zone (GMT minus 5 hours).
Capital: Richmond
Local Dialing Codes: 276 (eastern tip), 434 (mid-south), 540 (north, northwest), 804 (Richmond area), 757, (southeast corner), 703/571 (northeast corner).
Famous Figures: Several presidents have come from Virginia including William H. Harrison, Thomas Jefferson, James Madison, James Monroe, Zachary Taylor, John Tyler, George Washington and Woodrow Wilson; statesman Patrick Henry, confederate general Robert E. Lee, jazz singer Ella Fitzgerald, and explorer Meriwether Lewis of Lewis and Clark.

Useful Addresses

Virginia tourist information
Division of Tourism, 901 East Byrd Street, Richmond, VA 23219
Tel: 800-847-4882
Web: www.virginia.org
Richmond tourist information
Richmond Visitors Bureau
401 N. 3rd Street
Tel: 804-782-2777
Toll-free: 800-370-9004
www.richmondva.org

Richmond

FROM THE AIRPORT

Richmond International Airport is served by GRTC buses (tel: 804-358-4782). Otherwise taxis and rental cars are the only way into the central city.

WHERE TO STAY

The Berkeley Hotel
1200 E. Cary Street
Tel: 804-780-1300
www.berkeleyhotel.com
Located in the Shockoe Slip warehouse district, this elegant hotel is convenient to everything in downtown Richmond. 55 rooms. $$

The Jefferson Hotel
Franklin and Adams Streets
Tel: 804-788-8000
Toll-free: 800-424-8014
Originally opened in 1895, this is Richmond's finest hotel and well worth a visit or a stay. 274 rooms. $$–$$$

John Marshall Hotel
101 N. 5th Street
Tel: 804-783-1929
Fax: 804-644-2364
Elvis Presley and six US presidents are among those who have enjoyed the beautiful suites in this landmark Downtown hotel. Convenient for attractions and nightlife. $$–$$$

Linden Row Inn
100 E. Franklin Street
Tel: 804-783-7000
Toll-free: 800-348-7424
Centrally-located in the Downtown area and combining the best of a hotel and B&B stay. 71 rooms. $$

The Patrick Henry Inn
2300 E. Broad Street
Tel: 804-644-1322
Three comfortable suites with period decor and fireplaces in this 1850s Colonial-style inn, opposite St John's Church in the Church Hill neighborhood. The inn has an English pub, outdoor deck and magnificent garden and an excellent restaurant. $$–$$$

West-Bocock House
1107 Grove Avenue
Tel: 804-358-6174
Romantic B&B in the Fan district.

The house, built *circa* 1870, has a lovely veranda and garden. Rooms have French linens and fresh flowers. There's a plantation-style breakfast in the morning. **$$–$$$**

The William Catlin House
2304 E. Broad Street
Tel: 804-780-3746
Toll-free: 800-695-8284
Built in 1845 in the Church Hill residential area, this charming B&B has seven rooms filled with period furnishings, all with private bath and a fireplace. Close to Downtown, Capitol Square and Shockoe Slip. **$$–$$$**

The William Miller House B&B
1129 Floyd Avenue
Tel: 804-254-2928
Intimate B&B in a beautiful Greek Revival-style home dating from 1869, with period windows, a parlor and marble mantlepieces. There's two large guest rooms with sitting areas and private baths. Located in the Fan District. **$$$**

WHERE TO EAT

The best food in Richmond can be found in its neighborhood restaurants. Whether you're looking for a quick burger or salad, traditional Southern cooking, or a romantic spot for fine dining, ask the locals where they eat in areas like Shockoe Bottom, the Fan or the Museum district. Around town, you'll also find a great range of world cuisines.

Acappella
2300 E. Broad Street
Tel: 804 377 1963
Inspired Italian cuisine with a German twist, set in the Colonial atmosphere of the Patrick Henry Inn in Church Hill. Stretch out the evening in the lovely beer garden and cozy pub. **$$**

Bill's Barbecue
3100 N. Boulevard
Tel: 804-358-8634
Bill's is justly popular for lavish portions of succulent barbecue and excellent breakfasts. **$**

Joe's Inn
205 North Shields Ave
Tel: 804-355-2282

One of the historic Fan District's many excellent restaurants, featuring a wide array of American and Italian specialties in a casual neighborhood atmosphere. **$**

Millie's Diner
2603 E. Main
Tel: 804-643-5512
Enjoy excellent New Southern cooking in a remodeled traditional diner. **$$**

Southern Grill
550 E. Grace Street
Tel: 804-343-7200
Traditional pan-fried chicken, short ribs, and smothered shrimp and grits are among the Southern favorites served at this Downtown restaurant overlooking the Carpenter Center. **$–$$**

Strawberry Street Cafe
421 Strawberry St
Tel: 804-353-6860
A Fan District favorite, with American fare and an unusual twist — a salad bar contained in an old bathtub. **$$**

The Tobacco Company
1201 E. Cary Street
Tel: 804-782-9555
Web: www.thetobaccocompany.com
This restaurant features creative New American cuisine in a converted tobacco warehouse, **$$**

WHERE TO SHOP

The shops of Shockoe Slip on East Cary Street between 12th and 14th house upscale specialty shops in a restored tobacco warehouse.

Around Virginia

WHERE TO STAY

Charlottesville
Boar's Head Inn and Sports Club
200 Ednam Drive
Tel: 434-296-2181
Toll-free: 800-476-1988
An elegant place to stay or just eat a meal in the midst of history and horse country. 173 rooms. **$$**

Clifton – The Country Inn
1296 Clifton Inn Drive
Tel: 434-971-1800
Fax: 434-971-7098
Toll-free: 888-971-1800
www.cliftoninn.com
Elegant Federal and Colonial revival-style historic manor house surrounded by 40 wooded acres (17 hectares). Guest rooms are furnished with antiques and a wood-burning fireplace. Facilities include clay tennis courts, pool, whirlpool and award-winning cuisine. **$$$$**

The Inn at Monticello
118 Scottsville Road
Tel: 434-979-3593
This cozy country inn is close to Monticello and many other attractions. 5 rooms. **$$**

Mount Vernon Motel
1613 Emmett Street
Tel: 434-296-5501
Standard motel rooms in the university district. Complimentary breakfast, courtesy shuttle, seasonal outdoor pool and restaurant. **$**

Silver Thatch Inn
3001 Hollymead Drive
Tel: 434-978-4686
Fax: 434-978-6156
Toll-free: 800-261-0720
Web: www.silverthatch.com
This delightful clapboard home is one of the oldest buildings in central Virginia. Accommodations comprise seven guest rooms, all with private baths, and several with canopy beds and fireplaces. The uniquely appointed rooms are named after early Virginian-born presidents. There are three dining rooms and a bar. **$$$–$$$$**

Chincoteague
Channel Bass Inn
6228 Church Street

Tel: 757-336-6148
Toll-free: 800-249-0818
www.channelbass-inn.com
This is one of the Eastern Shore's
finest inns, with Victorian elegance
and Eastern Shore charm. Good
food is served, too. 5 rooms. **$$$**

Fredericksburg
Fredericksburg Colonial Inn
1707 Princess Anne Street
Tel: 540-371-5666
Pretty hotel reminiscent of an
earlier time. 30 rooms. **$**
Kenmore Inn
1200 Princess Anne Street
Tel: 540-371-7622
Toll-free: 800-437-7622
www.kenmoreinn.com
Huge old house built in 1796. 12
guest rooms. **$$**

Harrisonburg
Joshua Wilton House
412 S. Main Street
Tel: 540-434-4464
This wonderful Victorian B&B inn
can serve as a perfect Shenandoah
Valley base. Good food, too. 5
rooms. **$$**

Irvington
The Tides Inn
480 King Carter Drive
Tel: 804-438-5000
Toll-free: 800-843-3746
www.tidesinn.com
One of Virginia's most beloved re-
sorts, located right on a peaceful
river. 110 rooms. **$$–$$$**

Lexington
Historic Country Inns
11 N. Main Street
Tel: 877-283-9680
Fax: 540-463-7262
Web: www.lexingtonhistoricinns.com
This firm runs three inns in the
area: two in the Lexington Historic
District – the Alexander Withrow
House (see below) and McCampbell
Inn – and Maple Hall 6 miles (9
kms) to the north on 56 acres (22
hectares). All inns feature
fireplaces, fine dining, trails and
pool. **$$$–$$$$**
Alexander-Witherow House
11 N. Main Street
Tel: 540-463-2044

This 18th-century B&B inn is
situated right in Lexington's Historic
District. 7 rooms. **$$**
B&B at Llewellyn Lodge
603 Main Street
Tel/Fax: 540-463-3235
Toll-free: 800-882-1145
www.llodge.com
Six comfortable, individually
decorated rooms in an attractive
gray-brick Colonial building. The inn
is known for its tempting breakfast
menu featuring the innkeeper's
award-winning omelets. A health-
conscious menu is also available.
Other features include four-poster
beds, ceiling fans and a porch
swing. Situated close to Downtown,
this is the ideal base for visiting
Lexington's attractions. **$$$**

Luray
Luray Caverns Motel West
Route 211
Tel: 540-743-4536
Locally owned, clean and
convenient to Luray Caverns. 19
rooms. **$**
The Mimslyn
401 W. Main Street
Tel: 540-743-5105
A handsome hotel set high on a hill
in its own grounds. Sweeping dining
room and secluded nooks and
crannies convey an elegance not
reflected in the price. Suites also
available. **$$–$$$**
Shenandoah River Inn B&B
201 Stagecoach Lane
Tel: 540-743-1144
Toll-free: 888-666-6760
www.shenandoah-inn.com
This former stagecoach inn has
been welcoming guests since 1812.
Located on the river with fine
mountain views, facilities include
private baths, king/queen beds,
screened porches, and gourmet
breakfasts. Cabins available. **$$$**

Middleburg
Red Fox Inn
2 E. Washington Street
Tel: 540-687-6301
Toll-free: 800-223-1728
www.redfox.com
This historic inn was built in 1728
and is a popular place for regional
dining, too. 24 rooms. **$$–$$$**

Middletown
Wayside Inn
7783 Main Street
Tel: 540-869-1797
www.waysideofva.com
Historic inn and restaurant featuring
Southern hospitality and cuisine. 24
rooms. **$**

Mountain Lake
Mountain Lake Hotel
115 Hotel Circle
Tel: 540-626-7121
An historic mountain resort
featuring 2,600 acres (1,050 hectares) of tall trees, stunning mountain scenery, dining rooms
overlooking a clear mountain lake,
and a wide variety of
accommodation. 66 rooms. **$–$$$**

New Market
Blue Ridge Inn
2251 Old Valley Pike
Tel: 540-740-4136
www.blueridgeinn.com
Pleasant with cable TV and
refrigerators. **$**

Newport News
The Inn at Kiln Creek
1003 Brick Kiln Blvd
Tel: 757-874-2600
Pretty golf resort with adjoining
hotel. 16 rooms. **$–$$**

Petersburg
Petersburg Ramada
380 E. Washington Street
Tel: 804-733-0000
Toll-free: 800-473-0005
Modern and convenient to Old
Towne Petersburg. 200 rooms. **$**

Portsmouth
Holiday Inn Waterfront
8 Crawford Parkway
Tel: 757-393-2573
Toll-free: 800-465-4329
This waterfront hotel is convenient
to everything in the Tidewater area.
232 rooms. **$**

Roanoke
Patrick Henry Hotel
617 S. Jefferson Street
Tel: 540-345-8811
www.patrickhenryroanoke.com
This conveniently located historic

landmark is the ideal base in downtown Roanoke. 125 rooms. **$$**

Shenandoah National Park
For information about the park, tel: 540-999-2243. Lodgings within the park are managed by:
ARAMARK Services
Shenandoah National Park
PO Box 727, Luray, VA 22835
Tel: 540-743-5108
Toll-free: 800-778-2851
www.visitshenandoah.com
Big Meadows Lodge
Tel: 800-778-2851
(Open mid May – late October)
An attractive oak and chestnut structure, built in 1939, adjacent to the grassy "big meadow". Disabled access. **$$–$$$**
Lewis Mountain Cabins
Tel: 800-778-2851
Open May – October. These historic cabins are reasonably priced and ideal for families. Facilities include sheltered outdoor cooking, recreation area with fireplace and a picnic table. Wheelchair accessible. **$–$$**
Skyland Resort
Tel: 800-778-2851
Open March – early December. At 3,680 feet (1,122 m), this resort is located at the highest point of Skyline Drive. Fabulous views from airy suites and rustic cabins. Disabled access. **$–$$**

Staunton
Belle Grae Inn
515 W. Frederick Street

Price Codes

Hotels: Categories based on average cost of a double room for one night.
$ = under $65
$$ = up to $100
$$$ = up to $150
$$$$ = over $150

Restaurants: Categories based on average cost of dinner and a glass of wine, before tip.
$ = under $15
$$ = up to $30
$$$ = over $30

Tel: 540-886-5151
www.bellegrae.com
This city B&B inn features rooms in the main building and several outbuildings. 12 rooms. **$–$$**
Frederick House
28 N. New Street
Tel: 540-885-4200
Toll-free: 800-334-5575
www.frederickhouse.com
Located in the downtown area, this historic building houses a European-style B&B inn. 14 rooms. **$**

Strasburg
Hotel Strasburg
213 S. Holiday Street
Tel: 540-465-9191
Toll-free: 800-348-8327
www.hotelstrasburg.com
Massanhutten Mountain forms the backdrop for this former hospital, converted into a lovely hotel in 1915. Featuring creative Southern-style fine dining. **$$**

Virginia Beach
The Cavalier
42nd Street and Oceanfront
Tel: 757-425-8555
Toll-free: 800-446-8199
This pretty property is a Virginia Beach legend. The old section offers historic rooms with meals, while the new section provides modern options. 400 rooms. **$–$$**

Washington
The Inn at Little Washington
Middle and Main Streets
Tel: 540-675-3800
www.innatlittlewashington.com
This special Northern Virginia property features some of the finest accommodations and French meals in the entire state. 12 rooms. **$$$$**

Williamsburg
Kingsmill Resort
1010 Kingsmill Road
Tel: 757-253-1703
Toll-free: 800-832-5665
Located just 15 minutes from Colonial Williamsburg, this full-service resort is a popular getaway for relaxation, golf and other sporting activities. 407 rooms. **$$–$$$$**

Williamsburg Inn
Francis Street at S. England Street
Tel: 757-229-1000
Toll-free: 800-447-8679
If you want perfect elegance right in the Historic District, then plan to stay here. 235 rooms. **$$$–$$$$**

Yorktown
Duke of York Motor Inn
508 Water Street
Tel: 757-898-3232
www.dukeofyork.com
Located right on the York River waterfront, this is an ideal base for exploring Yorktown and the rest of the Historic Triangle. 57 rooms. **$**

WHERE TO EAT

Charlottesville
Blue Bird Café
625 W. Main Street
Tel: 434-295-1166
Appetizing lunches featuring steaks, fried chicken and crab cakes. **$$**
C&O Restaurant
515 E. Water Street
Tel: 434-971-7044
www.candorestaurant.com
Imaginative dishes with a French influence served in an attractively converted rail workers' layover. Try the sliced, marinated and seared flank steak. Elegant but casual atmosphere. **$$**
Court Square Tavern
5th and East Jefferson Streets
Tel: 434-296-6111
Authentic pub fare and a large selection of beers. **$**
Michie Tavern
683 Thomas Jefferson Parkway
Tel: 434-977-1234
www.michietavern.com
Historic inn with country cooking in a rustic atmosphere. **$–$$**
Millers
109 W. Main Street
Tel: 434-971-8511
An old-style and pleasantly smoky atmospheric bar, formerly a drugstore specializing in "Miller's Tonic" in the early 1900s. The current Millers dispenses great cheeseburgers and a nice grilled chicken salad. Sit on the outdoor patio with bubbling fountain and listen to live jazz. **$**

Fredericksburg
Kenmore Inn
1200 Princess Anne Street
Tel: 540-371-7622
www.kenmoreinn.com
Good steak-and-seafood restaurant
with live entertainment. **$$**
The Smythe's Cottage and Tavern
303 Fauquier St
Tel: 540-373-1645
This tavern, located in the city's
Historic District, offers Colonial and
regional cooking at its Virginia
finest. **$**

Lexington
The Palms
101 W. Nelson Street
Tel: 540-463-7911
This casual restaurant is frequented
by college students, professors,
and lots of locals, thanks to
interesting American cuisine and
cold drinks. **$**

Luray
Parkhurst Restaurant
2547 US Highway 211 W
Tel: 540-743-6009
This popular restaurant features
international cuisine with many
local touches, as well as an award-
winning wine list. **$–$$**

New Market
Southern Kitchen
9576 S Congress Street
Tel: 540-740-3514
Great fried chicken and regional
favorites. **$**

Price Codes

Hotels: Categories based on
average cost of a double room
for one night.
$ = under $65
$$ = up to $100
$$$ = up to $150
$$$$ = over $150

Restaurants: Categories based
on average cost of dinner and a
glass of wine, before tip.
$ = under $15
$$ = up to $30
$$$ = over $30

Norfolk
Doumar's
1919 Monticello Ave
Tel: 757-627-4163
The legendary local place for
barbecue sandwiches and curbside
service at the state's first drive-in
restaurant. **$**
Ships Cabin
4110 E. Ocean View Avenue
Tel: 757-362-4659
Overlooking the Chesapeake Bay,
this is a great place for seafood in
the Tidewater area. **$$**

Roanoke
Awful Arthur's
2229 Colonial Avenue SW
Tel: 540-777-0007
Much-loved seafood restaurant in
an attractive historic location.
Entrees include steamed crab,
oysters, clams and fresh fish. **$–$$**
The Library
3117 Franklin Road SW
Tel: 540-985-0811
One of Roanoke's all-time local
favorites, with an elegant
atmosphere and outstanding French
and Continental cuisine. **$$**
Roanoker
2522 Colonial Avenue
Tel: 540-344-7746
Short on atmosphere but long on
portions of delicious, Southern
cooking. A wide array of well-
prepared vegetable side dishes,
rich gravies, and other good
trimmings. **$**

Virginia Beach
Capt. George's Seafood Restaurant
1956 Laskin Road
Tel: 757-428-3494
2272 Old Pungo Ferry Road
Tel: 757-721-3463
With two locations and a following
popular with tourists and locals
alike, Capt. George's is the king of
seafood buffets in the Virginia
Beach area. **$$**
The Lighthouse
1st and Atlantic Avenue
Tel: 757-428-7974
Located directly on pretty Rudee
Inlet, this is a perfect place for a
hearty seafood buffet or try one of
their delectable seafood specials.
$$–$$$

Wakefield
The Virginia Diner
408 County Drive North
Tel: 757-899-3106
www.virginiadiner.com
This unusual restaurant, located
between Richmond and Norfolk, is
surely the state's peanut mecca.
You can buy a load of Virginia
peanuts here, but you can also
enjoy some excellent Southern
cooking in a friendly atmosphere. **$**

Williamsburg
Chowning's Tavern
109 Duke of Gloucester Street
Tel: 757-229-2141
Offering Colonial food and drink,
this is one of several Historic
District taverns that features period
food and atmosphere. **$$**
The Trellis
403 Duke of Gloucester Street
Tel: 757-229-8610
This award-winning restaurant with
its owner/chef has been hosting
Williamsburg guests for many years,
offering unusual regional cuisine in
a casual setting. **$$–$$$**

WHERE TO SHOP

Less than an hour's drive from
Fredericksburg towards Washington,
DC, is Potomac Mills (2700
Potomac Mills Circle, Prince
William, Virginia; on the internet
www.potomacmills.com). With more
than 220 stores, some offering
discounts of up to 70 percent, this
is one of the East Coast's largest
and most popular malls.

A range of motels and hotels in
all price categories has sprung up
around the area to cater to patrons
partaking of the "shoppertainment"
possibilities (the mall's word for the
Mills experience) which includes –
in addition to the stores – 18 movie
screens and 25 restaurants. An in-
mall television station broadcasts
up-to-the-minute bargains.

Major brands include Books-A-
Million, Nordstrom Rack, Off 5th
Saks Fifth Avenue, Donna Karan,
Gap, L.L. Bean, Tommy Hilfiger and
Brooks Brothers. Potomac Mills is
open 10am–9.30pm Mon–Sat,
11am–7pm Sun.

Further Reading

Fiction

Billy by Albert French. Moving but not very well-known novel about a 10-year-old black boy convicted of murdering a white girl in Mississippi in 1937.

The Complete Stories by Flannery O'Connor. One of the South's leading writers, Georgia-born O'Connor is known for her novel *Wise Blood*, powerfully filmed by John Huston, but this collection of short stories shows the true range of her talent.

Crazy in Alabama by Mark Childress. Hilarious and bizarre novel in which Lucille Vinson kills her husband and takes a trip from Alabama to Hollywood, with his head in a hatbox.

Fried Green Tomatoes at the Whistle Stop Café by Fannie Flagg. Actress/novelist Flagg's acclaimed account of the life of the 80-year-old Cleo Threadgoode, from Whistle Stop, Alabama.

Intruders in the Dust by William Faulkner. Hard to choose from the Nobel Laureate's work, but this thriller-like story of an elderly black farmer arrested for the murder of a white man is especially accessible.

Jolie Blon's Bounce by James Lee Burke. One of the best of Burke's crime novels featuring the Louisiana detective, Dave Robicheaux. They all drip with steamy Southern atmosphere.

Life on the Mississippi by Mark Twain. The seminal and beautifully written story of Samuel Clemen's journey as a riverboat pilot.

The Secret Life of Bees by Sue Monk Kidd. Set on a peach farm in South Carolina in the 1960s, this is a beautiful tale of a girl's maturing, and her awareness of racism.

A Time to Kill by John Grisham. Grisham's first novel, the gripping tale of racial killings in a small town in Mississippi.

To Kill a Mockingbird by Harper Lee. Classic novel set in the Deep South of the 1930s, about a black man accused of raping a white girl and defended by an honorable white lawyer, played in the movie by Gregory Peck. Set in a fictionalized version of Lee's home town, Monroeville, Alabama.

General Non-fiction

Midnight in the Garden of Good and Evil by John Berendt. This "factual" account of a murder in steamy Savannah in 1981 became a cult best-seller, and there are even now "Midnight" tours of the town.

Praying for Sheetrock by Melissa Fay Greene. True story of the 1970s political awakening of the tiny black community of Sheetrock, in McIntosh County, Georgia.

Redbirds: Memories from the South by Rick Bragg. Bragg's account of how he grew up in poverty in rural Alabama, and went on to become a Pulitzer Prize-winning novelist.

Sitting Up with the Dead by Pamela Petro. The author travels across the South from the Carolinas to Louisiana, in search of the traditional oral storytellers and listening to their tales.

History & Civil Rights

Heritage of the South by Tim Jacobson. The history of Dixie from the Native Americans until now.

Mine Eyes Have Seen the Glory by Douglas Brinkley. Biography of Rosa Parks, the dignified woman who began the Montgomery Bus Boycott when she refused to give up her seat on the bus to a white man.

Stride Toward Freedom by Martin Luther King Jr. Dr King's account of the early days of the Civil Rights struggle, in particular the pivotal 1955–56 Montgomery Bus Boycott.

Music

The Blues Highway by Richard Knight. A travel and music guide of a route stretching from New Orleans to Chicago, though much inevitably focuses on the South's rock, jazz, country and blues roots.

Blues Traveling: The Holy Sites of Delta Blues by Steve Cheseborough. A detailed guide to the blues landmarks of Mississippi and the surrounding area, from the backroads to the big city.

Good Rockin' Tonight by Colin Escott with Martin Hawkins. Marvelous account of the birth of rock 'n' roll at Sun Records in Memphis, Tennessee, where Elvis, Johnny Cash, Roy Orbison, Jerry Lee Lewis and Carl Perkins all made their earliest recordings.

It Came from Memphis by Robert Gordon. The roots of rock 'n' roll, and much else besides, in an off-beat trawl through Memphis's recent history.

Travel

Backroad Buffets & Country Cafes by Don O'Briant. A guide to the best in backroads cooking.

In God's Country by Douglas Kennedy. London-based journalist and novelist travels through the Bible Belt, taking in Christian heavy-metal music to Death Row.

No Place Like Home by Gary Younge. A journalist who grew up black in Britain journeys through the South and explores the notion of racial identity.

Recommended Country Inns – the South by Carol and Dan Thalimer. Dreamy places to lay your head.

A Turn in the South by V.S. Naipaul. Nobel Prize-winning novelist's memorable journey through the South, from gaudy Graceland to the struggles of the Civil Rights Movement.

Other Insight Guides

North American destinations are strongly represented in Insight Guides' global range of more than 560 guidebooks and maps. A few of the companion books to this one include *Insight Guides* to New Orleans, New York, California, San Francisco, Las Vegas, Texas, Florida and Washington, DC. Some titles from the laminated, easy-fold *FlexiMap* range include Atlanta, New Orleans, New York, Dallas, Las Vegas and San Francisco.

ART & PHOTO CREDITS

INSIGHT GUIDE
New South

Cartographic Editor **Zoë Goodwin**
Production **Linton Donaldson**
Design Consultants
Klaus Geisler
Picture Research **Hilary Genin**

Map Production Stephen Ramsay
©2004 Apa Publications GmbH & Co.
Verlag KG (Singapore branch)

Index

A
B
C
D
F
G
H
I
J
a
b
c
e
f
g
h
i
j
k
l

INSIGHT GUIDES

The classic series that puts you in the picture

Alaska	Denmark	Lisbon	Rome
Amazon Wildlife	Dominican Rep. & Haiti	London	Russia
American Southwest	Dublin	Los Angeles	St Petersburg
Amsterdam	East African Wildlife	Madeira	San Francisco
Argentina	Eastern Europe	Madrid	Sardinia
Arizona & Grand Canyon	Ecuador	Malaysia	Scandinavia
Asia's Best Hotels	Edinburgh	Mallorca & Ibiza	Scotland
& Resorts	Egypt	Malta	Seattle
Asia, East	England	Mauritius Réunion	Shanghai
Asia, Southeast	Finland	& Seychelles	Sicily
Australia	Florence	Melbourne	Singapore
Austria	Florida	Mexico	South Africa
Bahamas	France	Miami	South America
Bali	France, Southwest	Montreal	Spain
Baltic States	French Riviera	Morocco	Spain, Northern
Bangkok	Gambia & Senegal	Moscow	Spain, Southern
Barbados	Germany	Namibia	Sri Lanka
Barcelona	Glasgow	Nepal	Sweden
Beijing	Gran Canaria	Netherlands	Switzerland
Belgium	Great Britain	New England	Sydney
Belize	Great Gardens of Britain	New Orleans	Syria & Lebanon
Berlin	& Ireland	New York City	Taiwan
Bermuda	Great Railway Journeys	New York State	Tanzania & Zanzibar
Boston	of Europe	New Zealand	Tenerife
Brazil	Greece	Nile	Texas
Brittany	Greek Islands	Normandy	Thailand
Brussels	Guatemala, Belize	Norway	Tokyo
Buenos Aires	& Yucatán	Oman & The UAE	Trinidad & Tobago
Burgundy	Hawaii	Oxford	Tunisia
Burma (Myanmar)	Hong Kong	Pacific Northwest	Turkey
Cairo	Hungary	Pakistan	Tuscany
California	Iceland	Paris	Umbria
California, Southern	India	Peru	USA: On The Road
Canada	India, South	Philadelphia	USA: Western States
Caribbean	Indonesia	Philippines	US National Parks: West
Caribbean Cruises	Ireland	Poland	Venezuela
Channel Islands	Israel	Portugal	Venice
Chicago	Istanbul	Prague	Vienna
Chile	Italy	Provence	Vietnam
China	Italy, Northern	Puerto Rico	Wales
Continental Europe	Italy, Southern	Rajasthan	Walt Disney World/Orlando
Corsica	Jamaica	Rio de Janeiro	
Costa Rica	Japan		
Crete	Jerusalem		
Croatia	Jordan		
Cuba	Kenya		
Cyprus	Korea		
Czech & Slovak Republic	Laos & Cambodia		
Delhi, Jaipur & Agra	Las Vegas		

INSIGHT GUIDES

The world's largest collection of visual travel guides & maps